THE CHIEF EXECUTIVE IN TEXAS

A Study in Gubernatorial Leadership

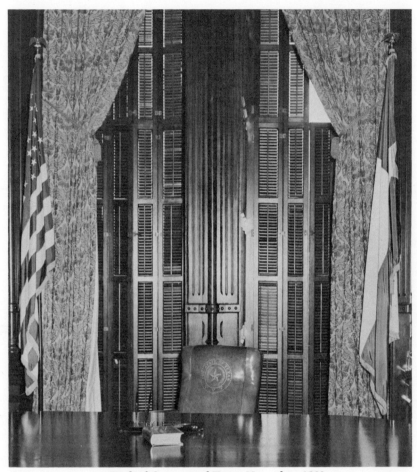

Desk of Governor of Texas, November, 1963

THE CHIEF
EXECUTIVE
IN TEXAS

A Study in Gubernatorial Leadership

by FRED GANTT, JR.

 UNIVERSITY OF TEXAS PRESS

Library of Congress Catalog Card No. 63–16063

Copyright © 1964 by Fred Gantt, Jr.
All Rights Reserved

Manufactured in the United States of America

Acknowledgments of permissions to quote
are listed in the Permissions section.

To the memory of my beloved parents
FRED GANTT, 1894–1963, and
MARGARET ELIZABETH GANTT, 1897–1956,
who would have shared with me
both the good and bad of this work

FOREWORD

The extensive literature of American state government contains a wealth of information on the office of governor, especially as it has evolved during the present century. In addition, many biographies of individual governors have been published. Very few studies, however, have confined themselves in any comprehensive or exhaustive way to the governorship alone, either as a comparative evaluation or as an analysis of the office within a single state. The Presidency of the United States has been analyzed frequently as a position of power and leadership, but the governorship of a great many of our states has not been examined in this way. Hence, this important and uniquely American office with its many variations from state to state is ill-understood by most Americans. In fact, many of the best-informed citizens in most states are not too well aware of what their governor can or cannot do, and even they often praise or blame him for what he cannot control.

Dr. Fred Gantt, Jr., therefore, in making this exceptionally thorough study of the governorship of Texas, has performed a great service to the people of this state and to students of government in general. While he confines himself largely to the office of chief executive as it has developed under the present Constitution of 1876, he does not neglect its origins under Spanish and Mexican rule and its character under the republican and the earlier state constitutions. In his full treatment of the office since 1876 he gives equal consideration to every compartment and facet of the governor's powers and role of leadership—executive, administrative, legislative, and political. Both formal and informal aspects are given adequate attention, as are the personal qualities and contributions of individual governors. Finally, the evolution of the office amidst the stupendous social, economic, and political changes of the last eighty-odd years is well handled.

Seemingly, every possible source of information, written and unwritten, official and informal, has been tapped. Especially worthy of note is Dr. Gantt's extensive use of personal interviews with the incumbent governor and former governors and many members of their staffs, as well as with a host of administrators, legislators, newspaper men, and others whose knowledge and experience were acquired at some time during the last forty to fifty years.

x *Foreword*

The Chief Executive in Texas: A Study in Gubernatorial Leadership is, then, a thorough and exhaustive piece of work which should serve as a model for similar studies in most other states and which is of inestimable value to all who are interested in Texas government.

O. Douglas Weeks
Professor of Government
The University of Texas

Today, perhaps as never before in history, the American people are in need of capable leaders in government. At the state level the modern governor enjoys unprecedented public attention and is looked to for leadership in his state. Despite his important role, little research has been undertaken on the office he occupies, and the public is ill-informed about his responsibilities.

Though numerous biographies have been written on outstanding governors in many states, only two definitive studies encompassing the office of governor on a comparative, nationwide scale appear in the literature. Leslie Lipson's volume, *The American Governor from Figurehead to Leader,* embodied the initial exploration of the office per se, but it was not until almost two decades later that Coleman B. Ransone's work, *The Office of Governor in the United States,* appeared. The office has been analyzed in several states (Arkansas, Florida, Maryland, and Nevada), but the paucity of research prompted one writer to suggest a need for comparative study and research on the office. He noted that, while the states differ widely in their circumstances, they have significant similarities, and he concluded, "States generally would benefit from a study of the governor's office."[1]

Inspired by this challenge, in 1960 I undertook an extensive investigation of materials concerning the gubernatorial office in the state of Texas. I found many provocative books and articles on individuals who have occupied the office, but no single volume in which the office of governor of Texas was analyzed. This book was written with a view toward at least partially filling this gap. Both the legal and the personal aspects of the office have been emphasized because it is necessary to see the office and the man who occupies it as an entity. To this end I have drawn freely upon the experiences of executives in this state who, through the years, have responded to the multiplicity of situations with which they have been confronted, and I have considered how they have utilized the facilities at their command to furnish leadership in the state. Although the office of governor must be viewed as a whole in which the various functions and powers cannot be compartmentalized satisfactorily, for purposes

[1] Lynton K. Caldwell, "Perfecting State Administration," *Public Administration Review,* VII (Winter, 1947), 25.

of discussion this work is divided into four major parts: development of the governorship, the governor as executive-administrator, the governor and the Legislature, and the political role of the governor. The treatment of each of these aspects overlaps the others to some extent, for it is within the total framework that the incumbents must operate.

Examples to illustrate the functions of the office have been drawn from the administrations of the twenty-four governors who have served under the present Constitution from its adoption in 1876 to 1963, with major emphasis being attached to the development of the office within the past three or four decades; however, throughout the work illustrations from earlier years have been included. National trends in state government are discussed and comparative examples show how governmental practices in Texas coincide with or deviate from comparable functions in other states.

In collecting material over a three-year period, I drew heavily upon the official records and archival material of the state of Texas. Public papers of the governors were examined carefully, although during a part of the time I was at work, the materials in the State Archives were being consolidated into a new permanent building adjacent to the Capitol and the papers were not arranged in any systematic order but were in the boxes in which they had been received from outgoing administrations. Statutes, court cases, *Journals* of the Senate and House of Representatives, and reports of many state agencies were reviewed, along with books, articles, and newspaper accounts of various administrations. Equally as important, and frequently more enlightening, were interviews conducted with practitioners of government. I was able to confer personally with either the governor or a member of the governor's staff for every administration since World War I, and I consulted a seemingly unending number of administrative officials, newspapermen, legislators—indeed anyone at hand who had a knowledge of the practical workings of Texas government.

It is my hope that this beginning in exploring the office of the governor of Texas will motivate further studies to examine more thoroughly the many facets of this important office in this important state.

FRED GANTT, JR.

Texarkana, Texas

ACKNOWLEDGMENTS

Due to the limitations of space, individual acknowledgment of everyone who has contributed information and ideas that have gone into this work cannot be made, but grateful appreciation is extended to all who cooperated so generously by sharing their views on the various aspects of the governorship. Names of individuals who have been quoted are listed in the Bibliography; without their assistance the work would have lacked much that has been included.

Special appreciation goes to former Governor Price Daniel, the incumbent governor during the preparation of most of this work, and to his chief assistants, George Christian and John Goldsum, who, despite a crowded schedule, spent much time in furnishing information to explain the operations of the office. I am likewise indebted to former Governor Allan Shivers, who spent an entire afternoon sharing his views of the chief executive's duties, and to Weldon Hart, longtime confidant of Governors Shivers and Jester, who answered my numerous questions on many different occasions and supplied many documentary materials which would not have been available otherwise. Thanks are due former Governor Coke Stevenson, who cordially received me in Junction for an interesting and informative session. Finally, I am appreciative of the help accorded me by Governor John Connally and his staff after assuming office in January, 1963. Frank Miskell, administrative assistant to Governor Connally, was particularly helpful in making introductions to his fellow staff members and in supplying materials of value.

Two staff members of earlier administrations must be singled out because their insights helped me to understand far better the governorship of Texas. William J. Lawson, executive secretary to former Governor W. Lee O'Daniel, furnished from his personal files copies of campaign speeches and weekly broadcasts from the Governor's Mansion, many of which would not have been available elsewhere. He also provided a complete file of press releases issued from the executive office during his service there. Ghent Sanderford, secretary to former Governor Miriam A. Ferguson, spent many hours enlightening me about the colorful era with which he was associated.

Appreciation is expressed to the Political Science Department of the University of Houston for making available the transcript of a television interview with Governor Price Daniel on the governor's office. Dr. Dorman Winfrey, director-librarian, Texas State Library; James R. Sanders, director, Legislative Reference Service, Texas State Library; and Miss Doris Connerly, former director, were quite helpful in furnishing detailed information on a multitude of subjects. Raymond Brooks, longtime political reporter, gave me much valuable information; and Allen Duckworth, political editor of the *Dallas Morning News*, was also most helpful.

For assistance in preparing maps and tables utilizing his ability as a draftsman, I am grateful to Charles T. Pettigrew. The book has been made a better one by the inclusion of a number of pictures collected with the help of the following: Mrs. Dan Moody, Mrs. James V. Allred, Miss Ima Hogg, Mrs. Allan Shivers, Mrs. Price Daniel, Miss Bertha Porter, Mrs. Marie Shultz, and Dr. Llerena Friend.

My obligation to Professor O. Douglas Weeks, Department of Government, The University of Texas, can never be repaid. As teacher and friend, he has long been a source of inspiration to me. His patient guidance, wise counsel, and scholarly interest throughout every phase of this study are largely responsible for whatever contribution it may make. I am also indebted to my other professors at The University of Texas for their many suggestions and helpful comments during the days of writing and revising the manuscript; each has been valuable in his own way.

Finally, I would be an ingrate if I did not mention the assistance received from my own father. Not only did he help to finance the research and typing, but he willingly shared the thankless task of proofreading the original manuscript and also raised questions which were puzzling from the layman's point of view. In the last analysis, his kindly words of encouragement at propitious moments probably contributed more to the culmination of this study than did any other single factor.

F. G.

Acknowledgment is made of permission to quote from the following materials:

Council of State Governments
  The Book of the States, 1960–61
American Assembly, Columbia University
  The Forty-Eight States: Their Tasks as Policy Makers and Administrators
Bureau of Public Administration, University of Alabama
  Hallie Farmer, *The Legislative Process in Alabama*
  Coleman B. Ransone, Jr., *The Office of Governor in the South*
University of Alabama Press
  Alexander Heard and D. S. Strong, *Southern Primaries and Elections, 1920–1949*
  Coleman B. Ransone, Jr., *The Office of Governor in the United States*
  Warner E. Mills, Jr., *Martial Law in East Texas*
Social Science Research Bureau, Michigan State University
  Joseph A. Schlesinger, *How They Became Governor*
Arnold Foundation, Southern Methodist University
  S. D. Myres, Jr. (ed.), *The Government of Texas: A Survey*
A. H. Belo Corporation, *Texas Almanac, 1961–1962*
Holt, Rinehart and Winston, Inc.
  William Anderson, *et al., Government in the Fifty States*
Vanguard Press, Inc.
  Robert S. Allen (ed.), *Our Sovereign State*
Governmental Research Center, University of Kansas
  Byron Abernethy, *Some Persisting Questions Concerning the Constitutional State Executive*
Texas State Historical Association
  Walter Prescott Webb and H. Bailey Carroll (eds.), *The Handbook of Texas*
Department of Political Science, Tulane University
  L. Vaughan Howard and John H. Fenton (eds.)
  State Governments in the South: Functions and Problems
University of North Carolina Press
  Alexander Heard, *The Costs of Democracy*
Texas Tech Press
  S. S. McKay, *Texas Politics, 1906–1944*
  ——, *W. Lee O'Daniel and Texas Politics, 1938–1944*
Brookings Institution
  Stanley Kelley, Jr., *Political Campaigning*
Doubleday & Company, Inc.
  Rexford G. Tugwell, *The Enlargement of the Presidency*
  George Fuermann, *Reluctant Empire*

Macmillan Company

Harold Zink, *Government and Politics in the United States*

James Bryce, *The American Commonwealth*, Vol. I

Naylor Company

James T. DeShields, *They Sat in High Place: The Presidents and Governors of Texas*

Ouida Ferguson Nalle, *The Fergusons of Texas*

D. C. Heath and Company

W. Brooke Graves, *American State Government*

University of Oklahoma Press

Cortez A. M. Ewing, *Primary Elections in the South: A study in Uniparty Politics*

Homer E. Scace, *The Organization of the Executive Office of the Governor*. By permission of the author.

Appleton-Century-Crofts, Inc.

Chester C. Maxey and R. Y. Fluno, *The American Problem of Government*, 6th ed. Copyright © 1957, Appleton-Century-Crofts, Inc.

Finla G. Crawford, *Readings in American Government*, rev. ed.

University of Chicago Press

Leslie Lipson, *The American Governor from Figurehead to Leader*. Copyright 1938 by The University of Chicago

Harold D. Lasswell, *Psychopathology and Politics*. Copyright 1930 by The University of Chicago

Prentice-Hall, Inc.

Wilbourn E. Benton, *Texas: Its Government and Politics*. © 1961 by permission of Prentice-Hall, Inc., Englewood Cliffs, New Jersey

Rupert N. Richardson, *Texas, the Lone Star State*, 2d ed. © 1958 by permission of Prentice-Hall, Inc., Englewood Cliffs, New Jersey

Institute of Public Affairs, The University of Texas

O. Douglas Weeks, *Texas Presidential Politics in 1952*

———, *Texas One-Party Politics in 1956*

———, *Texas in the 1960 Presidential Election*

A Guide to Texas Agencies, with *1960 Supplement*

The Texas Constitutional Amendments of 1960

Public Affairs Comment

McGraw-Hill Book Company

Charles R. Adrian, *State and Local Governments*

Stuart A. MacCorkle and Dick Smith, *Texas Government*, 4th ed.

The Steck Company

Rae Files Still, *The Gilmer-Aikin Bills: A Study in the Legislative Process*

Ralph W. Steen, *Twentieth-Century Texas: An Economic and Social History*

———, *The Texas Story*

Alfred A. Knopf, Inc.

V. O. Key, Jr., *American State Politics: An Introduction*

———, *Southern Politics in State and Nation*

David B. Truman, *The Governmental Process*

R. N. Current, T. Harry Williams, and Frank Friedel, *American History: A Survey*
Random House, Inc.
  Robert S. Babcock, *State and Local Government and Politics*
  Donald R. Matthews, *The Social Background of Political Decision-Makers*
Thomas Y. Crowell Company
  Austin F. Macdonald, *American State Government and Administration*, 6th ed.
  Belle Zeller, *American State Legislatures*
Pat M. Neff, *The Battles of Peace*. By permission of Pat M. Neff, Jr.

F. G.

CONTENTS

ILLUSTRATIONS

TABLES

FIGURES

PART ONE

The Development of the Governorship in Texas

1

The Executive Office

While attending the convention which drafted the United States Constitution in 1787, James Madison, frequently designated as the architect of that document, is reputed to have remarked, "The Executives of the States are in general little more than cyphers; the Legislatures omnipotent."[1] Notwithstanding such an inauspicious beginning, the position of the governors of the states of the Union has slowly but steadily exceeded Madison's expectations in both theory and practice of American government. True, the legislatures were paramount in 1787, but the formation of the Union marked the genesis of a new trend in the status of the governor, for the example of balanced government and a relatively strong executive at the federal level soon began to make its impact felt upon the states. In like manner, the declining confidence of the people in state legislatures, accompanied by the rise of Jacksonian democracy in the first half of the nineteenth century, further enhanced the position of the state executive.

By 1850 the governor, freed from legislative domination, had come to represent a coordinate, as opposed to a subordinate, branch of government, and the concept of the executive as the "sole representative of the whole state" had begun to emerge.[2]

James Bryce observed in 1888 the increasing importance of American state executives:

[1] Charles S. Tansill (ed.), *Formation of the Union of American States*, p. 398.
[2] Byron R. Abernethy, *Some Persisting Questions Concerning the Constitutional State Executive*, p. 3. Hereafter cited as Abernethy, *The State Executive*.

The decline already noted in the respect and confidence felt for and in the legislatures has latterly, in some States, tended to attach more influence to the office of Governor, and has opened to a strong and upright man, the opportunity of making it a post of effective leadership. The people are coming to look upon the head of their commonwealth as the person responsible for giving them a firm and honest administration. When they are convinced of his rectitude, they regard him as the representative of their own best will and purpose, and have in some instances shown that they are prepared to support him against the legislature and to require the latter to take the path he has pointed out.[3]

But, simultaneously, the executive department of most state governments was being weakened by internal division—occasioned by the aura of Jacksonian democracy, which demanded the popular election of the governor's major subordinates. State administration thereby became a virtual fourth branch of the government, largely independent of either executive or legislative control, and responsible only to an indifferent electorate. By the end of the century, the typical state executive department was a sprawling, multiheaded organization whose power was diffused among many officials. If there was a plan to the typical state administrative organization, "it would appear to have been a planned planlessness, a conscious attempt at decentralization and disorganization designed to prevent concentrated authority at any point in state government."[4]

Early in the twentieth century many leading scholars and practitioners of government had become apprehensive over the existent chaotic situation and the administrative impotency that characterized the states. About 1909 the first concrete proposal to correct the evils of administrative disintegration was advanced by the Peoples' Power League in Oregon, which urged the state "to concentrate executive power in the hands of the governor—checked only by an independent auditor—and to establish vital connections between the governor and the legislature."[5] Such action prompted several sister states to create study commissions on the executive structures within their jurisdictions.[6] The first tangible evidence of the studies was the adoption of the Illinois Civil Administrative Code of 1917, which

---

[3] James Bryce, *The American Commonwealth*, I, 501.

[4] Abernethy, *The State Executive*, p. 5.

[5] W. Brooke Graves, *American State Government* (4th ed.), p. 370.

[6] For a list of the states, see Charles G. Haines, *The Movement for the Reorganization of State Administration*, University of Texas Bulletin No. 1848, August 25, 1918.

abolished more than one hundred boards, commissions, and agencies, and consolidated all of their functions into nine major departments responsible to the governor.[7] The Illinois action inaugurated the Administrative Reorganization Movement, which revived interest in the state executive departments as it spread to the far corners of the nation. Regardless of the fact that many states, including Texas, turned a deaf ear to pleas for reorganization, the role of the governors received unprecedented public attention. The Great Depression a few years later added to the prestige of the executives when citizens turned to them for firm leadership in a social-service state as a hoped-for palliative for personal economic problems and insecurities.[8]

While the country was engaged in World War II, one writer noted that even then the governors were "coming back into their own." He continued:

> After some groping, they seem to be finding their proper places of power, influence, and usefulness in a new dispensation of cooperative relationships with the Federal Government, which, if wisely utilized, will be the means of saving our federal-state system of government in the United States. . . . It is not too much to say that the governors will be the chief influence in saving our system, if it is to be saved. . . . All in all, the governors have met the constant need in a democracy of a stabilizing influence.[9]

"THE DECADE OF THE GOVERNORS"

If the amount of national and international publicity achieved by the executives of the American states may be used as a guide, the 1950's might well be described as "the decade of the governors."[10] As a result of the increasing use of mass media of communication, actions of the state executives have come to be scrutinized more carefully by the citizens, and the names of some governors have come to be well known in most households. Today, as a group, the heads of the fifty states occupy a position of prestige and receive publicity unparalleled in gubernatorial history.

As the governors have come more into the limelight, their re-

[7] Abernethy, *The State Executive*, p. 7.

[8] Charles R. Adrian, *State and Local Governments: A Study in the Political Process*, p. 254. Hereafter cited as Adrian, *State and Local Governments.*

[9] Thomas L. Stokes, "The Governors," *State Government*, XVII (June, 1944), 344–345.

[10] S. R. Solomon, "Governors: 1950–1960," *National Civic Review*, XLIX (September, 1960), 410.

sponsibilities have multiplied. In one analysis, Professor S. R. Solomon has suggested that the gubernatorial problems of the last decade might be identified as the "five r's"—revenue, race, reapportionment, reorganization (administrative), and revision (constitutional).[11] The solution of these complex problems demands leadership of the highest quality, as well as a re-evaluation of the executive's position. A recent book states the challenge succinctly:

> The twentieth century has summoned the governor to a new role. The tangled problems of the machine age require a kind of leadership that state legislatures have been unable to supply. The mantle has fallen on the governor. The people have come to look to him for leadership and programs. He may fail as an executive, as general manager of the routine business of the state, and still be forgiven; but if he fails as a political leader, he will be deemed an unsuccessful governor. That our tripartite form of government makes it highly difficult for the governor to play the leading part successfully makes no difference in the expectations of the people. They look to the governor more than to the legislature and the judiciary; they expect the governor to be able to carry the legislature with him on important policies, and hold him responsible if he fails. On the other hand, if he succeeds, they honor and exalt him. He becomes a national figure.[12]

Probably an even greater position of importance will attach to the governor's office in the future as the complexities of modern society mount. Undoubtedly, Americans will need to search more diligently than ever for enlightened leadership in government, for the survival of the federal system will rest upon the leaders who are chosen through the democratic processes. Certainly the citizens cannot evade their responsibility for selecting wise and competent leaders; to fulfill their obligations the voters must know and appreciate the attributes of the offices which they are called upon to fill through the exercise of their franchise.

THE GOVERNOR IN TEXAS

The office of governor of Texas is the highest position within the power of Texans to bestow in state government, but most citizens of the state have little conception of the workings of the office in all its ramifications. Many do not realize that Texas government, which the

[11] *Ibid.*, p. 411.
[12] Chester C. Maxey and Robert Y. Fluno, *The American Problem of Government* (6th ed.), pp. 300–301.

Governor nominally heads, has become an operation spending some $2 billion a year[13] and employing 66,325 persons on a monthly payroll of approximately $18,514,900.[14] In an attempt to demonstrate the role and the importance of the chief executive in this milieu, the present study has been undertaken. In the chapters that follow, the most important activities of the office have been explored and assessed. It is to be hoped that future studies will inquire even further into various facets of the office. But in the years that lie ahead, all citizens of Texas should know and understand more about their leader, his duties, responsibilities, and opportunities, if they are to choose wisely who occupies the gubernatorial chair. The quality of leadership which Texas voters demand will determine in large measure the role that Texas is to assume in the American system of government.

LEGAL QUALIFICATIONS

The legal qualifications for becoming governor of Texas are few and simple. One must be at least thirty years of age, a citizen of the United States, and a resident of Texas for at least five years immediately preceding election.[15] Although no specific religious requirement is set, neither the governor nor any elected state official, may be excluded from office because of his religious sentiments, "provided he acknowledges the existence of a Supreme Being."[16] Presumably, therefore, an atheist would be barred from the office, although the probability of his being elected at all might be practically nil. Interestingly enough, the governor is not required to be a qualified voter, and on at least one occasion the victor in the election was unable to cast a vote.[17] He is prohibited from practicing any profession and from holding any other office—civil, military, or corporate—during the term for which he is elected, though the courts have ruled that this limitation does not extend to his ex-officio membership on state boards.[18]

---

[13] *Annual Report of the Comptroller of Public Accounts*, State of Texas, 1960, Part I, pp. b and c.

[14] *The Book of the States, 1960–1961*, p. 163.

[15] Constitution of Texas, Art. IV, Sec. 4.

[16] Constitution of Texas, Art. I, Sec. 4.

[17] Stuart A. MacCorkle and Dick Smith, *Texas Government* (4th ed.), p. 90. It is reported that W. Lee O'Daniel had not paid his poll tax when first elected in 1938.

[18] *Arnold* v. *State*, 9 S.W. 120 (1888); *Missouri, Kansas, and Texas Ry. Co. of Texas* v. *Shanon*, 100 S.W. 138 (1907).

Candidates for governor may be nominated (1) by the primary system or (2) by the convention system.[19] A political party whose gubernatorial candidate in the preceding election received more than 200,000 votes must hold a primary, but parties whose candidates received less votes may use either method. In practice in Texas, this has usually meant that the Democratic Party has nominated candidates by the primary method, while the Republican Party has used the convention method, although it may well be that candidates of both parties will be nominated consistently by primaries in the future.[20] The primaries are held on the first Saturday in May of even-numbered years, with a runoff primary four weeks later in the event no candidate receives a majority of the votes cast. Some six months thereafter, on the Tuesday following the first Monday in November, a general election is held in which the governor and other officials are elected. Prior to the 1960's the general election amounted to little more than a compliance with the law, as nomination by the Democratic Party was tantamount to election. However, in 1961, the Republicans elected a United States senator—the first statewide race they had won since the days of Reconstruction after the Civil War. Undoubtedly they will capture still other offices in the years ahead, perhaps including the governorship.

The returns of the general election are delivered to the secretary of state, who transmits them to the speaker of the House of Representatives as soon as the speaker is chosen by the regular session in the January following the election. During the first week of the session the speaker opens and "publishes" the returns in the presence of a joint session of the Legislature.

The person having the highest number of votes . . . and being constitutionally eligible, shall be declared by the Speaker, under sanction of the Legislature, to be elected. . . . But if two or more persons shall have the highest and equal number of votes for . . . said office, one of them shall be immediately chosen to such office by joint vote of both houses of the Legislature. Contested elections . . . shall be determined by both houses of the Legislature in joint session.[21]

---

[19] A detailed analysis of the nomination procedure appears in Chapter 11.
[20] The Republican Party has been required to hold primaries in 1926, 1930, 1934, 1954, 1958, and 1962.
[21] Constitution of Texas, Art. IV, Sec. 3.

Since more than a million votes have been cast in elections in recent years, the eventuality that a tie will have to be broken by the Legislature would appear to be remote.[22]

TERM, RESIDENCE, AND COMPENSATION

So far as the term of office is concerned, Texas is among the minority of states which still cling to that fast-fading relic of the Jacksonian era—the two-year gubernatorial term. Most states have abandoned the short term in favor of a four-year term, but Texas has not seen fit to follow suit; however, the number of two-year terms which an incumbent may serve is unlimited.[23] Prior to the 1940's there was an "unwritten law" against a third term for Texas governors, but when President Franklin D. Roosevelt broke a similar tradition at the national level, Texans fell in line and overthrew the state precedent of many years. Coke Stevenson had served almost one and one-half years of his predecessor's term (W. Lee O'Daniel had left the governorship to become United States Senator) and had been re-elected in his own right, when at the height of World War II, in 1944, he was re-elected to a second full term; thus, when he retired from office he had the distinction of having served longer as Texas governor than had any other individual in history. Allan Shivers achieved an even greater distinction by being elected to three full terms after having served more than half of his predecessor's term— a total of seven and one-half years. (Beauford Jester, who preceded Shivers, died of a heart attack while in office.)

Shivers' successor, Price Daniel, was elected to three full terms, and in 1962 became the first person ever to seek a fourth elective term, but his candidacy was this time rejected by the voters. At least two candidates in that race pledged to support an amendment which would limit the number of terms which a governor could serve in Texas. John Connally, a proponent of a maximum of two terms consisting of two years each, won the Democratic nomination and the election.

For his services to the state the governor receives a compensation

[22] For example, in the election of 1960, Price Daniel, Democrat, received 1,627,698 votes to 609,808 for William M. Steger, Republican. *Texas Almanac, 1961–1962*, p. 460.

[23] In 1962 only fifteen states had a two-year term; thirty-five had a four-year term. *The Book of the States, 1960–1961*, Supplement II, p. 1. Minnesota switched to the longer term in 1962, and a new Michigan constitution providing for a four-year term was adopted by the voters of that state in April, 1963.

fixed by act of the Legislature. The initial salary was set by the Constitution of 1876 at "$4,000 and no more," and that figure remained in effect until 1936, when it was increased to $12,000 by constitutional amendment. In 1954 the voters authorized the removal of a constitutional limit and vested authority to fix the governor's salary in the Legislature, with the proviso that a sum lower than $12,000 should not be set.[24] Shortly thereafter an annual stipend of $25,000 was established by the Legislature, placing the chief executive of Texas among the nation's higher-paid governors.[25] In addition, the governor and his family live in the Executive Mansion, opposite the State Capitol.[26] The Legislature makes an annual appropriation for the upkeep of the Mansion; the courts have held that none of this money may be spent for food, liquors, or engraved cards or invitations for the governor's private use.[27]

SUCCESSION TO THE OFFICE

The lieutenant governor of Texas is first in line of succession to the highest office. He becomes the chief executive "in case of the death, resignation, removal from office, inability or refusal to serve, or of the Governor's impeachment or absence from the State," and serves until another is chosen at the next election and is duly qualified, or "until the Governor impeached, absent, or disabled, shall be acquitted, return, or his disability be removed."[28] If, during the lieutenant governor's service, he should become incapable of performing the duties, the president pro tempore of the Senate assumes the executive power.

Under the terms of an amendment added to the Constitution in 1948, the exigency of the death or incapacity of the governor-elect

[24] Constitution of Texas, Art. IV, Sec. 5. See also Art. III, Sec. 61–a.
[25] Only five states pay more than Texas: New York, $50,000; California, $40,-000; Pennsylvania, $35,000; Illinois and New Jersey, $30,000. The states of Alabama, Alaska, Hawaii, Missouri, and Ohio pay the same salary as does Texas. *The Book of the States, 1960–1961*, p. 126.
[26] Located at 1010 Colorado Street in Austin, the Executive Mansion, an imposing structure occupying a city block, was built in 1856. Mrs. Price Daniel, hostess of the Mansion from 1957 to 1963, has prepared for publication a comprehensive history of the Executive Mansion. Mrs. Daniel and her assistant, Mrs. Marie Shultz, also added a collection of mementoes for display in the public reception rooms. The collection includes an item presented by each of the families who have occupied the residence.
[27] *Terrell, Comptroller of Public Accounts v. Middleton*, 187 S.W. 367 (1916).
[28] Constitution of Texas, Art. IV, Sec. 16.

prior to inauguration is covered.[29] If the governor-elect dies in this interim, the lieutenant governor-elect acts until after the next general election, or in case of his disability or failure to qualify, the lieutenant governor-elect serves until a person has qualified. If both the governor-elect and lieutenant governor-elect are permanently disabled, the Legislature, in joint session, is authorized to elect someone to fill the office.

In 1959 the Emergency Interim Executive Succession Act was passed,[30] in compliance with the 1948 amendment which authorized the legislators to provide by statute for a further line of succession. The statute places fifteen officials in line for the post after the governor. Pursuant to its terms, the present line of succession is established as governor, lieutenant governor, president pro tempore of the Senate, speaker of the House of Representatives, attorney general, and the chief justice of each of the Courts of Civil Appeals, in numerical order of their supreme judicial districts.

~ Since 1876 only four lieutenant governors have succeeded to the high office as a result of the death, inability, or resignation of a governor. Of these cases, one vacancy resulted from a death, another from impeachment, and two from resignations to accept a seat in the United States Senate. Except for those serving for a few days during the temporary absence from the state of both the governor and the lieutenant governor, the line of succession has never gone beyond the lieutenant governor.

REMOVAL FROM OFFICE

Chief executives of Texas may be removed from office before the expiration of their terms only through the process of impeachment. In such cases the House of Representatives brings the charges, and the Senate, sitting as a court of impeachment, hears the case. Conviction requires a two-thirds vote of the senators present, and judgment extends only to removal from office and disqualification from holding any other office of honor, trust, or profit under the state. A convicted person, however, is also subject to indictment, trial, and punishment according to law.[31] In practice, "impeachment is a convenient political weapon, and almost every governor who attempts

[29] Constitution of Texas, Art. IV, Sec. 3–a.
[30] *Acts of 1959*, Fifty-sixth Legislature, Chapter 232.
[31] Constitution of Texas, Art. XV, Secs. 1–5.

to provide legislative leadership will be threatened with its use," says one writer.[32]

Although many governors throughout the nation have been impeached and threats of impeachment have been even more frequent, only a few have been convicted. Texas has the distinction, if such it be, of having been one of three states to convict and remove a governor on impeachment charges.[33] Perhaps there is no more dramatic story in Texas political history than that of the impeachment of Governor James E. Ferguson in 1917. Centering mainly upon his alleged misuse of public funds and his attempt to dominate the Board of Regents of The University of Texas when they refused to dismiss several faculty members with whom the Governor disagreed, Ferguson was charged on twenty-one counts by the House of Representatives. After a long and heated trial during the months of August and September, 1917, the Senate found him guilty on ten of the charges, and he was removed and disqualified from holding other state offices.[34] Years later the Legislature passed a bill granting amnesty to Ferguson (after the voters had elected his wife governor), but the Texas Supreme Court declared the amnesty bill to be in violation of the Constitution.[35] The trial of Ferguson and his resurgence in politics was a source of amazement to many observers. In the words of one recent writer:

> Considering the nation as a whole, it is doubtful if any other state has contributed as much as Texas to the "law of impeachment." It could not be otherwise in view of the trial and removal of Ferguson, the election of his wife as first citizen, and the litigation, legislation, and advisory opinions resulting from their entrance in Texas politics.[36]

THE GOVERNOR AS LEADER

Within this legal framework, the governor of Texas must operate to lead his state. To do so, he is endowed by the Constitution and stat-

[32] Adrian, *State and Local Governments*, p. 273.

[33] Other governors removed via impeachment include Sulzer of New York (1913), Walton of Oklahoma (1923), and Johnston of Oklahoma (1927).

[34] One of the most thorough coverages of the Ferguson impeachment trial appears in daily reports in the *New York Times*, in August and September, 1917. The official report of the trial may be found in *House Journal*, Thirty-fifth Legislature, second called session, pp. 35–494.

[35] *Ferguson* v. *Wilcox, et al.*, 28 S.W. (2d) 526 (1930).

[36] Wilbourn E. Benton, *Texas: Its Government and Politics*, p. 260. By permission of Prentice-Hall, Inc.

utes with numerous powers and responsibilities, the most important of which may be classified as executive, administrative, and legislative. Furthermore, his position in the hierarchy of his political party affords a useful "extralegal" medium of power and influence. Collectively, the executive, legislative, and political powers equip him with the tools, albeit insufficient ones, which he must use to exert leadership in the state.

Mere powers alone, however, are not enough. As a recent textbook on state government states:

> Particular powers may be inadequate for this or that purpose, but put together the various powers, the prestige of the governorship, the leadership that is expected from the incumbent, and a shrewd, genial, and dynamic man in the office, and the combination becomes an engine of public power that can accomplish great things.[37]

During the campaign of 1962 the *Houston Chronicle* editorialized that an "ideal" person for the office of governor of Texas needs: (1) brilliance of mind, (2) legal knowledge, (3) political experience, (4) administrative skill, (5) sound knowledge of business and industry, and (6) a nationwide acquaintance.[38] Needless to say, officeholders have not always possessed this combination, for seldom does human nature or society achieve the ideal. Nevertheless, Texas has been generally fortunate in selecting men of high caliber for the highest office in the state. In the words of one observer:

> . . . the Governors of Texas may be taken to represent fairly the highest type of her public men throughout the years covered by their services. It is true here, as elsewhere, even in the United States at large, that the ablest men have not always attained the position of rulership, and that some of those who have thus succeeded have not always measured up to the ideal standard of chieftainship in the State. But considered from all points of view . . . the list of rulers whom the people of Texas have chosen in the past years contains the names of her truly great men, and even the humblest in the catalogue has been gifted with qualities of head and heart that found appreciation in the affection and confidence of a discerning constituency.[39]

[37] William Anderson, Clara Penniman, and Edward W. Wiedner, *Government in the Fifty States*, p. 269.

[38] *Houston Chronicle*, May 27, 1962.

[39] James T. DeShields, *They Sat in High Place: The Presidents and Governors of Texas*, p. xxiii. Hereafter cited as DeShields, *The Presidents and Governors of Texas*.

At best, the task of being governor of Texas is not an easy one. Incumbents are confronted with problems more diverse than those that face any other executive in the state, are subjected frequently to abuse and criticism by the public, and are circumscribed in the exercise of their functions by legal and constitutional restrictions. In the view of the chief executive at the turn of the century, Joseph Draper Sayers, "A Texas Governor has only two happy days: the day he is inaugurated and the day he retires."[40] Similar sentiments were expressed by a successor of two decades later, Pat M. Neff: "The Governor's office is not the primrose path of pleasure. Every time you throw yourself in opposition to what somebody wants, you immediately become the target for many a poisoned arrow."[41] Neff, however, also said of the executive office, "It thrills; it inspires; it humbles; it is a challenge to the highest, the noblest and the best."[42]

Although the job of the chief executive in Texas may be made more difficult by restrictions which weaken it legally, the nature of the executive function and the gubernatorial office endow the governor with certain potentialities of leadership which can make him in actuality stronger and more powerful than would seem to be the case on the surface. Granted that the limitations fixed by the Constitution and statutes, plus a disintegrated administrative system reminiscent of the nineteenth century, restrict the Texas executive more than is true of some of his counterparts in other states of the union, the inescapable fact remains that he is the logical public official to lead the state. He assumes a role of leadership enjoyed by no other in the state when he recites the oath of office, which Governor Neff labelled "retrospective, introspective, and prospective."[43]

I, ——, do solemnly swear (or affirm) that I will faithfully execute the duties of the office of Governor of the State of Texas, and will to the best of my ability preserve, protect, and defend the Constitution and laws of the United States and of this state; and I furthermore solemnly swear (or affirm), that I have not, directly nor indirectly paid, offered, or promised to pay, contributed, nor promised to contribute any money, or valuable thing, or promised any public office of employment, as a reward for the giving or withholding a vote at the election at which I was elected. So help me God.[44]

[40] Ross Phares, *Texas Tradition*, p. 192.
[41] *Messages of Pat M. Neff*, pp. 34–35.
[42] *Ibid.*, p. 1.
[43] *Ibid.*
[44] Constitution of Texas, Art. XVI, Sec. 1.

2

The Development of the Executive
Article in Texas Constitutions

The inhabitants of Texas are reputed to boast endlessly of a long and colorful history under six flags as province, republic, and state. Less well known is the stimulating fact that the office of chief executive in Texas predates the founding of the American union and the Presidency of the United States by almost a century. The lineage of the office of governor of Texas can be traced directly through the ninety-five incumbents who have held the position during more than two and one-half centuries.[1]

The first individual to become governor of Texas was designated by a *cédula real* from the King of Spain in 1691. Don Domingo Terán de los Ríos, commissioned *gobernador de Tejas* at a salary of 2,500 pesos annually, departed immediately with fifty soldiers to carry herds of cattle and horses to the missions that were being built by the Roman Catholic priests among the Indians east of the Trinity River. Returning to Mexico the following year, he left enough animals to establish the great herds which were found 125 years later when

---

[1] *Texas Almanac, 1961–1962*, p. 441. The entity of Texas as a political subdivision is usually accepted as dating from the appointment of Don Domingo Terán de los Ríos in 1691, following the expedition of Captain Alonzo de Leon and Father Massenet into east Texas and the founding of San Francisco de los Tejas and other early missions. Some authorities, including the late Dr. C. E. Castañeda of the Latin American Collection of The University of Texas, would place several early royal governors from Spain among those properly belonging to a list of governors of Texas. Dr. Castañeda would include four: Francisco de Garay (1523–1526), Panfillo de Narvaez (1523–1528), Nuño de Guzman (1528–1530), and Hernando de Soto (1538–1543).

the American colonists arrived. Historians record this founding of the cattle industry as the major contribution of the first governor of Texas.[2]

After the completion of this journey, political authority was relaxed for a while and little attention was given Texas until the administration of Martín de Alarcón, Governor of Coahuila and Texas, who founded the mission of San Antonio de Valero and the presidio of San Antonio de Béxar in 1718. The first nobleman to hold the office of governor, the Marqués de San Miguél de Aguayo, was appointed by the Viceroy and sent to watch the French in Texas, lest they seize control from the Spaniards. By 1722, largely as a result of the Marqués' efforts, the dominion of Spain was definitely established between the Rio Grande and the Rivière Rouge—a situation that was to prevail for the following century. During the years of Spanish control of Texas thirty-seven individuals held the title "Gobernador de Tejas."[3]

When independence from Spain was declared the first governor of Texas to be selected by the Mexican government was Felix Trespalacios. While the state remained under the flag of Mexico turnover in the chief executive's office reached an all-time high. Between 1822 and 1836 fifteen persons held the position, the average tenure being somewhat less than twelve months.[4]

The intervening years have witnessed a far-reaching change from the complicated and obsequious ceremonials that surrounded the dominating Excellencies of the days of Spanish and Mexican rule. Compared with the environments of those magistrates, chief executives of later years have found themselves in far simpler surroundings, but it adds "something to the dignity of the office and to the pride of its incumbents to be able to trace a lineage so ancient and so genteel"[5] as that evidenced in the following list.

CHIEF EXECUTIVES OF TEXAS FROM 1691 TO 1964

GOBERNADORES DE TEJAS

1691–1692   Domingo Terán de los Ríos
1693–1716   Texas unoccupied but included Coahuila

[2] DeShields, *The Presidents and Governors of Texas,* p. xi.
[3] *Texas Almanac, 1961–1962,* p. 441.
[4] *Ibid.*
[5] DeShields, *The Presidents and Governors of Texas,* p. xiii.

1716–1719 Martín de Alarcón appointed governor of Texas on December 7, 1716 (On August 5, 1716, he had been appointed governor of Coahuila.)

1719–1722 The Marqués de San Miguél de Aguayo, governor of Coahuila and Texas

1722–1726 Fernando Pérez de Almazán

1727–1730 Melchor de Media Villa y Ascona

1730– Juan Antonio Bustillo y Zevallos

1734– Manuel de Sandoval

1736–1737 Carlos Benites Franquis de Lugo

1737– Fernández de Jáuregui y Urrutia, governor of Nuevo León, governor extraordinary and *visitador*

1737–1740 Prudencio de Orobio y Bazterra (governor ad interim)

1741–1743 Tomás Felipe Wintuisen

1743–1744 Justo Boneo y Morales

1744–1748 Francisco García Larios (governor ad interim)

1748–1750 Pedro del Barrio Junco y Espriella

1751–1759 Jacinto de Barrios y Jáuregui. Barrios was appointed governor of Coahuila in 1757, but was retained in Texas until 1759 to complete a task.

1759–1766 Angel de Martos y Navarrete

1767–1770 Hugo Oconór (governor ad interim)

1770–1778 The Baron de Ripperdá

1778–1786 Domingo Cabello

1786– Bernardo Bonavía appointed July 8, but apparently did not serve.

1787–1790 Rafael Martínez Pachecho appointed February 27; removal approved October 18, 1790.

1788– The office of governor was ordered suppressed and the province put under a presidial captain.

1790–1799(?) Manuel Muñoz

1798(?)– Josef Irigoyen, apparently appointed but did not serve.

1800(?)–1805 Juan Bautista de Elguezábal

1805–1810 Antonio Cordero y Bustamante

1810–1813 Manuel de Salcedo

1811 (Jan. 22–March 2) Juan Bautista Casas (revolutionary governor)

1814–1818 Christóbal Domínguez

1817– Ignacio Pérez and Manuel Pardo (governors ad interim)

1817–1822 Antonio Martínez

1822–1823   José Felix Trespalacios
1823(?)–1824   Luciano García

GOBERNADORES DE COAHUILA Y TEJAS

1824–1826   Rafael Gonzáles
1826–1827   Victor Blanco
1827–1831   José María Viesca
1831–1832   José María Letona
1832–1833   Juan Martín de Beramendi
1834–1835   Juan José Elguezábal
1835–   Augustín Viesca
1835–   Ramón Eca y Músquiz

PROVISIONAL GOVERNORS DURING THE TEXAS REVOLUTION

Nov. 14, 1835–March 1, 1836   Henry Smith
Jan. 11, 1836–March 1, 1836   James W. Robinson[a]

PRESIDENTS OF THE REPUBLIC OF TEXAS

March 17, 1836–Oct. 22, 1836   David G. Burnet
Oct. 22, 1836–Dec. 10, 1838   Sam Houston
Dec. 10, 1838–Dec. 13, 1841   Mirabeau B. Lamar
Dec. 13, 1841–Dec. 9, 1844   Sam Houston
Dec. 9, 1844–Feb. 19, 1846   Anson Jones

GOVERNORS OF STATE OF TEXAS AFTER ANNEXATION TO UNITED STATES

Feb. 19, 1846–Dec. 21, 1847   J. Pinckney Henderson
May 19, 1846–Nov. –, 1846   A. C. Horton[b]
Dec. 21, 1847–Dec. 21, 1849   George T. Wood
Dec. 21, 1849–Nov. 23, 1853   P. Hansborough Bell
Nov. 23, 1853–Dec. 21, 1853   J. W. Henderson[c]
Dec. 21, 1853–Dec. 21, 1857   Elisha M. Pease
Dec. 21, 1857–Dec. 21, 1859   Hardin R. Runnels
Dec. 21, 1859–March 16, 1861   Sam Houston[d]
March 16, 1861–Nov. 7, 1861   Edward Clark

[a] Robinson was elected by the Council after Smith had been deposed and the office of governor declared vacant by the Council. Thereafter both men claimed the right to exercise the executive authority.

[b] Lieutenant Governor Horton served as governor while Governor Henderson was away commanding troops in the war with Mexico.

[c] Lieutenant Governor Henderson became governor when Governor Bell resigned to take his seat in Congress, to which he had been elected.

[d] Houston refused to take the oath of allegiance to the Confederacy and was deposed. He was succeeded by Lieutenant Governor Edward Clark.

Nov. 7, 1861–Nov. 5, 1863	Francis R. Lubbock
Nov. 5, 1863–June 17, 1865	Pendleton Murrah[e]
July 21, 1865–Aug. 9, 1866	Andrew J. Hamilton (provisional)
Aug. 9, 1866–Aug. 8, 1867	James W. Throckmorton[f]
Aug. 8, 1867–Sept. 30, 1869	Elisha M. Pease
Jan. 8, 1870–Jan. 15, 1874	Edmund J. Davis[g]
Jan. 15, 1874–Dec. 1, 1876	Richard Coke (resigned to enter U.S. Senate)
Dec. 1, 1876–Jan. 21, 1879	Richard B. Hubbard
Jan. 21, 1879–Jan. 16, 1883	Oran M. Roberts
Jan. 16, 1883–Jan. 18, 1887	John Ireland
Jan. 18, 1887–Jan. 20, 1891	Lawrence Sullivan Ross
Jan. 20, 1891–Jan. 15, 1895	James S. Hogg
Jan. 15, 1895–Jan. 17, 1899	Charles A. Culberson
Jan. 17, 1899–Jan. 20, 1903	Joseph D. Sayers
Jan. 20, 1903–Jan. 15, 1907	S. W. T. Lanham
Jan. 15, 1907–Jan. 19, 1911	Thomas M. Campbell
Jan. 19, 1911–Jan. 19, 1915	Oscar Branch Colquitt
Jan. 19, 1915–Aug. 25, 1917	James E. Ferguson (impeached)
Aug. 25, 1917–Jan. 18, 1921	William P. Hobby
Jan. 18, 1921–Jan. 20, 1925	Pat M. Neff
Jan. 20, 1925–Jan. 17, 1927	Miriam A. Ferguson
Jan. 17, 1927–Jan. 20, 1931	Dan Moody
Jan. 20, 1931–Jan. 17, 1933	Ross S. Sterling
Jan. 17, 1933–Jan. 15, 1935	Miriam A. Ferguson
Jan. 15, 1935–Jan. 17, 1939	James V. Allred
Jan. 17, 1939–Aug. 4, 1941	W. Lee O'Daniel (resigned to enter U.S. Senate
Aug. 4, 1941–Jan. 21, 1947	Coke R. Stevenson
Jan. 21, 1947–July 11, 1949	Beauford H. Jester (died)
July 11, 1949–Jan. 15, 1957	Allan Shivers
Jan. 15, 1957–Jan. 15, 1963	Price Daniel
Jan. 15, 1963–	John Connally

Source: Derived from Rupert N. Richardson, *Texas, the Lone Star State* (2d ed.), pp. 443–446, and *Texas Almanac, 1961–1962*, p. 441.

[e] Murrah's administration was terminated by the fall of the Confederacy. Murrah retired to Mexico, and for a period (May–June, 1865), Lieutenant Governor Fletcher S. Stockdale was acting governor.

[f] Throckmorton was removed by the military. Pease, provisional governor who succeeded him, resigned September 30, 1869.

[g] Davis was appointed provisional governor after he had been elected governor.

A contemporary author has concluded that the story of the chief executive in a typical American state has been one of progression

from detested minion of Royal power, to stepson of legislative domination, to popular figurehead, to effective executive. . . . The American governorship was conceived in mistrust and born in a strait jacket, the creature of revolutionary assemblies.[6]

Tracing the evolution of the executive article through the various Texas constitutions should determine whether Texas has been "typical."

MEXICAN FEDERAL CONSTITUTION, 1824, AND CONSTITUTION OF THE STATE OF COAHUILA AND TEXAS, 1827

Constitutional government in Texas was begun in 1824 with the adoption of a provisional government under the *Acta Constitutiva de Federacion de 1824*. That document called for a strict separation of powers among the legislative, executive, and judicial departments, and for the organization of internal government in the various states of the Mexican Federation.[7] Some nine months later, in October, 1824, the Mexican Federal Constitution was adopted, and the provisional governments were made permanent. Mexican fundamental law was influenced by both the American and the Spanish constitutions but it was probably more closely akin to the Spanish Constitution of 1812.[8] This document provided for division of the country into states, departments, and municipalities, one such state being Coahuila and Texas, which adopted its first constitution on March 11, 1827. The executive power of the state was vested in a governor and a vice governor, but there was also this additional provision: "For the better discharge of the duties of his office the governor shall have a body for consultation, to be styled the *Executive Council*, which shall be composed of three voters proper, and two substitutes, of all whom only one can be an ecclesiastic."[9] These councillors, along with the governor and the vice governor, were to be elected on the day after

[6] William H. Young, "The Development of the Governorship," *State Government*, XXXI (Summer, 1958), 178.

[7] *Acta Constitutiva de Federacion Mexicana de 1824*, Arts. 20–25.

[8] Walter P. Webb and H. Bailey Carroll (eds.), *The Handbook of Texas*, p. 396.

[9] Constitution of the State of Coahuila and Texas, Tit. II, Sec. III, Art. 121. The idea probably was taken from the Spanish Constitution of 1812, in which a Council of State was provided to advise the king (Title IV, Art. 168).

the election of deputies to the Congress of the State of Coahuila and Texas.[10]

The formation of the Executive Council to assist the governor was an interesting addition to the executive article, although the precedent for such a body had been set by many of the colonial and early state governments in the United States. Specifically, the group was charged with these duties: (1) to give written reports to the governor on all business required by law or requested by the governor; (2) to watch over the observance of federal and state laws and to apprise the Congress of violations; (3) "to promote establishment of, and give activity to, all branches of prosperity of the state";[11] (4) to propose nominations of three for filling the offices required by law; (5) to concur with the permanent deputation agreeably on the convocation of Congress to extra session, and (6) to explain the accounts of all public funds and transmit the same to Congress for approval.[12]

Notwithstanding the authority of the Council, the governor alone possessed certain responsibilities offering the opportunity for real leadership.[13] One of his more important functions was the promulgation of laws enacted by the Congress. Although not the direct veto power in the Anglo-American tradition, this promulgation function provided him with some influence over Congress. The constitution declared that if the governor approved of the laws, he was to promulgate them immediately; however, if he should not agree, he was to "make observation upon the laws and decrees of Congress . . . suspending their publication until said Congress resolves thereon."[14] At the rehearing of the laws the executive was to designate a public speaker to represent him at the debate.[15]

Other functions of the governor included the preservation of internal order in the state, seeing to "the fulfillment of the law," appointing all officers of state not elected by the people, and proposing to the permanent deputation (after hearing the advice of the Executive Council) the convocation of extra sessions of Congress.

[10] *Ibid.*, Tit. II, Sec. III, Art. 129.

[11] *Ibid.*, Sec. III, Art. 127.

[12] *Ibid.*

[13] *Ibid.*, Tit. II, Sec. 1, Art. 113, divided the powers of the governor into Prerogatives, Attributes, and Restrictions. Spanish tradition prevailing at that time required that the powers of the executive be explicitly outlined. See William A. Whatley, "The Formation of the Mexican Constitution of 1824" (unpublished M.A. thesis), p. 134.

[14] Constitution of the State of Coahuila and Texas, Tit. II, Sec. I, Art. 112.

[15] *Ibid.*, Tit. I, Sec. IV, Arts. 102–103.

Two rather uncommon provisions added much to stature of the chief executive. He was authorized to see that justice was promptly and fully administered by tribunals and courts of justice of the state and that their decisions were executed. Such a provision seemingly placed the executive on a plane at least as high as that of the judiciary or possibly higher—a unique situation for those days when executive power was greatly feared. A second real power was in the field of personnel management, i.e., the chief executive could suspend from office (up to three months) and deprive of one-half salary during that time "all officers of the executive department, and of his appointment or approval, on violating his orders or decrees, transmitting the data on the subject to the respective tribunal, should he think there is a proper ground for action."[16] Undoubtedly, this provision allowing for disciplinary action was the strongest of its kind ever to appear in a Texas constitution.

The governor of Coahuila and Texas possessed two unique duties not usually performed by the executive of a state. He was the superintendent of the manufacture of tobacco (a monopoly held by the federal government), and he was responsible for authorizing the negotiation of contracts for the maintenance of churches in the state.[17]

One feature of this Constitution, later to prove highly distasteful to the people, was the decree power vested in the Congress, but often delegated to the chief executive. Frequently the use of decrees reflected to some extent the degree of rest or unrest prevalent in the state; when danger threatened, the executive's powers were increased by decree, only to be reduced again when security was restored. Used on 325 occasions before Texas rebelled, the decree power covered such emergencies as those of 1826 and 1829, when the governor was authorized to arrest and confine without legal procedure any person whom he suspected as a disturber of the peace, and of 1834, when he was authorized to organize troops to defend federal institutions and take, on his own authority, any measures that might be necessary for securing public tranquility in the state.[18]

Obviously, the first fundamental law of the state allowed for extensive power—at times absolute—to be vested in the governor.

---

[16] *Ibid.*

[17] William S. Brandenberger, "The Administrative System of Texas, 1821–1836" (unpublished M.A. thesis), pp. 30–32.

[18] The text of all 325 decrees are published under the title *Laws and Decrees of the State of Coahuila and Texas,* translated by J. P. Kimball, M.D.

Nevertheless, in keeping with the Spanish tradition, specific limitations were fixed. The incumbent of the office could not assume personal command of the state militia without the consent of Congress. Neither could he interfere during criminal trials nor deprive an individual of his liberty. He was prohibited from taking private property "unless it should be necessary for a purpose of manifest public utility in the judgment of the executive council." Finally, he could not "impede or embarrass" popular elections or leave the capital for more than a month without the consent of Congress.[19]

Despite the specificity of the Constitution of 1827 on the executive power, the use of decrees was displeasing to many citizens. Furthermore, even though Coahuila and Texas were one state under the Mexican Federation, Coahuila had much greater representation in the national government than did Texas. One has only to read the Texas Declaration of Independence to find a succinct cataloguing of the grievances held by Texans against such despotic Mexican rule. Logically enough, citizens of the Texas portion of Coahuila and Texas joined in taking steps against those who were in control, and on March 2, 1836, the Declaration of Independence from Mexico was signed at Washington-on-the-Brazos.

CONSTITUTION OF THE REPUBLIC OF TEXAS, 1836

If ever a constitution was born of a revolution, the Texas Constitution of 1836 was that one. The same delegates who declared independence drafted immediately a basic law for the newly organized Republic. Calling for a unitary government, the document was "a composite structure of portions of the Constitution of the United States and of several state constitutions in effect. It does not appear that any one state was followed."[20]

Framed in the heyday of Jacksonian democracy, Articles III and VI dealt with the office of the executive. They instituted a President who was popularly elected for a three-year term and who was ineligible to succeed himself—the latter provision, no doubt, inspired by an aversion of the Mexican system, where presidents had used their powers on numerous occasions to influence elections. The President of the Republic was required to be thirty-five years of age, to be a

---

[19] Constitution of the State of Coahuila and Texas, Tit. II.

[20] Rupert N. Richardson, "The Framing of the Constitution of the Republic of Texas," *Southwestern Historical Quarterly*, XXXI (January, 1928), 209.

citizen of the Republic, and to reside within Texas for three years prior to election. His powers closely resembled those of the American President, except that he was forbidden to lead the armies without consent of Congress—again a carry-over from the Mexican Constitution of 1824. There was a provision for a Cabinet, with the President empowered to appoint a Secretary of State and such other department heads as might be created by law. He had the power to remit fines and forfeitures, to fill vacancies, to receive foreign ministers, to negotiate treaties, and to recommend legislation. Also, borrowing from the American Constitution, he was required to see "that the laws be faithfully executed."

The Republic of Texas existed for only nine years, but its Constitution had the attributes of a fundamental law in the truest sense. It was brief, concise, and not excessively restrictive of public officials; it was to become a model from which to pattern another constitution once Texas was admitted to the United States.

FIRST STATE CONSTITUTION, 1845

When Texas became a part of the Union in 1845, the chief executive of Texas became again the governor. The group that framed the first state constitution has been described as probably "the ablest assembly that has ever served the state."[21] The basic law of which they were the authors is generally conceded to be the best of all the constitutions produced by Texas since it became a state and was highly regarded by citizens of other states. United States Senator Daniel Webster, though opposing the annexation of Texas, called it the best of all state constitutions of that day.[22]

The document was indeed far ahead of its time; it incorporated many of the ideas which later were to be associated with the Administrative Reorganization Movement launched in the American states in the early part of the twentieth century. It was a basic charter in the strictest sense, brief and simple, outlining the powers and functions of the three branches of government without incorporating the endless amount of statutory detail which its successors have included so freely.

The executive under the Constitution of 1845 was in a position to

[21] Rupert N. Richardson, *Texas, the Lone Star State* (2d ed.), p. 126. By permission of Prentice-Hall, Inc.
[22] Webb and Carroll (eds.), *Handbook of Texas*, p. 398.

offer real leadership. He appointed other executive officials, who were responsible to him—a carry-over from the powers of the President of the Republic. Under this fundamental law the chief executive of the Lone Star State hit his peak of power and prestige, from a constitutional standpoint; never again has the governor been accorded so much independence and freedom as an official, with powers commensurate with responsibilities.

At the Convention of 1845, a committee to frame an executive article was one of the first to report to the assembly.[23] Its recommendations called for a governor to be elected for a two-year term and to be ineligible to serve more than four years in any six. He was to "take care that the laws be faithfully executed," to grant pardons and reprieves, and to appoint "all officers not otherwise provided for," including judges of the courts. All these powers were approved by the Convention without much debate.

The question of the governor's veto power received considerably more discussion. The committee had recommended that his veto could be overridden by a simple majority vote, but a substitute motion was offered on the floor to raise the requisite vote for overriding to a two-thirds majority. Many of the outstanding members of the Convention were sharply divided in their views on the question. Urging the adoption of a veto provision, Isaac Van Zandt argued that "power is dangerous" and that the only way to disarm it is to divide it; he added that if unlimited power to enact laws were vested in the Legislature alone, it would produce "more confusion and disorganization than any power vested in the governor." He was joined in these views by Thomas J. Rusk, presiding officer of the Convention, who believed that the veto would prevent "hasty legislation" and "too much legislation." A. S. Lipscomb admitted that the veto would have a "wholesome and salutary effect upon legislation," but thought it would be inconsistent with the principles of all free governments for the will of the majority to be thwarted by the governor's veto. Others objected because they were unwilling to have the governor participate in any manner whatsoever in the legislative power. Despite the opposition, the veto power, with the two-thirds overriding provision, was adopted as a part of the Constitution by a large majority.[24]

[23] Annie Middleton, "The Texas Convention of 1845," *Southwestern Historical Quarterly*, XXV (July, 1921), 34.
[24] *Debates of the Texas Constitutional Convention of 1845*, pp. 134–146 *passim*.

The only other section of the committee report to receive much discussion on the floor of the Convention was the proposal for the popular election of a secretary of state. Notwithstanding the widely held notion of the Jacksonians throughout the nation that all public officials should be elected by the people, many of the delegates to the Texas Convention were strongly opposed to the idea.[25] The most prevalent thought seemed to be that the secretary of state would be the governor's right-hand man, and as the two would be working so closely together, more harmonious relations would be promoted if the governor were allowed an appointee of his own choice. After much debate, R. Bache, of Galveston County, proposed that the secretary of state should be appointed by the governor, with the consent of the Senate, for a term to coincide with his own but that the treasurer and comptroller of public accounts should be elected by joint ballot of both houses of the Legislature.[26] With the adoption of these two clauses the executive article was indeed forward looking because it placed the chief executive in position to exert effective leadership in the state government. Shortly after its adoption President James K. Polk signed the joint resolution annexing Texas to the United States on December 29, 1845.

The Civil War erupted only fifteen years after this "best state constitution of the day" had become effective. Chief executives of the new state had not had time to establish high prestige or a position of leadership for the office. The period between annexation and the war was a hectic one for a Texas governor, and the office was plagued by frequent turnover, with eight individuals occupying the chair during those years. The first governor was called away for six months to command troops in the war with Mexico, and the lieutenant governor acted in his stead. A few years later another lieutenant governor became the chief magistrate for a month when the incumbent resigned to take a seat in Congress.

One of the best-known figures of Texas history, Sam Houston, had held the office only fifteen months when he was deposed for failure to take the oath of allegiance to the Confederate States. Had Houston remained governor, the position would surely have grown stronger through the influence of his leadership. Certainly, as President of the Republic and earlier as governor of Tennessee, he was an effective

---

[25] *Ibid.*, pp. 118–132 *passim.*
[26] *Ibid.*, p. 354.

executive.[27] Under Texas' 1845 Constitution the gubernatorial powers were tailored for such a leader, but the outbreak of the Civil War abruptly changed the picture.

CONFEDERATE CONSTITUTION, 1861

The affiliation of Texas with the Confederate States of America necessitated the drafting of a new state constitution. Actually the Constitution of 1861 did little more than effect a change of allegiance from the United States to the Confederacy,[28] and amend the previous Constitution through the elimination of the clauses made obsolete by the change. So far as the executive article was concerned, the governor was required to be a citizen of Texas rather than a citizen of the United States, and was made commander in chief of the militia, except when it was called into the service of the Confederacy. Two other changes fixed the executive's salary at $3,000 per annum and required that the offices of state treasurer and comptroller of public accounts be made elective. With these few exceptions, the executive article remained essentially the same.[29] The powers, duties, and responsibilities of the chief executive were not altered, but because of wartime conditions, incumbents during the next five years were not in position to exert effective leadership in the state.

FIRST RECONSTRUCTION CONSTITUTION, 1866

Following the end of the Civil War, the national government briefly attempted a reconstruction policy in the South pursuant to the plan contemplated by Abraham Lincoln. President Andrew Johnson appointed a provisional governor for Texas, and the state was ordered to draft a constitution in keeping with the changes wrought by the victory of the Union.

The Constitution of 1845 again served as the pattern, but in the main, the Constitution of 1866 was made to conform with the outline of Lincoln's reconstruction plan. So far as the executive article was concerned, the major alteration was the lengthening of the governor's

[27] This possibility was discussed with Dr. Llerena Friend, biographer of Sam Houston, who concurred generally with the writer in this belief.

[28] *Journal of the Secession Convention of Texas, 1861*, ed. Ernest W. Winkler, *passim*.

[29] Constitution of Texas, 1861, Art. V.

term from two to four years, with the limitation that no one could hold the office for more than eight years out of any twelve. The new term was to begin on the first Thursday following organization of the Legislature "or as soon thereafter as practicable."[30] More stringent residence qualifications were placed upon gubernatorial candidates: the length of state residence was doubled, and candidates were required to have resided in Texas for six years preceding election—an attempt, no doubt, to preclude those who had migrated to the state during the war from holding the highest executive office. The governor was given the unique prerogative of convening the Legislature at a place different from the seat of government if that city "should be dangerous by reason of disease or of the public enemy." Another noteworthy provision called for an increase in the chief executive's salary to $4,000 "until otherwise provided by law," thus giving the Legislature power to adjust the compensation—a policy which coincides with present-day thinking that salaries are more appropriately the subject of statutes than of constitutions.

Perhaps the most important section of this constitutional article was the one which gave the governor the power to veto items in appropriations bills—a right which remains to this day with the chief executive of Texas. Other Southern states were following this practice, and such a power had been vested in the President of the Confederate States. In its original form, Section 17 read:

> The governor may approve any appropriation, and disapprove any other appropriation in the same bill. In such case, he shall, in signing the bill designate the appropriation disapproved, and shall return a copy of such appropriations, with his objections, to the House in which the bill shall have originated; and the same proceedings shall then be had as in the case of other bills disapproved by the Governor; but if the Legislature has adjourned before the bill is returned to the House, he shall return the same to the Secretary of State with his objections, and also to the next session of the Legislature.[31]

The appointive power of the governor remained about the same as it had been under the two previous constitutions, with only the state treasurer and the comptroller of public accounts being elected.

This proposed constitution was submitted to the voters in June, 1866, and was approved by only a slim margin, 28,119 to 23,400. The

---

[30] Constitution of Texas, 1866, Art. V.
[31] *Ibid.*

closeness of the vote has been attributed to the dissatisfaction of many citizens over the increases in salaries.[32] The document, however, was not to remain the state's fundamental law for long.

SECOND RECONSTRUCTION CONSTITUTION, 1869

The President of the United States was soon thwarted in his attempt to effectuate the Lincoln plan of reconstruction. Control of the national Congress had fallen into the hands of a group of radical leaders with anti-Southern sentiments who believed that the South had not been adequately punished. These extremists enacted legislation known as the Congressional Reconstruction Acts of 1867. Passed over President Johnson's veto, the laws provided much stiffer control of the affairs of Southern states. They resulted in the disfranchisement of many leading white citizens, the enfranchisement of Negroes on a widespread scale, and the establishment of military government. All civil officers were replaced by appointees of military leaders in Washington, who also "suggested" the propriety of another constitution.

Accordingly, a convention assembled in Austin in 1868 to draft a new fundamental law in conformity with the congressional statutes. The Reconstruction Convention was composed of ninety delegates, only twelve of whom were friendly to the native element of the state. About thirty were moderate radicals, and the remainder, including nine Negroes, were extremists of the carpetbagger and scalawag type.[33]

Apparently most of the discussion regarding the executive branch of the government was done in committee, for the *Journal of the Reconstruction Convention* indicates little real debate or discussion of powers and duties of the governor on the floor of the Convention. The comments of the chairman of the Committee on the Executive, L. Lindsay, indicate the feeling that seemed to prevail:

It was the unanimous opinion of the Committee, that it was the best plan they could suggest, after all the deliberation which they have been able to give to the subject. It will be found to conform, in all its main features, to the Republican principles embodied in most of the state Con-

[32] Webb and Carroll (eds.), *Handbook of Texas*, p. 398.
[33] C. Perry Patterson, Sam B. McAlister, and George C. Hester, *State and Local Government in Texas* (3d ed.), p. 35.

stitutions, and in the Constitution of the United States, differing only in some of its details from constitutions adopted in other states.[34]

More disintegration of the executive power than ever was effected. Under the influence of Jacksonian democracy Texas had begun to diffuse the executive power among several officials in 1850, but the Constitution of 1869 called for eight executives: governor, lieutenant governor, secretary of state, comptroller of public accounts, treasurer, commissioner of the General Land Office, attorney general, and superintendent of public instruction. Only the attorney general and the secretary of state were to be appointed; all others were to be elected for four-year terms.[35]

One interesting feature of this Constitution was the oath demanded of all public officials. In addition to the customary pledge of support for the laws of the nation and the state, they were required to swear (1) that they had not fought a duel with a deadly weapon nor sent or accepted a challenge to fight a duel; (2) that they were not disqualified by the recently adopted Fourteenth Amendment to the United States Constitution; and (3) that they were qualified to vote. Another provision was intended to allow only the "right" people to be elected to public office. This goal was to be achieved by the establishment of a highly centralized election procedure under which the voters could cast their ballots only in their county seats in an election that would last from 8:00 A.M. to 4:00 P.M. for four consecutive days.[36] Under such a plan, presumably the returns could be "adjusted" at the end of each day to favor the candidates acceptable to the reconstructionists.

In the Convention itself most of the discussion centered around the salaries to be paid the executive officials. Delegates were far more concerned with the matter of compensation than with the powers and functions of officeholders. A committe report recommended that the salary of the governor be fixed at $5,000 until otherwise provided by law. During the debate on the floor, motions were offered both to raise and to lower that figure, but none mustered sufficient support for passage, and the chief executive became the best-paid official in the history of the state up to that time.[37]

[34] *Journal of the Reconstruction Convention*, p. 296.
[35] Constitution of Texas, 1869, Art. 12.
[36] *Ibid.*
[37] *Journal of the Reconstruction Convention*, pp. 477, 529.

The Constitution of 1869 did not represent the true sentiments of native Texans. Historian Walter Prescott Webb commented: "It was the longest and most unsatisfactory of Texas Constitutions, but the greatest dissatisfaction of the people living under it came from abuses by state officials elected under it rather than from constitutional defects."[38] Indeed, state government reached its lowest ebb under this document.

The carpetbag legislature vested extraordinary powers in the governor. He was given complete control over the registration of voters, and he was empowered to appoint persons to a number of offices which the 1869 Constitution had made elective. An even more flagrant violation of the principle of local self-government was the extension of the executive's appointing power to the governing bodies of the towns and cities. The governor was authorized to designate in each judicial district a newspaper that should be the official organ and do the public printing for that district. No public notice could be legally advertised except in this organ. An attempt was made to organize a general system of public schools under a state superintendent of education, the schools of each county to be managed by the county police court.

In various areas of the state, lawlessness was rampant, so the reconstruction government established a militia which was to be called out in event of a general resistance to the laws. For the apprehension of individual offenders or of those acting in small bodies, a state police system was established. Both the militia and the police were under the control of the governor whose power was reinforced by a provision enabling him to establish martial law in any troublesome district. The governor's police force might have been a good thing, except that some of the worst desperadoes in the state were accepted by the force. Under its shield of authority they committed many high-handed outrages, barefaced robbery, arbitrary assessments upon helpless communities, unathorized [sic] arrests, and at times even murders. The police force was used so often to enforce the arbitrary will of the governor that it became an emblem of despotic authority. The governor so shaped the laws and the administration that his power over the people of Texas was as truly totalitarian as that which had been wielded by the military commanders. In actual fact the liberty and life of every citizen lay in the governor's hands.[39]

Such despotism was not to be tolerated for long, and in 1872 the citizens rebelled by electing a majority of antiadministration mem-

[38] Webb and Carroll (eds.), *Handbook of Texas*, p. 399.
[39] Citizens Advisory Committee on Revision of the Constitution of Texas, *Interim Report to the 56th Legislature and the People of Texas*, March 1, 1959, pp. 20–21.

bers to the Legislature and pressing for revision of the "radical" Constitution. The prevailing opinion was that the existing document was
so bad that no argument was required to show that a new one would
be more desirable, because the existing Constitution had permitted
the "obnoxious acts" of the Republican regime.[40] By 1874 a new constitution had become an inevitability, and the governor and the Legislature felt impelled to call a convention to comply with public sentiment.

CONSTITUTION OF 1876

Convention delegates who assembled in Austin in September, 1875,
were to draft a constitution which would serve the state for the more
than eight decades to follow. So interested were they in trying to overcome the abuses to which they had been subjected by recent governmental officials that they moved with record speed to produce their
version of a new fundamental law designed to limit the power of
officials and to curb the extravagance of irresponsible spenders. The
assembly was able to complete its work within eleven weeks, but
its handiwork turned out to be excessively long and cumbersome,
for everything possible was done to limit powers of all branches of
government.

Membership in the Convention was composed mainly of "old-time
Texans" who had been prominent in previous conventions and in
public affairs. One of the members had been at the Convention of
1845; eight had attended the Secession Convention in 1861; and one
had helped write the Constitution of 1866, although obviously, none
of this group had participated in the Reconstruction Convention held
seven years previously. Nineteen had served in the Texas Legislature,
and four in the legislatures of other states. More than a score had
been officers of high rank in the Confederate Army, and three had
been members of the Union Army. Several had held judicial posts.[41]
Almost half of the ninety delegates were farmers, and twenty-nine
were attorneys. In political affiliation seventy-five were Democrats
and fifteen Republicans. There were six Negro delegates.[42]

The competency of the delegates, as a group, was about average.
A contemporary newspaper commented, "We know that the conven-

---

[40] Seth S. McKay, *Making the Texas Constitution of 1876*, p. 45.
[41] *Ibid.*, p. 74.
[42] Richardson, *Texas, the Lone Star State* (2d ed.), p. 221.

tion has relatively but a few able men in its composition, but those we deem very able, with clear sound judgments."[43] Many years later, one observer assessed the assembly as follows:

> With all deference to the memories of those who wrote the Constitution, they were merely an average group of men, with no marked aptitude for determining for all time how Texas should be governed. They were not possessed of any particular prescience; they were more interested in the present and the immediate past than in the future. They confronted a difficult task and performed it as best they could under the circumstances. The result was, at best, a very poor compromise.[44]

As in previous conventions, the Constitution of 1845 was used as a working model for this assembly, and the constitutions of several other states, particularly those of Louisiana and Pennsylvania, were frequently consulted. The Convention of 1875 was in no mood to return without reservation to the provisions of the first state constitution. Remembering their recent experiences under military government, the delegates were determined to curb the powers of the governor to avert renewal of despotic control over state and local administration. Consequently they adhered to the principle of decentralization of authority and provided for popular election of all officials in the executive branch, with the exception of the secretary of state, in effect making the department heads independent of gubernatorial control and responsible only to the electorate. To provide a more frequent check upon the executives, the terms of office were reduced from four to two years. The governor was prohibited from holding any other office or commission, civil, military, or corporate, and from practicing any profession for profit while in office. In keeping with the retrenchment theme, salaries were reduced and duties specified in great detail.[45]

Most of these provisions were agreed upon in committee, but, unfortunately, no records were kept of the work of the committees, and a motion was lost early in the meeting to have stenographers take down a verbatim report of the debates of the whole Convention. Only a few newspapers carried daily summaries of the proceedings. There-

---

[43] *San Antonio Herald,* September 20, 1875.

[44] S. D. Myres, Jr., "Mysticism, Realism, and the Texas Constitution of 1876," *Southwestern Political and Social Science Quarterly,* IX (September, 1928), 183.

[45] Citizens Advisory Committee on Revision of the Constitution of Texas, *Interim Report to the 56th Legislature and the People of Texas,* March 1, 1959, p. 22.

fore, an account of what happened must be pieced together from several sources.[46]

Judge W. P. Ballinger was chairman of a committee to consider the executive department. The number of members on his committee is not known, but most committees contained between five and fifteen. Only three weeks had elapsed when Chairman Ballinger presented the recommendations, and the Convention ordered two hundred copies of the report printed for public distribution.[47] Discussion concerning the executive began on the floor three days later, October 4, 1875. During the debates of the first day, the office of superintendent of public instruction was abolished, but motions to make the governor ineligible for more than two terms, to abolish the office of lieutenant governor, and to make elective the office of secretary of state were all defeated.[48]

As had been true in the preceding constituent assembly, one of the hottest discussions was ignited when the matter of compensation of executive officials was brought up.[49] Since economy was the motto of this Convention, several motions were offered from the floor to reduce the $5,000 gubernatorial salary suggested by the committee report. Delegate F. S. Stockdale condemned the idea of reducing the salary, saying it was an "office requiring the highest order of talent, probity, and integrity, and the very credit of the state, and its future as well as its present honor and glory require that it [the salary] should not be reduced beyond the figures reported by the Committee."[50] The other side of the argument was presented by a delegate named Flournoy, who countered that the office should never be sought as a remunerative one and that the salary of $333 a month plus house was "fairly reasonable and ought to be sufficient."[51] Judge Ballinger closed the discussion by arguing that governors should not have to supplement their incomes by practicing law on the side, as several of the recent incumbents had found it necessary to do.[52] After amendments to fix the salary at $3,000, $3,500, and $4,500 respectively had failed,

---

[46] The best sources are the *Journal of the Constitutional Convention Begun and Held in Austin, September 6, 1875*, hereafter cited as *Journal of the Convention of 1875*; and *Debates in the Texas Constitutional Convention of 1875* (ed. Seth S. McKay), hereafter cited as *Debates in the Convention of 1875*.

[47] *Journal of the Convention of 1875*, p. 234.

[48] *Ibid.*, pp. 283–284.

[49] *Ibid.*, pp. 285–286.

[50] *Debates in the Convention of 1875*, p. 152.

[51] *Ibid.*, p. 154.

[52] *Journal of the Convention of 1875*, pp. 286–290 *passim*.

a roll-call vote resulted in a 44-to-32 decision to compromise by setting the compensation at $4,000 where it remained until 1936.

Much discussion on the floor of the Convention centered around the limitations to be placed upon the power of the governor to call out the militia. Because of bitter experience with the abuse of military power under the Constitution of 1869, the delegates understandably wanted to be cautious in vesting that power in the governor. There was no contest over the provision that the governor should have the power to use the militia to suppress insurrections and to repel invasions; the difficulty lay in attempting to give specificity to the occasions on which he could use that prerogative. Clauses were introduced to the effect that it should be used to repel "raiders from the Mexican Republic," or to repulse invaders if the state were attacked by "troops under the direction or control of other States or governments or by predatory bands therefrom," or to defend itself if invaded by "armies or by bands of lawless men."[53] None of these attempts to amend was successful, but on roll-call vote a clause was added that the militia might be called to suppress insurrections and repel invasions "and protect the frontier from hostile incursions by Indians or other predatory bands."

The last attempt to alter the committee's report was a motion to eliminate the governor's veto power because it "belonged to the Legislative Department." That motion lost on voice vote.[54] Most of the convention members were inclined to accept the recommendations of the committee without question. Only seven roll-call votes were taken during the discussion on the executive and on the thirty-sixth day of the Convention, October 16, 1875, the article, as amended, was adopted by the overwhelming vote of 65 to 8.[55] Article IV thus came into being with its distintegrated, decentralized executive power, its short terms of office, and its low pay.

The campaign for ratification of the Constitution did not produce much opposition to Article IV. The major criticism concerned the low compensation allotted to executive officers. The press of the day, claiming that it reflected public opinion, played up this matter. The state's leading daily newspaper, the *Galveston News*, reported that the Convention had reduced salaries almost to the starvation point,[56]

---

[53] *Ibid.*, p. 292.
[54] *Ibid.*
[55] *Ibid.*, pp. 374–375.
[56] *Galveston News*, October 13, 1875.

and the *Houston Telegraph* suggested that the Convention might have provided that only single men could be elected to office. It continued:

> Texas has been advertised as an El Dorado with inexhaustible resources, a sort of paradise. But now we have proposed to engraft upon her organic law a feature which indicates a narrow, contracted, parsimonious policy, and proclaims to the world that her public servants must be salaried as if they were paupers . . . The few thousand dollars which, by the cutting down of salaries, is hoped to be saved to the state, will be a most costly economy to Texas . . .[57]

The state capital paper, the *Austin Statesman,* declared that "Grangerism" had succeeded well in the effort to fix small salaries; it unmercifully ridiculed the "bounteous provision" the Convention had made for the governor and other executives.[58]

   The criticism was relatively minor, and the popular vote in February, 1876, favored the Constitution, 136,606 to 56,652. The greatest support came from the rural areas, with towns and larger cities being generally unfavorable, but only 20 of the 150 counties failed to report a favorable vote.[59]

Taken as a whole, the Constitution satisfied the majority of the people of Texas, who generally felt that practically anything would be an improvement over the Constitution under which the state had been operating. The main effort of the Convention had been devoted to the restraining of individuals from wrongdoing in governmental positions. Nothing could have been more in keeping with the spirit of the times, and certainly the effort was complete as far as the executive branch was concerned.

Changes in the Executive Article since 1876

   The executive article of the Texas Constitution remains today essentially as it came from the Convention of 1875. Of the three coordinate branches of government, the executive has undergone the least number of changes at the hands of the electorate. Since its adoption only ten amendments affecting Article IV have been considered by the voters and one-half of those have been rejected. As at the Convention, many of the later amendments dealt with salary adjustments.

---

[57] *Houston Telegraph,* October 8, 1875.
[58] *Austin Statesman,* October 20, 1875.
[59] Patterson, McAlister, and Hester, *State and Local Government in Texas* (3d ed.), p. 39.

After four refusals to increase the salaries of the governor and other executives, the voters finally granted an upward adjustment in 1936, and in 1954 they empowered the Legislature to fix salaries of elective executive officers by statute—a procedure not unlike that allowed by previous fundamental laws.

The powers of the chief executive have been curtailed only twice —both times much to the relief of the officeholder. In 1936 a Board of Pardons and Paroles was created to advise the governor on reprieves, commutations of punishment, and pardons. No doubt any governor would have attested that the power to pardon was one of the most difficult he had to exercise and that it was a relief to have some assistance with it. In 1940 the appointment of notaries public was removed from the hands of the governor and given to the secretary of state. Again governors approved, because the task had become routine, requiring thousands of signatures of the chief executive each year.

An omission in the original article was the failure to include a provision for succession to office in the event of the death of the governor-elect. An amendment adopted in 1948 clarified what was to be done in that situation and authorized the Legislature to establish a line of succession to the office.

The first and only attempt to give constitutional status to another elective executive failed in 1907 when the voters rejected a plan which would have created a Department of Agriculture, to have equal rank with the several other departments set up by Article IV. Although the voters did not approve the amendment, the Department was later organized by statute, which also provided that its head, the commissioner of agriculture, was to be "one of the executives" in Texas government.

A final amendment to Article IV (Section 11a), in 1935, had little, if anything, to do with the executive. Logically, it should have been placed in the article on the judiciary because it gave the courts of original jurisdiction the right to suspend sentences and to place defendants on probation.

The progress of these amendments to Article IV is traced in Table 1.

SUMMARY

Comparison of the several executive articles reveals that, although the powers accorded the chief executives under the various state constitutions were more similar than different, several noteworthy

TABLE 1

Proposed Amendments to the Executive Article (IV),
Constitution of Texas

Legislature	Year	Purpose of Amendment	Section of Article IV	Action of Voters
30th	1907	To give constitutional status to Department of Agriculture, with a subordinate Bureau of Labor	27	Rejection: 19,736– 60,733
30th	1907	To increase governor's salary from $4,000 to $8,000; to give lieutenant governor $2,500 annual salary	5, 17	Rejection: 47,396–112,430
36th	1919	To increase governor's salary from $4,000 to $10,000	5	Rejection: 108,536–193,359
37th	1921	To increase governor's salary to $8,000; to increase that of secretary of state to $5,000; to increase that of attorney general to $7,500 and eliminate provision for fees; to increase comptroller, treasurer, and commissioner of General Land Office to $5,000 each	5, 21 22, 23	Rejection: 25,778– 68,223
41st	1929	To increase governor's salary to $10,000 annually	5	Rejection: 49,664– 76,166
44th	1935	To increase governor's salary to $12,000; to increase salary of secretary of state to $6,000; to increase salary of attorney general to $10,000 "and no more"	5 21 22	Adoption: 326,856–275,060
44th	1935	To create Board of Pardons and Paroles to assist governor	11	Adoption: 422,224–167,916
44th	1935	To authorize courts of original jurisdiction to suspend sentences and place defendants on probation	11a	Adoption: 245,285–216,549
46th	1939	To authorize appointment of notaries public by secretary of state	26	Adoption: 318,061–155,964
50th	1947	To authorize Legislature to fix successsion to the governorship	3a	Adoption: 548,195–130,119
53rd	1953	To provide for salary of governor and other executive officers to be fixed by statute	5, 21 22, 23	Adoption: 308,066–193,895

Source: *General and Special Laws of the State of Texas,* Fifty-sixth Legislature, regular session, 1959, pp. 1228–1236.

changes have been effected since Texas achieved statehood.[60] Obviously, the governor's position under the first state constitution (1845) was the most favorable from the standpoint of modern administrative theory. He was an executive in fact as well as in name, and his power to appoint department heads and exercise administrative control over them has never been equalled since. In fact, he appointed all executive officials with the exception of the comptroller of public accounts and the treasurer, both of whom were at first elected by the Legislature, later by the electorate. His appointive power, following the pattern of the national government, extended to the judiciary. Gradually, however, the appointive power was whittled down, until by 1869 the secretary of state was the only major department head to be selected by the governor; all others had become elective in true Jacksonian tradition, as had the judges of the courts. This disintegrated administrative system continues to the present day.

The term of office of the governor has also varied. Originally set at two years, it was increased to four years in both of the state's Reconstruction constitutions, only to be reduced again in 1876. The salary paid the chief executive rose slowly until after the Civil War, when it was reduced in keeping with the general retrenchment theme of the times; but adjustments have since been made.

All Texas' constitutions have given the governor the power to veto, subject to being overridden by a two-thirds vote of both houses. One innovation after the Civil War added the power to veto items in appropriations bills, and the three most recent constitutions have possessed such a clause.

The question is often raised as to whether the governorship in this state has followed the pattern, said to be typical, of progressing from "detested minion of Royal power, to stepson of legislative domination, to popular figurehead, to effective executive." On the basis of legal and constitutional considerations alone, chief executives of Texas have fallen into each of these categories at one time or another, although opinion is divided as to whether the "typical" order of progression has been followed. In subsequent chapters an analysis will be made of the modern governor's role as executive, as legislative leader, and as politician, but, first, the backgrounds of the individuals who have held the office under the Constitution of 1876 will be examined, with a view to projecting the "composite" governor of Texas.

[60] Appendix I presents in tabular form a summary of the powers of the chief executives under the various constitutions, and Appendix II offers a comparison of the terms, qualifications, and salaries of the executive under those documents.

3

Occupants of the Executive Office

Most executive positions, whether in business, industry, or government, are molded to some extent by their incumbents. Laws, rules, or traditions that define the offices shape in very large measure the decisions and actions of the officeholders; but, simultaneously, influence flows also from the personality of the occupants. Generally, public executives are more circumscribed by public opinion and custom than are their counterparts in the business world; but substantial room remains for public officials to exercise discretion in the decision-making process, and numerous channels exist through which leadership may be exerted. Regardless of the office in which a person finds himself, he will tend to emphasize as much as possible that aspect of his job which best fits his personality.[1] Researchers have reported:

The conviction that the political decision-maker's behavior and decisions are influenced by his personal life experience not only has a long and honorable history but also is substantiated by modern psychological and sociological research. We are told that human beings are selective in what they perceive, or experience through their senses, and that identical events or facts have different meanings for different people.[2]

To date, almost no systematic research has been undertaken on the relationship between an individual's personality and his behavior in public office; yet students in the field generally agree that conduct in public office and personality are in continuous interaction.[3]

---

[1] Donald R. Matthews, *The Social Background of Political Decision-Makers*, p. 41. Hereafter cited as Matthews, *Political Decision-Makers*.
[2] *Ibid.*, p. 2.
[3] David B. Truman, *The Governmental Process*, pp. 343–350; Harold D. Lasswell, *Power and Personality*, pp. 63, 101.

History is replete with examples of broad interpretations of the public executive's power and of the influence of his personality. Many occasions could be cited in which actions taken by executives were considered bold and different at the time but later came to be functions accepted by successors in office and the public. Perhaps the best-known examples of broad interpretations of executive power in public jurisdictions are actions that have been taken by Presidents of the United States.[4] Thomas Jefferson's purchase of the Louisiana Territory, Abraham Lincoln's Emancipation Proclamation, and Franklin D. Roosevelt's Lend-Lease agreement were all unprecedented moves at the time they were taken, but each came to be accepted as being within the appropriate purview of the executive. Andrew Jackson's pronouncement that he was a "tribune of the people" and would use all of the powers of his office to further their cause was equally bold. In time, however, it became a policy followed by the stronger American executives at both national and state levels.

Chief executives of American states have in many instances broadly interpreted their constitutional powers and made effective use of "extralegal" channels to carry out their programs. In his first address to the New Jersey Legislature, Governor Woodrow Wilson adapted the Jacksonian concept of the executive to the governorship. Never before had such an approach been followed in that state. Wilson declared:

I have become the responsible leader of the Democratic Party in the State. . . I am the only person in the whole state, however, to express approval or disapproval on behalf of all the people, and I will express that approval or disapproval by determining what we should do.[5]

This view of the gubernatorial office has been recently described as being much closer to our times than to those of Wilson, and even ahead of the present day in many respects.[6]

In Illinois, Governor Frank O. Lowden left an indelible imprint on the government of his own state and on American state government as a whole. Seizing upon the research of the eminent political scientists John A. Fairlie and William F. Dodd, he inaugurated the Administrative Reorganization Movement in 1917—an effort, which

[4] See, for example, Rexford G. Tugwell, *The Enlargement of the Presidency.*
[5] Quoted in Claudius O. Johnson, *American State and Local Government* (2d ed.), p. 84.
[6] Joseph E. McLean, "Early Modern Governor," *National Municipal Review,* XLVI (January, 1957), 20.

spread throughout most sections of the country, to promote efficiency and economy in state government.[7]

In Wisconsin, Governor Robert M. LaFollette, Sr., made history in opposing a political machine of long standing and crusading for a higher level of politics in the state. He was also the initiator of a number of progressive reforms in state government, including the initiative, the referendum, and the recall.[8]

Texas has its examples in which the incumbents have influenced the office. To mention only a few, Governor John Ireland used the prestige of his high office to appeal for an end to the "fence-cutting war" on ranches of West Texas.[9] The well-known James Stephen Hogg was able to get support for his railroad regulation plan, despite much opposition from the press, by going to the people.[10] The Governors Ferguson so freely exercised the pardoning power as to bring about a constitutional amendment curbing its use by the governor.[11] Governor Allan Shivers made highly effective use of lobbyists in promoting his own legislative program.[12]

Incumbents have sometimes taken too broad a view of their prerogatives. James E. Ferguson was impeached—an action that represented

the failure of his attempt to apply his seventeenth century conception of the executive power of the state as expressed by him in his statement, "I am Governor of Texas. I don't have to give reasons." It came as a natural consequence of the abuse of executive authority, and the desire on the part of the Governor to have the government of the state operated in accordance with his personal prejudices, and the personnel of state institutions changed in accordance with his whims.[13]

Years later, when Governor Ross Sterling declared martial law in the East Texas oil fields and maintained military control for six months,

---

[7] Louis Brownlow, "Lowden of Illinois," *National Municipal Review*, XLVI (October, 1957), 446.

[8] Harold Zink, *Government and Politics in the United States* (3d ed.), p. 758.

[9] Maggie R. Smith, "The Administration of Governor John Ireland, 1883–1887" (unpublished M.A. thesis), pp. 81–90.

[10] Mizell F. Kennedy, "A Study of James Stephen Hogg, Attorney-General and Governor" (unpublished M.A. thesis), pp. 125–130.

[11] Constitution of Texas, Art. IV, Sec. 11, providing for a Board of Pardons and Paroles to advise the governor, adopted in 1936.

[12] Interview with C. Read Granberry, administrative assistant to former Governor Shivers, May 17, 1960.

[13] Ralph W. Steen, "The Political Career of James E. Ferguson, 1914–1917" (unpublished M.A. thesis), p. 165.

a Federal District Court held his declaration unwarranted by Texas law and the maintenance of martial law a deprivation of due process of law.[14]

Personalities do in fact influence executive offices. Legal limitations have remained virtually the same throughout the years, but, depending a great deal upon the interpretations they place upon their roles, some executives are considered strong and others weak. In any event an executive is in a position to wield many kinds of "extralegal" influences during his administration. Given modern mass communication, even governors who might under other circumstances be weak, may become leaders, for to the average citizen the governor personifies state government. The office is the highest state office within the gift of the people, and the chief executive's every move is worthy of front-page reporting. "Governors live in goldfish bowls and cannot call their lives their own until they leave office"[15] is an accurate comment. Professor Harold Zink has described the office as follows:

The position of the governor regardless of whether weak or strong is almost always regarded with considerable esteem by the citizen of a state and consequently even in those instances where executive authority is lacking the incumbent is likely to be frequently in the limelight.[16]

QUALIFICATIONS FOR TODAY'S GOVERNOR

A position conferring such prestige naturally requires that the incumbent have broad qualifications. One contemporary writer has suggested that the following characteristics appear to be shared by most governors: good luck; great energy and drive; above-average intelligence; likeable personality; vanity; love of the limelight; a sense of knowing what the public wants, fears, or approves of, and a willingness to identify with felt needs; and a talent for collecting more credit than is their due.[17]

The requirements of the position are summed up in another way by the former executive secretary of the Council of State Governments—the person who for more than three decades probably had more dealings with more different governors than anyone else during this century. He has written:

[14] Warner E. Mills, *Martial Law in East Texas*, p. 40.
[15] Coleman B. Ransone, *The Office of Governor in the United States*, p. 154.
[16] Zink, *Government and Politics in the United States* (3d ed.), p. 750.
[17] Charles R. Adrian, *State and Local Governments: A Study in the Political Process*, p. 276.

. . . the Governor needs to be a man of breadth. He must be ambidextrous, and then some. An individual might be a wonder, a genius, and a great public benefactor in any one of numerous professions, and still be a flop as governor. For every Governor should have—and if he is to be an outstandingly successful Governor he must have—the gifts of popular leadership, executive ability, decisiveness, studious inquiry, and the skill of political competence in the broadest and most constructive sense.[18]

American state executives, including those of Texas, have not always measured up to these high standards. Indeed, many have been almost totally lacking in qualifications. At one time or another almost every kind of person has held the office in at least one of the states of the Union. One survey of incumbents in gubernatorial offices categorized twentieth-century state executives as belonging to one of six major types: the strong leader, the figurehead, the "man of the people," the grafter, the showman, and the reformer. Texas has had its examples of each.[19]

TYPES OF GOVERNORS

THE STRONG LEADER

Although strong leaders are always in the minority, most states have at times, accidentally or otherwise, elected such men governors. New York appears to have been most fortunate in this respect, with such outstanding leaders as the two Roosevelts, Charles Evans Hughes, Alfred E. Smith, and Thomas E. Dewey. Other states have produced fewer in number, but such men as Woodrow Wilson of New Jersey, Robert M. LaFollette, Sr., of Wisconsin, and Gifford Pinchot of Pennsylvania were renowned for their leadership.

Generally, such a man has better-than-average intelligence, a reasonable understanding of human nature, attractive personal characteristics, a measure of persistence, an appreciation of the role of state government, and a substantial amount of courage and independence. In Texas, Governor Allan Shivers demonstrated many of these attributes and is considered by many to be one of the strongest leaders ever to serve the state. Not only was he able to get many of his legislative proposals enacted, but he was a major force in leading the

[18] Frank Bane, "The Job of Being a Governor," *State Government*, XXXI (Summer, 1958), 184.
[19] Zink, *Government and Politics in the United States* (3d ed.), pp. 754–758. The examples from Texas were provided by the present writer.

state in a revolt against the presidential candidate, Democrat Adlai Stevenson, of his own political party in both 1952 and 1956.[20] With the Governor's influence and backing, coupled with other factors, the Republican candidate, Dwight D. Eisenhower, carried Texas in both elections. Had a governor of lesser stature attempted such a party bolt, the attempt would probably have been abortive. In 1960, after four years in private life, Shivers again backed the Republican presidential candidate, speaking in behalf of Richard Nixon in Texas and other states. His speeches attracted enthusiastic audiences despite the fact that he did not hold an official position, but in the election, the Democratic candidate, John F. Kennedy, carried Texas.

THE FIGUREHEAD

Contrasting diametrically with the strong-leader type is the weak, colorless, sometimes stupid creature kept in office by a political boss or machine. Not every governor of this type is supported by a boss, nor is every governor who is supported by a boss a complete figurehead. Now and then, however, a governor is controlled by those who have usurped power. This type of governor seldom has a contribution to make—no courage, no fresh ideas, no leadership qualities; he merely serves the men behind the scenes. Many have accused Huey P. Long of maintaining a figurehead governor in Louisiana after Long was promoted to the United States Senate.

Texas may have had an example of the figurehead governor when it had "two governors for the price of one." Disqualified because of his impeachment, James E. Ferguson entered the name of his wife, Miriam A. Ferguson, in gubernatorial politics in 1924. For two terms she sat in the governor's chair, but Mr. Ferguson maintained a desk in her office and was consulted on most major decisions.[21] Fortunately, figurehead governors have not loomed large in the political history of this country.

THE "MAN OF THE PEOPLE"

At any given time a majority of governors will probably be "men of the people"—neither outstanding in their ability, nor fools. They

[20] For an analysis of Governor Shivers' role in leading the state into the Republican camp, see O. Douglas Weeks, *Texas Presidential Politics in 1952*, pp. 82–96, and *Texas One-Party Politics in 1956*, pp. 44–50.

[21] Ouida Ferguson Nalle, *The Fergusons of Texas*, p. 170. Mrs. Nalle was the elder daughter of the Fergusons.

are not originators of programs, yet they are not satisfied with doing nothing. They are not representatives of bosses, but they do not generally display outstanding courage. They are fairly typical of the rank and file of citizens, their greatest drawback being that they have no very definite ideas as to what a governor can do, and hence follow a policy of drifting and opportunism. The great problem they present is that they unintentionally promote mediocrity in the field of state government by failing to provide adequate leadership.

As in the nation as a whole, it is likely that the majority of Texas governors would fall into this category, but two examples will suffice. Upon the death of Governor L. S. (Sul) Ross, in 1898, the *Galveston News* editoralized:

> He was not masterful in the art of politics, but, better than this, he was a well-balanced man from whatever standpoint one might estimate him. In his public relations he exhibited sterling common sense, lofty patriotism, inflexible honesty, and, withal, a character so exalted that he commanded at all times not only the confidence but the affection of the people.[22]

A later governor, Charles A. Culberson, has been evaluated in these words: "It would seem in retrospect that the Governor and his associates were not altogether free from the taint of political opportunism..."[23]

THE GRAFTER

The true grafter does not find the governor's office a safe place to operate because it is constantly in the limelight. During the present century, at least five states have had governors whose conduct led to their trial in impeachment proceedings or on criminal charges in the courts. New York, Oklahoma, and Texas have removed governors from office through impeachment trials, and North Dakota removed one through a recall election. A chief executive of Indiana was placed in a federal penitentiary following conviction in court, and a governor of Louisiana served a prison term after he had completed his term of office. More common than outright graft is the "honest graft" available to governors—filling offices with friends who do not possess the highest qualifications, influencing purchases of supplies from particular sources, or doing a favor for the promise of a profitable retainer upon retirement from office. Impossible to measure, such "honest

[22] *Galveston News*, January 5, 1898.
[23] Robert L. Wagner, "The Gubernatorial Career of Charles Allen Culberson" (unpublished M.A. thesis), p. 103.

graft" may become degrading to the entire level of state government. Few states, if any, have not experienced such practices to some degree.

THE SHOWMAN

The twentieth century has provided numerous examples of the spectacular political campaign designed to attract sizeable crowds, especially in the South and Southwest. Vaudeville acts, cowboy singing, boxing matches, hog-calling contests, hillbilly bands, and helicopter or parachute landings have proved popular in many states. "Alfalfa Bill" Murray of Oklahoma was a master showman, who gained a widespread reputation for eating the tops of vegetables, such as beets, carrots, and potatoes; a mouthful of chewing tobacco became his trademark, as did the practice of removing his coat when speaking. Governor Eugene Talmadge of Georgia adopted a pair of red suspenders as a part of his dress and was proud to show them off on the political platform. Governor Jimmy Davis of Louisiana, a guitar-playing song writer, no doubt received many votes because of the popularity of his composition, "You Are My Sunshine," which was played at his rallies.

— Texas has produced its share of political showmen, but none can measure up to W. Lee O'Daniel, who acquired the name "Pappy" from a favorite song of his hillbilly band: "Please Pass the Biscuits, Pappy." O'Daniel, who had migrated to Texas from Kansas to join a flour-manufacturing firm, formed a hillbilly band, the "Light-Crust Doughboys," and served as master of ceremonies on a daily statewide radio program to advertise his flour. Only thirteen years after moving into the state, he astonished the political world by adapting his radio techniques to a race for the state's highest office. Well-known to thousands of listeners, O'Daniel attracted unprecedented numbers to his political rallies with his lively shows. Even after his election he kept the band and entertained the citizenry with a Sunday morning radio broadcast from the "living room of the Governor's Mansion to the rank and file of the common citizens of Texas."[24]

THE REFORMER

Occasionally a governor is elected on the basis of some reform he has carried out in another office or which he promises to carry out if elected chief executive. During the post-World War I period, Robert

[24] The scripts for many of these programs appear in the W. Lee O'Daniel File, Barker Texas History Center Library, The University of Texas.

M. LaFollette, Sr., as governor of Wisconsin, was highly successful in promoting such measures at the initiative, the referendum, and the recall. In 1924 he ran for President of the United States on the Progressive Party ticket, amassing more popular votes than any other minor-party candidate in history. During World War II, Ellis Arnall of Georgia was able to secure the adoption of a new state constitution which abolished the poll tax and lowered the voting age to eighteen—an exceptional feat for a state in the Deep South. District Attorney Thomas E. Dewey of New York City, capitalizing upon the reputation he had gained from ridding the city of gambling and vice, was elected as a "clean-up" governor of New York. After a successful administration in Albany, he was nominated for the Presidency by the Republican Party in 1944 and 1948. These and other candidates have been successful as reformers at various times in political history, but today the reformer is less popular than he was some three or four decades ago.

Texas has produced some leaders who have sponsored needed reforms in the state. James S. Hogg pressed for statutes to effect railroad reform just before the turn of the century; Dan Moody revamped the prison system and established the Highway Commission; and James V. Allred championed programs of social welfare in Texas in the 1930's while Franklin Roosevelt's New Deal was changing the nation. Each of these governors moved into the high office from the attorney generalship.

The above classification suggests very strongly the importance of considering public-policy makers' attitudes and frames of reference. Along with the study of institutions, the study of men is valuable. Professor Harold D. Lasswell has written, "Political science without biography is a form of taxidermy."[25] The actions of individuals are heavily influenced by their previous experiences; therefore the study of social and economic backgrounds contributes to a deeper understanding of decisions of those in political authority. Although the majority of political scientists have shown little interest in this area, a few have been doing research for half a century, and there is much evidence that the present trend in the study of political science is toward increased emphasis upon the behavior of public servants. In the past decade, the literature of political science has been expanded by many studies of this nature in all three branches of government.[26]

[25] Harold D. Lasswell, *Psychopathology and Politics*, p. 1.
[26] Matthews, *Political Decision-Makers*, p. 2.

Governors of American states have been the subject of a number of studies emphasizing the social, economic, and political backgrounds of political decision makers and extensively covering the backgrounds of chief executives serving since 1900. Researchers have uncovered many interesting and informative trends. In the current edition of his well-known textbook on American state government, Professor Austin F. Macdonald has observed:

> Most of the men who have been elected governors of American states have possessed considerably more than average ability and training. In recent years, at least, more than half of them have been college graduates. Most of them have stood quite high in the occupational scales—as lawyers, educators, merchants, manufacturers. It may be fairly said that they have been representative of the better class of business and professional men in their respective communities.[27]

BACKGROUNDS OF TEXAS GOVERNORS

If individuals influence offices, a corollary would be that the office of governor in Texas is in great measure what it is today because of the contributions of those who have occupied the chair. In studying the governorship, the office and its occupant should be considered as an entity.[28] Comparing trends in one state with those that obtain throughout the country[29] can help develop such a viewpoint.

No single study has been made of the social, economic, and political backgrounds of all Texas governors, but an analysis can be made

[27] Austin F. Mcdonald, *American State Government and Administration*, (6th ed.), p. 176.

[28] William Anderson, Clara Penniman, and Edward Weidner, *Government In The Fifty States*, p. 270.

[29] Over the past three decades, chief executives of American states have been the subject matter of a number of helpful studies emphasizing the backgrounds of decision makers in the states. These studies have covered rather comprehensively the first half of the present century, and a number of interesting general trends are apparent. See Austin F. Macdonald, "American Governors," *National Municipal Review*, XVI (November, 1927), 715–719 (covering the period 1900 to 1910); S. R. Solomon, "American Governors Since 1915," *National Municipal Review*, XX (March, 1931), 152–158; John A. Perkins, "American Governors— 1930–1940," *National Municipal Review*, XXIX (March, 1940), 178–184; S. R. Solomon, "United States Governors—1940–1950," *National Municipal Review*, XLI (April, 1952), 190–197; Cortez A. M. Ewing, "Southern Governors," *Journal of Politics*, 10 (May, 1948), 385–409; John K. Gurwell, "Governors of the States: A Review of the Background and Experience of the Men Who Are the Governors of the 48 American States," *State Government*, 14 (July, 1941), 157–158, hereafter cited as Gurwell, "Governors of the States."

of the chief executives who have served under the present Constitution. As this document has been the fundamental law of the state for some eight and one-half decades, during which time the modern conception of the governorship has come into being, the twenty-four individuals who have been governor of Texas from 1876 to 1963 will supply an adequate sample for determining whether the office requires or develops significant characteristics in its incumbents.

What manner of men have served in the highest office in the Lone Star State? Under the terms of the Constitution of 1876, a governor must be a citizen of the United States, at least thirty years of age, and a resident of the state for five years immediately preceding his election.[30] Since these qualifications were written, a veritable cross section of humanity has held the executive chair in Texas. Its governors have ranged from the quiet man to the boisterous, from the self-educated frontiersman to the university scholar, from the son of a tenant farmer to the son of a congressman, from the flour salesman to the housewife, and from the young attorney general elected at thirty-three to the sage old lawyer chosen at sixty-three. The group has represented most phases of social, economic, and political life in the state (see biographical data in Appendix III.) The following analysis will delve first into socioeconomic factors affecting the executive office and then into other aspects deemed to be equally important in the governors' backgrounds.[31]

OCCUPATION OF PARENTS

A favorite myth of American politics is that the path to the White House runs from the log cabin; and it is generally believed that the political arena is one place in which Horatio Alger-like success is possible for anyone. Some who have questioned the myth, however, have concluded that leading politicians tend to come from among families ranking high in America's system of social stratification. They argue that the political chances of an individual are improved if he comes from parents whose occupation is considered to be of high

---

[30] Constitution of Texas, Art. IV, Sec. 4.

[31] Data for the discussion in the remainder of this chapter were taken from the biographical files of Governors of Texas found in the Archives of The University of Texas and in Barker Texas History Center Library at the University. The files include clippings from contemporary newspapers, official manuscripts, some personal letters of governors, and other material relevant to the administration of the particular individual. The files also frequently contain campaign posters and literature.

social status.[32] Few would dispute that occupation is an important criterion in determining rank among one's peers, although occupations enjoying high public regard do not always enjoy equally high economic status. In fact, a Texas historian has pointed out:

> The opportunity of any citizen to be Governor of Texas is greatly enhanced by being the son of poor parents, by having been a laboring man and a farmer for a number of years, and then by having made a moderate success of some enterprise.[33]

A partial compilation of the occupations of fathers of Texas governors substantiates this idea that social status may be important but that high economic status may not be helpful in politics. Biographical data on the economic status of parents of executives were not available in all cases but, from the information obtainable, it appears that being reared in a "poor" family has been no detriment to the Texas politicians. Many of the governors under consideration came from "poor" homes, and at least two were born in log cabins, while five were from families that were moderately "well-to-do." Governor Ireland, born in 1827, was known as "Ox-Cart John" (he was also known as "Honest John"), and this association with a humble mode of transportation apparently had its political value. Regardless of economic status, family interest in public affairs was present in nearly all the families. Several fathers of future executives had been elected to local public offices, and one had served in the United States Congress for twenty years. Others had attended one of the constitutional conventions held in the state or had been active in the affairs of the Democratic Party—the only viable political party in Texas at that time.

An analysis of parental occupations reveals that the largest number of chief executives came from farm homes: a total of eleven parents were farmers, ranging from large plantation owners to tenant farmers. Professions also were well represented: four parents were lawyers, one was a teacher, one a minister, and one a physician. Only one parent in the group was a businessman—and he was bankrupt when he died. One father was both an editor of a weekly newspaper and a real-estate man, and another was a military man. Two of the fathers were employed by government—one by the federal government as a

[32] Matthews, *Political Decision-Makers*, p. 23.
[33] Steen, "The Political Career of James E. Ferguson, 1914–1917" (unpublished M.A. thesis), p. 167.

rural mail carrier and the other by the state as a Texas Ranger captain.

Parental occupations, consequently, were generally of acceptable social standing, although at many times the families did not enjoy high economic levels. Summarized below, occupations of the fathers of governors were:

Occupation of Father	Number So Employed	Percentage of Total
Land-owning Farmer	9	37.5
Tenant Farmer	2	8.34
Lawyer	4	16.68
Soldier	1	4.17
Minister	1	4.17
Doctor	1	4.17
Merchant	1	4.17
Teacher	1	4.17
Editor	1	4.17
State Employee	1	4.17
Federal Employee	1	4.17
Information not available	1	4.17

RELIGIOUS BACKGROUNDS

Just as an acceptable occupation of parents appears to be significant in the rise of an individual to the governor's chair, religious affiliation may also play a part. The effect of one's religious views upon his election to office cannot be assessed with accuracy, but to some people religious issues are a factor, particularly in a state such as Texas where fundamentalist sects have loomed large. In the presidential campaigns of 1928 and 1960 the Catholic religion of the Democratic candidates was discussed nationally. The political significance of religion in this state was underscored in 1959 when the Baptist General Convention of Texas passed a resolution calling upon members of that denomination, the largest Protestant group in the state, to reaffirm their stand on separation of church and state.[34] This move was interpreted by some to oppose a Catholic candidate for the Presidency. Despite the fact that the Roman Catholic Church has been one of the largest denominations in the state for some time,[35]

34 *Corpus Christi Caller-Times,* November 5, 1959.
35 The latest tally compiled by the Texas Council of Churches indicated a total of 5,822,235 church members in the state. Breakdown of that total by percentage is approximately as follows: Baptists, 35.8; Roman Catholics, 31.7; Methodists,

members of that faith have not usually been elected to state offices other than the Legislature. In recent gubernatorial elections the one Catholic candidate was unsuccessful in an attempt to unseat an incumbent running for re-election. Undoubtedly factors other than religion were more compelling but the matter of religion was discussed in some quarters.[36]

In 1961 the Protestant population of the state approximated two and three-fourths million. The total number has grown through the years, but the proportion of each denomination to the total population has not changed significantly since records of church affiliation have been kept.[37] The two largest Protestant groups—Baptists and Methodists—have furnished about 70 per cent (eighteen) of the governors of Texas. Eleven of the governors (45.87 per cent) have been Methodists, and seven (29.19 per cent) have been Baptists. The Disciples of Christ have supplied three governors (12.51 per cent), and the Episcopal Church two (8.34 per cent).[38] The only other faith

---

14.3; Church of Christ, 6.9; Presbyterians, 2.9; Lutherans, 2.3; Episcopalians, 1.9; Disciples of Christ, 1.9. All other denominations had less than 1 per cent of the total membership. Figures furnished by the state office of the Texas Council of Churches.

[36] In 1958 State Senator Henry B. Gonzalez opposed Governor Price Daniel for a second term. The writer was a resident of Northeast Texas and during the campaign talked to a number of voters in that area about the candidates. Three issues were most discussed: (1) that custom decrees a second term for governors who have had at least moderate success, (2) that the Senator was of Spanish-American ancestry, and (3) that the Senator was a "liberal" and a Catholic.

[37] Protestant denominations in Texas in 1960 reported the following numbers of members to the Texas Council of Churches: Baptist, 1,579,139; Methodist, 832,746; Church of Christ, 400,000; Presbyterian, 165,481; Lutheran, 134,866; Disciples of Christ, 114,814; Episcopal, 95,725. An official of the Council of Churches indicated that the total number of church members has grown steadily over the years but that the proportions by denomination had not changed significantly since records have been kept, although the Baptists have gained "slightly" more than other major sects.

[38] Mrs. Ferguson was a member of the Methodist Church in her early life, but by the time she became governor she had changed her affiliation to the Episcopal Church. Information provided by her daughter, Mrs. Stuart Watt of Austin. Dan Moody belonged to the Baptist Church, as had his father, for most of his life but often attended the Methodist Church with his mother, who was a Methodist. At one time he taught a Sunday School class in the Methodist Church, and for years he was in the habit of attending services almost every Sunday at both the First Methodist Church and the First Baptist Church in Austin, going to the early service at one and the 11:00 o'clock service at the other. A few years ago, he and Mrs. Moody joined the First Methodist Church. Information in a letter from Dan Moody, Jr., June 14, 1963. In the table below, which gives affiliations at the time the person was governor, Mrs. Ferguson is counted as an Episcopalian and Mr. Moody as a Baptist.

to be represented has been the Presbyterian Church, with one governor.

Religious affiliations of the twenty-four governors under consideration are tabulated as follows:

Church	Number of Governors	Percentage
Methodist	11	45.87
Baptist	7	29.19
Disciples of Christ	3	12.51
Episcopal	2	8.34
Presbyterian	1	4.17

Some Southern politicians believe that affiliation with the Masonic Lodge is almost as important as religious connections for those seeking public elective office.[39] That Masonic membership is not a handicap politically is illustrated by the fact that only four governors since 1876 have not been Masons, and one of those obviously could not be a member because she was a woman.[40] Undoubtedly, the contacts made in the Masonic organization prove useful in political campaigns.

EDUCATIONAL BACKGROUNDS

American public servants are not chosen solely upon the basis of fortunate birth or cultural inheritance. Such a headstart helps, but it is not enough. American politicians usually must also display a considerable amount of personal achievement before their political chances for high office are very good, and studies reveal that the top political officeholders are among the better educated of all occupational groups in the United States. There is a good deal of variation in the educational level within the group, but a majority of those

[39] Ewing, "Southern Governors," *Journal of Politics*, 10 (May, 1948), 394.

[40] The following excerpt is contained in a letter dated March 20, 1951, from Dr. Llerena Friend, Librarian, Barker Texas History Center, The University of Texas, to H. G. Secrest, of Taylor, Texas: "J. J. Gallaher, grand treasurer of the Grand Lodge, Waco, informs me that the following Texas Governors were NOT Masons: Peter H. Bell; Pendleton Murrah [both of whom held office prior to adoption of the present Constitution]; J. S. Hogg; T. M. Campbell; O. B. Colquitt; and Mrs. M. A. Ferguson. Colquitt became an Entered Apprentice but did not finish his work." "Governors' Folder on file in the Barker Texas History Center.

John Connally, elected in 1962, is not a member of the Masonic Order. Information given this writer by Connally's press secretary.

elected in recent years have come from the 10 per cent of the population who have attended college. The trend is toward even more highly educated decision makers, but they appear already to have had education superior to that of the citizenry at large.[41]

The percentage of state executives with higher education has risen steadily over the past half century. Studying the educational background of all governors in the United States between 1915 and 1950, Professor Solomon indicated that between 1915 and 1930, 64 per cent of the officeholders had attended institutions of higher education; during the 1930's the figure rose to 77 per cent; and between 1940 and 1950, 88 per cent of America's governors were college-trained.[42] At the end of the period studied, the median number of school years completed by the total population of the country was only slightly over nine,[43] but by 1960 only six of the nation's fifty governors had not attended college.[44]

Similarly, the education of Texas governors has been superior to that of the general population of the state. In 1960, when college enrollment in the state hit an all-time high, the median number of years of education completed by the adult Texas population (25 years of age and over) was 10.4 years,[45] but over the years, two-thirds of the governors in this study (16 of the 24) had some college training. Several attended small colleges which are now defunct, but others went to well-known, out-of-state institutions such as Harvard, William and Mary, Virginia Military Institute, the University of Virginia, and the University of Alabama. The training they received ranged from one year of undergraduate study through professional law degrees.

Not until 1921 was a governor elected who had obtained a degree from a Texas institution of higher learning; since that time all the governors who attended college (seven out of ten) received at least a part of their education within the state. Of Texas institutions still functioning, The University of Texas, Baylor University, and Rice University have been alma maters of governors. Degrees granted have usually been the Bachelor of Arts or the Bachelor of Laws. Pat

[41] Matthews, *Political Decision-Makers,* p. 30.
[42] Solomon, "U.S. Governors—1940–1950," *National Municipal Review,* XLI (April, 1952), 191.
[43] U. S. Department of Commerce, *Statistical Abstract of the United States, 1958,* p. 112.
[44] Council of State Governments, *The Governors—Their Backgrounds,* p. 2.
[45] U. S. Department of Commerce, Bureau of the Census, *1960 Census,* pp. 45–330.

Neff earned a Master's degree, and several have been the recipients of honorary doctorates. Within the past forty years only three incumbents have not had college training. The trend in the state, as in the nation, has been toward electing better-educated persons to high office.

OCCUPATIONAL BACKGROUNDS

Occupational backgrounds of political figures are highly important. Most governors have had some standing in their communities and most have sprung from families who displayed an interest in public affairs. Added to family background has usually been personal business success or professional attainment of some kind. A number of years ago, one writer reported that, occupationally, state legislatures were more democratic in composition than either the national Congress or state governorships; he also found that the occupational level of American public decision makers has been very much the same during the past century and a half.[46]

The legal profession has traditionally supplied many public leaders in American history, and lawyers have sometimes been called "the high priests of American politics," probably because they

meet what seems to be the first prerequisite of top-level political leadership: they are in a high-prestige position. . . . [Furthermore] the skills developed by the lawyer in the practice of his profession give him an advantage in the race for office, if not actual training for the performance of public duties. His job involves skill in interpersonal mediation and conciliation and facility in the use of words. Both of these skills are indispensable to the politician. Moreover, the lawyer in private practice operates in large part as the expert adviser to decision-makers.[47]

The predominance of lawyers in statehouses always has been striking, and the number has been growing. During the first decade of the twentieth century, incumbent governors in 48 per cent of the states had received legal training.[48] By mid-century the percentage had risen to 53.[49] In the South, the number is generally higher than the national norm; a few years ago, Professor Cortez Ewing found that

[46] H. D. Anderson, "Educational and Occupational Attainment of Our Rulers," *Scientific Monthly*, 40 (September, 1935), 512.

[47] Matthews, *Political Decision-Makers*, pp. 30–31.

[48] Macdonald, "American Governors, 1900–1910," *National Municipal Review*, XVI (November, 1927), 715.

[49] Solomon, "U.S. Governors—1940–1950," *National Municipal Review*, XLI (April, 1952), 191.

69.6 per cent of Southern governors had received legal training.[50] In promoting lawyers to the gubernatorial chair, Texas is typical of the South. Seventy per cent of her governors since 1874 have been lawyers, and an even larger number had legal training although they primarily practiced some other vocation.

Trailing far behind the legal profession as a source of chief exccutive talent is the newspaper business. Two editors have been governor of the state, but no other vocation has had more than one representative. Those having other occupations included: a banker, an executive in the oil business, a flour manufacturer-salesman, a professional soldier, and a housewife. Strangely enough, no small-town merchant or college professor has ever attained the office, although two governors became college presidents upon leaving office, and one became a professor. Occupations of the twenty-four governors at the time of election were:

Occupation When Elected	Number So Employed	Percentage
Lawyer	17	70.8
Editor	2	8.34
Soldier	1	4.17
Banker	1	4.17
Oil Company Executive	1	4.17
Flour Manufacturer	1	4.17
Housewife	1	4.17

PRIOR PUBLIC OFFICES HELD

Perhaps even more important than socioeconomic factors in the background of the chief executive is his apprenticeship in public life before becoming the first citizen of his state. An extensive analysis of the national pattern of promotion to the governorship over a period of eighty years reveals that almost all governors had some previous experience in holding public office.[51] Twenty years or more of private and/or public experience is usually required to reach the gubernatorial chair, the average age at inauguration being fifty-one years.[52]

Probably no public office, with the exception of the Presidency,

---

[50] Ewing, "Southern Governors," *Journal of Politics*, 10 (May, 1948), 394.

[51] Joseph A. Schlesinger, *How They Became Governor: A Study of Comparative State Politics, 1870–1950*, p. 13. Hereafter cited as Schlesinger, *How They Became Governor.*

[52] Solomon, "U.S. Governors—1940–1950," *National Municipal Review*, XLI (April, 1952), 192.

has not at some time been held by a future state governor; however, only a few classifications of employment have been important as steppingstones to the highest state position. A study, covering nearly a century, of governors in all states reveals that state legislatures have provided an important opportunity to gain background experience, more than half of the governors at one time or another during their careers having served as legislators. Next in importance has been the law-enforcement category, with 32 per cent of the governors having held such jobs. Other positions, in order of importance, have been administrative jobs in government, local elective offices, statewide elective offices, and federal elective offices. Only 9 per cent of America's governors at the time of the study had held no previous public office.[53]

The most clearly defined path to the governorship is through state-wide elective office. . . . Men usually come to these positions with prior office experience and hold them just prior to the governorship. The pattern consists of a minimum of two offices before the governorship: (1) legislative office and (2) state office (usually lieutenant governor). Legislative leadership (either as Speaker or President of the Senate) is frequently a third stage in the process of advancement. Thus we have here a highly ordered pattern, which enables one to project the future governors of a state over a period of from four to six years and possibly more.[54]

No state had a rigid ladder of promotion which had been climbed by all governors, but in more than half of the states a typical office career had been followed by at least one-third of the incumbents.[55]

Statewide elective offices seem to be most likely to lead to the governorship where one party is dominant.[56] Thus, "the South remains a section in which a young man still has the opportunity to reach high political preferment. Its politics are tumultuous. Long apprenticeship is not a requirement for election to high office. This [probably] is a corollary of the uniparty system."[57]

Even with a possibly rapid rise to the office, Southern governors have traditionally had more experience in political office than have governors of other sections. The typical pattern of Southern political success still consists of early election to the state legislature, a tour of

[53] Schlesinger, *How They Became Governor*, p. 11.
[54] *Ibid.*, p. 16.
[55] *Ibid.*, p. 19.
[56] *Ibid.*, p. 26.
[57] Ewing, "Southern Governors," *Journal of Politics*, 10 (May, 1948), 391.

duty as district attorney or county judge, then a plunge into the larger area of statewide politics.[58] Unlike other sections, the South recruits few of its governors from the ranks of business executives, a fact that derives from the very personal nature of Southern politics—with its one-party, double-primary system—and from the absence, until recently, of large-scale business activity.[59]

With the declining prestige of state legislatures in general, service in the legislature has become less important as an immediate stepping-stone to the chief executive's position. At the same time, law-enforcement backgrounds have become increasingly important in gubernatorial careers. The number of public attorneys going directly to the executive chair has been large, due to the fact that decisions on what to investigate and prosecute frequently represent important political decisions.[60]

In his national study Professor Schlesinger cites Texas as a primary example of a state in which law-enforcement careers, especially the office of attorney general, have led to the governor's office. He explains this situation with the following thesis: (1) Texas is a state in which the maintenance of order has been, and is today, of primary political importance; (2) the sharp clash of interests characteristic of a rapidly expanding economy has focused political attention upon the law-enforcement official; and (3) the development of regulatory agencies to control important elements of the economy has provided an opportunity to use this type of office as a means of advancing to the governorship.[61]

The average age of Texas governors at inauguration has been 47¾ years, a figure slightly below the national average of 51. Since 1876 five governors have been inaugurated in their thirties, eleven in their forties, eight in their fifties, and only one above sixty. The number of executives who held no prior office has also been higher in Texas than in most states. Seven of the incumbents, more than one-fourth, had not previously been elective officeholders, although one of that number had served several years as an appointed chairman of the State Highway Commission, and another had served as United States Secretary of the Navy. A detailed list of prior offices held by the governors appears in Appendix IV.

[58] *Ibid.*, p. 395.
[59] *Ibid.*, p. 397.
[60] Schlesinger, *How They Became Governor*, pp. 51, 81.
[61] *Ibid.*, p. 83.

Examination of public elective offices held by Texas governors substantiates Professor Schlesinger's contention that law-enforcement positions have loomed large as training grounds for the state's executives. Five served as attorney general and six as county or district attorneys. Service in the Texas Legislature was also of importance; nine governors were legislators at some time in their pregubernatorial careers. Five served as lieutenant governor, four of these gaining the governor's office by succession, then being re-elected in their own right. A compilation of prior public service of Texas governors follows:

Former Position Held	Number	Percentage
Lieutenant Governor	5	20.8
Attorney General	5	20.8
Member of U.S. Congress	3	12.48
U.S. Secretary of the Navy	1	4.16
Texas Legislator	9	37.44
Public Attorney (District or County)	6	24.96
Judicial Officer	4	16.64
State Administration Officer	5	20.8
Officer of Local Government	5	20.8

There have been several governors who have held two or more offices during their careers, but, overall, the office of attorney general has been the single most important steppingstone to the top office. Of those having legislative service, three had been elected speaker of the House. Of the judges coming to the executive office, one had been chief justice and two others had been associate justices of the Texas Supreme Court. The group with prior administrative experience in state government contained two members of the Railroad Commission, one state revenue agent, and a chairman of the Texas Highway Commission. Local offices held included mayor, justice of the peace, sheriff, and city attorney. One early governor had been a member of the Alabama Legislature before migration to this state, and a second had served as the sheriff of a Kentucky county. Three of the group were members of the Secession Convention of 1861, and one had participated as a member of the Constitutional Convention that drafted the executive article under which he served.

Since 1900 Texas has elected to the governorship one member of the United States House of Representatives, one United States Senator, three lieutenant governors (by succession), one highway commissioner, two railroad commissioners, two attorneys general, one former state legislator who had retired to private life preceding his election, one who had been United States Secretary of the Navy, and four persons possessing no previous political experience. No clear pattern, therefore, emerges for advancement to the governorship. Nevertheless, an office which can serve as a sounding board to gain statewide attention is undoubtedly helpful in progress toward the governorship. Law-enforcement positions and regulatory agencies provide such an opportunity in Texas, where there are vast geographic areas and conflicting economic interests to deal with, but a person without benefit of previous office can make a successful assault on the governorship. What is clear is that the Legislature, although undoubtedly an important training ground, is not a place from which high state officers are likely to be directly chosen.

INFLUENCE OF GEOGRAPHICAL ORIGINS

Undoubtedly, the area from which a politician comes plays an important part in his political career. Both his place of birth and his "official residence" at the time of election may affect his attainment of position. Several years ago a survey of the nation's governors revealed that about one-third of the executives in American states were "foreigners," i.e., born outside of the states they governed.[62] By 1960 this number had dropped to one-fifth.[63] In Texas the trend has been more and more toward the election of native-born sons to office, with fourteen governors (58.33 per cent of the twenty-four in this survey) having been born in the state. Of the executives not native born, only two were born north of the Mason-Dixon line—one in Iowa and the other in Ohio. The future Governor Lawrence S. (Sul) Ross, born in Iowa, was brought to Texas as a child by his parents and was reared in this state. W. Lee O'Daniel, a native of Ohio, moved to Kansas at an early age, where he grew to adulthood in the city of Kingman. After working for a flour-milling company there, he migrated to Texas in 1925 when he secured a salesman's job in Fort Worth. The Southern states which have supplied Texas with governors since 1876 are South Carolina and Georgia, two each (Roberts, Lanham, Hubbard, Colquitt), and Kentucky, Virginia, Alabama, and Mississippi, one each (Ireland, Coke, Culberson, Sayers).

[62] Gurwell, "Governors of the States," *State Government,* XIV (July, 1941), 158.
[63] Council of State Governments, *The Governors—Personal Histories,* p. 1.

Among areas of Texas where future governors were born, East Texas has provided the most, closely followed by Central Texas. Sectionally, the distribution of birthplaces of native Texans follows:

Section of Texas Where Born	Number of Governors	Percentage Native-born
East Texas	5	35.7
Central Texas	4	28.56
Southeast Texas	2	14.28
West Texas	2	14.28
South Central Texas	1	7.14

Probably more important from a sectional standpoint is the official residence of the governors at the time of gaining office. For many years East Texas was the center of official residences of governors and other leading political dignitaries. About the turn of the century the city of Tyler, in deep East Texas, had become in actuality the political center of the state. To alleviate that situation a number of prominent men determined to take the leadership of Texas politics from the "Tyler gang."[64] The attempt was successful to some extent; however, it may be that the westward shifting of the state's population would have diminished East Texas control sooner or later.

Statistics show that Central Texas, which has been the official residence of one-third of the governors since 1876, has furnished more chief executives than has any other single section of the state. No governors have come from South Texas, Southwest Texas, and the Panhandle area. Only two West Texans have been elected, a situation perhaps to be expected as that region includes the most sparsely populated counties in the state. Areas of Texas where governors resided when elected are shown below, and the map in Figure 1 details the official residences as well as the birthplaces of chief executives since 1876.

Official Residence	Number of Governors	Percentage
Central Texas	8	33.36
North Texas	5	20.85
East Texas	5	20.85
Southeast Texas	4	16.68
West Texas	2	8.34

[64] Grady S. St. Clair, "The Hogg-Clark Campaign" (unpublished M.A. thesis), p. 35.

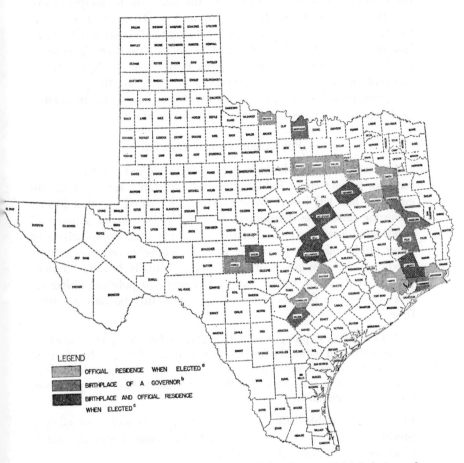

F<small>IG</small>. 1—Map of Texas showing geographical distribution of birthplaces and official residences of governors of Texas.

a3 each from Smith and McLennan Counties
2 each from Jefferson and Tarrant Counties
b2 each from Cherokee and Bell Counties
c2 from Bell County

Most chief executives have maintained their official residences in the medium-sized or small cities of the state—in municipalities of less than 100,000 population. Tyler, in East Texas, and Waco, in Central Texas, have the distinction of being the "hometown" of three governors each. Temple, in Central Texas, produced two governors, the Fergusons, from the same family. Fort Worth, in North Texas, has sent two citizens to the governorship, including the present incumbent, John Connally. Only four executives have come from cities ranking among the top five in population in the state.

POSTGUBERNATORIAL CAREERS

Activities of those who have held a state's highest office frequently have an impact upon public affairs of the state even after the incumbent has left office. In most states the activities of a former governor cannot be discounted, because he is "usually a potential candidate for re-election, no matter how many years out in private or other public office,"[65] according to Professor Solomon, who in 1931 predicted that the governorship would eventually become "a stepping-stone to fame rather than a toboggan to political oblivion." Over the nation the governorship has apparently become a shuttle train.

It is not only a stepping-stone to federal office but also an office to which ex-governors and national officeholders may return, because they find the governorship more desirable or to point for higher federal or other post or . . . [even] to provide a vantage point from which to scrutinize policies of the federal government.[66]

Promotion in public office within a state appears to be not solely a product of internal politics but to reflect to some degree the state's place in the promotional hierarchy.[67]

Insofar as the Executive Mansion is used as a step to higher positions, Texas hardly fits into the national pattern of promotion. The fact that Texas is a Southern, one-party state may account for the fact that her governors have never figured prominently in the presidential picture. Three years after his impeachment James E. Ferguson ran

---

[65] Solomon, "U.S. Governors—1940–1950," *National Municipal Review*, XLI (April, 1952), 196.
[66] *Ibid.*, p. 197.
[67] Schlesinger, *How They Became Governor*, p. 196.

for President of the United States on the ticket of the American Party, but, of course, his was only a token candidacy.

Despite the fact that former governors of Texas have not figured in the national political scene, one cannot overlook their importance in state and regional public life, for a majority of them have remained somewhat active in Texas politics. Their major role, however, has not been in campaigning as active candidates for office but in espousing some candidate or issue in which they were interested. The presidential campaign of 1960 is a case in point. All former governors of the state except one endorsed the Republican candidate, Richard M. Nixon, and two, Moody and Shivers, worked hard for his election, the latter making many speeches throughout the nation. Only former Governor Miriam A. Ferguson and the incumbent, Governor Price Daniel, supported the Democratic candidate in that election. The votes that were swung by such public endorsements cannot be estimated with any degree of accuracy, but of course some voters were influenced, perhaps particularly among elderly citizens not in touch with the current situation but loyal to the leadership of the Fergusons, or Hobby, or Moody, or O'Daniel.

The United States Senate has sometimes been called an "ex-governors club," but the title is hardly appropriate where Texas is concerned. Since 1876 only three Texas governors (Coke, Culberson, and O'Daniel) have been "promoted" to that body, although over the years six governors have been defeated for seats in the Senate. Price Daniel took the rather unusual step of resigning from the Senate to become governor of Texas.

Some governors continued to hold public office after the expiration of their tenures in the state's highest office. Governors Sayers and Neff later served in state administrative agencies, and former Governor Ross was appointed to the Railroad Commission, but declined the appointment to remain as president of A. and M. College. Colquitt and Neff became affiliated with the federal government in administrative capacities, and Allred occupied the bench as a federal district judge for many years. Hubbard was rewarded for his services as temporary chairman of the Democratic National Convention by being appointed to the post of United States Minister to Japan. Sayers and Lanham served on the Board of Regents of The University of Texas, and Hobby served on the Board of Regents of Texas Technological College.

Political comebacks have been the exception rather than the rule in Texas. Those who have run for any office after leaving the governorship have been generally unsuccessful. Mrs. Miriam Ferguson was the only person to be elected governor for two nonsuccessive terms, but she was defeated for governor on three other occasions. Former Governors Ireland, Campbell, Jim Ferguson, Moody, Allred, and Stevenson were defeated for United States senator; and the most recent attempt at a comeback—when former Governor and Senator W. Lee O'Daniel ran for governor in 1958—resulted in the ex-Governor's running a poor third.

By and large, Texas governors have returned to private life upon retirement from the executive office, although of the twenty-four, only Lanham declared his complete retirement upon finishing his term. The majority have remained active in some profession or business. Six took up the practice of law, three affiliated with business establishments, two served as newspaper editors, and one returned to his ranch. Three entered the field of education: Lawrence S. Ross became president of Texas A. and M. College, Pat Neff became president of Baylor University, and Oran Roberts was named professor of law at The University of Texas, where he became affectionately known as "The Old Alcalde" (mayor). Roberts and Hubbard published books (not including speeches or public papers) and Neff published an account of his campaign for office.[68] Table 2 shows the activities of Texas governors upon leaving the Executive Mansion.

Four Eras in the Governorship of Texas

Before drawing conclusions about a "composite Texas governor," a survey of events over the period covered may reveal whether there have been any significant chronological trends. For this purpose, the years since 1876 have been divided into four periods of approximately twenty years each. The classification is admittedly arbitrary, but not without logic, as the periods have been broken so that each begins with the inauguration of a new governor.

The first period, 1876 to 1898, was an era in which the newly written Constitution was being adapted—a period of readjustment after the Civil War and a time in which new regulatory functions were instituted in government. It was the age in which many of the

[68] Roberts, *Fifty Years of Political, Legislative, and Judicial History of Texas;* Hubbard, *The United States in the Far East;* Neff, *The Battles of Peace.*

TABLE 2

Postgubernatorial Careers of Texas Governors

Governor	Public offices held after Governorship	Other Offices Sought	Principal Occupation
Richard Coke	U.S. Senator*		Government
Richard B. Hubbard	Minister to Japan		Attorney and Author
Oran M. Roberts			Professor of Law, The University of Texas
John Ireland		U.S. Senator (defeated)	Attorney
Lawrence S. Ross			President, A.&M. College of Texas
James S. Hogg			Attorney
C. A. Culberson	U.S. Senator* (Minority Leader)		Government
Joseph D. Sayers	Board of Regents, U. of Texas; Chm., Industrial Accident Bd.; Member, Pardons Board		Attorney
Samuel W. T. Lanham	Board of Regents, U. of Texas		Retired
Thomas M. Campbell		U.S. Senator (defeated)	Attorney
Oscar B. Colquitt	U. S. Mediation Bd.; Attorney, Reconstruction Finance Corp.*		U.S. Government Official
James E. Ferguson		Governor U.S. Senator President of U.S. (defeated for all)	Newspaper Publisher
William P. Hobby	Board of Regents, Texas Technological College		Newspaper Editor
Pat M. Neff	U.S. Mediation Bd.; Chm., Texas Railroad Commission		President, Baylor University
Miriam A. Ferguson		Governor (defeated 3 times)	Housewife

* Died while holding this office.

TABLE 2 (Continued)

Postgubernatorial Careers of Texas Governors

Governor	Public offices held after Governorship	Other Offices Sought	Principal Occupation
Dan Moody		U.S. Senator (defeated)	Attorney
Ross S. Sterling			Oil Company Executive
James V. Allred	U.S. District Judge*	U.S. Senator (defeated)	U.S. District Judge
W. Lee O'Daniel	U.S. Senator	Governor (defeated 2 times)	Insurance Executive
Coke Stevenson		U.S. Senator (defeated)	Rancher
Beauford H. Jester**			
Allan Shivers			Business Executive
Price Daniel		Governor (defeated)	Attorney

* Died while holding this office.
** Died while in office as governor.
Source: Compiled from Biographical Files, Barker Texas History Center, The University of Texas, and from Scrapbooks on Texas Governors, The University of Texas Archives.

last ties to the Confederacy were broken, and during this time most of the governors were either veterans of the Army of the Confederate States or sons of veterans of that Army. On the whole, they were well trained in both education and experience; it was fortunate for the state that men of such caliber were chosen to serve during the readjustment days.

The second period, 1899 to 1920, witnessed the beginning of the new century, with its emphasis upon reform and progressivism. Also, it saw the world engaged in a conflict which up to that time was the largest war in history. Two of the governors of this period showed deference for the position by giving up seats in the national Congress to become chief executive of the state. At this time the new method of nominating public officials through the direct primary was begun— a democratization which was to influence the type of candidate chosen in subsequent years.

The next two decades, 1921 to 1941, were the period of business expansion after World War I and of a major financial depression which resulted in a re-evaluation of the social functions of the state. During these decades governors were chosen who had less prior public experience than had those of any years since 1876. Texas had the distinction of electing the first woman governor in the nation, and political showmanship hit its peak in gubernatorial contests.

The last period, 1941 to 1963, included another world war, inflation, and unprecedented prosperity. The old two-term tradition was broken, and governors generally had better education and experience in public affairs, particularly legislative affairs, than ever before. A new interpretation of the governor's role as a leader developed in Texas and throughout the nation in these years.

The analysis by time period may be summarized as follows:

Date	No. of Governors	Average Age at Inauguration	Percentage with College Training	Percentage of Lawyers	No. Yrs. Previous Public Service		
					National Office	State Office	Local Office
876–1898	7	$47^4/_7$	71	83	2 Avg.(.29)	37 (5.3)	22 (3.1)
899–1920	6	49	33.3	50	30 Avg.(5)	24 (4)	2 (.33)
921–1941	6	$46^4/_7$	67	50	0 Avg.(0)	17 (2.8)	8 (1.3)
941–1963	5	48	80	100	5 Avg.(1)	40 (10)	8 (2)
TOTALS (1876–1963)	24	$47^3/_4$	66.6	75	37 Avg.(1.55)	118 (4.26)	40 (1.74)

"THE COMPOSITE TEXAS GOVERNOR"

The detailed analysis of biographical material of twenty-four governors who have held office under the present Constitution does not bolster the theory of a "typical" governor of this state. One could not identify any appreciable number of chief executives by going out into the highways and byways with any single preconception—a fact which may primarily be a result of the operation of free democratic processes. But despite the great heterogeneity of incumbents, it is possible to hypothesize a "composite" governor.

What, then, may one expect the governor of Texas to be like? A combination of data indicates that he will be a man, about forty-eight years of age when he begins his occupancy of the Executive

Mansion on Colorado Street. He will have had some experience in public service, most likely in state government. Almost certainly he will have come from one of the small towns of the state. He will be a native son of Texas, born to parents of poor or modest means, who, however, enjoyed a position of moderate social standing in their community by virtue of the father's occupation and/or participation in public affairs. In most cases, the "governor" will have had at least some college education, perhaps even hold a degree or two; and the chances are quite good that he will be a lawyer by profession.

He will be married and the father of several children, and he will be a "joiner." He may have membership in the American Legion or another veterans' organization. He will belong to a major Protestant denomination—almost surely either Methodist or Baptist—and he will be a Mason.

The "typical Texas governor" will have been born in Central or East Texas. He will have seen service in the Texas Legislature and probably have held a statewide elective office, most likely a law-enforcement position. He may expect to remain as chief executive at least four years, and perhaps even longer.

Unless the "governor" goes immediately to another elective office he probably will be unsuccessful in trying for a seat in Congress or even in returning to the governor's chair. But he will continue his interest in public affairs after his retirement from office, inevitably to the extent of endorsing, and sometimes actively campaigning for, other candidates—for governor, for the United States Senate, or for the Presidency of the United States. He will be sought out for his advice on candidates and issues as the press of the state continues to keep in touch with him.

After he retires from public office the "composite governor" will enter a profession or the business world and live for many years. At the time of this writing, six former Texas governors are living, who have together served the state for more than fifty years, in every decade but the first one of the twentieth century. One of these is an octogenarian; three are over seventy; and two are in their fifties. Only one chief executive of this state has died in office in this century.

PART TWO

The Governor as Executive and Administrator

4

The Executive Office: Duties and Staff

Almost a quarter of a century has elapsed since a British political scientist, migrating to the United States to study executives at the state level, reported that the typical American governor had been elevated from the status of figurehead to that of leader. Basing his conclusions largely on the outgrowth of the Administrative Reorganization Movement begun in 1917, Leslie Lipson found the executive of the 1930's to be "the chief purveyor of services to his fellow citizens."[1] Continuing in the same vein some two decades later, another student of the governorship, this time an American, categorized the functions of a state executive at mid-century into three groups: policy formation, management, and public relations. He found that the policy formation function was undoubtedly the most imporant and the public relations function the most time consuming.[2]

Frank Bane, for over twenty-five years executive director of the Council of State Governments, said, in 1958, that "the most spectacular and important change that has taken place with respect to the office of the Governor has been the great expansion of its duties and responsibilities."[3] Increased activities have thrown the executive into many diverse roles until he has come to personify the state government to the citizenry. One contemporary writer describes the governorship of the sixties as an institution, declaring:

[1] Leslie Lipson, *The American Governor from Figurehead to Leader*, p. 249.
[2] Coleman B. Ransone, Jr., *The Office of Governor in the United States*, pp. 116–118.
[3] Frank Bane, "The Job of Being Governor," *State Government*, XXXI (Summer, 1958), 184.

. . . to the people, it is a symbol of the unity of society within the state; to the governor, his staff, and his many advisors, it is an image to be carefully constructed and then disseminated through the mass media of communication until it influences every politically conscious person in the state. The governorship is many things, as is the Presidency, and the governor must play many social roles and must learn to help the public to keep them individually identifiable. The governor is chief of state, the voice of the people, chief executive, commander-in-chief of the state's armed forces, chief legislator, and chief of his party.[4]

DUTIES OF THE GOVERNOR OF TEXAS

Describing these various roles of the governor of Texas some years ago, a capital-city newspaper called the position "really a devil of a job," adding, however, that "there are few among Texas' 6,808,813 people who wouldn't be proud to hold it."[5] Though expressed in the vernacular, this portrayal of the public image of the office may not be an oversimplification, for the job is indeed demanding, requiring much time and talent. In his position as the state's first citizen, the governor of Texas must provide leadership to the state and its government in many ways, both formal and informal, although in some cases where leadership is needed, the governor may find himself lacking sufficient authority to act effectively. Compared with executive offices in some states, "the office of governor of Texas is a weak one and occupies a position similar to that of most state executives in about 1850 or 1875."[6]

This "weak" position does not mean, however, that the governor does not have a multitude of duties and responsibilities; it means rather that he may have to call into play all of his skills or even use devious means to exercise authority. He is in a position that commands a degree of prominence and prestige not attaching to other state offices; consequently, he is inherently in a position to exercise leadership, however inadequate, because the willingness of the people to accept executive leadership is historically evident.[7]

As leader of the state government, the governor is charged by the Constitution and statutes of the state with numerous specific duties

[4] Charles R. Adrian, *State and Local Governments: A Study in the Political Process*, p. 255. Hereafter cited as Adrian, *State and Local Governments*.

[5] *Austin American*, September 20, 1947.

[6] Stuart A. MacCorkle and Dick Smith, *Texas Government* (4th ed.), p. 100.

[7] Leonard D. White, "On Governors," *Public Administration Review*, IV (Winter, 1944), 69.

and responsibilities. In its *Manual of Texas State Government* the Texas Legislative Council outlined the powers of the Executive Office as follows:

I. Executive Powers and Duties
 1. Law Enforcement
 2. Represents State
 3. Appointments
 4. Removal
 5. Membership on Boards
II. Legislative Powers
 1. Messages
 2. Special Sessions
 3. Veto
III. Clemency Powers
IV. Executive Authority
 1. Contacts with state agencies and institutions
 2. Investigation and planning for development of the state and its resources and the general well-being of the people.[8]

The staff of Governor Price Daniel wrote a pamphlet consonant with that outline, explaining the executive's constitutional and legal obligations.[9] Written in layman's language, for distribution to the public, this brochure classifies the governor's functions as executive, legislative, and judicial, and discusses his duties under the headings given below.

EXECUTIVE FUNCTIONS

Law enforcement. The governor is charged with the responsibility of seeing that the laws of the state are faithfully executed. To do so, he may call forth the militia (the Texas National Guard) to suppress insurrections and repel invasions; assume command and direct activities of the Department of Public Safety to cope with public disaster, riot, or insurrection, or to meet any dangerous resistance to enforcement of the law; declare martial law in areas where civil authorities need assistance in maintaining law and order; require reports from all administrative agencies on the conduct of their affairs; and "exercise other miscellaneous powers and the influence

[8] Texas Legislative Council, *Manual of Texas State Government,* Staff Research Report 51–56, pp. 1–3.
[9] "Duties and Powers of the Governor of Texas." Each of these functions is dealt with in detail elsewhere in this study.

of his office in providing leadership for the State government."

Military. Except when they are called into service of the national government, the governor is commander in chief of the military forces of the state (National Guard or state militia). He selects an adjutant general to serve as his agent in the administration of the military forces and to carry out his orders.

Appointments. With the advice and consent of two-thirds of the Senate, the chief executive appoints the secretary of state; the adjutant general; the commissioner of labor statistics; members of numerous state boards and commissions, most of which have an overlapping membership serving for six-year terms; and certain local officers such as pilot boards and branch pilots at various ports; public weighers; special weighers; and quarantine and health officers if needed to enforce quarantines proclaimed by the governor.

He also fills vacancies in state and district offices (except those in the Legislature) and issues writs of election to fill vacancies in the Legislature, the United States Senate, and the United States House of Representatives. In the case of the United States Senate, he has the power to name an appointee to fill a vacancy until the next election.

Interstate and state-federal relations. The governor conducts the business of the state with all other states and with the United States. He represents Texas on the Interstate Oil Compact Commission and the Board of the Southern Regional Education Compact. He requisitions other states for fugitives wanted by Texas law-enforcement officials. He also may grant or refuse requests from governors of other states for extradition from Texas of fugitives from their states. He may offer rewards for the apprehension of criminals.

Ex-officio and miscellaneous duties. The governor is an ex-officio member of some ten boards and commissions, including the School Land Board and State Building Commission. He issues commissions, both official and honorary, and proclamations, some of which have the force of law when authorized by law, but most of which are ceremonial.

LEGISLATIVE FUNCTIONS[10]

Messages. The governor may give messages to the Legislature at any time, although the Constitution requires him to present only an opening message (which is sometimes called the "State of the State

[10] The Legislative functions are discussed and analyzed in detail in Chapters 7 to 10.

Message") at the beginning of each session and a "valedictory" message upon his retirement from office. The legislative program of the governor is usually embodied in his opening message, but he may from time to time submit special messages requesting the enactment of specific laws.

Veto. Every bill which passes both houses of the Legislature must be sent to the governor for his approval or veto. If he signs the bill, it is filed with the secretary of state, but if he vetoes it, he returns it to the house of origin with a message stating his objections. Upon receipt of a veto the two houses may override the governor by a two-thirds vote of members present.

During legislative sessions the governor has ten days, excluding Sundays, in which to act on a bill, but if it reaches him during the last ten days of a session or after adjournment, he has twenty days after adjournment, excluding Sundays, in which to act. Under such circumstances, a veto is absolute, as the Legislature has no chance to reconsider. No matter when a bill is received, however, if the governor does not either sign or veto, it becomes law without his signature.

Finances. The governor is the chief budget officer of the state. He is required to make recommendations concerning appropriations for the operation of various departments and agencies of the state, and to make recommendations for raising needed revenue. If a department is unable to finance its operations for a complete fiscal year, the governor may supplement its original appropriation with deficiency grants, upon request of the department. In recent years the governor has had $200,000 per biennium—the maximum allowed by the Constitution—at his disposal for such exigencies.

The governor may require information in writing from any state official relating to the expenses of his respective office and may also inspect its books, accounts, and vouchers.

Special sessions. The governor may call the Legislature into special session, specifying the reasons why the session is being convened. At such special sessions, the Legislature may pass laws only upon matters submitted by the governor, although it may perform other functions, such as passing on gubernatorial appointments, instituting impeachment proceedings, and conducting trials of impeachment.

JUDICIAL FUNCTIONS

On recommendation of the Board of Pardons and Paroles the governor may grant reprieves, commutations of punishment, and pardons; approve paroles; and remit fines and forfeitures. On his own initiative he may grant one thirty-day reprieve and stay of execution in capital cases and may revoke paroles and conditional pardons. In cases of treason he may grant clemency, with the advice and consent of the Legislature.

Major Routine Duties of the Office

Though the above duties are spelled out with specificity, the mere recital of formal powers fails to reveal adequately the complete picture of the operation of the office. Citizens frequently cannot understand what a governor does with his time, but anyone with a knowledge of the office can testify that the occupant of the gubernatorial chair is heavily burdened with innumerable time-consuming details, such as, to mention only a few, signing official papers, answering correspondence, issuing proclamations, meeting people, speaking to civic groups, attending dedications, and cutting ribbons. Nevertheless, such functions are a "must" if the executive is to maintain popularity with the public, and such tasks are frequently credited with being the best way for an officeholder to feel the pulse of the public.[11]

Because of the many details requiring his attention, the governor of Texas must spend many long hours in the discharge of his duties. "Regardless of the calendar or clock, his time belongs to the people who elected him . . . and it might be added that a governor is not paid on a portal-to-portal basis,"[12] as a Houston newswriter has commented.

In describing the day-to-day routine and the demands on the governor's time, Governor Price Daniel said:

The governor's job is a night-and-day job; I usually get up in the morning about seven and start answering the telephone, and then look over the mail that has come in late the day before. I sign mail before going over to the office and then have interviews most of the day, meeting on state boards or with people who want to discuss problems of state government. And then in the evening at the Mansion, where we have a state highway patrolman on duty at all times, I take calls and messages until late in the night some-

----

[11] In separate interviews with the writer, Coke Stevenson, Allan Shivers, and Price Daniel concurred that it is not only desirable but vital for the governor to attend as many public functions as possible in order to keep up with current public opinion, as well as to keep himself in the public eye for political reasons.

[12] E. L. Wall, "Biggest Job in the Biggest State," *Houston Chronicle Magazine,* April 27, 1947, p. 12.

times. It's a big state—so many people. It is true that the governor's job is almost a full-time proposition day and night.[13]

Numerous attempts have been made to describe the "typical day" of a governor; running through most of these accounts is the theme that the job entails long hours and unlimited minutiae. While serving as governor of New York, Alfred E. Smith once observed that an executive's energy was so consumed with trivial details of a clerical or subordinate nature that little time was left for the more important functions of office.[14] Smith's observation is applicable to some extent to Texas governors, as may be seen when one goes behind the formal duties and considers some of the day-to-day requirements.

COMMUNICATIONS

As might be expected, the handling of communications in the governor's office constitutes one of the most time-consuming burdens. In 1950, for example, the Texas Legislative Council found that incoming calls averaged 187 a day, incoming letters and telegrams usually totaled about 300 a day, and the governor received an average of 500 personal visits each day (counting groups of students, clubwomen, and citizens' groups). These findings

in part reflect the fact that it is quite customary for the people of the State to communicate with the Governor regarding the conduct of State activities in their many ramifications—to them the Governor is government personified and the one who can "get things done" . . .[15]

A decade later, citizens apparently still shared this view, although the form of communications with the governor's office had changed. Whereas the written medium was used predominantly in 1950, within ten years the telephone call had become more popular. During the year 1960 the governor's staff estimated that one thousand telephone calls came in daily, averaging two per minute and lasting generally five minutes. At the same time, approximately 150 letters

[13] Interview of Governor Price Daniel with Miss Pauline Yelderman of the University of Houston, April 5, 1960. Script of the interview, which was used in an educational television program, was made available to the writer by the University of Houston Department of Political Science. Hereafter cited as Daniel-University of Houston television interview.

[14] Alfred E. Smith, "How We Ruin Our Governors," *National Municipal Review*, X (May, 1921), 278.

[15] Texas Legislative Council, *Manual of Texas State Government*, Staff Research Report 51–56, p. 3.

were received daily. In addition, the governor was receiving about 50 requests a year to write articles on particular subjects, each of which required some research to be done.[16]

The number of contacts generally bears some correlation with the situation at hand; for example, it is not unusual for correspondence and/or telephone communications to double when a controversial issue is being debated during a legislative session, and it is likely that contacts will increase during an emergency. Some governors have encouraged citizens to communicate with them. Hardly a week passed from 1939 to 1941 that Governor W. Lee O'Daniel did not implore the citizens to "write a letter telling me your views."[17] His plea was heeded and he was deluged by mail in unprecedented proportions. Some indication of its volume may be obtained from a letter written by his secretary to a constituent apologizing for a six-weeks delay in answering. The aide wrote:

> I trust you will pardon delay in answering your letter of January 25 addressed to Governor O'Daniel . . . I am sure you will understand when I tell you that this office has been receiving *from two to three thousand letters daily* since the inauguration, and the Governor's correspondence necessarily has been neglected.[18] (Italics mine)

The volume of mail O'Daniel received broke the record for the governor's office, according to the recollections of a long-time employee. Hugh Greene, a Negro porter who became almost a legendary figure in the Capitol, was employed during the administration of Governor O. B. Colquitt (1911–1915). He became adept at imitating signatures of the governors and one of his functions came to be the signing of papers, official and unofficial, on behalf of the current governor. Greene claimed that Governor O'Daniel's mail was the heaviest of any received by the nine governors he had served. Certainly he was in a position to know, as he reportedly signed "all copies of pardons and paroles as well as reams and reams of other official correspondence."[19] Later accounts indicate that succeeding

---

[16] Figures furnished by John Goldsum, administrative assistant to Governor Price Daniel, June 21, 1961.

[17] The scripts of several of O'Daniel's Sunday morning broadcasts are available in his biographical file at Barker Texas History Center, The University of Texas.

[18] Letter from Reuben Williams, executive secretary to Governor O'Daniel, to S. T. Ellington, San Antonio, March 10, 1939. Box T–610, O'Daniel Correspondence Files, Texas State Archives.

[19] *Austin Daily Tribune*, November 19, 1939.

administrations did not receive nearly so much mail as did O'Daniel, although one newspaper reported in 1951 that Governor Allan Shivers received "as a rule about 1,000 letters a day and about 200 telegrams."[20]

To determine the nature of requests flowing into the governor's office, this writer examined the correspondence files in the State Archives of several administrations, and found that the governors received letters from persons in practically every walk of life—from the lowliest citizen, whose penmanship was almost illegible and whose grammar was illiterate, to the President of the United States or members of his Cabinet. The predominant subject was employment, either in applications from persons desiring public employment or in letters recommending individuals for jobs on the state payroll. During the days of extensive public works programs the most voluminous files contained correspondence connected with the Works Progress Administration.[21]

In addition, governors received scores of requests for photographs, autographs, or mementoes to be sold at church bazaars or by civic clubs. In fact, there is practically no request imaginable that has not been made of a governor at some time. A few examples will illustrate the diversity of requests. Governor Allred received the following:

A request from Pearl Baker of Chillicothe, Missouri, to help locate "a man named Baker," potential heir to $37,000, who was thought to be on relief rolls in Texas. (Upon publication of this letter, scores of other letters were received from persons claiming to be Baker—or to know him.)

A request from a man in Ohio to get him a job as a ranch hand.

A request for the governor to draw up a will "to comply with state law."

A letter seeking help in getting out of a mental hospital in Washington, D.C.

A plea from a Bishop College student, B. F. Bell, Jr., to remedy the situation in the Longview jail, where Negroes were "badly treated."

A letter notifying the governor of the prevalence of gambling in Belton and Bell County.[22]

Governor O'Daniel's correspondence was equally varied. He re-

[20] *Austin Statesman,* January 16, 1951.
[21] Correspondence Files of Governors Allred, O'Daniel, Stevenson, and Jester, the most recent available to the public as of 1963, were searched.
[22] Taken from Box T–1935, Allred Correspondence Files, Texas State Archives.

ceived many requests to use his weekly radio program to locate relatives or missing persons. He was also asked to

Evaluate old coins.

Secure a patent on an invention of a "safety transfer seat," to transfer prisoners.

Get a son released from Fort Leavenworth Penitentiary, where he was serving a term for making illegal whiskey.

Help in bringing a nephew from Poland to become a naturalized citizen.

Assist a Bishop, California, schoolgirl, Wanda Scott, by sending "all the information on the Neutrality Act. The reason I ask you to do this is that Texas is my home state."[23]

During the administration of Governor Beauford H. Jester, a daily summary of incoming mail, including the name of the correspondent and the nature of his communication, was distributed to the staff. At the end of each month an analysis was made of the number of pieces of mail handled during each working day. The volume of mail for the month of May, 1948, is shown in Table 3.

In 1951 an Austin newspaper reported that Governor Shivers had received 543 applications for tickets to The University of Texas–Southern Methodist University football game, along with 202 requests for aid in securing hotel reservations in Austin for the game weekend.[24]

This brief sample amply points up the fact that at one time or another, governors have been asked by the citizens to do practically everything. Apparently there is nothing that some people would not ask of their executive. Regardless of the impossibility of complying with a demand, most communications require at least a token acknowledgement of receipt, which alone is no small task.

PUBLIC APPEARANCES

The prestige of almost any public gathering is automatically enhanced by the attendance of the governor, and all chief executives are the recipients of a tremendous number of invitations. Ordinarily, the governor is one of the most sought-after speakers for public meetings, and the occupants of the office have generally found it politically advantageous to keep themselves fairly well before the public, with

[23] Taken from Box T–610, O'Daniel Correspondence Files, Texas State Archives.
[24] *Austin Statesman,* January 16, 1951.

TABLE 3

Analysis of Incoming and Outgoing Mail in the
Office of the Governor of Texas
in May, 1948

Beauford Jester Administration

Date	*Mail Report For 25 Working Days Of May, 1948* Incoming Pieces of Mail	Outgoing Pieces of Mail
May 1	67	90
May 3	75	42
May 4	46	54
May 5	66	91
May 6	56	37
May 7	68	57
May 8	56	51
May 10	73	75
May 11	57	84
May 12	43	90
May 13	52	76
May 14	65	84
May 15	65	956
May 17	49	68
May 18	71	45
May 19	59	26
May 20	49	58
May 21	53	45
May 22	39	55
May 24	56	68
May 25	37	147
May 26–27	59	69
May 28	52	28
May 29	52	48
Totals	1,365	2,444
Daily Average	54.7	97.8

Source: Jester Correspondence Files, Box GC–79, Texas State Archives.

the result that problems often arise as to which invitations to accept. Years ago the difficulties of transportation precluded the acceptance of some invitations, for it was physically impossible for a governor to be in opposite corners of so expansive a state during the same day. He simply could not speak in the Red River Valley in the morning and in the Rio Grande Valley that evening because the train or the automobile could not transport him fast enough. With the coming of air transportation, however, the possibilities changed considerably. No longer could a governor plead that he be excused from attending a meeting in El Paso because he had already agreed to appear in Texarkana the night before. In fact, it is not now possible for a governor to reject an invitation on the grounds that he will not have time to travel, for within a few hours the airplane will carry him anywhere in Texas. In the words of one former gubernatorial assistant, "Airplanes have virtually wrecked the governor's schedule."[25]

As a consequence, the modern governor finds it necessary to accept more and more invitations throughout his state. In 1951 one newspaper called Governor Allan Shivers "Texas' speakingest governor of all times." Alluding to the fact that he received one hundred requests a day to attend functions, the report commented that Shivers filled some fifteen engagements weekly over and above his work in the executive offices, with a majority of the invitations coming from outside Austin.[26] These figures, no doubt, included all appearances, whether he made a formal speech or informal remarks. Of course the governor is always expected to say something.

Governor Shivers also undoubtedly earned the title of "Texas' most-travelled governor"—up to his time. Figures computed for his journeys out of the capital during his first term showed that in 1950 he travelled 29,410 miles and that in 1951—a year in which the Legislature was in session for four months, requiring the governor to stay close to his desk—he travelled 18,260 miles.[27] In 1954, when he was seeking a third term against the most formidable opposition he had encountered, Shivers travelled extensively and made the largest number of appearances of any year of his tenure. An examination of his itinerary for that year, exclusive of formal campaign appearances, is presented in Appendix V.

The appointment books of Governor Shivers for the years 1949 to 1956, inclusive, reveal that he made 281 formal speeches for which texts were prepared, 89 of which were in other states, as detailed in Table 4.

Price Daniel, his successor, continued the pace set by Shivers. An analysis of Daniel's appearances for 1960, an election year, shows that he delivered 105 speeches for which formal texts were prepared, and an approximately equal number of informal "off-the-cuff" remarks.

---

[25] Interview with Weldon Hart, executive secretary to Governors Jester and Shivers, in Austin, March 21, 1961.

[26] *Austin Statesman*, January 16, 1951.

[27] Record kept by Weldon Hart, executive secretary to the governor. Figures furnished the writer by Mr. Hart.

TABLE 4

Prepared Speeches of Governor Allan Shivers, 1949–1956

Year	Out-of-State Speeches	Total Number of Prepared Speeches
1949	4	18
1950	2	46
1951	15	35
1952	17	43
1953	13	23
1954	16	61
1955	13	19
1956	9	36
Total	89	281

Source: Derived from Governor's appointment books for each of the years. Made available by Weldon Hart, executive secretary to Governor Shivers.

In addition, he recorded some 100 radio and television messages on such topics as safety, holiday greetings, and comments on specific problems for study groups, conventions, or similar meetings.[28]

Although there is no way of evaluating the impact of such public appearances upon the political careers of the executives, one thing seems certain: most governors believe that the time spent in travel, making speeches, and doing the necessary research in preparation for the addresses is not wasted time. Governor Connally's daily schedule for two weeks, as presented in Appendix VII, gives further insight into the travels and activities of a governor of Texas.

PERSONAL CONFERENCES

Notwithstanding the fact that the executive meets a host of people on his swings around the state, a large segment of the population still finds its way into his office in the Capitol to seek an audience with him. Callers—famous, obscure, important, psychotic, desperate, curious, publicity seeking, "apple polishing"—a veritable cross section of humanity—all descend for multifarious reasons, necessitating some "weeding out" by a staff member. Nevertheless, as Governor Price Daniel confirmed, the executive still spends "most of the day" seeing people. Such personal conferences always have been, and undoubt-

[28] Information furnished by John Goldsum, administrative assistant to Governor Daniel, in an interview in Austin, June 21, 1961.

edly always will be, a part of the politician's job. Naturally, some incumbents are more accessible than are others; some, in fact, openly encourage the public to call on them.

Probably larger numbers of people were successful in securing personal conferences during the Ferguson administrations than in any other administration, for it was a Ferguson practice to see any and all who came. One aide to Governor Miriam Ferguson recalls that the reception room was continuously jammed with constituents waiting to see "one of the governors." Staff members were under instructions to determine the business of the visitor, to relay the information to higher echelons, and then to inform the individual that he would be seen if he would wait his turn. Sometimes a lengthy wait would eliminate a caller, but usually those who came stayed and saw the executive. As a consequence, citizens descended en masse seeking favors of many kinds—jobs, contracts, clemency, proclamations, and the like. Some came solely to exchange greetings, to thank the governor for a favor, or just to glimpse the "oddity"—the woman governor whose husband's desk was alongside hers.[29]

As time has passed and calendars have become more crowded, governors have become less accessible to the public. Some have tried to compensate by seeing people in groups. Governor W. Lee O'Daniel invited Texans to come see him at his inauguration, to make it a homecoming of common citizens.[30] He drew the largest inauguration crowd in Texas history, but, of course, few of the 60,000 visitors talked to him personally. He later invited as many as could be accommodated to drop by the "living room of the Governor's House" to witness his Sunday morning broadcasts and to talk with him before and after the program.[31] For his second inauguration he invited "all" the people of Texas to come to a barbecue of beef, mutton, and buffalo on the grounds of the Mansion so he could shake their hands and talk with

---

[29] Interview with Ghent Sanderford, secretary to Governor Miriam A. Ferguson, in Austin, April 13, 1961. Mr. Sanderford related a number of interesting events; one involved a caller who had escaped from the Texas Penitentiary and had come to see the governor about a pardon. Mr. Ferguson talked to him, sternly lectured him about escaping from Huntsville, but promised that if the man would return voluntarily and complete his sentence he would be pardoned in due course. Mr. Ferguson then wrote a "To Whom It May Concern" letter identifying the man and saying that he was returning to prison. The man, unaccompanied, returned as promised and when he had completed his sentence he received a pardon, sent via telegraph to him at Huntsville.

[30] S. S. McKay, *W. Lee O'Daniel and Texas Politics*, p. 132.

[31] *Ibid.*

them. More than 20,000 ate with him that day,[32] while his hillbilly band rendered luncheon music.

In more recent years some governors have attempted to see larger numbers of people by setting aside a particular time each day in which the governor comes into the official reception room to greet callers who desire a personal audience but whose business does not warrant a private conference. During the Shivers tenure the executive appeared to receive the public at 11:30 each morning he was in the Capitol. Governor Daniel also used this plan from time to time, and Governor Connally continues it. Connally also issues many signed, decorative "commissions" to various honorary positions, such as "Ambassador of Good Will" or "Honorary Texas Citizen." At the reception hour he usually signs and presents such commissions to several persons.

The public reception approach has proved to be particularly effective as a time-saving device in seeing student organizations, women's clubs, Chamber of Commerce tours, and similar groups; it permits a governor to meet numbers of constituents whose only business in the Capitol is a desire to shake the chief executive's hand. One such public reception in August, 1963, might be described as a typical session. Running about twenty minutes behind his announced 2 P.M. reception hour, Governor Connally, accompanied by two administrative assistants, entered the Governor's Reception Room adjacent to his private office. Immediately he began to circulate among the twenty-three adults who were awaiting his arrival. After shaking hands with each and extending a personal greeting, he signed and presented Honorary Texas Citizen commissions to a couple, citizens of a foreign country, who had spent the summer as faculty members at The University of Texas and who were soon departing for their homeland. Next he signed a proclamation calling upon Texans to support the drive for the relief of muscular dystrophy, and was photographed with a victim of that disease who was confined to a wheel chair.

The governor then received two groups of Boy Scouts totalling some fifty-seven members. A spokesman from the Cub Scouts presented him with a scrapbook containing newspaper clippings about the chief executive which the group had compiled. A representative from the Eagle Scouts presented him with an honorary membership certificate in the organization. After being photographed with each

[32] *Ibid.*, p. 356.

boy who made a presentation, Governor Connally requested that the Scouts file past him to shake hands. During the course of the hand-shaking he had a personal comment for each boy, such as "My name is John, too," "How many brothers do you have?" "I have a boy about your age named Mark." Group photographs were taken with the Scouts surrounding the governor at his desk.

Within a span of some twenty-seven minutes, Connally had issued a proclamation, signed commissions, chatted with a score of voters, and greeted some eighty persons, each of whom undoubtedly went away with a feeling of satisfaction at having been so cordially received by the state's first citizen. Obviously, the governor's public reception can be a device to increase the public contacts which are so important to the politician.

Not every constituent, however, is willing to settle for being received with a group. Many still seek a more private reception. When they do seek to see the executive personally, what are the usual reasons they advance? Although it was not possible to determine the frequency of the business given in requests for appointment, one staff assistant, intimately familiar with the operations of the office, extracted from Governor Shivers' appointment books a list of requests which appeared to be typical. The following outline, not necessarily arranged in order of importance, illustrates business transacted in conferences with the governor.

Protests about action, or lack of action, on the part of some state agency. For example, the Board of Control has turned down a "lowest bid" on a state contract; the Liquor Control Board contemplates moving, or not moving, a certain agent; the Highway Department is not performing satisfactorily in the matter of a farm-to-market road designation and/or right of way; the State Board of Insurance has declined to issue a requested license, etc.

Requests for the governor to write a letter to a national organization. State chapters bidding for a national convention usually feel that a letter from the governor will be helpful to their cause. Such a delegation calling on the governor might include officials of the organization, Chamber of Commerce representatives, personal friends of the governor in the expectant host city, and the local senator or representative, or perhaps both of them.

Requests for clemency. Some seek pardons or paroles on behalf of themselves or friends or relatives. Frequently, pleas for restoration of driver's licenses or hunting licenses are received.

Conferences on appointments to public office. Applicants and/or

their supporters visit the executive to promote their cause by inform-
ing him of their qualifications and experience for an office to be filled.

Conferences on speaking engagements. Groups or individuals come
to extend personal invitations to cut the ribbons at a county fair, a
public building, or a highway opening; to speak at a local historical
commemorative event; to attend a testimonial dinner for a veteran
public servant, civic leader, or party stalwart; or to address a civic
club, make a commencement address, etc.

Conferences on proposed legislation. Spokesmen both for and
against a bill to be proposed or under consideration desire to air
their views before the executive acts, or to urge that he change his
stand.

Conferences with department heads. Matters of general policy are
discussed at meetings, initiated at the request of the department official or of the governor.

Departmental requests for deficiency appropriations. Various agency representatives present their cases for additional money, seeking
to justify their asking.

Requests to intervene in labor disputes.

Swearing-in ceremonies for important public appointees. Such a
ceremony frequently includes taking pictures.

Ceremonial presentations. For example, in July 1951, the adjutant
of the American Legion, Department of Texas, presented Governor
Shivers, on behalf of the Philippine Association, Incorporated, a piece
of stone from the Rock of Corregidor as a "symbol of friendship."
Picture taking accompanies such presentations.

Ceremonial signing of bills, proclamations, etc. The governor signs
bills in the presence of their authors. Proclamations designating certain "Days," or opening charitable drives or campaigns, are signed
before interested citizens. Photographers are usually present.

Receiving important visitors from other places. For example, officials of foreign countries or of the United States may be visiting Austin with a mission, but more frequently they merely pay a courtesy
call. Governors of Mexican and American states pass through and
wish to exchange greetings.[33]

These "typical" visits to see the governor in person suggest that

[33] Prepared for the writer from appointment books (1950–1956) of Governor
Allan Shivers, by Weldon Hart, who has custody of the records of the Shivers
Administration and is preparing them for transmittal to the state. The writer is
heavily indebted to Mr. Hart for this contribution and others noted at various
points.

the major portion of the executive's day is consumed in meeting and greeting people from all walks and stations of life. Even this list fails, however, to consider the additional scores of constituents who might be fortunate enough to secure an appointment to bring some matter to the governor's attention.

Two detailed schedules are given in Appendix VII of Connally's appointments and activities as governor. One schedule is for a week when the Legislature was in session and one is for a week when it was not in session.

In view of the multiplicity of minutiae in the performance of such routine functions as answering correspondence and telephone calls, traveling to diverse points, making hundreds of addresses, and seeing innumerable people in his office, it is at once obvious that the governor alone cannot possibly attend to all of the demands made upon his time. He is obliged to recruit a corps of capable assistants on whom he can rely for aid in removing some of the burdens of office from his shoulders. Governors of most states have come to rely heavily upon their staffs to assist them in performing their functions.

THE GOVERNOR'S STAFF

Upon completion of a survey of the operation of the executive branch of the United States government in 1937, the President's Committee on Administrative Management reached an expected conclusion, "The President needs help."[34] Undoubtedly, a comparable observation would have been equally appropriate for the governor of any of the then forty-eight states or, indeed, for practically any top-level executive in a large governmental or business establishment whose responsibilities had multiplied at a rapid pace as the functions of his organization expanded. The effect of the report was a new impetus to attempting to solve the problems of staffing the offices of public executives, with the result that more attention than ever came to be focused upon the importance of adequate aid for America's chief executives. Commenting upon his own need for help, James V. Allred, who was governor of Texas at the time, observed:

No one man has time enough to see or do the things he should do; generally he is so tired at the end of the day that he never catches up; so many people see him that he never gets to make up his own program. . . . In

[34] U.S. President's Committee on Administrative Management, *Report With Special Studies*, p. 5.

other words, the biggest difficulty is the office itself—the difficulties of attaining it, keeping up with it and trying to be reelected.[35]

Apparently, adequate staff assistance for public executives has been a problem from the beginning of the Republic. A typical Revolutionary governor, De Witt Clinton of New York, is reputed to have written in 1778, "I am so Circumstanced at present so much to do & no Body to assist me that I can hardly steal a Moment to write to my Friends."[36] Though later governors have not found themselves in so desperate a plight as that, few states have provided their executives with adequate staffs to meet the demands of their positions, prompting one writer to raise the question as to whether, in transforming the governor from figurehead to leader, the states might not have created an "armless wonder,"[37] without adequate assistance to perform his tasks.

Adequate staffing becomes a problem of even greater proportions for the chiefs of American states as their duties continue to increase. The need for assistance in carrying out the functions of office was underscored recently by a panel discussion at the National Governors' Conference in 1958. The concensus of the executives was that "whether a Governor has top flight assistants . . . goes to the heart of the matter in determining whether a chief executive can do an adequate job."[38]

The broad scope of a modern governor's duties makes his staff a matter of vital concern because his assistants serve

as additional eyes and ears, as handlers of routine, as reviewers, analyzers, and proposers. They can bring skills to the task which a governor may lack. They can work within his stated policies and privately known values. Without them his full role as a leader cannot be realized.[39]

The popular conception that "men around the governor" really run the state holds considerable truth, for the executive process is indeed

[35] Robert R. Martindale, "James V. Allred, The Centennial Governor of Texas" (unpublished M.A. thesis), p. 118.
[36] Quoted in Leonard D. White, "On Governors," *Public Administration Review*, IV (Winter, 1944), 68.
[37] Homer E. Scace, *The Organization of the Executive Office of the Governor*, p. 1. Hereafter cited as Scace, *The Executive Office of the Governor*.
[38] "The Business of Being Governor—A Panel Discussion," *State Government*, XXXI (Summer, 1958), 148.
[39] American Assembly, Graduate School of Business, Columbia University, *The Forty-Eight States: Their Tasks as Policy Makers and Administrators*, p. 107. Hereafter cited as American Assembly, *The Forty-Eight States*.

a collective process, producing a collective product in government much as does management in big business.[40] The personal staff of the governor is really the nerve center of the executive branch; around it revolve the activities of planning, policy formulation, public relations, and administrative management. Although aides cannot give an executive the personal qualities of endurance, decisiveness, persuasiveness, responsibility, and intellectual capacity required for leadership, an organization can be set up with sufficient flexibility to enable each governor to staff it with men loyal to him, responsive to his particular nature, and capable of compensating for some of his own weaknesses. Such a setup is a necessity if he is to have a program reflecting his philosophy of government and if the executive office is to project his personality and policies in contacts with the public.[41]

In the words of Professor Coleman B. Ransone:

The key thing to remember in staffing is that the governor's staff should be designed to take care of as many details on management and public relations as possible and to assist but not replace the governor in the realm of policy formation. . . .The number and kinds of persons which the governor needs depend upon a variety of factors including the governor's personal work habits, his program, the traditions and customs of office in a given state, the size of the state and its population and a number of other not-so-easily-categorized factors.[42]

Ideally, the staff should be kept small because the maximum results will be obtained only if the governor can engender a team spirit among the key men around him. The most important thing is to get capable people and to keep the staff small enough to allow the governor to keep in close contact with his assistants, advises a governor, out of his own experience.[43]

As the organization is identified with the governor's job, it must be a highly flexible apparatus, varying somewhat from state to state and from time to time within a given state. Within a single state the organization will vary as the state undergoes periods of general economic emergency or stability and prosperity, and executives of widely different experience will find it necessary to make adjustments to utilize the abilities and interests of the men available for appointment

---

[40] Adrian, *State and Local Governments*, p. 255.
[41] Scace, *The Executive Office of the Governor*, p. 2.
[42] Ransone, *The Office of Governor in the United States*, p. 361.
[43] Interview of the writer with Governor Price Daniel, in the Executive Office, Austin, November 30, 1961.

to key positions.[44] In any event, staff members must be persons of considerable ability who are willing to serve as the alter ego of the executive, and normally they must remain somewhat anonymous.

Although assignments within the staff group will vary, the general responsibilities of a governor's staff in modern times usually include at least the following functions:

1. Developing policy recommendations to be presented to the public during campaigns and to the Legislature during sessions. Assistants must supply the executive with information, do his research, and frequently prepare the texts of his speeches.

2. Assuming general responsibility for public relations. Although the press secretary will usually frame important releases, each staff member must be constantly alert to any possible situation upon which can be built a news story favorable to the governor.

3. Maintaining liaison with various state, local, and federal agencies. The governor cannot know personally what is going on in all agencies and must rely on his staff to keep him informed as to problems, budgetary situations, and the workings of various pressure groups vis-à-vis state agencies.

4. Answering routine correspondence, deciding which mail should go personally to the governor, and referring such items to state agencies as may be necessary.

5. Maintaining liaison with the Legislature. One member is usually assigned to observe the activities of the lawmakers and to confer on matters of concern to them.

6. Handling personal callers.

7. Maintaining liaison with the governor's political party.[45]

In short, it has been said that the duty of the staff is "to aid the governor in drawing up his program, in selling it to the public and to the legislature, and in providing some control over the various agencies in the executive branch."[46] And, of course, the staff must relieve the executive of as much of the detail of office as is possible.

MINIMUM STAFFING: 1876–1921

During the first four decades following the adoption of the Constitution of 1876 no official records were kept as to how the various occupants of the office organized the work of their assistants, but re-

[44] Scace, *The Executive Office of the Governor*, p. 5.
[45] This outline of functions follows that found in Adrian, *State and Local Governments*, pp. 256–258.
[46] Scace, *The Executive Office of the Governor*, p. 3.

ports of the comptroller of public accounts reveal that during the forty-year period the staffs remained consistently small and varied little from one administration to another, at least so far as job titles were concerned. Apparently, most of the executives during the 1880's operated with a staff of three: the governor himself, a private secretary, and a porter.[47] Near the end of the decade an item appeared in the appropriations for "additional clerical help."[48]

The first real indication of the need for a larger staff came in 1893 during the administration of Governor James S. Hogg, who requested an appropriation of $1,500 annually for extra help in his office. Once the Legislature authorized the addition, however, Hogg felt compelled to use the item veto to strike it out because the state had become hard pressed financially. Some light is thrown on the problem of staffing in the 1890's by Hogg's veto message:

> You have generously allowed the executive office at my request $1500 each year as "salary for file and corresponding clerk." While the accumulated and fast increasing business of the office make such assistance desirable, it is not proper and absolutely necessary. If exigencies demand, I can and will add one or two more hours of service a day to the other employees of the department and do some extra work myself, to the end that public interests shall not suffer by striking out this item.[49]

The budget for the biennium shows that with the deletion of the extra personnel, Hogg's staff was left with a private secretary, a stenographic clerk, and a porter. Total expenses allowed to the Executive Department came to $32,270.[50] (The term Executive Department is used frequently to connote the Governor's Office and is so used in this chapter.)

According to the comptroller's reports, the first major addition to the governor's staff occurred in 1901 when salaries for the Board of Pardon Advisers and the State Revenue Agent appeared as items in the Executive Department budget.[51] These officers, along with the private secretary, stenographer, and porter, constituted the personnel

---

[47] *Annual Report of the Comptroller of Public Accounts, State of Texas,* 1884, p. 153; see also *ibid.,* 1887, p. 200.

[48] *Ibid.,* 1888, p. 175.

[49] *House Journal,* Twenty-third Legislature, regular session, p. 1209.

[50] *Annual Report of the Comptroller of Public Accounts, State of Texas,* 1893, p. 114.

[51] *Ibid.,* 1901, p. 90.

of the governor's staff through the administrations of Lanham, Campbell, and Colquitt (1903–1915).[52]

Even at the beginning of World War I, when "big government" became the order of the day, the staff of the governor of Texas remained small and highly personal in its operation. The secretary to Governor William P. Hobby recalls that only five persons were in the office in 1918—the governor, his secretary, an assistant secretary, a stenographer, and a porter. Each person was directly responsible to the executive, and the office was run on a highly informal basis. No adjunct activities were attached to the office.[53]

STAFFING IN THE 1920's AND 1930's

With the creation of the State Board of Control in 1919[54] the first of a long line of executive agencies that were to be established in Texas came into existence, and with the growth of the number of boards, many of which made the governor an ex-officio member, came the need for expansion of the staff of the governor's office. Given the responsibility for drawing up a budget, the Board of Control at once recognized the need for help in the Executive Department by including an additional assistant secretary and two extra stenographers, bringing the staff in 1921 to a total of eight persons.[55] Two years later a custodian of files was added.[56] Although this was the largest number of assistants the office had employed to that time, the incumbent, Pat Neff, made little use of his aides. In the view of one member of the staff, Neff was a perfectionist who preferred to handle as much detail as possible himself.[57] Neff's successor, Governor Miriam A. Ferguson, upon advice of her husband, took the unusual step of inviting some members of the Neff staff to stay on during her administration, and several chose to remain.[58]

---

[52] *Ibid.*, 1906, p. 83; and 1908, p. 94.

[53] Interview with Raymond Brooks, secretary to Governor Hobby, in Austin, March 3, 1961.

[54] *Vernon's Annotated Civil Statutes, State of Texas*, Art. 601.

[55] State Board of Control, *First Biennial Appropriation Budget*, 1921–1923, p. 26.

[56] *Ibid.*, *Second Biennial Appropriation Budget*, 1923–1925, p. 9.

[57] Interview with J. H. Johnson, secretary to Governor Neff, in Austin, March 17, 1961.

[58] Interview with Ghent Sanderford, secretary to Governor M. A. Ferguson, in Austin, April 13, 1961. Mr. Sanderford told the writer that he was instructed to go to the Governor's Office and extend the invitation to certain employees to remain with the Ferguson Administration. It was his belief that such a course of action was unique at that time, as ordinarily a new governor brought in a com-

In 1927 the first reduction in staff took place when one assistant secretary and one stenographer were eliminated.[59] However, both were reinstated during the subsequent biennium,[60] and during most of the 1930's the staff remained relatively stabilized at eight persons, the only additions occurring in 1937 when two more stenographers were employed.[61]

THE GROWTH OF THE STAFF: 1939–1962

When Governor W. Lee O'Daniel was inaugurated in 1939 additions to the staff of the Executive Department became necessary. A political novice, O'Daniel needed help from seasoned advisers, and he also continued his weekly radio broadcast, which necessitated much planning and coordination. As a result of his radio programs, the volume of mail to the governor's office skyrocketed, and a third assistant secretary was soon added, bringing the staff to eleven.[62]

Describing the organization of work during the O'Daniel incumbency, a close associate recalled that the functions were divided into political matters and administrative matters, with an executive secretary heading each section. The work was thus separated according to category and handled by the respective divisions.[63] This period, the same in which the Executive Office of the President was created at the national level, may well have marked the beginning in Texas of a realization of the importance of the governor's staff as identified in modern administrative theory. The staff was the largest ever up to that time, and the Governor himself (perhaps because of his lack of experience in public office) seemingly began to rely more heavily upon assistants for help in carrying out his duties.

This trend was accentuated by World War II when the activities of the office were increased in connection with national defense efforts, such as rationing and selective service. When O'Daniel resigned

---

pletely new staff. Governor Ferguson's action may have set a precedent, for similar invitations have been issued by some other administrations since then.

[59] State Board of Control, *Fourth Biennial Appropriation Budget*, 1927–1929, p. 26.

[60] *Ibid.*, *Fifth Biennial Appropriation Budget*, 1929–1931, p. 29.

[61] *Ibid.*, *Seventh Biennial Appropriation Budget*, 1933–1935, p. 70 and *Eighth Biennial Appropriation Budget*, 1935–1937, p. 193 and *Ninth Biennial Appropriation Budget*, 1937–1939, p. 204.

[62] *Ibid.*, *Tenth Biennial Appropriation Budget*, 1939–1941, p. 200.

[63] Interview with William J. Lawson, executive secretary to Governor O'Daniel, in Austin, March 13, 1961. Mr. Lawson handled political matters in the Governor's Office, and Reuben Williams, executive secretary, handled administrative affairs.

to become United States Senator, Governor Coke Stevenson retained several key assistants, including a personal secretary who was to remain through four administrations. While Stevenson was in office the staff numbered twelve. In an attempt to improve relations with Mexico a Good Neighbor Commission was created as an adjunct to the staff.[64]

After the war the activities of the governor were further accelerated by the industrial and economic expansion which the state was experiencing, and the state government began to play an expanded role in civilian defense, an activity which was attached to the Executive Department. Governor Beauford Jester retained a veteran staff member, William McGill, who had served his two immediate predecessors in the gubernatorial office. He also employed Weldon Hart, a well-known journalist. Both McGill and Hart remained on the staff through his administration and then joined his successor, Allan Shivers.

The most knowledgeable account of the organization and staffing of the office of the governor of Texas ever written by a key assistant came from the pen of William McGill in 1949. Replying to a questionnaire which had been sent to all states by the Institute of Public Administration as a part of the research on its forthcoming report on *The Executive Office of the Governor*,[65] the executive secretary to Governor Shivers explained in detail the organization and division of labor then obtaining in the Governor's Office. The letter, addressed to Luther Gulick, read as follows:

. . . Before leaving, [Governor Shivers] discussed with me your letter regarding the study you are making . . .

As in other states, the Executive Secretary to the Governor of Texas is the head of the Governor's staff. He occupies an office on the floor below the Governor's private office and has a reception room and staff separate from the public reception room upstairs and different from the Governor's personal staff. The overflow of callers from the Governor's reception room, and various delegations and individuals whom the Governor is unable to see come to the office of the Executive Secretary.

The heads of State Departments and institutions and, frequently, members of the Legislature come initially to the Executive Secretary for the discussion of micellaneous matters.

The Executive Secretary employs and supervises the personnel in the

[64] Interview with Coke Stevenson, in Junction, Texas, February 27, 1961.
[65] McGill's letter supplied information which was incorporated into the study made by Homer E. Scace, *The Executive Office of the Governor*.

Governor's office. A bookkeeper looks after the details of the payrolls, requisitions for supplies and so forth—reporting to the Executive Secretary.

The staff consists of approximately thirty people.

The Executive Secretary looks after function of planning and research, calling upon other departments and agencies of the State for expert advice and assistance.

The Executive Secretary directs the activity of an inter-agency committee on the economic development of the State. He is also the coordinator for the State Disaster Relief organization and for civil defense activities. He also screens all clemency matters.

An administrative assistant in the organization looks after radio and press relations, prepares proclamations and public statements, maintains the files on recommendations for appointment to public office, and assists in the planning and research functions above mentioned.

Another administrative assistant keeps the Governor's calendar, screens visitors, handles invitations, and usually accompanies the Governor on out-of-town trips.

An assistant executive secretary reads all mail and telegrams, preparing a mail list describing in a few words the character of each communication and indicating to which staff member the communication has been referred. When the Governor is in the city, she also handles his personal telephone calls. Extradition matters are handled by this staff member.

The actual preparing of the executive budget is done by the Budget Division of the State Board of Control. When this budget is presented to the Legislature, the Governor sends in a budget message outlining his recommendations on State Finances.

Each bill passed by the Legislature is sent to the Assistant Secretary of State, a lawyer who serves as counsel for the Governor's office in reading all bills. He attaches a memorandum to the bill in which he passes on the validity of the measure and points out flaws which may make it necessary for the bills to be withdrawn for correction or vetoed. The bill with the lawyer's memorandum attached goes to the Executive Secretary of the Governor for study and recommendation to the Governor.

The Governor is of course the Commander-in-Chief of the State Militia.

The variation in the Texas plan from the others described in your outline may be explained by the fact that the present Executive Secretary and Assistant Secretary have served the past three Governors in addition to the present Governor. One of the administrative assistants above mentioned has been with two administrations.[66]

Corroborating this information, the Texas Legislative Council reported four years later that the staff included approximately thirty

[66] Letter from William McGill, executive secretary to Governor Shivers, to Luther Gulick, dated December 29, 1949. Copy in files of Governor Shivers, made available by Weldon Hart.

people under the direction of the executive secretary. The duties of the principal assistants remained essentially as McGill had explained, except that the function of preparing the executive budget had been shifted from the Board of Control to the Governor's Office. In 1953, therefore, a director of the Budget Division was a member of the staff of the executive.[67]

In discussing the actual operating procedures of the office during the Shivers administration, Weldon Hart, who succeeded McGill as executive secretary, said that staff meetings were held twice a week during legislative sessions and once a week at other times. At such staff meetings specific assignments of functions were made, as it was the practice to work more on an individual assignment basis than by delegating responsibility for various activities on a permanent basis.[68] The actual organization of the staff was perhaps more formalized, however, than it had ever been before. An organization chart which shows the setup during the Shivers administration appears in Figure 2.

STAFFING IN THE SIXTIES

When Governor Price Daniel assumed office in 1957 he brought with him several aides who had served him while he was United States Senator, and there was a high turnover of personnel in the Executive Department. Being especially interested in certain projects, Governor Daniel within a few months added several staff members assigned to specialized functions, such as traffic safety, tax matters, and problems of the aged.

In August, 1961, the number of employees in the Executive Department had reached the all-time high of fifty-six full-time and fifteen part-time workers. The organization, graphically presented in Figure 3, was headed by an executive assistant, who was the "governor's right-hand man." Immediately below him were three administrative assistants, one of whom was in charge of legal problems and research, another who handled press matters, and a third who handled appointments and travel schedules.[69] Also, there were a traffic safety director, a budget officer, a coordinator of civil defense, and a tax

[67] Texas Legislative Council, *Manual of Texas State Government*, p. 3.

[68] Interview with Weldon Hart, executive secretary to Governor Shivers, in Austin, July 21, 1961.

[69] Information furnished by George Christian, executive assistant, and John Goldsum, administrative assistant to Governor Daniel, in interviews July 15, 1961.

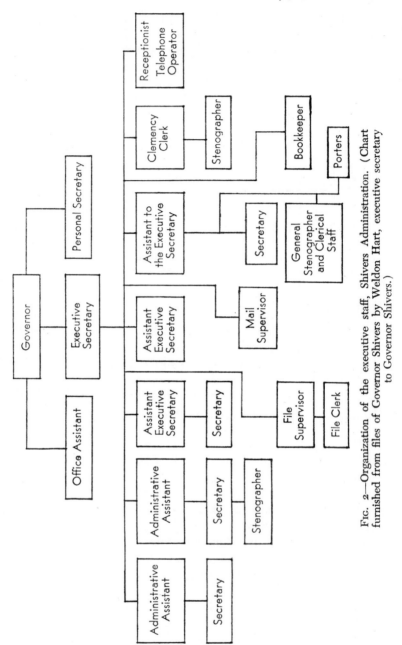

FIG. 2—Organization of the executive staff, Shivers Administration. (Chart furnished from files of Governor Shivers by Weldon Hart, executive secretary to Governor Shivers.)

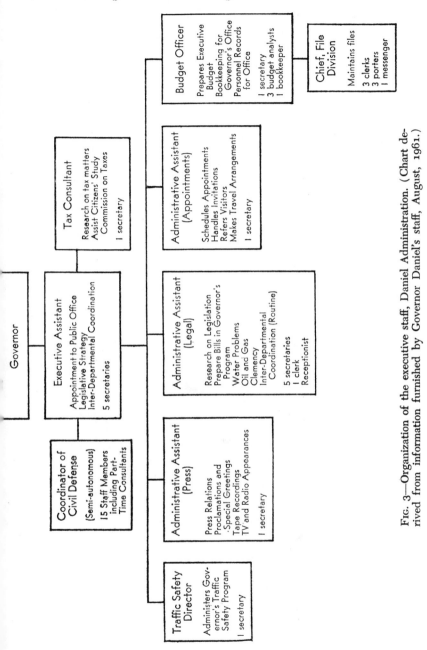

FIG. 3—Organization of the executive staff, Daniel Administration. (Chart derived from information furnished by Governor Daniel's staff, August, 1961.)

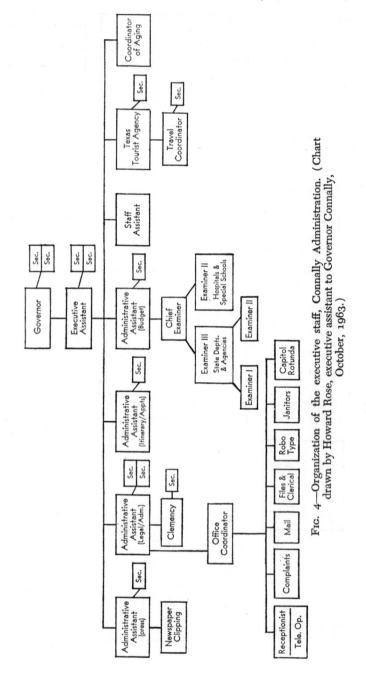

Fig. 4—Organization of the executive staff, Connally Administration. (Chart drawn by Howard Rose, executive assistant to Governor Connally, October, 1963.)

consultant. Later in the year a coordinator for services to the aged was added to the staff.

For the fiscal year ending August 31, 1962, the Legislature appropriated $256,309 for salaries and wages in the Governor's Office, and $254,285 for the following year.[70] In line with the classification plan adopted in 1961 to cover most state employees,[71] thirty-six "classified" positions were allotted to the Governor's Office and eleven to the civil defense organization.[72] Summarized in Table 5 are appropriations for the Governor's Office for the biennium 1962–1963.

Immediately after his inauguration in January, 1963, Governor John Connally recognized that the varied duties of his new office could be fulfilled only if he were authorized to employ additional staff members and to offer more attractive salaries for existing positions. He requested additional funds for staffing his office. After some discussion, the Legislature agreed to allot some $90,000 for that purpose; the Legislature subsequently appropriated a record $1.25 million for the biennium 1964–1965. A detailed analysis of appropriations for that period is shown in Table 6.

In keeping with his campaign theme of offering the state new leadership, Connally lost no time in reorganizing his staff. One of his first moves was to effect the transfer to the Department of Public Safety of the civil defense and traffic safety functions which had been operating within the Governor's Office. His interest in the development of tourism in Texas was reflected in the placing of the Texas Tourist Agency within the organization of the governor's staff. He employed two additional administrative assistants and indicated an interest in an expanded budgetary setup within the Executive Department. Under the general surveillance of the executive assistant, the breakdown of responsibility generally found an administrative assistant in charge of each of the following functions: press relations, research, legal matters, political-legislative relations, and office administration. Reorganization was completed with the assignments depicted in the organization chart shown in Figure 4.

On August 1, 1963, the payroll of the Governor's Office contained sixty-eight full-time and twelve part-time employees. Reflecting the

[70] *Supplement to Senate Journal,* Fifty-seventh Legislature, first called session, p. 97.
[71] *Vernon's Annotated Civil Statutes,* Art. 6252–11.
[72] *Supplement to Senate Journal,* Fifty-seventh Legislature, first called session, p. 98.

TABLE 5

Appropriations for the Governor's Office, 1962–1963

	For Year Ending	
	August 31, 1962	August 31, 1963
Salaries and Wages:		
Governor	$ 25,000	$ 25,000
Lt. Governor while Acting Governor	5,000	Unexpended Balance
Executive Assistant	15,000	15,000
Administrative Assistant (2)	24,000	24,000
Traffic Safety Director	12,000	12,000
Administrative Assistant	10,000	10,000
Coordinator for Services to the Aged	5,200	5,200
Salaries of Classified Positions	148,847	151,823
Seasonal Help	11,262	11,262
Total Salaries and Wages	$256,309	$254,285
Miscellaneous:		
Travel, membership in Governors' Conference and Council of State Governments, rewards for law enforcement, Texas' Share of Interstate Oil Compact Commission Expenses, Consumable supplies, etc.	114,320	114,320
Governor's Mansion Maintenance and Upkeep	18,552	18,552
Total Governor's Administrative Office	$389,181	$387,157
Deficiency Grants:		
(for aid in emergencies and legal defense of State officials)	200,000	Unexpended Balance
Civil Defense and Disaster Relief:		
Salaries of Classified Positions	57,922	59,080
Travel, supplies, operating expenses	28,600	28,600
Total Civil Defense and Disaster Relief	$ 86,522	$ 87,680
Grand Total	$675,703	$474,387

Source: *Supplement to Senate Journal,* Fifty-seventh Legislature, first called session, pp. 96–97.

need for increased staff assistance, the appropriations bill for the biennium 1964–1965 authorized the governor to hire a maximum of seven administrative assistants. Although at the time of writing, several of these positions remained unfilled, such legislative recognition of the increased functions of the Executive Department could portend even further expansion of the gubernatorial staff.

AN INSTITUTIONALIZED OFFICE?

Following the lead of the national government after it created the Executive Office of the President on the recommendation of the Presi-

TABLE 6

Appropriations for the Governor's Office, 1964–1965

	For Year Ending	
	August 31, 1964	August 31, 1965
Out of the General Revenue Fund:		
For Salaries and Wages—		
Governor	$ 25,000	$ 25,000
Lt. Governor while Acting Governor	10,000	Unexpended Balance
Executive Assistant	15,000	15,000
Administrative Assistants NTE $15,000 per year	78,000	78,000
Coordinator for Services to the Aged	5,200	5,200
Salaries of classified positions, wages, and seasonal and part-time help	203,091	203,091
Subtotal, Salaries and Wages	$336,291	$326,291
Travel expense (including expenses of the Secretary of State and Lt. Governor when traveling for the Governor), consumable supplies and materials, current and recurring operating expenses, capital outlay, receptionist supplies, leaflets and equipment, and other expenses for which no other provisions are made	$ 54,600	$ 54,600
Contributions incident to memberships (including Interstate Oil Compact Commission and Council of State Governments)	63,000	63,000
Mansion expenses (including salaries of classified positions, wages and labor, consumable supplies and materials, current and recurring operating expenses and capital outlay)	64,146	62,646
Deficiency Grants: For the payment of claims arising prior to the convening of the next Legislature by the Governor in accordance with Article 4351, R.C.S.; and for grants to aid in cases of drouth, flood, disaster, catastrophe or calamity, the need for and the amount of such aid to be determined by the Governor; and for legal defense of state officials, and employees against whom indemnity actions may be brought	200,000	Unexpended Balance
Grand Total, Governor's Office	$718,037	$506,537

Source: Verifaxed copy of the Appropriations Bill furnished by James R. Sanders, director, Legislative Reference Division, Texas State Library.

dent's Committee on Administrative Management, several states attempted to cast the office of governor in the same mold by institutionalizing it. Such a practice was far from universal, but states generally did become more aware of the problems of staffing, and governors began to show more interest in securing capable assistants for their offices.[73] One group of political scientists urged institutionalization of the office in these terms:

> . . . the office must be *institutionalized* [italics mine] if it is really to play an important role.
>
> One form of institutionalization is purely political. In some states the governorship is in the hands of a group or faction for which the governor himself is merely chief spokesman. Another form is in the development of staff for the governor. In many states an important reason why the governor has limited influence and control is that he has too small a staff. The governor requires staff assistance in his relationship with the legislature and the public, and he also needs help in his relationship to administrative agencies. Only if the governor has a personal staff able to discover matters of administrative importance and to advise him on them can he be effectively responsible for what goes on.[74]

The foregoing review of staffing in Texas would hardly lead to the conclusion that the office of the governor in this state has become institutionalized to any great degree—at least not so far as staffing is concerned. Indeed, there still exists a situation in which personal relationships are paramount, and key personnel frequently change as governors come and go. But the number of people on the staff has increased severalfold within the past two decades, and some new activities have been added as the governor's direct responsibility. Some notable instances may be cited where highly placed staff members have served more than one administration. For example, William McGill and Weldon Hart were on the staffs of both Governors Jester and Shivers during the 1940's and 1950's, and the personal secretary of Governor O'Daniel was also to serve his three successors—Stevenson, Jester, and Shivers.

In the most recent transition of administrations, fifteen employees who had worked for Governor Daniel were retained by Governor Connally. While a majority of the carry-overs were on the clerical level, Joe Moore, who had been Daniel's tax consultant, became the chief budget examiner under Connally. Bill Cobb, a veteran employee

---

[73] Scace, *The Executive Office of the Governor*, p. 45.
[74] American Assembly, *The Forty-Eight States*, p. 122.

of the Legislative Budget Board, was designated as the governor's budget officer, and Frank Miskell, a researcher for the Texas Legislative Council, moved to the executive branch to become an administrative assistant to the governor. The same assistant in matters of clemency has served both Daniel and Connally, as has the accountant handling the payroll for the Governor's Office; the latter was originally employed during the Shivers incumbency. George Christian, who headed the Daniel staff as executive assistant, was soon summoned by Governor Connally to become an administrative assistant in charge of press relations. Whether such appointments are indicative of a trend remains to be seen. Further institutionalization of the governor's staff would perhaps offer a partial solution to the strengthening of the governorship in Texas, for it can be said with even greater emphasis than a quarter of a century ago, "The governor needs help."

5

The Governor in the Executive Branch:
Primus inter Pares

DIFFUSION OF EXECUTIVE POWER IN STATE GOVERNMENTS

The governor is not the executive; he is but a single piece of the executive. There are other pieces coordinated with him over which he has no direct control, and which are of less dignity than he only because they have no power to control legislation, as he may do by his veto, and because his position is more representative perhaps of the state government as a whole, of the people of the state as a unit. . . .

Of state officials associated with the governor . . . it may be said . . . that both in law and fact they are colleagues of the governor, in no sense his agents or subordinates, except perhaps in formal precedence. . . . Nor do they serve him after election. They are not given him as advisers; they are on the contrary coordinated with him.[1]

So wrote Woodrow Wilson, the professor of political science, in 1889. Despite reorganizations and attempted reorganizations that have occurred in many states since that time, this assessment has, by and large, remained valid. The Commission on Intergovernmental Relations, appointed by President Dwight D. Eisenhower, observed at mid-century that "few states have an adequate executive branch headed by a governor who can be held generally accountable for executing and administering the laws of the state."[2] This report merely pointed up a well-known fact: the executive branches of state

[1] Woodrow Wilson, *The State and Federal Governments of the United States*, p. 68.

[2] Commission on Intergovernmental Relations, *A Report to the President for Transmittal to the Congress*, p. 42. Hereafter cited as Commission on Intergovernmental Relations, *A Report to the President*.

governments have become highly fragmented organizations composed of many executives whose functions are largely divorced from one another.

The reasons for such fragmentation are not difficult to ascertain. History recounts the bitter experiences with royal governors in colonial America which produced a fear and distrust of executive power, and, though modified over the years, this fear persists to a degree in the public of most of the states.[3] The earliest state constitutions, written during the Revolutionary era, reflected this feeling by instituting a powerless governor, subordinate to and frequently chosen by the legislature. Years later, under the influence of Jacksonian democracy, major state offices were made elective, thus dividing the executive power among several persons responsible to the electorate. Simultaneously, the spoils system for the selection of governmental personnel was introduced on a broad scale. Throughout the remainder of the nineteenth century provisions for a plural executive were written into most state constitutions. In the present century, further disintegration of executive power has been effected by the common use of boards or commissions whose members serve for overlapping terms, the sum total of which are longer than the term of the chief executive. This situation caused the Commission on Intergovernmental Relations to conclude in 1955:

Typically . . . the governor is the nominal chief of a sprawling State administration consisting of scores of separate departments, commissions, and agencies. . . .

In 40 States, the people elect from 5 to 12 administrative officials or agency heads, in addition to the governor. Since the agencies are in some cases headed by boards, the actual number of persons elected may run even higher, being over 20 in 4 states. This arrangement seriously divides or hides responsibility and makes difficult the achievement of unity of command and consistency of action within a State administration.[4]

TEXAS' DISINTEGRATED ADMINISTRATIVE SYSTEM

Perhaps no better example of a disintegrated executive branch can be found anywhere than in Texas state government. The product of a period when service in government was held in low public esteem and when the citizens were particularly distrustful of executive power

[3] J. Alton Burdine and Tom Reavley, "Toward a More Effective Administration," *Texas Law Review,* 35 (October, 1957), 939.

[4] Commission on Intergovernmental Relations, *A Report to the President,* p. 43.

because of their bitter experiences in the Reconstruction era, the Constitution of 1876 made certain that the governor of Texas would share authority with half a dozen others by the following provision:

> The Executive Department of the State shall consist of a Governor, who shall be the Chief Executive Officer of the State, a Lieutenant Governor, Secretary of State, Comptroller of Public Accounts, Treasurer, Commissioner of the General Land Office, and Attorney General.[5]

With the exception of the secretary of state, all these offices were made elective, and in later years more elective positions were created: three places on a Railroad Commission,[6] a commissioner of agriculture,[7] and twenty-one places on a State Board of Education.[8]

Even greater diffusion of power was brought about after the turn of the century by the creation of a host of boards and commissions to regulate specific activities of government. The governor appoints the members of a majority of such boards and commissions, but they are largely insulated from his control because he is without legal power to remove them. Under such an arrangement, each regulatory activity is provided with its own governing body composed of from three to fifteen members from throughout the state who attend periodic meetings but whose real job is to select a full-time administrator. Many of the major activities of this state have come to be so operated.

Where, then, does the governor of Texas fit into this fragmented picture, and what degree of control does he exert within the executive branch, of which he is the nominal chief? The answers to these questions are not readily forthcoming, but the general position of the governor vis-à-vis elected officials and appointed boards and commissions can be studied and some conclusions drawn as to his executive-administrative role.

THE GOVERNOR'S RELATION TO ELECTED EXECUTIVES

The governor is specifically designated as the chief executive officer of the state. In this role he is required to "cause the laws to be faithfully executed."[9] Such, however, is the primary duty of all

---

[5] Constitution of Texas, Art. IV, Sec. 1.

[6] *Ibid.*, Art. XVI, Sec. 30; *Vernon's Annotated Civil Statutes*, Art. 6447.

[7] *Vernon's Annotated Civil Statutes*, Art. 47.

[8] *Ibid.*, Art. 2654–2.

[9] Constitution of Texas, Art. IV, Sec. 10. In this duty, his obligation is similar to that of governors in forty-five other states (*Index Digest of State Constitutions*, p. 473).

elected executives, and the governor of Texas is given little or no means of carrying out his responsibility other than the declaration of martial law and the use of the Texas Rangers.[10]

The only power specifically bestowed on the governor in relation to his colleagues in the Executive Department is that he may require reports and inspect the books of the departments. His authorization reads:

> An account shall be kept by the officers of the Executive Department, and by all officers and managers of State institutions, of all moneys and choses in action received and disbursed or otherwise disposed of by them, severally, from all sources, and for every service performed; and a semi-annual report thereof shall be made to the Governor under oath. The Governor may, at any time, require information in writing from any and all of said officers or managers, upon any subject relating to the duties, condition, management and expenses of their respective offices and institutions, which information shall be required by the Governor under oath, and the Governor may also inspect their books, accounts, vouchers, and public funds; and any officer or manager who, at any time, shall wilfully make a false report or give false information, shall be guilty of perjury, and so adjudged, and punished accordingly, and removed from office.[11]

Inasmuch as the governor has no means of discipline, this power in actuality is almost worthless and really amounts only to the ability to "request reports," with no sanctions if he is ignored.[12] This being the case, governors must search for other means of working with executive officials of the state.

A GOVERNOR'S CABINET

One approach aimed at promoting better understanding was a governor's cabinet which would hold regular meetings to discuss problems of the executive branch. Following an idea advanced in a legislative report some fifteen years earlier,[13] Governor Beauford H. Jester invited all of the elected executives to join him in such a cabinet. Reporting to the people in a statewide broadcast, Jester said:

> Early in my administration, I invited various heads of State agencies to join me in membership in an Administrative Cabinet—an organization

---

[10] Stuart A. MacCorkle and Dick Smith, *Texas Government* (4th ed.), p. 95.
[11] Constitution of Texas, Art. IV, Sec. 24.
[12] MacCorkle and Smith, *Texas Government* (4th ed.), p. 95.
[13] Texas Legislature, Joint Legislative Committee on Organization and Economy, *The Government of the State of Texas*, Part I, p. 58.

for the discussion of our several responsibilities and functions and for the development of ways and means in which we could coordinate our activity and be helpful to one another.

The Cabinet has had most interesting and useful meetings, and I think we have a better State government and a happier family of State officials as a result of its existence.[14]

Despite Jester's enthusiasm his Cabinet did not become a permanent fixture, and it is doubtful that it really accomplished its desired results. Questioned about its use, two men who have served as governor of Texas since then, both of whom were included in Jester's Cabinet, differed as to its utility. Allan Shivers was indifferent to the cabinet idea, saying that he preferred instead to deal with elected officials in his administration on an individual basis. Ever mindful of the fact that he had no legal authority over the elected officials and that they were not bound to accede to his wishes, he worked constantly to maintain close relationships with the group by visiting them informally in their offices and, from time to time, attending social gatherings in various departments.[15]

Price Daniel was more inclined toward the use of a cabinet but not in the way Jester used it.[16] He indicated that he thought cabinet meetings could be useful on specific matters, as opposed to general discussions, but said he would include only those department heads who had some part in the function under discussion. In practice this would amount to little more than sporadic conferences on particular problems.

A GOVERNOR'S ENDORSEMENT OF CANDIDATES

A unique action was taken by W. Lee O'Daniel in 1938 after his nomination in the first primary. Although O'Daniel did not face a runoff, some candidates did, and the gubernatorial nominee surprised everyone with the following statement:

I feel I can better carry out your wishes and give you the kind of government you want if you will vote for and elect the following men: Walter Woodul for Attorney General; C. V. Terrell for Railroad Commissioner;

[14] "Report to the People, May 21, 1948." Mimeographed script of the broadcast is in the Jester biographical file, Barker Texas History Center, The University of Texas. The Cabinet included all elected executives and some appointive officials.
[15] Interview of the writer with former Governor Shivers, in Austin, December 4, 1961.
[16] Interview of the writer with Governor Daniel, in Austin, November 30, 1961.

Bascom Giles for Land Commissioner; and Coke Stevenson for Lieutenant Governor.[17]

This unprecedented move rocked the state, and, although emotions were mixed, the reaction of the general public was decidedly unfavorable.[18] In the wake of the publicity, one of the most spirited runoffs ever waged in Texas took place. Although two of the four men endorsed by O'Daniel won, evidence does not indicate that administrative relationships were more than ordinarily cordial between them and the Governor. To the contrary, press reports frequently hinted of ill will, bringing a public denial of disharmony from O'Daniel himself.[19]

DISAGREEMENTS WITH COLLEAGUES

Instances may be cited of highly publicized disagreements between the chief executive and one of his colleagues in the executive branch. At times such disputes have been over policy matters; at others they have been purely political in nature, particularly when a member of the administration has aspired to the top office himself. Illustrations from three administrations of different periods will show what can happen.

The administration of Governor O. B. Colquitt (1911–1915) was apparently more rent with strife in the official family than any other has ever been. Certainly Colquitt had more than his share of open bickering. He seemed always to be at odds with the attorney general's department.[20] Because of Colquitt's predilection for deciding constitutional questions for himself, a feud erupted between him and Attorney General Jewel P. Lightfoot. The Governor ordered the state treasurer to withhold payments for two special assistants to the Attorney General, but he was overruled in mandamus proceedings in the courts.[21] Failing in this discipline, he sent a list of people holding federal liquor licenses, but no state licenses, to the Attorney General, with the charge that the latter had failed to enforce the law.[22] He then vetoed one-half of the biennial appropriation for the Attorney

[17] S. S. McKay, W. *Lee O'Daniel and Texas Politics, 1938–1942*, p. 62.
[18] *Ibid.*
[19] Press release from Governor O'Daniel's office, February 8, 1940, copy of which is in files of William J. Lawson, his executive secretary.
[20] George P. Huckaby, "Oscar Branch Colquitt: A Political Biography" (unpublished Ph.D. dissertation), p. 256.
[21] *Austin Statesman*, March 7, 1911.
[22] *Ibid.*, March 23, 1911.

General's department, saying he would finance the department from the Governor's deficiency fund if necessary.[23] On every possible occasion he publicly harassed Lightfoot until the Attorney General decided not to seek re-election, and even resigned before his term expired.[24] Another quarrel took place between Governor Colquitt and the commissioner of the General Land Office, J. T. Robison, over the Prohibition issue. Robison charged:

> We have a Governor going all over the State advising the people to defy the law. I say that this man at the head of the Ship of State is under contract with the liquor people to make this fight.[25]

After several exchanges, Robison accused the Governor of misrepresenting the facts concerning the Land Office. He wrote:

> Since I began work in this Department . . . I have not seen you in it as much as thirty minutes all put together. You are invited to come over and stay long enough to learn something of its work, importance, and responsibility. I must decline to be drawn into any further controversy at this time. I am too busy trying to do the work for which I was elected.[26]

Governor Colquitt had apparently met his match. He never accepted the invitation, and relations failed to improve.

Open differences between executive officials also occurred during the first administration of Governor Miriam A. Ferguson (1925–1927). Almost from the beginning, Attorney General Dan Moody was hypercritical of the Governor and her husband, especially in regard to their policies concerning pardons and highway construction. Mr. Ferguson dominated the issuance of contracts for road building to such an extent that opponents charged that contracts were made more from the standpoint of friendship than from the best interests of the state.[27]

Becoming the chief spokesman of the Ferguson critics, Moody uncovered some corruption in the handling of highway contracts and filed suit against two construction companies, alleging that they would realize a profit of over $5 million.[8] This litigation resulted in

[23] *Ibid.*, March 12, 1911.
[24] Huckaby, "Oscar Branch Colquitt: A Political Biography" (unpublished Ph.D. dissertation), p. 258.
[25] *Austin Statesman*, July 10, 1911.
[26] Quoted from the Colquitt Papers in Huckaby, "Oscar Branch Colquitt: A Political Biography" (unpublished Ph.D. dissertation), pp. 260–261.
[27] S. S. McKay, *Texas Politics, 1906–1944*, p. 146.
[28] *Austin American*, June 6, 1926.

a modification of the procedure for awarding contracts. Other comparable episodes concerning Mr. Ferguson's role in awarding contracts were found in various agencies, leading Moody to charge that Texas had "government by proxy." He vowed to fight "Fergusonism" to the end and ran against Mrs. Ferguson in the primary of 1926. In one of the bitterest political campaigns in Texas history he unseated the chief executive.

A more recent public disagreement among the state's constitutional officers occurred in 1961 when Attorney General Will Wilson appeared before the House Committee on Taxation and Revenue to oppose the tax plan advocated by Governor Price Daniel. Daniel rebuked Wilson for getting into the tax fight, which he considered to be a matter between the Governor and the Legislature, implying that Wilson's motives were purely political. In an open letter to the Governor, Wilson said that he had not only the right but the duty to urge the chief executive not to "force the state to waste a half million dollars in still another special session, which in the end is bound to pass a general sales tax." Criticizing Daniel for his position, the Attorney General wrote:

Well, Governor, if calling [the sales tax] the Will Wilson tax will ease your pain, I am quite content that it be so called. If by that device we can finance our schools and hospitals, I am willing to carry the political load which a Governor should carry, and which under most governors, the Attorney General would not have to assume. . . . You took office with a comfortable surplus on hand, but under your administration the situation has steadily deteriorated until we are now eighty-odd million dollars in the red.[29]

Several weeks later, in a surprise appearance before the State Democratic Executive Committee in Austin, Wilson opened fire on the chief executive by accusing him of plotting to run United States Secretary of the Navy John Connally as a candidate for governor in 1962, while Daniel himself would seek the lieutenant governorship, from which post he could continue to run the state.[30] The charge evoked the following comment from Daniel:

It is sad that any man honored with a high public office by the people of Texas would conduct himself so desperately as the Attorney General did before the State Democratic Committee. Any fair-minded person who

[29] *Austin Statesman*, July 31, 1961.
[30] *Houston Chronicle*, October 11, 1961.

reads the entire statement is bound to know it is false and a concoction of his imagination.[31]

The two squared off again on the question of who was responsible for failure to make banks surrender dormant accounts to the state. By letter, Daniel urged Wilson to "make some investigations and hold some courts of inquiry on this subject." He continued: "I am sure you will find that several million dollars of lost deposits have been charged off and transferred to bank profits . . . and that many of these accounts were subject to escheat by the state."[32] A few hours later Wilson called a press conference to reply. Reminding the Governor that as a former attorney general he should be more familiar with escheat laws, Wilson said, "In reality, you have publicly called for me to enforce a law which you have failed to pass during three terms as governor."[33]

The breach deepened and became complete in the campaign for the Democratic nomination for governor in 1962. Throughout the campaign Daniel was a principal target of Wilson, who criticized the Daniel Administration as having been "dilly-dallying" and "leaderless."[34]

GENERAL COOPERATION AMONG EXECUTIVES

Notwithstanding such scattered incidents of hostility within the executive branch, elected officials in Texas generally have cooperated remarkably well with their chief executives, particularly in view of the absence of legal controls by the governor. Noting the cooperation of "most constitutional officers," Governor Price Daniel remarked: "Though the governor has no authority over them, still they will work on nearly anything that is for the good of the state, and they will help the governor in his program, most all of them."[35]

Speaking on the same point, former Governor Shivers agreed that most officials desire to be cooperative. He stressed, however, that a governor "must be prudent in attempting to exercise influence" on officials who have been elected the same as he. He continued:

[A Governor] realizes that, in the public view, he will be held more or less responsible for all actions and conditions, good or bad, in state gov-

[31] *Dallas Morning News,* October 11, 1961.
[32] *Ibid.,* December 9, 1961.
[33] *Ibid.*
[34] *Houston Chronicle,* March 1, 1961, and March 18, 1961.
[35] Daniel–University of Houston television interview.

ernment. His cue, then, is to try to secure cooperation of other officials in a friendly, informal way. If the Governor has prestige, i.e., stands high with the public, he can be persuasive with other officers who would hesitate to face an open break with him.[36]

The prevailing attitude of the majority of elected officials is well summarized by a veteran officeholder, Robert S. Calvert, comptroller of public accounts under four governors, who says that, in his judgment, most elected officials are desirous of working on the governor's "team" regardless of who the incumbent might be.[37] Despite the fact that the officials are responsible to the people who elected them and not to the governor, much is to be gained by maintaining harmony in the official family. Not only will such cooperation create a better public image of the governmental process, but when the executives work with one another they can do a better job severally as well as individually. Invariably the result of a cooperative attitude is a more efficient job in the particular department and in the state government as a whole, according to Calvert.

The Governor's Relation to Appointed Executives

Governor James V. Allred once remarked that "from the moment a governor or other state official is nominated until after his appointments are made, ninety per cent of his time is taken up in interviewing people wanting appointments or desiring to endorse others for appointment."[38]

The job of selecting personnel is as difficult as it is time-consuming. Perhaps any governor or staff assistant would attest that making appointments is probably *the most difficult* function of the office. Competent persons who will reflect credit upon the administration must be chosen, while at the same time political consequences must be considered. As one newspaper editorialized, "For every one appointed to public office, half a dozen are disappointed."[39] Whatever the decision, new political enemies may be made.

[36] Interview of Allan Shivers for a television program sponsored by the University of Houston, April 1, 1960. Script furnished by Weldon Hart. Hereafter cited as Shivers–University of Houston television interview.

[37] Interview of the writer with Robert S. Calvert, comptroller of public accounts, in Austin, August 2, 1961.

[38] *House Journal*, Forty-sixth Legislature, regular session, p. 31.

[39] *Austin American*, September 20, 1947.

The appointive power of the governor of Texas is extensive. While the exact number of positions subject to gubernatorial appointment is indeterminate, it is generally conceded to be in the neighborhood of 1,000.[40] Only one constitutional officer—the secretary of state—and two statutory department heads—the commissioner of labor statistics and the adjutant general—are selected by the governor. However, there are many other appointive positions on some 110 boards and commissions, and in addition, numerous vacancies occur in the executive and judicial branches at both the state and district levels. Furthermore, the governor may fill vacancies in the United States Senate and in certain local offices such as those of public weighers, branch pilots, and governing boards of river authorities and conservation districts.

The volume of appointments made annually may be illustrated by the year 1960, in which Governor Daniel appointed 275 members of various boards and commissions, 80 public weighers, 74 branch pilots, 26 judges to fill vacancies, and 39 special judges. For each job filled there were approximately three candidates, and in one case forty-five persons sought the job.[41]

In making appointments, the executive faces certain limitations. All appointments require confirmation of two-thirds of the senators present—[42]a large number when compared to the simple majority vote which the President of the United States must secure for his appointments. Moreover, members of most boards and commissions serve overlapping terms so that, barring deaths and resignations, a governor is unable to get a majority of his appointees on those bodies until late in a second term. Some offices require technical qualifications of an appointee which the governor must be sure are met, and other positions must, by statute, be held by representatives from different economic or professional groups or geographical sections of

---

[40] *Texas Almanac, 1961–1962*, pp. 366, 370. The governor appoints "an indefinite number" of commissioners of deeds "at will to take acknowledgment and proofs of the execution of any deed, mortgage, or other conveyance of lands, tenements, etc." and an indefinite number of commissioners of pilots "to examine application for office of deputy pilots and examine misconduct of pilots."

[41] Statistics supplied by John Goldsum, administrative assistant to Governor Daniel.

[42] Constitution of Texas, Art. IV, Sec. 12. An interpretation of this section may be found in *Denison* v. *State*, 61 S.W. (2d) 1017 (Tex. Civ. App., 1933, writ of error refused).

the state. In a few cases he must choose appointees from lists submitted by governmental agencies or private groups.[43] Undoubtedly the major limitation, however, is the strong tradition of "senatorial courtesy," under which the Senate will decline to confirm an appointee if the senator from the district in which he resides objects to the appointment.

How then are appointments to public office actually made? Obviously, the executive cannot know personally everyone he selects and must rely upon the recommendations of others in many instances. As Governor Price Daniel pointed out, the procedure varies somewhat with the importance of the office to be filled. If the position is a highly desirable one, many will be interested in it; if the place to be filled is a minor one, there may be some difficulty in securing a capable person. This dilemma means that appointment making is the most difficult job the governor has.[44]

Inevitably the spoils system affects the appointing process. The executive consults with his supporters about appointments and frequently is beseiged with mail from would-be officeholders or their supporters. The role of the senator concerned may vary. Occasionally a senator may suggest an appointee, but the more general practice seems to be that he is consulted after a decision has been made but prior to public announcement of the appointment. At that point the senator could "veto" the appointment if he objected, since custom decrees that an executive will choose only those acceptable to the senator from whose district the appointee hails. In the view of one veteran newspaperman, it is good politics for the governor to approach a potential officeholder on his availability before contacting the senator because if the candidate knows he is being considered, the senator will be less inclined to object than if he is asked beforehand about the matter. In this way the governor can more nearly select the people he wants with less probability of objection.[45] Regardless of the stage at which a senator is consulted, however, "senatorial courtesy" is a potent force in the appointing process in Texas.[46]

The actual appointing procedure may be illustrated from archival material of the Jester Administration—the most recent administration

---

[43] MacCorkle and Smith, *Texas Government* (4th ed.), p. 93.

[44] Interview with Governor Daniel in Austin, November 30, 1961.

[45] Interview with Stuart Long, Capitol News Bureau, in Austin, June 28, 1961.

[46] This point of view was expressed by former Governors Stevenson, Moody, Shivers, and Daniel in separate interviews with the writer. A large number of their former staff members concurred.

whose records were available to the public when this research was done, in 1962. Apparently the "patronage man" in the Jester Administration was Secretary of State Paul H. Brown, who contacted the Governor's supporters in local areas to ask advice on appointments. The filling of the office of district attorney of the Twenty-fifth Judicial District of Gonzales County in October, 1947, is a case in point. Brown contacted A. G. Blackwelder, asking for a recommendation for the post from local supporters of the Governor. In reply, the name of Willis E. Ellison was submitted. The Governor then wired Senator R. A. Weinert of his intention to appoint Ellison, and upon approval from the Senator, announced the choice publicly.[47] (Copies of the correspondence illustrating the entire procedure appear in Appendix VI.)

Another example involves the appointment of a member of the Board of Regents of The University of Texas. On February 20, 1947, Governor Jester received a confidential memorandum from William L. McGill, his executive secretary, as follows:

My grapevine tells me that University Officialdom is saying prayers this afternoon that you will see fit to name someone from the northwestern part of the state.

They feel that the present attack of the West Texas Chamber of Commerce will not by any means be the end of the fight to take away the endowment of the University and A. & M., and they feel that it is a matter of great importance that someone be on the Board from the Northwest.

I pass this on for such edification as it may be to you.[48]

Heeding the advice contained in the memorandum, Governor Jester decided to appoint "one of the Swenson boys" from Stamford. He directed Paul Brown to contact his Jones County campaign manager, Bernard Buie, for advice as to whether to appoint W. G. (Bill) Swenson or A. M. G. ("Swede") Swenson to the position. Mr. Buie replied that either man would be good, but suggested that "Swede" Swenson, because he had been a prominent football player, would be better known. He wrote: "Am of the opinion that on the announcement that "Swede" Swenson had been appointed as a member of the Board of Regents of The University, not less than 50,000 people all over the state would feel that he was a man they knew, and favored."[49]

[47] Governor Jester's Correspondence Files, Box GC–79, Texas State Archives.
[48] *Ibid.*, Box GC–80, Texas State Archives.
[49] *Ibid.*

Following this advice from the "grass roots," Jester nominated A. M. G. Swenson, and the Senate confirmed the nomination.

If a governor disregards recommendations by local people and the senators, he may be in for difficulty, as was W. Lee O'Daniel, who "had more trouble with his appointments than any other governor in the state's history [up to his time]. All records were broken in the number of his nominations rejected by the Senate."[50] His unorthodox approach may be illustrated by his attempts to fill the office of chief justice of the Supreme Court of Texas in 1940. He first offered the place to Attorney General Gerald C. Mann, whose election he had opposed only a few months previously. Mann declined on the grounds that he lacked the seven years of experience in the practice of law required by the Constitution. O'Daniel offered to wait the six months needed for Mann to accumulate the requisite experience, but Mann felt that such action would violate the spirit of the Constitution.[51] O'Daniel then sent a wire to Eugene P. Locke, an attorney in Dallas:

> The importance of the office of Chief Justice of the Supreme Court of Texas is so great to the people of this state that I think the job should seek the man and not the man seek the job. Therefore, without consulting you, I am tendering you the appointment as Chief Justice of the Supreme Court.[52]

Locke also declined the post. Significant was the fact that neither the appointees nor the senators were consulted prior to the making of the offers.

Governor Coke Stevenson also met with difficulties in securing confirmation of certain appointments, despite the fact that he had recently been presiding officer of the Senate. Reporting the rejection of two Stevenson appointments—J. W. Page for adjutant general and W. J. Lawson for secretary of state—the *Houston Post* called the move "an eyebrow raiser," saying there was a supposition that Stevenson might have agreed to submit the names because his predecessor, O'Daniel, had tendered the appointments before his resignation. The newspaper said bluntly that Stevenson had "enough friends in the Senate to get whomever he wants confirmed."[53]

[50] McKay, *W. Lee O'Daniel and Texas Politics*, p. 146. McKay gives a complete account of O'Daniel's difficulties in securing senatorial confirmation of appointments on pages 150 to 153.

[51] Press release dated April 10, 1940, a copy of which is in files of William J. Lawson, O'Daniel's executive secretary. Made available by Mr. Lawson.

[52] *Ibid.*, April 11, 1940.

[53] *Houston Post*, February 5, 1943.

Another appointee was also rejected for secretary of state when Senator Claude Isbell, who wanted the job himself, objected; consequently, Stevenson appointed Isbell, who was confirmed immediately.[54] In 1945 Senator Weaver Moore, who became Stevenson's archfoe on appointments after he was bypassed for the vacancy of attorney general, created an unusual situation with regard to the Senate's role of advice and consent. He obtained passage (12 to 10) of a resolution to reconvene the Senate the following year in "solo session" to act on any appointments made "between now and then." Control of the state Unemployment Compensation Commission and $150 million were at stake. Moore declared, "It's an open secret that Claude Williams, director and Chairman of the Commission, is soon to resign. We want a voice in picking his successor."[55]

When the Senate convened it received no appointments from the Governor; a member finally presented the recess appointments certified by the secretary of state. Later, the Board of Control refused to pay an account for the printing of the *Senate Journal* for the session, and the Supreme Court ruled that such sessions, convened by resolution solely for passing on appointments, were unconstitutional.[56]

A recent and spectacular controversy over the confirmation of a gubernatorial appointment occurred in 1963, during the regular session of the Fifty-eighth Legislature. One of the first names submitted to the Senate by Governor Connally was that of W. St. John Garwood, for appointment to the Board of Regents of The University of Texas. A prominent citizen of the state and former associate justice of the Texas Supreme Court, Garwood had agreed to accept the appointment, although he had voluntarily retired from politics some years before. In one of the greatest surprises of the session, the Senate refused confirmation, acting upon the matter, contrary to Senate custom, while the senator from Garwood's home district, Charles Herring, was absent because of illness. Although the Senate considered the appointment in executive session (a practice which was severely attacked by one of its own members) and the discussion was therefore secret, there was speculation that Garwood's "liberal" position concerning racial integration at The University of Texas and his

[54] Interview with former Governor Coke Stevenson at Junction, Texas, February 27, 1961.

[55] *San Antonio Light*, June 3, 1945.

[56] *Walker* v. *Baker, Chairman of Board of Control, et al.* 196 S.W. (2d) 324 (1946).

outspoken support of the United Nations might have caused some senators to vote against him.

Despite occasional conflicts with the Texas Senate, governors of Texas have usually had most of their appointments confirmed with little question or opposition, whether because of close adherence to the unwritten rule of "senatorial courtesy" or because of political acumen or wisdom in selecting capable people.[57] The fact remains that the power of appointment is probably the governor's most important executive function today.

THE GOVERNOR'S REMOVAL POWER

Frequently the power to remove is considered to be incident to the power to appoint, but certainly no such presumption is valid in Texas, or for that matter, in most state governments. Usually, if the governor has any removal authority, it must be specified in the constitution or statutes.[58] Although the Texas Constitution permits the removal of all elective executive officers by impeachment proceedings,[59] it further authorizes the Legislature to provide for "the trial and removal of all officers of this state, the modes for which have not been provided in this Constitution."[60]

Pursuant to this provision, four modes of removal for executive officials have emerged: impeachment, joint address, quo warranto proceedings, and action by the governor alone. Through statutory enactment, impeachment has been extended to the offices of secretary of state, banking commissioner, commissioner of insurance, and "all other state officers and heads of State departments or institutions of any kind, and all members, regents, trustees, or commissioners having control or management of any state institution or enterprise."[61] Upon joint address of two-thirds of both houses of the Legislature, the governor must remove the commissioner of agriculture, the commissioner of insurance, or the banking commissioner.[62] The law also provides for "the trial and removal of any other public official" by

[57] MacCorkle and Smith, *Texas Government* (4th ed.), p. 93.
[58] William Anderson, Clara Penniman, and Edward Weidner, *Government in the Fifty States*, p. 268.
[59] Constitution of Texas, Art. XV, Sec. 2.
[60] *Ibid.*, Art. XV, Sec. 7.
[61] *Vernon's Annotated Civil Statutes, State of Texas*, Sec. 5961. This statute was enacted after Governor James E. Ferguson removed a University of Texas regent in 1917.
[62] *Ibid.*, Sec. 5964.

quo warranto proceedings;[63] the power residing in the governor alone is couched in these terms:

All State officers appointed by the Governor, or elected by the Legislature, where the mode of their removal is not otherwise provided by law, may be removed by him for good and sufficient cause, to be spread on the records of his office, and to be reported by him to the next session of the Legislature thereafter.[64]

While this law seemingly would vest some independent removal power in the governor alone, "for all practical purposes, the power simply does not exist, and the governor cannot remove any state or local official, either elected or appointed."[65] This anomalous situation springs from the judicial construction of the constitutional provision authorizing the Legislature to provide for "the trial and removal of public officers." The Supreme Court interpreted the word *trial* to involve the hearing of evidence according to law and the rendition of judgment by a legally constituted tribunal.[66] As a consequence, therefore, all state officials apparently must be afforded a trial in a court of law before their removal can be effected (in the event such action is demanded).[67] Even in those cases where the governor is specifically authorized to remove an official for cause—as for example, he was authorized to remove members of the State Board of Insurance for nonattendance at meetings—[68] it is extremely doubtful that such removals would be upheld since no "trial" would be involved.[69]

Regardless of these legal barriers, the governor is not without some recourse to rid his administration of certain officials. He is apparently free to remove an official as his personal representative on an interstate commission, as did Governor W. Lee O'Daniel when he wrote the following letter to Ernest O. Thompson:

Two years ago it became my duty to appoint a Member of the Interstate Oil Compact Commission to serve as my personal representative on this Commission. Notwithstanding the fact that you had been a candidate

[63] *Ibid.*
[64] *Ibid.*, Sec. 5967.
[65] MacCorkle and Smith, *Texas Government* (4th ed.), p. 93.
[66] *Knox v. Johnson*, 141 S.W. (2d) 698 (1941).
[67] The distinction between a "state official" and a "state employee" is unclear, but presumably the former category includes all who are appointed by the governor with the advice and consent of the Senate.
[68] *Texas Insurance Code*, Art. 1.03.
[69] Wilbourn E. Benton, *Texas: Its Government and Politics*, p. 279.

against me and had been rather severe and bitter in your criticism, I appointed you as my personal representative on this Commission, with the hope that it would best serve the interest of this state.

I beleive [sic] that the best interest of Texas would be served by having on this Commission a man who would devote his time to the problem of conserving the natural resources of Texas. I feel that as the man on this Commission is my personal representative, the place should be filled by someone in whom I have full confidence.

Therefore, this letter is to notify you that in order to promote the welfare of this State and bring about a more effective regulation and conservation of our natural resources, I have this day removed you as my personal representative from the Interstate Oil Compact Commission.[70]

In some cases the governor might use the press to publicize his grievances against an official, thus forcing a resignation by creating unfavorable public opinion against the man, or he might apply personal pressure on an official to secure a resignation.[71] Such a case is reported to have occurred in the first administration of Governor Miriam A. Ferguson. An eyewitness to the incident related the following episode. Hearing that one of the Governor's appointees, who headed a state agency, was engaging in unbecoming conduct, Mr. Ferguson and an aide went to the official's office to demand a resignation. Mr. Ferguson told the man that his misconduct with a subordinate was becoming a source of embarrassment to the Administration and asked for his resignation. When the man did not move fast enough, Mr. Ferguson directed the secretary accompanying him to draft a letter of resignation, saying, "He'll sign it," and, as predicted, he signed. Thus a private citizen, albeit the Governor's husband, removed a department head in the state government.[72]

This example may be unique, but there are probably many cases in which pressure applied by a governor has made a state official uncomfortable to the point of resigning, for the chief executive's office does carry prestige which is not easily ignored. To be sure, such an

[70] Press release of July 30, 1940, copy of which is in files of William J. Lawson, O'Daniel's executive secretary.

[71] The report is widely circulated that Governor Huey P. Long of Louisiana required undated letters of resignation of certain state officials as a prerequisite to their appointment. When he desired to terminate the official's employment, he filled in the date. Allen P. Sindler, *Huey Long's Louisiana: State Politics,1920–1952*, p. 63.

[72] Incident related to the writer by Ghent Sanderford, executive secretary to Governor Miriam A. Ferguson, in an interview in Austin, June 5, 1961. Mr. Sanderford wrote the letter of resignation which the official signed.

approach is slower and more difficult than possessing clear-cut removal power, but the ultimate accomplishment is the same. Allan
Shivers may have had such exigencies in mind when he said, "In
most cases the governor does not need statutory or constitutional
authority to remove appointive officers, as he could readily secure a
resignation by calling for it either privately or publicly."[73]

Questioned about his views, Price Daniel conceded that it might
be wise to "study" the possibility of allowing a governor to remove
his appointees for malfeasance in office, but he hastened to add, "I've
never seen the situation arise where I would want that kind of power
or needed it."[74]

A strong removal power is generally believed to be one of the
necessary prerequisites for a strong executive, but no one can claim
that such independent removal power is possessed by the governor of
Texas.

THE GOVERNOR'S RELATION TO THE MULTIHEADED AGENCIES

According to a former attorney general of Texas, "One of the most
vexing problems of modern Texas government is the present system
of state boards. These boards are like Topsy, they just growed and
growed."[75] Throughout the twentieth century the administrative
structure of Texas government has been plagued with a rash of
boards and commissions created to carry out a multiplicity of functions: administrative, managerial, educational, examining, and regulatory.

In 1933 the Joint Legislative Committee on Organization and
Economy reported the existence of 131 "practically independent
agencies" in the state,[76] and by 1950 Texas "had no less than
124 different state agencies, with twenty-seven ex-officio boards and
thirty-eight out of fifty-four departments also headed by boards or
commissions."[77] The most recent compilation showed that in 1961
there were eighty-six agencies headed by an individual officer or by
an entire board appointed by the governor; twenty-six agencies the

[73] Shivers–University of Houston television interview.
[74] Daniel–University of Houston television interview.
[75] John Ben Sheppard, *A Bureaucrat's Dilemma: Ex-Officio Boards*, p. 1.
[76] Texas Legislature, Joint Legislative Committee on Organization and Economy, *The Government of the State of Texas*, Part I, p. 1.
[77] L. Vaughan Howard and John H. Fenton (eds.), *State Governments in the
South: Functions and Problems*, p. 26.

members of which were "all or partly ex-officio and the Governor is one of the ex-officio members or appoints at least one member"; and eighteen agencies the members of which were "all or partly ex-officio . . . but all members are chosen by persons other than the Governor."[78] This superabundance of agencies has been aptly described as "organized disorganization."[79]

Today some 110 boards and commissions supervise and direct most of the major concerns of the state: banks, highways, health, water, higher education, game and fish, insurance, welfare, hospitals and special schools, and liquor control—to mention only a few. Some boards and commissions are ex-officio and constitutional officers hold places on many of them, but the personnel are in the main appointees of the governor. Even so, most of these bodies enjoy a peculiar type of freedom from legal control. They are on their own to become policy makers and to choose executives to effectuate their policies. Their independence is further increased by the fact that members serve long, overlapping terms and, barring unexpected vacancies, a governor must have been in office almost two terms before he has chosen a controlling majority on any one body. The usual situation is that the appointees of the governor's predecessor "run the show" during his first term, and he has no removal power over them.

If these agencies enjoy such a degree of independence, what is the governor's relation to them and what informal methods of control may he exert over their day-to-day working operations? The same general relationships obtain between the governor and the boards and commissions as between him and the elective officials, except, of course, his own appointees may have more personal interest in the administration of the executive who named them and feel a personal loyalty to him. Legally they owe no greater allegiance and are under no heavier obligation to the chief executive than are their elected counterparts.

Some executives of bygone days sought to impose their wills upon the multiheaded agencies, only to find that the administrative machinery was not well adapted for such tactics. The unsuccessful attempt of Governor James E. Ferguson to control The University of Texas through its Board of Regents is notorious in Texas history.

[78] Institute of Public Affairs, The University of Texas, *Organization Chart, The State Government of Texas, 1961.*
[79] Benton, *Texas: Its Government and Politics,* p. 296. By permission of Prentice-Hall, Inc.

One of the principals in that drama has reported that Ferguson called a meeting of the Regents and demanded the removal of several faculty members. In his words, "Mr. Ferguson was the first and he probably will be the last governor to call a secret meeting of the Board of Regents in the Executive Office."[80]

Although this action was one of the events leading to his impeachment, Ferguson attempted to control other boards during his wife's tenure as governor by sitting in conference with them and playing a major part in awarding contracts. In this way he allegedly directed the program of the Highway Commission.[81] When Mrs. Ferguson campaigned in 1932, her husband claimed that since her previous administration (1925–1927) the Highway Commission had become "arrogant, disrespectful, dictatorial, and incompetent," and Mrs. Ferguson pledged that she would "try to get the present highway commissioners removed."[82]

Although there is no evidence that he tampered directly with the operation of the agencies as had Ferguson, the impolitic W. Lee O'Daniel became probably the most outspoken and antagonistic critic of the board and commission system ever to occupy the Executive Mansion. Learning in his first term that he had been unable to appoint majorities on most boards and commissions, he opened fire on the system in the first speech in his campaign for re-election in Waco on July 2, 1940. He labeled the agencies "giant oligarchies and juicy play-pretties of the professional politicians," singling out the Board of Control, the Game, Fish, and Oyster Commission, and the Department of Public Safety as the chief targets of his vehement attacks at that time. In describing his position with the latter, he said:

I was Governor for about a year with all three members of that Board being appointed by a previous Governor. The members of that Board owe no particular allegiance to me because I did not give them their jobs, and if I would go to them to enforce some law violation, they could just tell me to go jump in the lake because they were under no obligation to me. I did not hire them and could not fire them. . . . Then if a group of you good citizens would come to the Governor . . . and tell me about some violation of the law in your neighborhood and ask me to fulfill my constitutional duty to see that the law was enforced, I would have to tell you the

[80] John A. Lomax, "Governor Ferguson and The University of Texas," *Southwest Review,* XXVIII (Autumn, 1942), 21.

[81] McKay, *Texas Politics 1906–1944,* pp. 147–148.

[82] *Fort Worth Star-Telegram,* May 22, 1932.

Governor's office had been stripped of that power and the Department of Public Safety is the only state law enforcement agency and it did not have to pay any attention to me as Governor because I did not appoint its members.[83]

Alluding to the fact that it would be about mid-point of his second term before he would have appointed a majority of the members, O'Daniel said further, ". . . they will then enforce the law when I tell them to for a short period of a few months on the tail end of my second term." In the meantime, he claimed former governors would have had more influence than the incumbent.[84]

O'Daniel then called the boards and commissions "the fourth branch of government," and dubbed the Game, Fish, and Oyster Commission the

Millionaire Sportsman Club, with all expenses paid by the Texas taxpayers, with all of its 74 boats, with its horde of Game Wardens and with its own bank account, and with its authority to actually sell some of the natural resources of the State and spend money in any manner it desires.[85]

The Commission responded to this attack by challenging the Governor to prove his charges or withdraw them. He was invited to meet with the members. When he did not appear, they released their answers to the press, and the bitter row became a campaign issue.[86]

Fortunately, not all relationships between chief executives and the state agencies have been so hostile. Over the long range a marked degree of amity has existed after both sides have become acclimated to their respective roles. In the opinion of many officials the board-commission plan has done an adequate job of administration in Texas.[87]

ADMINISTRATIVE RELATIONSHIPS IN PRACTICE

What is the usual situation that exists between the governor and the appointive boards and commissions? In searching for an answer

---

[83] A copy of the text of this speech, delivered at an open-air rally but not broadcast, was furnished by O'Daniel's executive secretary, William J. Lawson.

[84] *Ibid.*

[85] *Ibid.*

[86] McKay, *W. Lee O'Daniel and Texas Politics*, p. 320.

[87] Two major exceptions among these officials were former Governors Moody and Shivers, who in interviews with the writer, reiterated the stands they had taken in their respective terms recommending to the Legislature the short ballot and strengthened executive powers.

to this question, a number of interviews with gubernatorial appointees, both past and present, with legislators, and with executive heads of many state agencies elicited frank answers, after these officials were assured that their observations would be held in strict confidence. Certain generalizations may be drawn from the composite of answers to questions propounded to all.

Without exception, opinion was that the boards and commissions were, in fact as well as in theory, truly independent of gubernatorial control in the management of their respective functions. Several examples were cited where action taken by the agencies contravened the desires of the governor. Most appointees indicated that no promises were exacted from them as a condition of their appointment, though several said the governor had discussed in general terms the work of the agencies to which they were being appointed. One official described as typical a situation which occurred in 1957: after watching the swearing-in ceremonies of members of the newly organized State Board of Insurance, Governor Price Daniel reportedly told the members that they were thereafter "on their own."

The attitude of the chief executive toward appointed boards may be further illustrated by correspondence of the late Governor Jester. In 1947 the Board of Directors of the A. and M. College of Texas decided to remove some funds for which they were responsible from a bank in Bryan to another financial institution. The action evoked some objection, and protests were sent to Governor Jester. In replying to Harry Knox, secretary to the then United States Senator W. Lee O'Daniel, who had registered objections, Jester wrote:

> As I told you over the telephone, I will find out from my good friend and appointee on the Board, Tyree L. Bell, the reason why the Board of Directors voted to move this account.
>
> In my opinion, the Governor should not dictate details of administration to any Board or Commission, members of which he appoints. I believe a good way for a Governor to get in trouble would be to start a policy of telling members of Boards what to do and what not to do. However, when friends raise a question as to why a certain action, the Governor could, for the friends, undertake to find out the "why" without seeming to dictate to the Board or trying to influence any of its members' actions therewith. This I will be glad to do for you . . .[88]

Following his promise, but at the same time backing the Board,

[88] Letter of Governor Jester to Harry Knox, Washington, D.C., dated July 26, 1947, Jester Correspondence Files, Box GC–74, Texas State Archives.

Jester inquired of the incident from Tyree L. Bell, his appointee. He reaffirmed confidence in his appointees:

I never intend to meddle with the affairs of the Boards or Commissions. I know that the Board had a good reason for taking the action it did. Furthermore, I am not interested enough to want to know why the Board took its action, but since Knox telephoned me and then wrote me that he believed the action was taken because of the fact that Bryan [the banker] did not favor Gilchrist [the college president], it might be well for you to give me the facts so that I can uphold the Board's action whenever he talks to me about it when he comes to Texas.[89]

Regardless of the legal independence they enjoy, however, most members and executive directors of independent establishments apparently are desirous of cooperating with the current administration, whoever the governor might be at the time. As one official phrased it, "Even if they don't respect the governor, they respect the office of governor and generally try to get along."[90]

Persons appointed by a particular governor will naturally possess a loyalty to his administration which others may not feel; it follows that an *esprit de corps* will build up as more and more appointees of an incumbent governor assume their stations. In fact, one of the main criticisms levelled against third and fourth terms for chief executives in Texas is that an opportunity would be afforded for a governor to "control" a board or commission, since normally he would have appointed virtually all of the members of major agencies by the end of his third term.[91] One member of a large commission, reportedly close to the incumbent governor, said candidly:

If the governor appoints a man to office, then he owes loyalty and allegiance to the administration. If he feels otherwise, he should not accept the appointment in the first place. Quite obviously, when the governor who appointed me asks me to do something, I'm going to try my best to do it.

[89] Letter of Governor Jester to Tyree L. Bell, Dallas, Texas, dated July 26, 1947, Jester Correspondence Files, Box GC–74, Texas State Archives.
[90] Interview with Durwood Manford, chairman of the Board of Water Engineers, in Austin, August 10, 1961. Since then Mr. Manford, also a former speaker of the House of Representatives, has been appointed to the State Board of Insurance. (The name of the Board of Water Engineers has now been changed by legislative action to the Texas Water Commission.)
[91] In the Democratic primary of 1962 this charge was frequently levelled by several of his opponents at Governor Price Daniel, who was seeking an unprecedented fourth term. *Houston Chronicle*, March 18, 1962.

He added that since he had been appointed, eleven months previously, he had received "very, very few" such requests from the governor or his staff members.

In the absence of real controls, are there informal methods by which the chief executive may exert a modicum of influence over the sprawling administration of which he is nominally the head? In the interviews conducted, four methods of informal contact and control were mentioned most frequently by the operating officials: budget recommendations, required reports, informal conferences, and appointment of personnel.

Budget recommendations. As "chief budget officer," the governor is required to submit to the Legislature each biennium a budget including estimates for every administrative agency in the state government. Each of the officials mentioned the budget as one of the controls available to the governor, and there appeared to be a general respect for the use of the budget for such a purpose. Although it is generally conceded that the budget prepared by the Legislative Budget Board is more closely followed in the enactment of appropriations, new functions and services more frequently appear for the first time in the executive budget.[92] Consequently, if an agency anticipates expansion, it is highly desirable that it maintain good relations with the governor to receive favorable budgetary consideration.

Reports. As indicated above, the Constitution requires reports of the agencies to be submitted to the chief executive, who is authorized to inspect the books and accounts of any agency. The emphasis attached to this reporting function varied widely among the boards and commissions; some regarded such a report as virtually meaningless, while others believed it to be a perfect medium through which to proffer suggestions and reveal plans for expanded functions and services. One veteran executive director stated that his salary could be withheld pending the submission of his report, but no other official mentioned such an eventuality.

Informal conferences. A great deal of importance was attached to the value of informal conferences between the governor and his staff and representatives of the agencies. Former Governor Shivers agreed that much could be accomplished on broad policy questions by a free exchange of ideas. He pointed out that a governor feels closer to

---

[92] An analysis of the budgetary power appears in Chapter 8.

his appointees and freer to advise with them than with others, but he warned that the chief executive should never attempt to usurp power or to take over administrative direction of an agency.[93]

One Board member, a former legislator of prominence, said that matters pertaining to his organization were discussed quite freely and openly between the officials in his agency and the Governor's Office. He said that many "friendly disagreements take place under the best ethical circumstances" in the conferences and concluded that most governors were broad-minded men who sought and respected the opinions of their appointees. In his judgment, informal discussions were valuable to both sides as a tool in making policy decisions.

One veteran, who has served as an executive director of one of the state's largest agencies under five administrations, expressed the belief that the governor's "power of suggestion" was a potent factor with most agencies. He indicated that if a governor, as an extreme measure, should issue a press release criticizing his agency, or any other agency, for its acts of commission or omission, the result would probably be a crystallization of public opinion, which almost surely would eventually bear upon the policy of the agency.

Personnel appointments. Practically all agencies disavowed any undue pressure from a governor to hire particular persons, although several readily conceded that an executive's recommendation "did no harm" in securing employment for applicants in their organizations. Most agreed that they would be inclined to choose an individual recommended by the governor if the applicant met the qualifications for the job but added that it was unlikely a governor would urge appointment of an obviously unqualified person. Several said that they would heed recommendations for jobs from members of the Legislature above those from the governor.

The governor's role in personnel selection varies from one administration to the other, but regardless of who is in office, a routine reply will go out to letters from applicants or their endorsers. Sometimes the reply says that the letter is being referred to one of the agencies "for consideration"; at other times the job seeker is advised to contact the agency in which he wishes to work. Two replies sent by Governor O'Daniel's office in 1939 illustrate.

Since the day Governor O'Daniel was inaugurated as Governor he has strongly adhered to the policy of not taking any hand in the employment

[93] Interview of the writer with former Governor Allan Shivers, in Austin, December 4, 1961.

or discharge of any State employee for the reason that he believes this power should be vested solely with the heads of each department . . .[94]

At the present time there are no vacancies in the Executive Department, and Governor O'Daniel has stated in the press that he feels that hiring employees should be left up to the heads of the various departments of the State . . . It is suggested that you contact Colonel Homer Garrison, Jr., who is director of the Department of Public Safety in this matter, to see if an opening exists.[95]

A letter written during the Allred administration to the state director of the National Youth Administration may present a truer picture of the *modus operandi*.

                                                  September 28, 1937
Dear Jess:
    I am being called upon by students whose fathers may be friends of the Governor or who helped in the campaign, to intercede in their behalf for part-time employment either with a state department or under the N.Y.A. program.
    In the event I am *forced to write letters to you, please use your own judgment*. I appreciate all you have done in the past, and you may be assured that such favors will be returned with great pleasure. In the event this office is *really interested in someone*, I shall call you, although I do not anticipate such need [italics mine].
    With kindest regards, I am,

                                        Sincerely yours,
                                        s/George Clarke
                                        Secretary to the Governor[96]

    Questioned about his role in personnel selection below the executive level, Governor Price Daniel replied that, excluding his own office, he did not "have the power to give anyone a job in the state government." He acknowledged that he could recommend applicants and that occasionally some of the boards came to him to discuss personnel matters. He praised Texas for having "the finest setup for hiring on the basis of merit" without having a statewide comprehen-

---

[94] Letter from Reuben Williams, executive secretary to Governor O'Daniel, to the Rev. Forrest R. Waldrop, Corpus Christi, Texas, dated August 24, 1939. O'Daniel Correspondence Files, Texas State Archives, Box T–1953.

[95] Letter from Reuben Williams to Mrs. C. A. Nyquist of Lyford, Texas, dated September 26, 1939, Texas State Archives, Box T–1953.

[96] Letter from George Clarke, secretary to Governor James V. Allred, to J. C. Kellam, state director of NYA, Allred Correspondence Files, Texas State Archives, Box T–610.

sive merit system provided in its law. Alluding to a conversation in which he compared notes on this matter with the governor of Wyoming at a recent Governor's Conference, Daniel contrasted his own role with that of his fellow executive who, because he appointed department heads, could get people jobs throughout the government. He concluded that he would not like to be a "patronage type of governor" because more politics would be involved in the operation of the government. He proudly pointed out that on a per capita basis Texas had fewer state employees than any state in the Union, and that, with the exception of Tennessee, this state spent less for the operation of state government. Such a record he attributed to the processes of personnel selection in Texas.[97]

ADMINISTRATIVE REORGANIZATION?

The facts substantiate that informal methods and the power of suggestion are the governor's principal tools in exerting whatever control he has over the state administration. As was reported to the Commission on Intergovernmental Relations:

The Governor is not the chief administrative office, if by this we mean that he exercises wide directive and coordinative power. He is not without a certain influence, but he gains this in insignificant part from legal grants of power. . . . In short, each officer and agency of administration tends to supply its own direction without much consideration of the Governor and his desires.[98]

Since 1917, when the Administrative Reorganization Movement was launched, some states have been successful in strengthening their operations through integrated administrative systems with a strong governor at the apex. However, even in the face of strong pleas for reorganization in state government by many distinguished Texans—including a joint legislative committee,[99] two governors,[100] a state

[97] Interview of the writer with Governor Price Daniel, in the Executive Office in Austin, November 30, 1961.

[98] A report by O. Douglas Weeks and Wilfred D. Webb to the Commission. Quoted in Howard and Fenton (eds.), *State Government in the South: Functions and Problems*, p. 26.

[99] Texas Legislature, Joint Legislative Committee on Organization and Economy, *Government of the State of Texas*, Pt. I.

[100] Speech of Governor Dan Moody, *House Journal*, Forty-first Legislature, regular session, pp. 22–23, and inaugural address of Governor Allan Shivers, *House Journal*, Fifty-fourth Legislature, regular session, pp. 70–71.

auditor and efficiency expert,[101] civic organizations,[102] and prominent academicians—[103]very little has been accomplished in Texas. In his final inaugural address in 1955, Governor Allan Shivers urged the creation of a stronger executive to cope with mounting problems of the state:

> Over the years, the duties of the executive branch of our state government have multiplied manifold; but where the responsibility has been concentrated the authority has been diffused. New functions, new boards and new agencies have been added to the executive arm to serve new needs; but, in far too many instances, the line of authority and accountability has become dim and obscure. This is neither sound policy nor good government.
>
> I believe we should begin giving serious thought to reorganizing the executive branch. If the Governor is to be held accountable for the conduct of the executive branch, future Governors should have direct authority over—as well as responsibility for—the performance of administrative functions which are not policy-making in character. Those offices which are, in effect, a part of each Governor's administration should be subject to his appointment and removal. These changes would not lessen the burdens of the office of Governor, but they would increase the obligation for faithful and responsible service. . . . Our challenge is to build an example of state government at its finest.[104]

At present there seems to be very little sentiment among public officials and citizens for a change from the elected executive–board–commission type of administration to one of functional departmentalization under an integrated setup.[105] Perhaps people believe that Texas' system is still justified because it provides a safeguard against arbitrary exercise of power by the governor, or because it offers the

---

[101] *Annual Report on Condition and Fiscal Operations of the State of Texas,* 1939, p. 23.

[102] The West Texas Chamber of Commerce sponsored a limited reorganization plan in 1941. MacCorkle and Smith, *Texas Government* (4th ed.), p. 133.

[103] See, for example, "Reorganizing State Administration," by J. A. Burdine in *The Government of Texas, A Survey* (ed. S. D. Myres, Jr.), pp. 42–45; MacCorkle and Smith, *Texas Government* (4th ed.), pp. 124–135; Benton, *Texas: Its Government and Politics,* pp. 296–312.

[104] *House Journal,* Fifty-fourth Legislature, regular session, p. 70.

[105] In an extensive series of interviews, the writer found practically no one, with the exception of former Governor Shivers, who strongly advocated abandoning the board-commission plan. Former Governor Price Daniel told the writer that he believed that the present setup was a good one and that he would not favor a change.

governor political protection, or because it serves as a buffer.[106] Whatever their reasons, the prognosis for reorganization is poor. Every
sign points to the conclusion that the governor of Texas will, for the
foreseeable future, continue in his traditional role of *primus inter
pares* in the executive branch; for being an executive in all that the
term connotes is not one of the major activities of Texas' chief
executive. To provide leadership for the state he must rely heavily
upon other functions, the most outstanding of which are his roles as
legislative leader and political leader.

[106] Burdine and Reavley, "Toward a More Effective Administration," *Texas
Law Review*, 35 (October, 1957), 944.

6

Special Functions of the Governor of Texas

Because of the diversity of the functions and duties with which the governor of Texas is charged, not all of his activities fall into a neat categorical pattern. As might be expected of the state's foremost position, the duties are so multifarious and heterogeneous that some of them defy classification. Such duties cannot be discounted, however, for to do so would give a less-than-accurate portrayal of responsibilities of the office. For want of a better term, the miscellaneous duties may be labelled "special functions" of the governor, for, by virtue of the office, only he can perform them.

For purposes of discussion here, the "special functions" of the office include the following unique duties: the governor's activities as head of state and as the state's representative in intergovernmental relations, the governor's activities in international affairs, exercise of the governor's power to grant clemency, exercise of the governor's military power, and ex-officio activities of the governor.

The Governor as Head of State

An oft recounted anecdote in the corridors of the State Capitol in Austin relates that during the administration of Governor William P. Hobby a Negro maid in the Executive Mansion was married to a porter. As the ceremony ended, the officiating minister intoned, "And now in the presence of the Governor of Texas and Almighty God, I pronounce you man and wife." Undoubtedly the story overextends the public image of the governor, but it underlines the fact that, in the estimation of some citizens, the position of the chief executive is an exalted one.

Like the President of the United States, though in a much more modest fashion, the governor serves as the living symbol of his state. In this role he does not represent a political party, nor is he the man who struggles with the Legislature over a tax bill or some other controversial matter. As he opens a new highway, dedicates a new state building, or welcomes a national convention to Texas, he is the representative of all the people of the state.

As has been noted elsewhere,[1] he shakes hands with an untold number of people, travels thousands of miles, confers with innumerable citizens, and allows himself to be photographed with scores of groups. All such ceremonial functions permit him to make contact with constituents under favorable circumstances and with a minimum of the tension that might accompany appearances in his political role. It has been said that through such duties, "a governor can keep his physician's finger on the public pulse while allaying suspicion by appearing in his priestly garb."[2] Persons who would never think of voting for a particular executive will leave no stone unturned in their efforts to secure greetings from him for the annual convention of their favorite organization, for he symbolizes the state and its dignity.

PROCLAMATIONS

In his role as head of state, the chief executive is the recipient of hundreds of requests each year to endorse, support, or publicize the activities of many groups which may desire him to issue a gubernatorial proclamation designating a day, week, or month to honor or promote their interests. In recent years the governor of Texas has issued three hundred or more proclamations annually, urging citizens to give to worthy causes, such as the Heart Fund; to observe traditional holidays; or to be mindful of particular products which bolster the economy of the state.[3] Requests for proclamations run from the worthwhile to the bizarre and improbable. To mention only a few of the more unusual proclamations, in 1936 Governor James V. Allred designated: Buy-It-Made-in-Texas Week; Save Your Vision Week; Spirit-of-the-Church-in-America Days; National Tomato Week; and Texas History Study Week.[4] Five years later, in 1941, Governor W. Lee O'Daniel proclaimed: Eat More Meat Week; Kindness Week;

[1] See Chapter 4.
[2] Charles R. Adrian, *State and Local Governments*, p. 261.
[3] Interview with John Goldsum, administrative assistant to Governor Daniel, in Austin, June 26, 1961.
[4] Proclamations of Governor James V. Allred, 1936 (bound volume in Texas State Archives).

Bottled Soft Drink Week; Cotton Christmas Gift Month; and Black-eyed Pea Day.[5] In 1961 Governor Daniel designated: Egg Month; National Vending Machine Week; and Better Gardens Month.[6]

For each proclamation issued, the governor or his staff must do some research to find something complimentary to say about the event to be proclaimed; and as most requests for proclamations are spawned by the citizenry, each request must be surveyed to determine whether subtle policy questions are involved or whether the governor may get into political hot water by endorsing or recognizing the activities of a certain group.

On occasion the issuance of proclamations has entailed matters of far greater importance, which brought loud repercussions. When the governor uses his power to declare martial law, he issues a proclamation to that effect; one of the most significant proclamations ever issued in Texas was signed on March 2, 1933, by Governor Miriam A. Ferguson to declare a financial moratorium in Texas two days prior to the proclamation by President Franklin D. Roosevelt which accomplished the same end throughout the United States.

No better illustration of the governor's function as head of state can be found than in Mrs. Ferguson's declaration. Although actually lacking power to close the banks, the Governor, after consultation with numerous financial leaders, decided to assume authority for the bold action, since, in their judgment, a financial panic would be avoided by such action. The proclamation read, in part:

I, MIRIAM A. FERGUSON, Governor of the State of Texas, *by virtue of the authority and powers by me assumed,* do hereby proclaim a Financial Moratorium in the State of Texas, from this date until and including March 7th, 1933.

It is my order that within said time all State Banks, All National Banks, State Banks and Trust Companies, Trust Companies, Building and Loan Associations, Private Banks, and all other banking and financial institutions be prohibited and enjoined from paying to any depositor or creditor upon any account or deposit liability any amount during the period of time covered by this proclamation, and said institutions shall remain closed during such time.

While this is an extraordinary action, yet it is imperative that same be assumed and taken to protect the great masses of the people who have

---

[5] Proclamations of Governor W. Lee O'Daniel, 1941 (bound volume in office of secretary of state, Austin).

[6] Proclamations of Governor Price Daniel, 1961 (bound volume in office of secretary of state, Austin).

their all deposited in the various institutions of the State. If such action is not taken at once it will afford an opportunity for those who are informed to withdraw their deposits in full and leave the great army of small depositors in a position where it will not be possible for them to use their savings for their needs.

This action is taken after due consideration and with the approval of the State Banking Commissioner of our State, the Federal Reserve Bank authorities, and upon the earnest demand of the leading financial institutions of the State. I shall transmit to the Legislature promptly a message pertaining to my action and ask their prompt consideration of such legislation as may be meet and proper in the premises. In the meantime, I earnestly request the people to retain their usual composure until the Legislature acts, and I trust that we may have the full cooperation of all the financial institutions affected hereby.[7] (Italics mine.)

As promised, the Governor called a conference of leaders of the Legislature to discuss the necessary legislation to back up her proclamation, and the following day she transmitted a proposed bill along with a message which stated:

. . . I fully appreciate, and nobody understands better than I do, that this was an unusual proceeding. I would not have assumed the responsibility for such action had I not believed and known that the nation faces the greatest financial difficulty that ever afflicted the American people, and such being the case, these are times that try men's souls, and demand prompt and courageous action to deal with the problems that daily arise in official circles . . .[8]

Upon issuing the proclamation, directions were telephoned to banking institutions by the Governor's Office, and a few days later, legislation was enacted authorizing the banking commissioner to reopen banks under stipulated conditions; meanwhile the President of the United States had taken action similar to that of the Texas governor. As head of state she had helped avert a general panic.[9]

Some years later, Governor W. Lee O'Daniel used his proclamation power to order all Texans between the ages of eighteen and forty-five to register under the Selective Service Act of 1940.[10]

---

[7] Proclamation No. 13406, by Governor Miriam A. Ferguson, 1933. Original on file in Texas State Archives.

[8] *House Journal*, Forty-third Legislature, regular session, p. 645.

[9] Ouida Ferguson Nalle, *The Fergusons of Texas*, pp. 224–225.

[10] Proclamation No. 1836 by Governor W. Lee O'Daniel, 1940. Original on file in the office of the secretary of state in Austin.

INTERGOVERNMENTAL RELATIONS

As head of state, the governor is vested with the responsibility of conducting "all intercourse and business of the State with other States and with the United States."[11] He becomes, therefore, the channel of communication between his government and others. Undoubtedly the best-known function of this kind involves his responsibilities under the United States Constitution.[12] That document authorizes the governor of a state to determine whether a fugitive from justice shall be extradited to another state seeking his custody; conversely, requests for the return of a criminal to his own state are made in the governor's name. The frequency of such actions may be illustrated by the year 1961, during which Governor Price Daniel "delivered up" 173 persons to other states and requested the return of 205 prisoners to Texas.[13]

The introduction some thirty years ago of the concept of "cooperative federalism" into the American system of government further multiplied the duties of a governor in the field of intergovernmental relations. He was called upon to negotiate important compacts with other states, and in several instances he became an ex-officio member of the body administering the compact. By 1962 Texas was a member of some dozen interstate compacts on which the governor, or his personal representative, represented Texas. Some of the more important compacts included Interstate Oil Compact Commission; Southern Regional Education Compact; Interstate Civil Defense and Disaster Compact; Rio Grande Compact Commission; and the newly formed Southern Interstate Nuclear Compact.[14]

The governor also has become more involved in relations of the state with the nation. He is, of course, the representative of the state in signing agreements with the national government for the various grants-in-aid programs from which Texas received $346 million in 1960.[15] It is the governor who petitions the federal government for aid in emergencies caused by hurricanes, floods, tornadoes, and other

[11] Constitution of Texas, Art. IV, Sec. 10.

[12] Constitution of the United States, Art. IV, Sec. 2.

[13] Information furnished by John Goldsum, administrative assistant to Governor Daniel, in a letter to the writer dated April 6, 1962.

[14] Interview with John Goldsum, administrative assistant to Governor Daniel, in Austin, April 3, 1962. Other interstate compacts of which Texas is a member are listed in Texas Legislative Council and Institute of Public Affairs, *A Guide to Texas State Agencies*, p. 259.

[15] *Annual Report of the Comptroller of Public Accounts, State of Texas,* 1960, Part I, p. 20.

disasters; and when the interests of the state come into conflict with those of Washington, the chief executive becomes the principal spokesman for the state. Governor Shivers' controversy with the national government—even to the point of breaking with his own Democratic Party—over the ownership of the Texas tidelands is a well-known event of modern Texas history. In all such cases the governor acts as head of the state, promoting what he considers to be in its public interest. To underscore this role, the General Appropriations Bill for the biennium 1962–1963 empowered the governor to require all state agencies to clear their statements to agencies of other states and the federal government with him. The provision read:

The Governor's Office may require agencies of the State of Texas appearing before Federal agencies or agencies of other States to submit in writing to the Governor the purpose of such meetings and expression of the policies of the State agency concerning the subject matter of the meeting. After reviewing the policies, the Governor may require the State agency to conform to the policies of the State of Texas as outlined by the Governor and the Legislature before funds appropriated in this Act may be expended for necessary travel and other expenses.[16]

The governor also represents the state in national and regional organizations of state executives and in the Council of State Governments. During the post-World War II era Texas has fared quite well in this respect, two of her four chief executives serving in that period having been chairmen of governors' groups. In 1953 Governor Allan Shivers was chairman of the National Governors' Conference.[17] Governor Price Daniel completed a term as chairman of the Southern Governors' Conference in 1961.[18]

In a state in which the chief executive's position is constitutionally weak and the holder of the office is impelled to ferret out other means of exercising leadership, his role as head of state provides one useful avenue through which he can become the "voice of the people"—especially if he is imaginative and aggressive in that capacity.

THE GOVERNOR IN INTERNATIONAL AFFAIRS

Due to this state's geography and its ethnic composition, governors of Texas have frequently found themselves cast in a role not usually

[16] *Supplement to Senate Journal,* Fifty-seventh Legislature, first called session, p. 98.
[17] *State Government* (July, 1953), p. 214.
[18] *Houston Chronicle,* November 26, 1961.

associated with the duties of the governor of an American state—that of dealing with international affairs. Because Texas has a common boundary with Mexico that extends for approximately a thousand miles, and has more than two million inhabitants of Mexican descent,[19] her executives have been confronted from time to time with extraordinary problems involving relations between Texas and Mexico and even between the United States and Mexico.

For years following the annexation of Texas to the Union many Texans were apprehensive lest the amount of protection afforded by federal troops along the international boundary might prove to be insufficient, and the problem of greater security for the border was a perennial one until the turn of the century. During his incumbency Governor James S. Hogg came to grips with the "Mexican question" when the Texas Legislature passed a resolution in 1891 requesting an increase in the garrisons at posts along the Rio Grande.[20] Hogg complied by stationing all available Texas Rangers along the river, but he also worked diligently to foster greater international understanding and cooperation. In the words of his biographer:

. . . he made real progress in creating better relations with the state and federal officials of Mexico, both through the working agreements established between Texas and Mexican extradition agents and through his realistic approach to handling the problem of contagious diseases.[21]

Tangible benefits from his efforts were to be witnessed a few years later, when, after the disastrous flood of 1900, the city of Galveston was the recipient of $30,000 in relief funds from the Mexican government.[22]

An interesting sidelight on the governor's position during the Hogg era is cast by an incident which occurred during President Benjamin Harrison's tour of Texas in 1891. Wishing to honor Harrison by sending the governor of Chihuahua and a battery bearing firearms to meet him in El Paso, President Porfirio Díaz of Mexico dispatched a telegram to Governor Hogg, who was aboard the presidential train, requesting permission for his men to enter the United States bearing arms. According to the press covering the entourage, a good-natured debate ensued over who had the authority to permit the Mexicans to

[19] Texas Good Neighbor Commission, *Texas: Friend and Neighbor*, p. 115.
[20] *House Journal*, Twenty-second Legislature, regular session, p. 572.
[21] Robert C. Cotner, *James Stephen Hogg, A Biography*, p. 363.
[22] *Ibid.*, p. 366.

enter the country—the President or the governor. The report concluded, "The Republican president yielded to the states' rights argument and Hogg sent the telegram granting permission."[23]

President Díaz came to power in 1877—the year after Texas adopted its present constitution, and Mexico remained outwardly peaceful for more than thirty years under his strong dictatorship. Relations between Texas and Mexico were usually cordial. But in 1910 a violent revolution exploded in Mexico, at the instance of Francisco I. Madero, and fighting commenced a scant two months before Oscar B. Colquitt was sworn in as governor of Texas. During his entire two terms no other problem caused as much concern to Colquitt as did the question of how to handle the Mexican situation.[24] The policies he adopted soon embroiled him heavily in international relations and simultaneously in a long, acrimonious, verbal battle with the United States government.

One of Colquitt's first official acts was to proclaim the neutrality of Texas in the Mexican Revolution and to forbid Texas common carriers from hauling contraband of war.[25] Despite Texas' proclaimed neutrality, marauding bands of armed Mexicans periodically crossed the Rio Grande, pillaging and ravaging the countryside, molesting and even murdering some Texas citizens. At first Colquitt sought to work with federal authorities in protecting the border. In November, 1911, at the request of President William H. Taft, he doubled the Ranger force. He also ordered all Mexican revolutionists to leave Texas within forty-eight hours, and when the Mexican government sent 25,000 troops to patrol the border, Texans gave Colquitt credit for having averted another major battle in Mexico.[26]

In 1912 federal troops were stationed alongside the Texas Rangers on the border, and considerable friction resulted, causing many complaints to be lodged with Colquitt about the conduct of national officials. Americans detained in Mexico for various reasons increasingly began to appeal to the governor of Texas to extricate them. At first Colquitt referred such requests to federal authorities, but in August, 1912, he tired of federal inaction and proceeded to deal directly with the Madero regime—an action which incurred the wrath of United

[23] *Austin Daily Statesman,* April 24, 1891.
[24] George P. Huckaby, "Oscar Branch Colquitt: A Political Biography" (unpublished Ph.D. dissertation), p. 267.
[25] *Austin Statesman,* February 12, 1911.
[26] *Ibid.,* November 18, 20, 21, and 28, 1911.

States officials.[27] Upon Woodrow Wilson's accession to the Presidency, Colquitt sought smoother relations. He requested that Wilson appoint customs officials, consuls, district attorneys, and marshals who were in harmony with the state administration. The President agreed to Colquitt's request, but the harmony was short-lived.[28]

In November, 1913, the "Mexican problem" flared up again when Mexico sentenced several of its nationals for having smuggled arms through Texas. Governor Colquitt urged President Wilson to intervene and restore order in Mexico, and when the President adopted instead his policy of "watchful waiting," Colquitt released a long tirade declaring that he had been obliged to use Texas Rangers to make up for "the deficiency of the United States Government."[29] For the remainder of his term, he was at odds with Wilson's Mexican policies—a stand for which he received nationwide publicity, both favorable and unfavorable. In the meantime Mexico had witnessed the assassination of Madero, who was succeeded by General Victoriano Huerta, only to be forced out of office by Venustiano Carranza.[30]

James E. Ferguson, who succeeded Colquitt, became involved quickly in relations between the United States and Mexico. In his first year in office (1915) conditions along the border remained highly unsettled, due primarily to the efforts of Francisco (Pancho) Villa to overthrow President Carranza. When the United States gave *de facto* recognition to Carranza's regime, Villa was enraged and sought to create a state of war between the United States and Mexico by shooting several Americans and making a number of raids into Texas and New Mexico.[31] Public opinion in Texas was so inflamed that United States Secretary of State Lansing appealed to Governor Ferguson to assist in calming the people of the state. He telegraphed:

. . . a solicitous word from you to state and county officials . . . would prove most efficacious in allaying race prejudice and in restraining indiscreet conduct.[32]

Ferguson sent copies of the telegram to the indicated officials with

[27] Huckaby, "Oscar Branch Colquitt: A Political Biography" (unpublished Ph.D. dissertation), p. 271.

[28] *Ibid.*, p. 273.

[29] *Austin Statesman*, March 4, 1914.

[30] Richard B. Morris (ed.), *Encyclopedia of American History*, p. 302.

[31] Richard N. Current, T. Harry Williams, and Frank Friedel, *American History: A Survey*, pp. 648–649.

[32] *Dallas Morning News*, November 1, 1915.

the suggestion that "cooperation of our officials and citizens herein suggested is very essential."[33]

But when Villa's activities continued, Governor Ferguson called for intervention saying, "It is the solemn duty of the United States to enter Mexico and assume control of that unfortunate country, and give the Mexican people that stability of government, which they are now unable and helpless to establish."[34] President Wilson did not intervene in Mexico, but he sent General John J. Pershing with an expedition to pursue Villa, and ordered the National Guards of Texas, New Mexico, and Arizona to the border. Had not war with Germany been imminent, the United States perhaps would have become embroiled with Mexico. In any case, what some called Wilson's "muddled" intervention built prejudice and hostility against the United States on the part of the Mexican people.[35] In efforts to restore friendly relations since that time, governors of Texas have had a prominent part.

It well may be that an action of a Texas governor was the turning point in achieving a better understanding between the two countries, for it is sometimes said that Texas "recognized" the post-Revolution Mexican government three years before the United States did. This legend stems from the friendship that blossomed between Governor William P. Hobby and President Alvaro Obregón of Mexico, who was elected in 1920. The two met in El Paso, before Obregón took office, and Governor Hobby extended the Mexican President-elect an invitation to join his official party in attendance at the State Fair in Dallas.[36] Obregón accepted and so thoroughly enjoyed his visit that he reciprocated by requesting Hobby to attend and speak at his inauguration. The governor of Texas was well received in Mexico City, and although he did not represent the United States officially, his trip did not go unnoticed in Washington; a few months later this country recognized the Obregón government. Having become interested in Mexico, Hobby, during his closing months in office and after his retirement to private life, did much to further a "good neighbor policy" before a policy of that name was conceived in Washington.[37]

After a decade of trying experiences, therefore, Texas relations as

---

[33] *Ibid.*

[34] *Ibid.*, May 10, 1916.

[35] Current, Williams, and Friedel, *American History: A Survey*, p. 650.

[36] Interview with Raymond Brooks, Hobby's secretary, in Austin, April 3, 1962.

[37] James A. Clark and Weldon Hart, *The Tactful Texan: A Biography of Governor Will Hobby*, p. 142.

well as United States relations with Mexico became more amicable, and governors of Texas made substantial contributions to their betterment. Governor James V. Allred visited Mexico in 1937 to help promote the officially adopted "Good Neighbor Policy" of President Franklin D. Roosevelt. Allred was the second Texas governor to visit the Mexican capital in the century since Texas had declared its independence from Mexico. He drew large crowds wherever he went and proved to be a popular ambassador.[38]

Despite official rapport, however, Mexicans were often discriminated against in Texas. In the World War II period the national government called upon Texas executives to use their position to help blot out such discrimination as a matter of national policy. Secretary of State Cordell Hull was in frequent communication with Governors O'Daniel and Stevenson reporting specific instances of discrimination and soliciting the help of the state government. Both governors apparently gave full support to Hull's pleas by urging local officials in the border area to cooperate with national policy.[39] Governor Stevenson became so concerned that he pressed for the passage by the Legislature of a resolution calling for all persons of the Caucasian race to be "entitled to full and equal accommodations, advantages, facilities, and privileges of all public places of business or amusements . . ."[40] In conjunction with the resolution he issued a proclamation declaring it to be the public policy of the state of Texas.[41] A few months later, at the behest of Stevenson, the Texas Good Neighbor Commission was created as an adjunct to the Executive Department. Its mandate was "to devise and put into effect methods by which inter-American understanding and good will may be promoted and inter-American relations advanced without resort to punitive measures or application of civil or criminal sanctions."[42] Through this action, the governor of Texas created "a little State Department" for Texas.[43] Funds for initial operations were made available through the Office of the Coordinator of Inter-American Affairs of the United States Department of State, but in 1947 the Texas Good Neighbor

---

[38] *Dallas Morning News,* August 5, 6, and 11, 1937.

[39] Governor's Correspondence Files, O'Daniel and Stevenson Administrations, Texas State Archives, Box T–610; Box T–1926.

[40] House Concurrent Resolution No. 5, Forty-eighth Legislature, May 20, 1943, commonly referred to as the "Caucasian Race Resolution."

[41] Proclamation No. 7039, June 25, 1943, Department of State, Austin.

[42] Texas Good Neighbor Commission, *Texas: Friend and Neighbor,* p. 5.

[43] *Ibid.,* p. 139.

Commission was made a permanent agency of the state government.[44] During its existence, the Commission

has followed in an unswerving path of persuasion, education, and example in eliminating any existing prejudices toward Latin Americans in the state, . . . and it aims to promote cordial relationships with governmental representatives and all people in support of goals of the State Department.[45]

Taking cognizance of Governor Stevenson's avid interest in good Latin-American relations, President Franklin D. Roosevelt telephoned the Governor requesting him to join a good-will tour to Mexico in the fall of 1943.[46] In company with General of the Army George C. Marshall, Ambassador to Mexico George Messersmith, and Nelson Rockefeller of the State Department, Stevenson visited Mexico City and the capitals of five Mexican states in a tour described in the press as "the most extensive ever undertaken to the Mexican republic by a Texas official."[47] As he had so recently sponsored the establishment of the Texas Good Neighbor Commission, the Texan personified the Good Neighbor Policy of the United States and was warmly received wherever he went.[48]

Building upon the groundwork laid by Stevenson, later governors have devoted increasing attention to the promotion of better relations with Mexico. Governor Shivers made a number of visits to official functions there, such as the dedication of a new customs house in Nuevo Laredo (where he was a guest of President Alemán of Mexico), the inauguration of the governor of Tamaulipas, and a conference on highway problems in Chihuahua.[49] Governor Daniel entertained Mexican dignitaries in Austin, including President Lopez Mateos.[50] He also adopted the practice of attending Laredo's annual Washington's Birthday celebration (jointly observed there on both sides of the Rio Grande), where he met prominent Mexican officials on the International Bridge to renew ties of friendship between the American and Mexican peoples. Mrs. John Connally attended this

[44] *Ibid.*, p. 5.
[45] *Ibid.*
[46] Interview with Coke Stevenson, at Junction, Texas, February 27, 1961.
[47] *Dallas Morning News*, September 18, 1943.
[48] One of the Mexican governors presented Governor Stevenson with a live bear as an expression of friendship. Confronted with the problem of not needing a bear in Austin but not desiring to offend the Mexican official by declining the gift, Stevenson decided to have the bear sent to Baylor University as a mascot.
[49] Appointment book of Governor Shivers, 1950.
[50] *Austin American*, October 17, 1960.

celebration in 1963 as a replacement for the Governor, who was in the hospital for minor surgery. He apparently intends to continue participation in this traditional expression of amity between the two countries.

Evidence of the governor's role in international affairs today is attested by the increasing number of invitations he receives to official and unofficial functions in Mexico; the total has grown each year over the past decade.[51] If the governor is unable to accept, he usually sends a representative from the Texas Good Neighbor Commission. In recent years discrimination against Mexicans has been alleviated in many instances, and the new approach to better relations has centered on cultural and educational exchanges, encouragement of the study of Spanish by Texans, programs protecting migrant laborers, and the like.[52] If the postwar period can be used as a yardstick, there is every reason to expect that the role of the governor of Texas as a diplomat will continue to mount in importance. Certainly the actions of recent state executives have promoted better relations between Texas, the United States, and Mexico.

THE GOVERNOR'S POWER TO GRANT CLEMENCY

The ability to grant various forms of clemency to those accused of violating state laws is a traditional power of American governors. In Texas the extent of the executive's control over the issuance of pardons, reprieves, and paroles has varied from time to time, but governors of Texas have always possessed the power.

The Constitution of 1876 endowed the chief executive with almost absolute power in clemency matters, and for sixty years governors found it useful as a bargaining point on many occasions. As set forth originally, the section read:

> In all criminal cases, except treason and impeachment, he shall have power, after conviction, to grant reprieves and pardons; and under such rules as the Legislature may prescribe, he shall have power to remit fines and forfeitures. With the advice of the Senate, he may grant pardons in cases of treason; and to this end he may respite a sentence therefor until the close of the succeeding Legislature: provided, that in all cases of re-

---

[51] Interview with Glenn E. Garrett, executive director of the Texas Good Neighbor Commission since 1954, in Austin, April 3, 1962. Mr. Garrett frequently represents the governor when the chief executive cannot attend functions in Mexico.

[52] *Ibid.*

mission of fines or forfeitures, or grants of reprieve or pardon, the Governor shall file, in the office of the Secretary of State, his reasons therefor.[53]

Before this provision had been in effect for any length of time, it became obvious that the clemency power was growing into a responsibility so large that no executive could exercise it judiciously without help. In 1893 Governor James S. Hogg received 2,179 requests for clemency, and a Board of Pardon Advisers—composed of two qualified voters appointed by the governor—was created to relieve some of the burden.[54]

Even with the Board in operation, the clemency power became in many cases a "political football." In his two terms, Governor Thomas M. Campbell issued 783 pardons, and in his four years Governor Oscar B. Colquitt issued 403 full pardons and 1,172 conditional pardons.[55] When Governor James E. Ferguson began exercising the power he used it so frequently that he was accused of adopting an "open-door policy" at the Texas Penitentiary. Ferguson issued 2,253 pardons between 1915 and 1917. His successor, Governor William P. Hobby, ran a close second by issuing 1,518 pardons in some three and one-half years.[56] Such free use of clemency prompted Governor Pat Neff to reverse the policy by announcing in 1921 that he would issue no pardons except upon written recommendation of a district judge. Neff said that for the previous six years his predecessors had granted pardons and paroles at a rate of more than three a day, and in his view, "The too-freely granting of pardons weakens the law and makes its enforcement a farce. . . . This encourages violation of the law."[57] Later he mentioned that it had been "more or less authoritatively rumored that pardons were granted for a consideration."[58] In order to avoid such criticism of his actions, Neff adopted the policy of reviewing recommendations and interviewing persons desiring clemency, concentrating that activity within his office and not making use of the Board of Pardon Advisers.[59] He issued only 92 pardons and 107 conditional pardons during his entire four years in office.[60]

[53] Constitution of Texas, Art. 4, Sec. 11.

[54] Stuart A. MacCorkle, "The Pardoning Power in Texas," *Southwestern Social Science Quarterly*, XV (December, 1934), 222.

[55] *Ibid.*, p. 225.

[56] Alvah P. Cagle, *Fundamentals of the Texas Constitution*, p. 89.

[57] *Houston Post*, January 23, 1921.

[58] *Dallas Morning News*, December 14, 1924.

[59] Interview with John H. Johnson, secretary to Governor Neff, in Austin, March 17, 1961.

[60] MacCorkle, "The Pardoning Power in Texas," *Southwestern Social Science Quarterly*, XV (December, 1934), 225.

Governor Miriam A. Ferguson freely granted pardons, as had her husband several years previously. In two years she granted 1,161 pardons, and rumors began to fly that pardons were being sold. That approaches were made to "practically all members of the Ferguson family" was corroborated by the Governor's daughter, who reported a blatant offer of $5,000 if she would use her influence to secure a pardon.[61] An aide in the governor's office at that time recalled an attempt by a policeman to offer Mr. Ferguson some money in return for a pardon. Coming to the office to discuss clemency, the man placed several bills in James E. Ferguson's palm when he shook hands. The overture so infuriated Mr. Ferguson that he ordered the policeman out of his office with instructions never to come back.[62] The same aide said that it was commonplace at that time for legislators to ask the governor to grant a pardon to a constituent, or a client, in return for which the legislator would promise to vote for certain of the governor's favorite legislative proposals.[63] In describing the situation of the 1920's, one writer said:

> In Texas every conceivable form of pressure seems to be brought to bear on the Governor in an effort to influence his actions. Appeals to his emotions, as well as reason, are made constantly. Political pressure, personality, and family influences are played up . . .[64]

Despite the recurrent rumors of bribery in connection with the issuance of pardons at that time, no clear-cut evidence has ever been offered that money actually changed hands. A prominent student of the Ferguson era wrote a number of years later, "In my opinion no pardons were sold."[65] The allegations resulted, however, in the reform program of Governor Dan Moody, who recommended that the Legislature create a Board of Pardons and Paroles to be composed of three persons appointed by the governor for six-year, overlapping terms with "duties such as the governor may direct and as are consistent with the Constitution."[66] Moody's suggestions planted the seed of the idea.

[61] Nalle, *The Fergusons of Texas*, pp. 186–196.

[62] Interview of the writer with Ghent Sanderford, secretary to Governor Miriam A. Ferguson, in Austin, June 8, 1961.

[63] *Ibid.*

[64] MacCorkle, "The Pardoning Power in Texas," *Southwestern Social Science Quarterly*, XV (December, 1934), 227.

[65] Letter from Ralph W. Steen to Ghent Sanderford, dated April 25, 1955, furnished the writer by Mr. Sanderford.

[66] *Vernon's Annotated Civil and Criminal Statutes, State of Texas* (1929), Art. 6203.

From this beginning the proposal for a Board of Pardons and Paroles gained momentum. When James V. Allred campaigned for office in 1934, he proposed a constitutional amendment removing to a reorganized board much of the power formerly exercised by the governor. Allred's plan, adopted by the voters in 1936, called for a Board of Pardons and Paroles to be composed of three persons, one to be appointed by the governor, a second to be chosen by the chief justice of the Supreme Court, and another to be selected by the presiding judge of the Court of Criminal Appeals. Under the terms of the amendment, the governor, on recommendation of the Board of Pardons and Paroles, may grant pardons, reprieves, and commutations of punishment, and may remit fines and forfeitures. On his own initiative he may grant one reprieve, not to exceed thirty days, in a capital case and may revoke paroles and conditional pardons. With legislative approval, he may grant clemency in cases of treason.[67]

In evaluating the amendment many years later, its sponsor, James V. Allred—then a federal district judge—commented that it had been highly successful in operation, and said that although there might have been abuses, they were not as serious or as often as when the power was in the hands of the governor alone. Allred said:

> Strangely enough, while I had criticized the Fergusons for their abuse of the pardon power, I instituted a merit system which was carried out pretty faithfully and turned out more people (most of them on revocable parole, however) than had the Fergusons. . . . of the thousands thus discharged only one thereafter committed a really serious crime . . .[68]

He added that he was prouder of that particular reform than of any other action that occurred during his administration.

Since the adoption of this amendment the governor's powers have been drastically reduced and considerable pressure has been removed, much to the relief of most incumbents. Nevertheless, the executive still must decide each year whether some seven to ten persons will live or die.[69] And although the procedure eliminated some of the solo decisions of the governor, it did not reduce the total number of clemencies that have to be handled through the chief executive's office. In fact, the number has continued to mount.[70] Statistics from

[67] Constitution of Texas, Art. 4, Sec. 11.

[68] Robert R. Martindale, "James V. Allred, the Centennial Governor of Texas" (unpublished M.A. thesis), p. 66. The quotation is from an interview Mr. Martindale had with Judge Allred.

[69] *Austin American*, September 20, 1947.

[70] Interview of the writer with John Goldsum, administrative assistant to Governor Daniel, June 21, 1961, in Austin.

1960 show that the details of clemency function are time-consuming, the recent practice being to have one clerk assigned solely to perform the attendant clerical work. A total of 9,101 clemency actions were passed upon in 1960. Actions taken are shown in Table 7.

Clemency power ultimately resides with the governor. Although he may not grant clemency on his own except for one thirty-day reprieve, he is not required to grant clemency even if it is recommended by the Board of Pardons and Paroles. He also has the authority to grant a lesser degree of clemency than that recommended by the Board.[71] As a matter of policy, however, recent governors have tended to follow more or less routinely the recommendations made to them, for clemency is a responsibility which most governors would prefer not to possess. Governor Shivers is said to have avoided talking to anyone about clemency if he could do so. He preferred having a staff member handle such interviews on his behalf.[72]

TABLE 7

Clemency Actions Passed upon by the Governor of Texas in 1960

Full Pardons	119
Conditional Pardons	83
Paroles	2,890
Reinstatement of Paroles	40
Revocation of Paroles	618
Commutations of Sentence	62
Emergency Reprieves	384
Death Cases	6
Thirty-day Commutations (Blood-donor Cases)	4,864
Miscellaneous	34
Total	9,101

Source: Memorandum to Governor Price Daniel from the Board of Pardons and Paroles, January, 1961. Made available to the writer by John Goldsum, administrative assistant to the Governor.

In expressing his views on the pardon power, Governor Price Daniel probably voiced the attitude of most recent executives in a television interview.

I like to be divested of powers that can be handled best by someone else, instead of gathering them under me. A perfect illustration of too much

[71] *Ex Parte Lefors,* 303 S.W. (2d) 394 (1957).
[72] Interview with Weldon Hart, executive secretary to Governor Shivers, in Austin, July 15, 1961.

power in the governor's hands was the old laws where the governor could grant a pardon or parole to anyone he wanted to. And you know there were a lot of scandals under it. Politicians come in who have supported the governor, he hates to turn down a friend—a lot of politics and some bribes got into pardons and paroles in days gone by. So Governor Allred recommended a constitutional provision that a Board of Pardons and Paroles be set up so that the governor could not grant a pardon or parole without recommendation by the Board. Now I like that because it means that those three members have the responsibility of hearing all the evidence. They are not running for office, and I like for them to come up with recommendations; then if I think they have made good recommendations, I follow them. But in no event can I let someone out of the Penitentiary without that recommendation from the Board. And I like that![73]

So, apparently, do most others charged with final clemency responsibility.

THE GOVERNOR'S MILITARY POWERS

One of the oldest traditional powers associated with executive officers is that of being commander in chief of the military forces within their respective domains. According to Blackstone, such power lay with the English kings, and in due course the idea was transplanted to America.[74] State constitutions, therefore, customarily provide that the governor shall be the commander in chief of the state's militia, just as the President of the United States heads the armed forces of the United States. In the twentieth century this military power of governors has probably been used most to expedite handling of outbreaks arising out of industrial antagonism, such as strikes, riots, or labor disturbances.[75]

Every organic law under which Texas has functioned as a governmental entity has contained a provision placing the chief executive in command of the state militia. From the early frontier days, when the Texas Volunteers (later called the State Militia) furnished their own muskets and powder horns, the forces grew increasingly larger. During World War I, the United States Congress passed the National Guard Act, under which the national government made financial contributions for the support of state militias. Thereafter called the Texas National Guard, by the mid-1950's the militia had expanded to

[73] Daniel–University of Houston television interview.
[74] *Vernon's Texas Constitution*, I. Interpretive comment on p. 794.
[75] Sarah A. Llewellyn, "Martial Law in Texas" (unpublished M.A. thesis), p. 14.

an authorized strength of some 25,000 men, composing an Infantry Division, an Armored Division, an Armored Cavalry Regiment, an Artillery Corps Headquarters, and three separate company-size non-divisional units in the Army National Guard. The Air National Guard included a Fighter Interceptor Wing Headquarters, a Fighter Interceptor Group, and a Maintenance Supply Group.[76]

In discharging his military role, the governor of Texas operates through a state adjutant general, whom he appoints as his military aide and adviser. He also prescribes regulations for organization, appoints officers, and issues orders concerning the conduct of the Guard.[77] As its commander in chief, the militia is subject to the orders of the governor at all times except when called into the service of the United States.[78] To provide an additional reservoir of military strength, the Texas State Guard Reserve Corps was organized as a volunteer military organization, subject to call by the governor for special duty either independently of or supplementary to the National Guard and regular law enforcement officers. Essentially an internal security force, in 1959 the Texas State Guard Reserve Corps had a total authorized strength of 10,000.[79]

Probably the most significant aspect of the governor's military role is the possibility of its being used as a means of assisting him in seeing that the laws are faithfully executed. Charged with such responsibility by the Texas Constitution, the governor

shall have power to call forth the militia to execute the laws of the State, to suppress insurrections, repel invasions, and protect the frontier from hostile incursions by Indians or other predatory bands.[80]

This authorization is generally presumed to carry with it the right to declare and administer martial law in order to fulfill the express purposes enumerated.[81] Although martial law is not specifically mentioned in the Constitution or laws of the state, the governor has been declared to possess the power by both the courts and the attorney general of Texas.

---

[76] *Annual Report of the Adjutant General of Texas, Fiscal Year Ending August 31, 1956*, p. 3.
[77] *Revised Civil Statutes of Texas*, Arts. 5781, 5783.
[78] *Ex Parte Daily*, 246 S.W. 91 (1922).
[79] *Report of the Adjutant General of Texas, Fiscal Year Ending August 31, 1959*, p. 33.
[80] Constitution of Texas, Art. IV, Sec. 7.
[81] Llewellyn, "Martial Law in Texas" (unpublished M.A. thesis), pp. 23–24.

In litigation arising out of Governor Hobby's declaration of martial law in Galveston in 1920 (because of a longshoremen's strike), the Federal District Court, Southern District of Texas, upheld the declaration and the right of the executive to suspend certain civil officers and set up military officers in their place.[82] A few weeks later a state court declared:

The governor has the constitutional right to proclaim martial law when it is required for the enforcement of the law. He is the exclusive judge of the existence of such conditions as make this necessary. This is a political and not a juridical question.[83]

In 1939, the attorney general ruled that

the Governor is empowered by the Constitution to declare martial law for the purpose of executing the provisions of the law involved and for the purpose of suppressing or preventing any insurrection against such law.[84]

MARTIAL LAW FROM 1917 TO 1931

Since the chief executive possesses the power to invoke martial law, of what value has the power been to him in carrying out his function of law enforcement? According to General Jacob F. Wolters of the Texas National Guard, who has the distinction of having administered more martial law zones than any other Texan in history, "Martial law . . . constitutes the State's last weapon of defense *against an enemy which cannot be dealt with otherwise. Rare, indeed, are the occasions when it must be used*" [italics mine].[85]

He further observed:

The history of Texas attests that martial law has never been declared in a normal, peaceful, quiet spot. But when organized criminals flout the law; when those officers sworn to uphold and enforce the law become members of a criminal ring; when citizens fear to testify in open court but live in terror of the assassin's cowardly bullet that flies by night, martial law must be declared and enforced.[86]

As General Wolters indicated, the governors of Texas have used martial law sparingly. Perhaps this restraint is explainable by the

[82] *United States* v. *Wolters,* 268 Fed. 69 (1920).
[83] *A. P. Norman* v. *W. P. Hobby,* Fifty-sixth District Court of Texas, August 10, 1920.
[84] Attorney General of Texas, Opinion No. 0–308, dated February 9, 1939.
[85] Jacob F. Wolters, *Martial Law and Its Administration,* p. 27.
[86] *Ibid.*

nature of the power. In a thorough legal analysis, B. F. Looney, the attorney general of Texas (1918–1920), ruled that the power of martial law is primarily a legislative power and that the governor can declare and use it only in a qualified sense.[87] Although he may have called out the militia, the governor is really acting in a civil capacity in seeing that the civil laws of the state are executed.[88] Furthermore, according to a court ruling in 1923, martial law can exist and military power be exercised over property of the citizen only when the civil arm of the government is powerless because of invasion, insurrection, or anarchy. When the necessity ceases, the military power must end.[89]

Although used frequently during the days of the Republic of Texas and early statehood, the power of martial law then lapsed and was not utilized by a governor for many years. Once its use was resumed, however, it became a popular device for coping with emergency situations during the twenties and early thirties. Every occupant of the executive chair between 1915 and 1933, with the exception of Mrs. Ferguson, used it at least once.

The first declaration of martial law under the present Constitution did not occur until August 24, 1917, when, on the day before he was suspended in impeachment proceedings, Governor James E. Ferguson placed the city of Houston under martial law as the result of an outbreak of racial strife between white persons and Negroes during the erection of Camp Logan for the United States Army. The tension subsided within a few hours, but due to the press of more urgent matters, the new Governor, W. P. Hobby, who had become chief executive when Ferguson was suspended, never revoked the declaration. This first use of martial law in Texas in the twentieth century evoked very little comment.[90]

In July, 1919, martial law was proclaimed in Longview, in the far eastern part of the state, to restore order following a race riot, and in September of the same year it was used in portions of Nueces, Aransas, and San Patricio Counties, along the Gulf Coast, which had been struck by a tidal wave. In 1920 Governor Hobby declared Galveston to be under martial law when a longshoremen's strike threatened to paralyze the city's docks. During the four months that the city was

---

[87] Attorney General of Texas, *Biennial Report 1918–1920*, p. 668.
[88] *Ibid.*, p. 676.
[89] *Rose Mfg. Co.* v. *Western Union Telegraph Co.*, Civ. App. 251 S.W. 337 (1923).
[90] Llewellyn, "Martial Law in Texas" (unpublished M.A. thesis), pp. 31–32.

under military rule, Governor Hobby found it necessary also to suspend the Corporation Court and to institute another in its place—an action upheld by the Federal District Court.[91]

Early in 1922 Governor Pat M. Neff used the military for approximately two months in Limestone and Freestone Counties to quell the lawlessness which accompanied the oil boom in Mexia. No sooner had that situation quieted than Neff was forced into declaring martial law to maintain order in Denison, Grayson County, during a railway strike.[92] Neff's action was prompted by the threat of the United States Secretary of War to dispatch federal troops if the state failed to act. In the proclamation, the Governor stated: "It is of prime importance that the State should preserve its sovereignty, and without the necessity of federal intervention protect the life and insure the property rights of her citizens."[93] Following that, seven years passed before Governor Dan Moody declared martial law in the Borger oil boom in 1929. Declaring that Hutchinson County was being run by a criminal gang, he kept military troops on the scene for a month. In 1931 Governor Ross Sterling sent soldiers to Sherman, Grayson County, for ten days when a mob, erupting because of a rape case involving a Negro, burned down the courthouse.[94]

Between 1917 and 1931, therefore, martial law was used more frequently than during any other period in Texas history. Of the eight times it was invoked, three instances involved race trouble, two were brought about by labor troubles, two quieted periods of lawlessness, and one coped with a storm disaster. The duration of martial law ran from three days to four months, and, according to the findings of one student of the subject, its use was "always successful."[95]

MARTIAL LAW IN THE EAST TEXAS OIL FIELDS

The longest and most publicized period of martial law in Texas history occurred in the East Texas oil fields, when on August 17, 1931, Governor Ross Sterling proclaimed an emergency in Rusk, Gregg, Smith, and Upshur Counties.[96] Sterling's action was the culmination of a series of events that had built up over the months since

[91] *United States* v. *Wolters*, 268 Fed. 69 (1920).
[92] *Report of the Adjutant General of Texas, Biennium 1921–1922*, pp. 37–42.
[93] Proclamation Number 249, dated July 24, 1922.
[94] *Dallas Morning News*, May 13, 1931.
[95] Llewellyn, "Martial Law in Texas" (unpublished M.A. thesis), p. 79.
[96] The most thorough analysis of the situation is found in Warner E. Mills, Jr., *Martial Law in East Texas* (Inter-University Case Program No. 53). The facts contained here were taken from Mr. Mills' case study.

the Great Depression struck the oil industry in 1929. On October 3, 1930, the first "gusher" was brought in to mark the beginning of a vast new oil field—the largest discovered in the world up to that time. The rapid development of the field so greatly increased the production of oil that prices slumped steadily, and it became apparent that some governmental action would be desirable to eliminate unnecessary waste.

In March, 1931, Governor Sterling proposed to the Texas Legislature that a new conservation commission be created—a suggestion which motivated the Railroad Commission, the regulatory body then responsible for the conservation of oil and gas, to issue orders for proration in the East Texas field. The Commission's action proved to be highly unpopular with many producers and resulted in a number of lawsuits.

When the price of oil dropped to ten cents a barrel in July, 1931, Governor Sterling called a special session of the Legislature and requested new conservation laws. Near the session's end a conference committee worked out a statute, adopted by both houses, authorizing the Railroad Commission to apply more stringent measures to prevent the waste of oil. The Commission was required, however, to post a notice for ten days and then to hold public hearings before issuing proration orders. New orders could not be effected until after such hearings. In the interim, while the Commission was preparing to move, oil was being produced at a rate in excess of one million barrels a day in the East Texas field—three times the allowable fixed by the Commission under the old law.[97] Conditions quickly grew worse, and a mass meeting of 1,500 oil men in Tyler petitioned Governor Sterling to declare martial law

to the end that the present enormous physical waste may be eliminated and huge loss to the State of Texas be prevented and that life and property may be safe during this hiatus of the conservation law of the State and that said martial law be maintained and oil production completely shut down before and during the reasonable period necessary to put into effect the new order under the new law.[98]

Faced with this appeal and a report from an aide whom he had dispatched to the scene, Sterling made a hasty decision on August 15, 1931, to accede to the wishes of the citizens. He was assured by a

[97] *Ibid.*, p. 24.
[98] *Ibid.*, pp. 24–25.

delegation that violence was imminent unless he acted. Within a two-hour period, he prepared to move into the area because he believed the production of oil in excess of the maximum allowed by the Railroad Commission to be wasteful and immoral; he chose to use what he conceived to be his only means of coping with the situation—the declaration of martial law.

In the words of Professor Warner E. Mills, Jr., "The key to Sterling's use of martial law lies in his confusion of policy and law and of morality and law."[99] The Governor's proclamation recited the state's policy of conservation and the facts, as presented to him, of the possibility "of an organized and entrenched group of producers . . . who were in a state of insurrection against conservation laws . . . and in open rebellion against the efforts of the constituted civil authorities . . . to enforce such laws."[100] He asserted that these conditions had angered citizens and provoked threats that they would enforce the conservation laws if the state were unable to do so. In summary, he said, the situation amounted to a state of insurrection, tumult, riot, and breach of the peace, and with imminent danger of intensification.

Sterling placed the veteran administrator of martial law zones, General Jacob F. Wolters, in command, and shortly thereafter 1,192 military personnel moved into the district.[101] Martial law, which operated at a cost of approximately $4,383 a day, avowedly was declared to prevent riots and insurrections of people who objected to having the wells run wide open. In reality, it was declared to control the situation until the Railroad Commission could promulgate orders; afterwards it was left in force to carry out these orders. Its effect, however, was to fix prices.[102] One chronicler has said:

> When an injunction was issued to restrain the Railroad Commission from enforcing its orders, the Governor took over the duties of the Commission and acted not only as chief executive but as law giver as well. In practice, then, troops were used to enforce the allowables fixed by the Governor himself.[103]

On October 13, 1931, a case was brought in the Federal District

---

[99] Warner E. Mills, Jr., "The Public Career of a Texas Conservative: A Biography of Ross Shaw Sterling" (unpublished Ph.D. dissertation), p. 167.

[100] *Dallas Morning News*, August 18, 1931. "Insurrection" apparently was used in the popular sense in the proclamation rather than in the technical sense.

[101] Llewellyn, "Martial Law in Texas" (unpublished M.A. thesis), p. 90.

[102] *Ibid.*, p. 110.

[103] *Ibid.*, p. 111.

Court for an injunction to halt temporarily the enforcement of proration orders. In granting the injunction, the Court ruled that the Governor had exceeded his authority in declaring martial law initially and that he had been without warrant of law in interfering with and depriving the plaintiffs of their right to operate their properties in a prudent way.[104] Inasmuch as the courts had never previously reviewed the propriety of a governor's use of the military, Sterling appealed to the United States Supreme Court. In the meantime, however, the end of martial law came rapidly, with the Railroad Commission taking over the regulation of the oil fields once more.

The Supreme Court ruled against the Governor, upholding the decision of the Federal District Court.[105] A comparison of the decisions by the two courts reveals somewhat different concepts of the Governor's authority to invoke martial law.

The two courts agreed that Sterling's actions in administering the affairs of the oil field amounted to a deprivation of plaintiffs' property without due process of law. They agreed that the Governor's findings of fact could not be binding on the federal courts and could not preclude them from reviewing and determining the facts for themselves. But the District Court went out of its way to rule on Sterling's authority under the Constitution and statutes of Texas to declare martial law. This the Supreme Court refused to do, and, in refusing to do so, the Supreme Court undercut that part of the District Court's opinion. The District Court likewise went to great lengths to show that the declaration of martial law had been unnecessary, given the conditions in East Texas. While not disavowing the opinion of the District Court in this respect, the Supreme Court put the burden of its opinion on the lack of necessity to maintain martial law after the initial declaration. The Supreme Court opinion evidenced a greater sympathy for the heavy burdens of state governments than did the opinion of the District Court.[106]

This case was particularly significant in bringing about recognition that the state chief executive is vested with discretion in determining whether an emergency requiring military aid in executing the laws has arisen, and that his decision upon such a matter is conclusive. Nevertheless, it was held that his judgment of measures necessary to suppress violence and restore order are not above judicial review. For

[104] *Constantin* v. *Smith,* 57 Fed. (2d) 236 (1932).
[105] *Sterling* v. *Constantin,* 53 S. Ct. 190 (1932).
[106] Mills, *Martial Law in East Texas,* p. 40.

the first time in history, the courts looked behind a governor's proclamation of martial law.[107] Although defeated for re-election, Sterling, in retrospect, commented, "I have no apology for martial law in East Texas. It saved the state $6 million in taxes, and it saved the people of Texas $40 million in the value of their products."[108]

MARTIAL LAW SINCE 1931

Since Sterling's administration the use of martial law in Texas has been infrequent and almost inconsequential. Governor Allred invoked it in March, 1937, to cope with an emergency arising out of the gas explosion which obliterated the New London School.[109] Governor O'Daniel, alleging possible physical combat and bloodshed would result from enforcement of the law which limited trucks to a weight of 7,000 pounds, toyed with the idea of invoking martial law to permit the orderly movement of perishable fruits and vegetables out of the Rio Grande Valley. He was quickly informed by the attorney general that he had no power to suspend the laws in such matters, since that action could be taken only by the Legislature.[110] O'Daniel subsequently abandoned the idea.

Most recently, martial law was declared in Beaumont in 1943 by Senator A. M. Aikin, Jr., who was acting governor during the absence from the state of both the governor and lieutenant governor. With the full approval of Governor Coke Stevenson, and at the request of officials in the area, Aikin used the military to quell a race riot. His action averted further incidents, and the order was withdrawn shortly. A headline carried by one newspaper appropriately summarized the situation: "MARTIAL LAW EXCEPTION NOT RULE FOR TEXAS."[111]

Twenty years have passed since martial law was last declared in Texas. Whether the findings of the courts in the Sterling case caused later executives to proceed with more caution or whether the threat of martial law remains a "gun behind the door" which spurs local officials into taking care of local conditions more adequately than they formerly did may not be determinable. However, it is probably true that recent governors have had more facilities to cope with situations

---

[107] Llewellyn, "Martial Law in Texas" (unpublished M.A. thesis), p. 103.
[108] Mills, *Martial Law in East Texas*, p. 41.
[109] *Report of the Adjutant General of Texas, Biennium 1937–1938*, p. 23.
[110] Attorney General of Texas, Opinion o–308, dated February 9, 1939.
[111] *The State Observer*, June 21, 1943.

once dealt with by martial law. For example, the Civil Defense and Disaster Relief organization may now obviate the use of the military in many emergencies. Even more important is the ability of the governor to order the greatly enlarged force of the famed Texas Rangers into situations which once would have demanded the use of the military.[112]

Perhaps the modern governor's attitude toward the use of the military was best summarized by former Governor Allan Shivers who said, "The military power of the governor, specifically martial law, should be reserved for genuine emergencies."[113] Happily, such genuine emergencies seem to have diminished in frequency.

Ex-Officio Duties

In addition to duties as head of state and representative of state government, as a major influence in international relations with Mexico, as a dispenser of clemency, and as commander in chief of the state militia, the governor of Texas is charged with a number of ex-officio duties. While the chief executive is not an ex-officio member of as many boards as are some other elected officials, and although his responsibility for ex-officio duties has been lessened somewhat in recent years, the governor of Texas still finds that he is burdened with enough such duties.

Commenting upon the ex-officio responsibilities of the office, former Governor Allan Shivers said:

These are too great a burden, by far, upon the Governor, who could readily spend virtually all his time attending ex-officio board meetings. This is an anomaly in the Texas setup: While in general policy matters and vital administrative functions the Texas Governor has responsibility without authority, in the case of the vast detail work of the ex-officio boards he has authority without the time to exercise proper responsibility. This type of board should be replaced by an appointive board.[114]

A compilation of ex-officio boards in 1962 revealed that the Governor directly participated in the following:[115]

---

[112] *Neff* v. *Elgin*, Civ. App. 270 S.W. 873 (1925).
[113] Interview with former Governor Allan Shivers in Austin, December 4, 1961.
[114] Shivers–University of Houston television interview.
[115] Compiled from Texas Legislative Council and Institute of Public Affairs, The University of Texas, *A Guide to Texas State Agencies* and *1960 Supplement* thereto. See also *Texas Almanac, 1961–1962*, pp. 363–372.

Organization and Year Established	Number of Members	Composed of
State Board of Canvassers (1897)	3	Governor, Attorney General, Secretary of State
Board to Calculate the Ad Valorem Tax Rate (1907)	3	Governor, Comptroller, Treasurer
Board to Approve Contracts for Fuel and Public Printing (1876)	3	Governor, Secretary of State, Comptroller
School Land Board (1939)	3	Governor, Commissioner of the General Land Office, Attorney General
Commission on Interstate Co-Operation (1941)	18	Governor, Lieutenant Governor, Speaker of the House, five members of the Senate Committee on Interstate Co-Operation; five members of House Committee on Interstate Co-Operation; five members of the Governor's Committee on Interstate Co-Operation
State Building Commission (1955)	3	Governor (chairman), Attorney General, Chairman of Board of Control
State Planning Committee (1953)	18	Governor, Lieutenant Governor, Speaker of the House, and five members appointed by each
Committee on State Revenue Estimates (1959)	3	Governor, Director of Legislative Budget Board, State Auditor
Texas Traffic Safety Council Executive Committee (1957)	6	Governor (chairman), Director of Department of Public Safety, State Highway Engineer, Attorney General, Commissioner of Education, Commissioner of Public Welfare
Texas Development Board (1959)	3	Governor, Chairman of Texas Highway Commission, Chairman of Texas Industrial Commission

In addition to the above agencies, the governor's advice and counsel may be sought by numerous other groups in the myriad of state administrators. Obviously, such duties demand a considerable amount of the executive's time and energy, and it would seem desirable to free him of at least some of these duties to enable him to devote more attention to matters of greater importance. As a former attorney general has written, service on ex-officio boards contributes to "a bureaucrat's dilemma."[116] The multiplicity of the governor's responsibilities would seem to support such a contention.

[116] John Ben Sheppard, *A Bureaucrat's Dilemma: Ex-Officio Boards.*

PART THREE

The Governor and the Legislature

7

The Governor and the Legislature: The Veto

THE CHANGING NATURE OF LEGISLATIVE-EXECUTIVE RELATIONS

The multifold changes wrought by time and usage upon the American governmental system have been remarkable—upon occasion ironic—and the relations between the legislative and executive branches have been no exception. Developments in legislative-executive relationships have tended, in fact, to undermine a principle of American political theory as old as the government itself—the separation of powers.

As originally conceived by the founders of the federal government, all functions of government were divided among three separate and distinct branches—legislative, executive, and judicial—each of which operated within its own sphere without much regard for the other branches save in those instances where the Constitution provided for "checks and balances." Such separation was provided for in the national Constitution, and it was included in most early state constitutions in America. Because of the many bitter experiences of the colonists with arbitrary royal governors, however, the citizenry of the original states began to agree with James Madison that the legislative branch should be "omnipotent." In such a role the lawmaking body was expected to make public policy through the enactment of appropriate statutes after thorough discussion by duly elected representatives of the people. The prime function of the executive was to sit in his office and wait until laws were passed, then execute them. His veto power was considered at that time to be chiefly a device through which he could protect against encroachments upon his domain.[1]

[1] Kirk H. Porter, *State Administration*, p. 49.

So much confidence was placed by the practitioners of government in the doctrines of separation of powers and legislative supremacy that even a century later, the well-known Englishman James Bryce was able to observe that while the governor of an American state was "not yet a nonentity," the legislature was "so much the strongest force in the several states that we may almost call it the Government and ignore all other authorities."[2] Even as his words were being penned, however, attitudes in America on the matter of executive-legislative relationships were undergoing a fundamental reorientation, and only two decades later one of the nation's leading scholarly journals reported that the overshadowing position of the legislative branch (coupled with some abuses on the part of individual members) had created a popular distrust for representative assemblies—a situation then labelled as "one of the most striking political phenomena of the present day."[3] The writer continued:

True reform towards real democratic state government lies not in the direction of the popular nostrums, [the initiative and the referendum], but in the direction of the increasing control of the governor over the state's legislative product. . . . The increasing influence of the governor over legislation is the comparatively new role which he is now beginning to play, and which, in its relation to popular control of government, bids fair to become *one of the most important developments in the history of the state governments.*[4] (Italics mine)

The turn of events has proved this prognosis to be almost completely accurate. Indeed the readjustment of executive-legislative relationships that has come about in the past half-century has resulted almost without exception in increased functioning of the governor in policy making. An outstanding public executive, Theodore Roosevelt, noted this trend in his *Autobiography:*

In theory the Executive has nothing to do with legislation. In practice, as things are now, the Executive is or ought to be peculiarly representative of the people as a whole. As often as not the action of the Executive offers the only means by which the people can get the legislation they demand and ought to have. . . . More than half of my work as Governor was in the direction of getting needed and important legislation.[5]

[2] James Bryce, *The American Commonwealth,* I, 532, 534.
[3] John M. Mathews, "The New Role of the Governor," *American Political Science Review,* VI (May, 1912), 220.
[4] *Ibid.,* p. 221.
[5] Page 282.

Led by Governor Frank Lowden in 1917, the state of Illinois initiated the Administrative Reorganization Movement, which was designed to make the governor an executive in fact as well as in name. An accompanying result was that the governor became a spokesman for the people as well as for the state administration, emerging as the formulator of a comprehensive legislative program. Other states joined in the movement for reorganization, and even in those states not undergoing administrative reorganization, the impact was felt and the governor began to offer more leadership in policy formulation because of the ineptitude of legislatures to deal with the increasingly complex problems of the day. By the 1930's it had become commonplace for textbooks to refer to the governor as "chief legislator" of the state.[6] Executive officials began to draft legislation for introduction by members of the Houses, causing one observer to conclude that

lawmaking bodies are not only delegating their power to make legislative decisions in many of the bills they enact, but they are allowing other forces and agencies to dictate, or at least to suggest in large measure, what bills they shall consider and what the bills contain.[7]

Obviously this modification has done violence to the original separation-of-powers concept, but apparently it has met with favorable response from the public.[8]

This new legislative-executive relationship has become ingrained in the American system of government, being recognized within the past decade by the Committee on American Legislatures of the American Political Science Association—a group composed of some of the most eminent political scientists of modern times. In the words of the Committee:

The preparation and initiation of legislation is no longer the exclusive prerogative of the legislature itself, though final decision rests with that body. The last two generations have witnessed a remarkable increase in the role of the chief executive and the administrative agencies in the legislative process. Early in the twentieth century, the governor emerged as state-wide representative and spokesman of the people, the majority political or party leader, and the chief legislator. The state administration,

---

[6] See, for example, Arthur N. Holcombe, *State Government in the United States.*

[7] O. Douglas Weeks, "Initiation of Legislation by Administrative Agencies," *Brooklyn Law Review*, IX (January, 1940), 117.

[8] Porter, *State Administration*, p. 50.

as it has been subsequently expanded, has become a principal source of legislative proposals.

. . . Realistic students have recognized that the formulation of public policy is essentially an indivisible process that should be shared by both the legislature and the administration. . . . The fundamental problem is, therefore, not only that of rendering the legislature more effective in taking its part, but of bridging the gap created by the separation-of-powers system and of producing greater harmony between legislative and executive departments.[9]

One political scientist, a former lieutenant governor of Vermont, describes the change that has taken place as being inevitable. He believes that the governor cannot escape being chief legislator whether he likes the role or not, because it is he who is held responsible by the people for the success or failure of a program. As a political figure he stands or falls not by his administrative ability but by his legislative program. His position, though he is not a member as such of the legislature, makes him in fact the only lawmaker who has the entire state as his constituency; consequently, "on most broad issues of policy, the legislators are inclined to follow the governor's leadership, knowing that he is not only the spokesman for the entire state, but the man whom their constituents elected."[10]

One may conclude that today's legislatures are "not now the agencies which formulate legislative proposals [but that they] merely ratify or reject them, with or without revision."[11] Professor Harvey Walker calls the modern relationship of the legislature vis-à-vis the governor "strange," but he believes that it is the result of many factors. He feels the governor wields more influence because of his more prominent position, which is due to:

(1) his uniqueness as the head of the executive branch, which makes him a prime source of news; (2) his power of veto (which one state has had the fortitude to deny); (3) his power to send messages to the legislature and to secure wide publicity for his recommendations; (4) his exclusive power to convene special sessions (which should never have been permitted to slip out of legislative hands) and even to determine the agenda for such sessions (a lamentable violation of separation of powers as well as a denial of wholesome legislative independence); (5) his power

---

[9] Belle Zeller (ed.), *American State Legislatures*, pp. 163–164.

[10] Robert S. Babcock, *State and Local Government and Politics*, p. 208.

[11] O. Douglas Weeks, *Research in the American State Legislative Process*, p. 43.

of appointment to executive posts, which may be used to influence legislative action or inaction; and (6) his power to initiate the budget estimates (which few legislatures are equipped to examine with care and discrimination). . . . A considerable number of constitutional changes would seem to be desirable if the office of governor is to be confined to reasonable proportions in its relation to the legislative branch.[12]

Methods of leadership available to the governor may be put into two broad categories: (1) constitutional and statutory functions (including use of the veto power, transmitting of official messages, and the calling of special sessions of the legislature), and (2) extralegal methods (including the "organization" of the legislature by the governor, dispensing patronage, utilizing the prestige of the office, making personal appeals, exercising influence of the governor as party chieftain, and recalling custom or tradition).[13] The foregoing methods are available to some extent to most governors, but the value of each of them varies considerably in practice.

THE TEXAS LEGISLATURE

Before legislative-executive relationships can be appreciated fully in any given state, a general knowledge of the peculiarly local conditions must be surveyed. Therefore, a brief description of the arena in which these relationships occur in Texas is in order.

The Texas Legislature, easily "the most heterogeneous governmental organization in the state,"[14] is composed of 181 members representing "all ages and degrees of maturity, many grades of experience, and nearly every school of thought."[15] Through the years members have come from practically every occupation, business, or profession, but, in the main, lawyers have predominated, with one-third to one-half of the members usually having had legal training. The second largest group is normally composed of farmers, stockmen, and ranchers—about 12 per cent of the total membership.[16] In 1959, for example, the Fifty-sixth Legislature numbered among its members 88 lawyers, 24 ranchers and farmers, 21 persons in various fields of business, 8 persons each in teacher and student categories,

---

[12] Harvey Walker, "The Legislature Today," *National Civic Review*, XLIX (November, 1960), 533–534.
[13] Coleman B. Ransone, *The Office of Governor in the South*, p. 70.
[14] Stuart A. MacCorkle and Dick Smith, *Texas Government* (4th ed.), p. 44.
[15] *Ibid.*
[16] *Ibid.*, p. 45.

and representatives of a diversity of other occupations.[17] The majority are usually in their forties and fifties, but there are many "bright young men"—who may be expected to become the leaders of tomorrow. Compared with the population as a whole, a rather high percentage of the members have had some college or university training.[18]

The Texas Senate, which must confirm gubernatorial appointments, is composed of 31 members elected for four-year terms from districts created according to the number of qualified voters, with the restriction that no county may have more than one senator. In the House of Representatives, where revenue bills must originate, population is the basis of representation.[19] The 150 members are chosen for two-year terms from three types of districts: 84 come from single-member districts, 5 from flotorial districts, and 61 from sixteen multi-member districts composed of urban counties. The latter districts elect from 2 to 8 representatives each, according to a place system.[20] No county may have more than 7 representatives unless its population exceeds 700,000, and then only one representative is allowed for each 100,000 people in excess of 700,000.[21] These constitutional provisions insure that the Texas Legislature, unlike comparable bodies in many states, will be dominated by the rural areas at the expense of the urban centers; and, unless overturned by judicial action, such conditions may continue for many years, for it is the Legislature which must propose amendments to the Constitution.[22] Beginning in 1961, the compensation for members was fixed at the rate of $4,800 per

[17] Institute of Public Affairs, The University of Texas, *The Texas Constitutional Amendments of 1960*, p. 32.

[18] MacCorkle and Smith, *Texas Government*, p. 45.

[19] Constitution of Texas, Art. III, Secs. 2 and 26.

[20] O. Douglas Weeks, "Toward a More Effective Legislature," *Texas Law Review*, 35 (October, 1957), 931.

[21] Constitution of Texas, Art. III, Sec. 26–a.

[22] *Ibid.*, Art. XVII. In April, 1962, the United States Supreme Court held the matter of apportionment of state legislatures to be covered by the "equal protection of the laws" clause of the Fourteenth Amendment to the United States Constitution. In the case of *Baker* v. *Carr* (82 S. Ct. 691 1962), the Court directed the state of Tennessee to draw new legislative districts in compliance with the state constitution, because the state had not been redistricted since 1900. In July, 1963, a Federal District Court in Oklahoma, admitting that it might be overstepping its authority, ordered that state's legislature to be reapportioned on the basis of population, as provided for in the state constitution. The day of rural predominance in state legislatures may therefore, by action of the judicial branch of government, be nearing an end.

annum with $12 per day for expenses for a maximum of 120 days in regular sessions and 30 days in special sessions.[23]

Because Texas is dominated by the Democratic Party, factionalism has developed and Party cohesion is weak.[24] Temporary combinations in the Legislature frequently result in throwing section against section, conservative against liberal, local interests against statewide interests, rural areas against urban areas, and administration supporters against antiadministration elements. "Logrolling" alignments often form, with the consequence that the Texas Legislature has been quite vulnerable to pressure politics. Many powerful lobbies operate in the state, and some highly publicized scandals have developed from "influence peddling."[25] For many years, members of the Legislature were routinely retained as lobbyists by various interest groups;[26] but in 1957 that situation was apparently rectified to some degree by the enactment of three laws: the Representation before State Agencies Act,[27] a Code of Ethics for State Employees,[28] and the Representation before the Legislature Act.[29]

The presiding officers of both houses occupy outstanding positions of power and influence in the legislative process.[30] In addition to possessing the usual prerogative of recognizing or refusing to recognize members desiring to speak, they also appoint all standing committees and designate chairmen thereof, and decide upon the committees to which bills are to be referred. The governor is obliged to work with the speaker of the House and the lieutenant governor if he hopes to succeed in pressing a particular program, with the result that in practice a close liaison ordinarily exists between the chief executive and the Legislature in Texas.

Within this one-party setting, where local issues are strong and national issues are weak, where pressure politics is strong and party cohesion is weak, where alignments on issues are shifting constantly,

[23] Amendment adopted in November, 1960, to Art. III, Sec. 24.

[24] Zeller (ed.), *American State Legislatures*, pp. 190, 209.

[25] Ronnie Dugger, "What Corrupted Texas?" *Harpers* (March, 1957), pp. 68–74.

[26] C. Perry Patterson, Sam B. McAlister, and George C. Hester, *State and Local Government in Texas* (3d ed.), p. 59.

[27] *General and Special Laws of Texas,* Fifty-fifth Legislature, first called session, Chap. 12.

[28] *Ibid.,* Fifty-fifth Legislature, regular session, Chap. 100.

[29] *Ibid.,* Fifty-fifth Legislature, first called session, Chap. 9.

[30] Patterson, McAlister, and Hester, *State and Local Government in Texas* (3d ed.), pp. 37–38.

and where presiding officers are all-powerful, the chief executive of Texas must give leadership if he is to fulfill his role of formulating a program. To be sure, the situation does not offer the most healthful environment for a thriving leadership role; but Texas governors have been successful enough to avoid being characterized as weak in political leadership—as have been governors in six of the eighteen one-party states of the Union.[31]

How then does a governor get on with his program? In Texas his formal relationships with the Legislature are clearly specified by the state Constitution. For purposes of discussion they may be considered in three aspects: the veto power, the message power, and the ability to call special sessions.

The Veto in the United States

The power to veto is supposed to be the most powerful of the constitutional devices for gubernatorial control of a legislature.[32] Taken from the Latin word meaning "I forbid," the veto can be traced to the power wielded by the tribune of the plebes in ancient Rome to annul or suspend acts of public authority. In America it is an adaptation of ancient British custom transplanted to the American colonies.[33] Its use was defended by no less a personage than Alexander Hamilton, in the formative days of the Republic, in these terms:

> It may perhaps be said that the power of preventing bad laws includes that of preventing good ones; and may be used to the one purpose as well as to the other. But this objection will have little weight with those who can properly estimate the mischiefs of that inconstancy and mutability in the laws, which form the greatest blemish in the character and genius of our governments. . . . The injury which may possibly be done by defeating a few good laws, will be amply compensated by the advantage of preventing a number of bad ones.[34]

Originally, except for Massachusetts and New York, the powers of the legislatures were so broad as not to be limited by the executive veto,[35] but Hamilton's defense did not fall on deaf ears, and by 1812

---

[31] Zeller (ed.), *American State Legislatures*, p. 210.

[32] L. V. Howard and John H. Fenton, *State Governments in the South: Functions and Problems*, p. 23.

[33] Marvin P. Baker, "The Executive Veto in Texas" (unpublished M.A. thesis), p. 9.

[34] Alexander Hamilton, James Madison, and John Jay, *The Federalist*, No. 73, p. 478.

[35] Paul S. Reinsch, *American Legislatures and Legislative Methods*, p. 129.

nearly one-half of the states had adopted the veto. By the beginning of the Civil War, the power had become firmly entrenched,[36] and today only the state of North Carolina does not provide it.[37]

James Bryce recognized the veto as a potent factor in executive hands, describing it thus:

> The veto may be overridden . . . but generally kills the measure, because if the bill is a bad one, it calls the attention of the people to the fact and frightens the legislature, whereas if the bill be an unobjectionable one, the governor's motive for vetoing it is probably a party motive, and the requisite overriding majority can seldom be secured in favor of a bill which either party dislikes. *The use of his veto is, in ordinary times, a governor's most serious duty, and by his discharge of it is he judged.*[38] (Italics mine.)

An analysis of the veto power, as exercised in American states, reveals that its potential began to be fully realized in the twentieth century and that today its power is formidable, with a trend developing toward strengthening it even more.[39] It may well be that the veto or threat of veto will become an even more potent factor in executive-legislative relations.

THE VETO IN TEXAS

Every state constitution under which Texas has operated has provided for the executive veto, and the power has been strengthened considerably on two occasions. Following the Civil War the governor was authorized to strike out items in appropriations bills, allowing the remainder of such measures to stand, and the Constitution of 1876 lengthened the period of time for the governor's consideration of bills and also permitted him to exercise the veto after adjournment of a legislative session.[40] Professor Frank Prescott has therefore

[36] Frank W. Prescott, "The Executive Veto in American States," *Western Political Quarterly*, III (March, 1950), 98.

[37] *The Book of the States, 1960–61*, p. 51.

[38] Bryce, *The American Commonwealth*, I, 496.

[39] Prescott, "The Executive Veto in American States," *Western Political Quarterly*, III (March, 1950), 112.

[40] Constitution of Texas, Art. IV, Sec. 14, provides the veto power. During the period in which the Legislature is in session, the governor has ten days, excluding Sundays, to act upon a bill sent to him. If he objects, he returns it to the house of origin along with a message stating his objections. Upon reconsideration the bill may be passed over the veto by a vote of two-thirds of the members present in both houses. Bills not so returned become law without the governor's signature. If the Legislature has adjourned, the governor has twenty days to consider; if he vetoes, he files a message with the secretary of state. If he does not veto, the bill becomes law; he does not possess the "pocket veto" as does the President of the United States.

178 *The Chief Executive in Texas*

classified Texas among those states having a strong veto power.[41] He has also noted that "A fairly good correlation can be observed between the states which have strong constitutional provisions on the subject and the frequency and firmness with which the veto has recently been exercised."[42]

Comparatively speaking, all governors of Texas have made effective use of the veto power.[43] Between the admission of Texas into the Union, in 1845, and the end of 1963, a total of 1,044 vetoes was recorded by the chief executives of this state. Of these, 853 occurred under the present Constitution. On only 51 occasions was the veto overridden by the necessary two-thirds vote of both houses; and more than one-half of these, 26, took place prior to 1876. The chief executives serving under the first five state constitutions (1845 to 1876) may have been freer in their exercise of the veto prerogative, but they were not sustained in it with as much frequency as their successors have been.[44] However, it should be remembered that these early governors were in office during the trying times of initial adjustment to statehood and, later, of adjustment to Reconstruction. They could not exercise the item veto until after 1866 and did not possess the right of veto after adjournment until after 1876.

VETOES UNDER THE CONSTITUTION OF 1876

In practice, the veto power probably has been one of the most valuable means of gubernatorial control of public policy in Texas since

[41] Prescott, "The Executive Veto in American States," *Western Political Quarterly*, III (March, 1950), 99.
[42] Frank W. Prescott, "The Executive Veto in Southern States," *Journal of Politics*, 10 (November, 1948), 675.
[43] Baker, "The Executive Veto in Texas" (unpublished M.A. thesis), p. 53.
[44] A thorough compilation of vetoes for the period 1845 to 1920 may be found in Baker, *ibid.*, pp. 68–69. Harold J. Marburger, a member of the staff of the Legislative Reference Service, Texas State Library, compiled the vetoes from 1931 (the beginning of the 120-day session) through the end of the Shivers administration in 1957. In mimeographed form, his work appears under the title "Veto Messages by the Governors of Texas, 1931–1957," containing page references to all messages filed during that period. (Hereafter cited as Marburger, "Veto Messages 1931–1957".) Data for the years 1921 to 1930 were compiled by this writer from *Journals* of the Texas Senate and House of Representatives for those years and from searching the records on file in the office of the secretary of state for vetoes filed after adjournment during that period. The writer also compiled comparable statistics covering the administration of Governor Price Daniel (1957–1963) and the first year of Governor John Connally's administration. By adding the compilations from these sources, a record of vetoes since statehood is readily acquired. Unless otherwise noted, statistics on the number of vetoes throughout this chapter are taken from this compilation.

1876. Two hundred ninety-six veto messages were sent to the Legislature from 1876 through 1963, and only 25, or 8.5 per cent, were overridden—a respectable "batting average" for the twenty-four governors. No doubt the governors' success in vetoing bills has been abetted greatly by their ability to reject bills after adjournment of the Legislature. In such an event the governor simply files a veto message with the secretary of state, and unless the bill is reintroduced at a subsequent session as a new bill, it cannot be considered again by the lawmakers. Over 60 per cent—557 out of 853—were handled in this way. That the Legislature did not have an opportunity to consider these vetoes was no fault of the governors but of the dilatory legislative procedure which necessitates a rush of bills during the closing days of a session. The effect is to strengthen greatly the veto power, as the governor has the final voice in such matters—at least until the next session. It would be difficult to estimate the number of bills vetoed after legislative adjournment that are reintroduced and passed by later sessions. Coke Stevenson, who served as presiding officer of both houses in the Texas Legislature and also as governor, believes that the number is negligible in this state.[45] This opinion was earlier expressed by one writer, who surveyed the question and reported:

It seems to be the general opinion of experienced legislators that instances are rare indeed in which vetoed bills are reintroduced and passed without first having undergone sufficient amendment to meet, or at least to compromise, the objections to the veto. The single factor which might serve to make such later passage of a vetoed bill possible, namely, a change of administration, serves but to illustrate the political and legislative nature of the present power of veto.[46]

The record of Texas governors in the use of the veto since Texas acquired statehood appears in Table 8.

WHY GOVERNORS VETO BILLS

The reasons given for vetoes are of utmost importance to an understanding of the prerogative. As has been pointed out, the original conception of the power was that the executive should be in a posi-

---

[45] Interview with former Governor Coke Stevenson at Junction, Texas, February 27, 1961.
[46] Glenn R. Negley, "The Executive Veto in Illinois," *American Political Science Review*, XXXIII (December, 1939), 1053.

TABLE 8

Vetoes during the Statehood of Texas, 1845–1963

Years	Total Vetoes	Vetoes after Adjourn-ment	Vetoes during Session	Vetoes Overridden	Percentage Overridden
1845–1875	191	——	191	26	15.2
1876–1920	298	181	117	7	2.35
1921–1930	213	179	34	6	2.82
1931–1963	342	197	145	12	3.63
Total	1,044	557	487	51	5.24 (avg.)

Source: Derived from compilation of data referred to in Note 44, this chapter.

tion to prevent encroachments upon his domain.[47] This notion was soon displaced with the idea that the governor should also be a protector of the public interest as well as of his own power. A nationwide study in 1950 revealed that for the preceding decade, the reason most often given by governors for exercising the veto on legislation was that the proposal would be against the best interests of public policy; the reason given next most often was that the law was unnecessary; and the third most-given reason was that of economy.[48]

An analysis of vetoes in Texas for the period 1845 to 1920 likewise emphasizes the importance of public policy as a reason for vetoes. The reasons given for the 489 vetoes during those years were classified as follows:[49]

Reasons for Veto	*Number of Times Recorded*
Against public policy	183
"Bad business"	143
Unconstitutional	142
Unnecessary	83
Defective wording	32
Miscellaneous	26
	——
	489

[47] Matthews, "The New Role of the Governor," *American Political Science Review*, VI (May, 1912), 220–221.

[48] Prescott, "The Executive Veto in the American States," *Western Political Quarterly*, III (March, 1950), 109.

[49] Baker, "The Executive Veto in Texas" (unpublished M.A. thesis), p. 54.

Since that study was completed, an additional 555 vetoes have been registered. Analysis of a sample of them reveals that considerations of public policy continue to be the predominant cause of rejection, that reasons of economy loomed large during the Depression of the thirties, and that Texas governors are more prone to veto for reasons of constitutionality than are governors of most states.[50] The explanation of this may lie in the fact that an overwhelming number of them were trained as lawyers.

Many instances may be cited in which the veto was necessitated by carelessness or procedural mistakes on the part of legislative officials. Not infrequently, duplicate bills are introduced in both houses, and two identical bills then wind up on the governor's desk.[51] At one time, Governor Miriam A. Ferguson vetoed eleven bills as unconstitutional "because they have not been signed by the Lieutenant Governor and the Speaker of the House of Representatives as required by the Constitution of Texas."[52] Occasionally, the Legislature has sent bills to the governor, only to pass a concurrent resolution shortly thereafter recalling the bill.[53]

An interesting mix-up occurred in the summer of 1963. The Fifty-eighth Legislature passed a bill revising the code of criminal procedure in the state for the first time in a number of years. When the bill reached the governor's desk, it was found that an erroneous working copy had been signed by the officials of the Senate and forwarded to the chief executive. After some verbal exchanges trying to fix the responsibility for the error, the sponsors of the bill called upon the governor to veto the incorrect bill which did not encompass the intent of the Legislature. In accordance with their wishes, Governor Connally killed the bill with his veto.

One cannot escape the conclusion that the exercise of the veto power has been a strong force in shaping public policy in Texas. Per-

---

[50] Although no attempt was made to read all the messages, a random sample was taken of five veto messages from each of the ten governors during the period 1920 to 1961. Those messages were vetoed for reasons of public policy, 22; economy, 9; unconstitutionality, 6; lack of necessity, 6; defective wording, 4; miscellaneous reasons, 3.

[51] For example, see *House Journal*, Fifty-fifth Legislature, regular session, p. 2197.

[52] *General Laws, Resolutions, and Vetoed Bills*, Thirty-ninth Legislature, first called session (pages not numbered). On file in office of secretary of state.

[53] *House Journal*, Forty-first Legislature, regular session, pp. 1344, 1345, and 1373.

haps an examination of several excerpts from typical messages will bring into clearer focus the import of the veto power.

So long as I am Governor, I shall treat this sugar bounty with derisive contempt. . . . Such a practice is a perversion of a fundamental principle in the maintenance of which alone can free institutions be preserved. (Governor James S. Hogg, Veto of a bill accepting a bounty offered the state by Congress, 1891)[54]

It is a very bad precedent to let the University have any money for their maintenance and support as long as the faculty approved and permitted students to undertake to intimidate and coerce and browbeat the Governor of the State and the Board of Regents. (Governor James E. Ferguson, Veto of appropriations for The University of Texas, 1917)[55]

I feel that if this bill was to become law that the sainted Jim Hogg has lived in vain. It is not only wrong in principle but is against public policy. There is no difference in accepting a free pass and money. (Governor Miriam A. Ferguson, Veto of "Free Pass Bill" authorizing railroads to grant passes to legislators and/or their families, 1925)[56]

I am opposed to spending public money for members of the Legislature to lobby before Congress. I do not believe that this is a proper expenditure of public money. I know of no specific constitutional limitations on the spending of public money that would touch the provisions here made, nevertheless I feel that such use of public money as is contemplated by this resolution is contrary to the spirit of the organic law of the state. Independent of limitations or the lact [sic] of limitations in the Constitution, I am convinced that it is contrary to public policy to spend public money in such a manner. (Governor Dan Moody, Veto of concurrent resolution to pay legislators to go to Washington to get Congress to establish a Veteran's Hospital in Texas, 1929)[57]

In my opinion this bill involves a major change in the policy of the state. The trend has always been away from individual toll roads and bridges, and with the low population bracket contained in this bill, it would be possible for every county to be in the toll road business. Texas has always stood for free highway travel or for a well-planned overall State highway toll road system. This bill is a step in the opposite direction from this ex-

[54] *Senate Journal,* Twenty-second Legislature, regular session, p. 450.
[55] Vetoed Bills, Thirty-fifth Legislature, first called session. On file in office of the secretary of state.
[56] *House Journal,* Thirty-ninth Legislature, regular session, p. 839.
[57] Vetoed Bills, Forty-first Legislature, third called session. On file in office of the secretary of state.

pressed policy. In addition, the bill omits certain safeguards in the present law to prevent the possibility of interference with navigation. (Governor Allan Shivers, Veto of a bill authorizing counties to construct and maintain bridges from one county to another and to pay for them by revenue bonds, 1955)[58]

This appropriation falls into the category of *niceties* rather than *necessities*. I stated in my message to the Legislature that we must make do for a while on some of our building projects to meet other needs. This is one of those projects. (Governor John Connally, Veto of new streets and paving repairs for Crockett State School, 1962)[59]

THE ITEM VETO

Probably the major contribution of the Confederate States of America to the theory and practice of government was the use of the item veto in appropriations bills.[60] Copied by Texas and most of the Southern states, the practice soon swept to other sections so that today only eight of the fifty states do not allow this power to their chief executives.[61] In this one instance the governor of a state possesses more power than does the President of the United States.[62] The primary purpose of the item veto seemed to be the prevention of improper and unconstitutional appropriations, but before long that purpose became "subordinated to a demand that the governor extensively use his veto authority as a means of compelling the state to live within its means."[63]

In practice, the use of the item veto may not be as effective as is generally supposed. Professor Prescott has written:

Its effectiveness was found to depend upon the degree to which appropriations were itemized, the extent to which revenues were earmarked for

[58] *Senate Journal,* Fifty-fourth Legislature, regular session, p. 1526.
[59] Vetoed Bills, Fifty-eighth Legislature, regular session. On file in the office of the secretary of state.
[60] The man who fathered the idea of the item veto in the Confederate States gave two reasons for so doing: to allow the executive to separate improper expenditures from necessary ones without negating the entire bill, and to adapt English budget principles to American conditions in order to secure greater harmony between the executive and the legislature. Robert H. Smith, *Address to the Citizens of Alabama on the Constitution and Laws of the Confederate States of America,* pp. 7–11.
[61] *The Book of the States,* 1960–1961, p. 51.
[62] Charles R. Adrian, *State and Local Governments: A Study in the Political Process,* p. 268.
[63] Roger H. Wells, "The Item Veto and State Budget Reform," *American Political Science Review,* XVIII (November, 1924), 783.

specific objects and the growing realization that piecemeal reductions were inadequate as over-all devices of control. With the rise of the executive budget movement, and the adoption of more drastic measures to maintain fiscal stability during the depression, the item veto has reverted to its original status. *It remains a useful albeit somewhat rusty "gun behind the door" to be aimed at an occasional predatory prowler.* More modern weapons are demanded to meet irresponsible mass attacks upon the public treasury.[64]

Notwithstanding its limitations, the item veto has been used frequently because legislatures have evaded their responsibilities and placed the burden of cutting appropriations upon the governor.[65] In this regard, it probably has been most useful in Texas.

Since adoption of the item veto in the first Reconstruction Constitution (1866), the taxpayers of Texas have surely been saved millions of dollars. However, the services of the state to its citizens may have been proportionately reduced; for throughout history the use of the item veto has been tied to economy and retrenchment in state government. In one biennium Governor Hogg reduced expenditures by more than $350,000 by eliminating new building programs and rejecting additional help for his own staff.[66] Years later, Governor Pat Neff vetoed items aggregating more than $39 million, explaining that such was his duty so that the lawmakers could "have an opportunity to reconsider revenue and appropriations bills, to the end that the state may be kept on a cash-paying basis."[67] He also killed the proposed West Texas Agricultural and Mechanical College with the item veto, claiming that the appropriation for it violated the will of the state Democratic Party convention.[68] A later governor, James V. Allred, vetoed an appropriation for $817,000 for the construction of an insane asylum, noting: "Many members voted for the passage of this bill because it was commonly understood that I would not approve the building of two hospitals at this time."[69]

[64] Prescott, "The Executive Veto in Southern States," *Journal of Politics*, X (November, 1948), 673.

[65] Patterson, McAlister, and Hester, *State and Local Government in Texas* (3d ed.), p. 80.

[66] *House Journal*, Twenty-third Legislature, regular session, p. 1209.

[67] *Senate Journal*, Thirty-eighth Legislature, third called session, p. 65.

[68] *General and Special Laws of Texas, Vetoed Bills*, Thirty-eighth Legislature, third called session. On file in the office of the secretary of state, pages not numbered.

[69] *Public Papers of James V. Allred*, p. 196. Hereafter cited as *Allred Papers*.

Use of the item veto had appeared to be on the decline during the last several administrations, but in June, 1963, Governor John Connally struck out items totaling in excess of $12 million in the biennial appropriations bill. Disagreeing with the Legislature over the amount to be spent for higher education, Connally said that the sum which he item-vetoed would be set aside as a reserve to be used in the future for the state's educational needs, and that he would guard the funds "like an old mother hen." He accused the Legislature of "shortchanging" the colleges and universities of Texas.

Improved budgetary procedures established in 1949 provided that both the governor and the Legislative Budget Board are to submit budgets to the Legislature. Cooperation of the two agencies by holding joint hearings on requests weed out many items of doubtful validity prior to presentation of the budget to the Legislature and no doubt reduce the probability of later item vetoes.

The value of the item veto as a control device has been weakened by judicial restrictions placed upon it. The courts have held that the governor does not have the power to reduce items or to eliminate qualifications or directions for their expenditure placed on appropriations.[70] If the governor files objections to items in an appropriations bill during the session, he may not later veto other items in the same bill after adjournment of the Legislature.[71] The ability to reduce items obviously would give the executive much greater command of fiscal affairs.[72] Governor Allred summarized the position of Texas governors in his item veto of portions of the General Appropriations Bill in 1937:

I think in many instances the appropriations for specific items are too high but I am confronted with the proposition that I do not have the power to reduce appropriations. I have to either approve an entire item, or veto it entirely. If I did this throughout the bill, I would, of necessity, have to submit the matter to the Legislature again with no prospect that a better bill would be secured. For this reason, I am approving this bill, subject only to the items specifically vetoed.[73]

Experience with the item veto does not provide a completely accurate way to evaluate it, but we may conclude that as part of a

[70] *Fulmore v. Lane*, 140 S.W. 405 (1911).

[71] *Pickle v. McCall*, 24 S.W. 265 (1893).

[72] M. Nelson McGeary, "The Governor's Veto in Pennsylvania," *American Political Science Review*, XLI (October, 1947), 941.

[73] *Allred Papers*, p. 202.

broader veto power, the item veto undoubtedly strengthens the position of a governor.

Just as it is difficult to assess the value of the item veto, it is even harder to determine with any degree of accuracy the success of threats to veto. Professor John A. Fairlie has expressed the belief that a governor wields greater influence over legislation through his power of disapproval than is indicated by the number of bills disapproved.[74] Bills which the governor is known to disapprove will not be passed— or they may be changed to meet the governor's objections prior to passage. Fear that the executive may disapprove measures in which they are especially interested may also induce some legislators to attempt to curry favor by voting for other bills known to be favored by the governor.

Leslie Lipson agrees with such an assumption, saying that the legislature and administrative agencies must come to terms with the governor because of the threat he holds over them. He quotes a member of the Massachusetts Constitutional Convention of 1917–1918 as saying, "The potential veto shapes legislative action so constantly that the actual veto does not have to be used very frequently in practice."[75]

One political scientist-legislator, Robert S. Babcock, discerned from his experience in the Vermont Legislature that

the real power of the governor's veto . . . lies not in his use of it, but his threat to use it. Members of the legislature will often consult the governor before introducing doubtful legislation, and if the governor warns them that he will veto the measure, they will usually withdraw the offending bills. . . . A legislator cannot afford to waste his energy trying to find enough votes to override a veto.[76]

Two instances in Texas history which achieved opposite degrees of success illustrate that the time, issues, and parties involved may make the difference to a governor in deciding to threaten to veto. Early in his first term Governor Dan Moody wrote, "I am reluctant

---

[74] John A. Fairlie, "The State Governor," *Michigan Law Review*, X (March, 1912), 383.
[75] Leslie Lipson, *The American Governor From Figurehead to Leader*, p. 210.
[76] Babcock, *State and Local Government and Politics*, p. 206.

to exercise the veto power and believe it should be sparingly used and then only when necessary."[77] Time, and perhaps a few stubborn legislators, changed Moody's mind, however, for two years later he rebuked the fifth called session of the Forty-first Legislature and in no uncertain terms threatened the veto:

I will not approve appropriations beyond the revenues of the State. I want to do whatever can be done to meet these needs, but I will not consent to the appropriation of money beyond the funds available. Whatever you can do within the limits of the revenues of the State toward meeting these needs I think should be done, but you have had the opportunity to raise the revenue to meet these needs, and you have not done it, and I will not become responsible for approving appropriations except within the money that the state has in sight.[78]

Shortly thereafter, the Legislature passed an appropriations bill acceptable to him.

A decade later the threat of a veto by another governor was less effective. Governor Allred, who had also expressed a distaste for use of the veto,[79] nevertheless sent a message to the Legislature in which he declared:

If these conservation authority bills are passed with tax remissions, I shall be compelled to veto them. . . . I dislike to take responsibility of saying in advance that I will veto any bill; I do it because it is my duty and because I owe it to the Legislature to be fair and frank with you.[80]

But Allred was less successful in his threat than Moody had been, for only a week later a bill was passed authorizing a tax remission to Harris County. Allred vetoed it on the grounds that "I must look at the welfare of the State as a whole."[81] In the end his view prevailed and his veto was not overridden.

The threat of veto apparently has been used less in the past two decades than formerly because it has been superseded by attempts to work out problems in advance. Governor Coke Stevenson's policy was not to carry the "big stick" too far; rather he preferred to confer privately with authors of bills of which he disapproved and advise them of his objections in advance. If the author felt compelled to

[77] *Senate Journal*, Fortieth Legislature, regular session, p. 819.
[78] *Ibid.*, Forty-first Legislature, fifth called session, p. 289.
[79] *Allred Papers*, p. 169.
[80] *Ibid.*, pp. 168–169.
[81] *Ibid.*, p. 176.

push the bill, he could so inform the Governor, indicating that it was politically expedient for him to do so. It was not uncommon for a member to say that he would understand the Governor's position if the bill were vetoed but that he was forced by local conditions to sponsor it. Even if such a bill passed the Legislature, Stevenson's practice was to confer with the author before the veto; he never used the public threat, as some of his predecessors had done.[82] When Governor Beauford Jester came into office he expanded Stevenson's tactics by using messages to call attention informally to sections of bills to which he objected. The implication was that the bill would be vetoed unless these sections were removed or revised, and the technique frequently worked. Jester assigned a staff member to check all bills for technical errors as well as for policy considerations.[83] The Stevenson-Jester tactics have apparently become accepted practice, for in numerous cases differences of opinion are compromised prior to passage of bills. Such informal discussion has proved helpful both to sponsors of bills and to governors in reducing the number of vetoes.[84]

HOW SUCCESSFUL IS THE VETO IN TEXAS?

The facts substantiate Professor Prescott's conclusion that Texas has a "strong veto power." The governor has been sustained by the Legislature approximately 95 per cent of the time—a statistic which bespeaks the importance of the veto power in this state.

Governors generally have tended to use the power more frequently during their second terms than during their first terms, but increased use of the veto during later terms does not appear to have increased the frequency with which the Legislature overrides the executive.[85] This apparent anomaly may come about because a new governor ordinarily has a "honeymoon period" with his first legislature and, until basic differences develop, the lawmakers are likely to go along

---

[82] Interview with former Governor Coke Stevenson, February 27, 1961, at Junction, Texas.

[83] Called to attention of the writer by Miss Doris Connerly, Texas legislative reference librarian.

[84] Consensus of several former staff members in the Governor's Office. The open threat of veto was used by Governor Daniel during the regular session of 1961. Opposing a general sales tax, the executive told the press he would veto such legislation. Apparently the threat was successful, because that session adjourned without passing a bill embodying a general sales tax. See *Austin American*, May 22, 24, 28, 1961.

[85] Baker, "The Executive Veto in Texas" (unpublished M.A. thesis), p. 54.

with a large part of his program. However, the longer the executive is in office, the better he learns his job, and the more self-confidence he gains, the firmer stand for his proposals he may take. Therefore, the longer a governor remains in office, the more effective is the use of his veto in molding public policy.

Which governors of Texas have been most effective in their use of the veto? At the turn of the century Governor Charles A. Culberson had become known as the "Veto Governor" because he used the power more frequently than had any of his predecessors under the Constitution of 1876, and was sustained in every one of his thirty-three vetoes.[86] Compared with those who followed him in office, however, Culberson's use of this prerogative was modest indeed. Since his day, the postadjournment veto has become ever more popular with the executives, and during the twentieth century a majority of the governors have vetoed more bills after adjournment than during the legislative session.[87]

The all-time record in the use of the veto was set by Governor Dan Moody, who also called more special sessions of the Legislature (five) in one term than has any other governor. During his four years in office, Moody had eight legislative sessions, vetoed 15 bills during the sessions, and used the postadjournment veto 102 times[88]—a record which should readily earn him the title of "Veto Governor of Texas." Only one of his vetoes was overridden.

As might be expected because of his long tenure, Allan Shivers used the veto on many occasions—a total of 88 times during his seven and one-half years in office, and was sustained on every occasion.[89] Pat Neff used the veto freely also, but with less success; 5 of his 65 vetoes were overridden—a high percentage when compared with Moody's record.[90] Another frequent user of the veto was Oscar B. Colquitt, who vetoed 60 bills during his two terms, being reversed only once. Coupled with other aspects of his Administration, the use

[86] Robert L. Wagner, "The Gubernatorial Career of Charles Allen Culberson" (unpublished M.A. thesis), p. 91.
[87] Exceptions were Colquitt, Allred, O'Daniel, and Shivers. Marburger, "Veto Messages, 1931–1957," p. 1.
[88] Vetoed Bills, Fortieth Legislature, and Vetoed Bills, Forty-first Legislature. On file in the office of the secretary of state.
[89] Marburger, "Veto Messages, 1931–1957," p. 1.
[90] *House Journal,* Thirty-seventh Legislature, and *House Journal,* Thirty-eighth Legislature, *passim.*

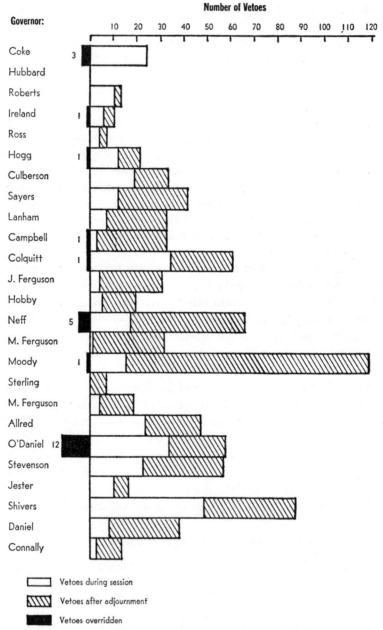

FIG. 5—Vetoes of governors of Texas, 1876–1964.

of the veto helped earn Colquitt the reputation of being "a little Napoleon."[91]

Two other governors have used the veto over 50 times. W. Lee O'Daniel vetoed 57 bills, only to gain the distinction, if such it be, of being the chief executive whose veto was overridden more than that of any other under the present Constitution. On a dozen occasions his action was not sustained. These rejections might be partially ex plainable by O'Daniel's complete lack of prior political experience as well as by the nature of the program he desired. His successor, Governor Coke Stevenson, used the veto 56 times during five and one-half years in office, but the majority of his vetoes were on the grounds that special legislation was involved in violation of the constitutional prohibition on such laws, and he was sustained in every case.[92]

The only governor never to exercise a veto during a session was Ross Sterling, a businessman lacking in political experience. Taking a limited view of the power, he concluded that it was not intended to permit the governor to substitute his judgment for that of the Legislature on constitutionality of laws but that it had been granted only to allow him to negate acts contrary to the public interest. He vetoed only 7 bills—all after adjournment of the Legislature. Exclusive of appropriations measures, he vetoed only four bills—all on the grounds of being contrary to the public interest.[93]

No one would claim that the veto is absolute in Texas, but none can deny that it is important. More than two decades have passed since the Legislature has chosen to override an executive veto—ample evidence of the significant, even though in this instance negative, role of the chief executive in policy making in Texas.

[91] Baker, "The Executive Veto in Texas" (unpublished M.A. thesis), p. 69.
[92] Interview with former Governor Coke Stevenson, February 27, 1961, at Junction, Texas.
[93] Warner E. Mills, Jr., "The Public Career of a Texas Conservative: A Biography of Ross Shaw Sterling" (unpublished Ph.D. dissertation), p. 145.

8

The Governor and the Legislature:
The Message Power

Unquestionably the most used, albeit at times the least effective, formal device for gubernatorial control of public policy is the message power. State constitutions usually require or enjoin the chief executive to send messages to the representative assemblies; and the message power of the governors has developed generally along the same line as that of the President of the United States. As has been pointed out,[1] state administrations have become in modern times a major source of proposed legislation, and it is through messages that a governor submits his legislative program.

Current usage divides gubernatorial messages into four groups: the State of the State Message delivered at the beginning of a legislative session, the budget message, the special messages, and the farewell message at the end of a governor's term of office.

Although the initial message to a legislative session can be expected to be rich in platitudes, it remains the chief vehicle for transmission of the governor's ideas which he desires to become law and frequently contains promises that he made during his campaign. The message customarily carries considerable prestige and is tantamount to an official declaration of policy. Shortly after its delivery various paragraphs of the message begin to crop up on the floor as administration bills. Although such bills must be introduced by legislators, sponsorship is admittedly a fiction, and all members are aware that these bills are products of the administration.[2]

[1] See Chapter 7.
[2] Robert S. Babcock, *State and Local Government and Politics*, pp. 204–205.

Inevitably, the contents of the governor's messages are well covered by all mass media of communication and become the object of public perusal. During the early part of the present century written messages were sent to both houses to be read by a clerk, but within the past two decades or so, the custom has been for the chief executive to deliver his message in person. The natural result is that widespread publicity surrounds the message, which is usually carried on statewide radio or television. Furthermore, since legislative leaders rarely present a comprehensive program, the governor's statement receives more popular consideration because of its inclusiveness and general appeal. Newspapers frequently carry it in full; it becomes the subject of editorial comment; and it is popularly discussed—to the advantage of the governor

because he has proposed and the legislature must dispose. If the governor strikes a popular note, then the action of the legislature, if contrary to his recommendations, is criticized. In case the legislature approves his recommendations, the governor gets credit.[3]

In addition to the message outlining his program, governors in most states are required to submit a budget to the lawmakers—a practice which has further enlarged the message power. By formulating estimates of the sums needed for the ensuing year or biennium and explaining his conclusions, the governor is able to bring the case for his financial policy to the attention of the citizens. Consequently, legislators can ill afford to ignore his recommendations.

Besides the initial message and the budget message, a half-dozen states require a "valedictory" address at the end of an executive's term, summarizing the accomplishments of his administration and making recommendations for needed legislation.[4] In almost every state governors have the prerogative of sending special messages on additional subjects as occasion demands. The use of this practice varies considerably from state to state and even from executive to executive within a state. In order to keep public attention focused on a few principal items, some governors follow the practice of sending a number of messages, each dealing with only one or two major subjects.

Just as practice concerning the frequency of messages varies, so the

[3] Finla G. Crawford (ed.), *Readings in American Government* (rev. ed.), p. 520.
[4] End-of-term messages are required in Arkansas, Illinois, Michigan, Missouri, Nebraska, and Texas. *Index Digest of State Constitutions* (2d ed.), p. 504.

effectiveness of their use varies with circumstances. One student of the legislative process (Professor Hallie Farmer) has concluded, however, that a large part of a governor's program advocated via messages will be enacted into law, for recommendations presented in gubernatorial messages are generally drawn from platforms upon which the executives ran for office. She believes that legislators frequently feel that a governor's platform is an expression of the peoples' will, which they should help to implement.[5]

THE MESSAGE POWER IN TEXAS

Of all states, Texas probably has one of the most comprehensive constitutional provisions concerning the message power. Not only is the chief executive required to supply information at the beginning of each session on the condition of the state, but he is bound also to give similar information at the close of his term and to *make recommendations* at that time. Furthermore,

... he shall account to the Legislature for all public moneys received and paid out by him ... and shall accompany his message with a statement of the same. And at the commencement of each regular session, he shall present estimates of the amount of money required by taxation for all purposes.[6]

Since 1951 the governor has been required by statute to present a budget to the Legislature within five days of the beginning of each regular session.[7] He may send as many special messages in addition as he deems appropriate, and there is no prohibition on his delivering messages to the public to rally public opinion for his recommendations.

Is the message power really valuable to an executive? A leading textbook has declared it to be not as effective in Texas as it is in two-party states and at the national level.[8] Nevertheless, it is important here and elsewhere because governors' messages probably reach more of the people than any other type of governmental reporting.[9]

The frequency, quality, and variety of messages will depend entirely upon the governor who is delivering them, but one writer has

[5] Hallie Farmer, *The Legislative Process in Alabama*, p. 171.
[6] Constitution of Texas, Art. IV, Sec. 9.
[7] *Vernon's Revised Texas Civil Statutes*, Arts. 688–689.
[8] Stuart A. MacCorkle and Dick Smith, *Texas Government* (4th ed.), p. 96.
[9] James L. McCamy, "Governmental Reporting in Texas State Administration" (unpublished M.A. thesis), p. 183. Hereafter cited as McCamy, "Governmental Reporting in Texas."

reported, "Most messages, like party platforms and the Apostles' Creed, will deal with such a breadth and variety of subjects that conclusions can be at best only general."[10] A study is undertaken below of the effectiveness of the message power as it was used by representative governors during different periods.

MESSAGES OF JAMES S. HOGG

James S. Hogg (1891–1895) was the first governor of this state to exercise what may be called the modern concept of the gubernatorial role of leadership. Professor E. C. Barker has said that probably only two other men, Sam Houston and Stephen F. Austin, left their impression so deeply on Texas history as did Hogg, and that perhaps only Houston affected popular feeling so strongly.[11] One of Hogg's contemporaries called him the "most unique personality that ever figured in Texas politics" and continued:

> His speeches and state papers evidence that he is a great practical statesman, who has ever been animated by a lofty desire to promote the general good, and whose efforts have found fruition in wise laws that must ever remain monuments to and honorably perpetuate his fame. . . . He has strong personal magnetism. His very appearance on the platform frequently electrifies the whole audience with enthusiasm and the battle is half won before a word is spoken.[12]

In view of this description, it was probably unfortunate that during Hogg's era the custom was to send messages to the Legislature rather than to deliver them in person, but he was able to use his pen so as to be quite successful in advocating his ideas in written messages. The problems of his day were less complex than were those in some succeeding administrations, and his messages were infrequent. He did not make extensive use of special messages to guide policy; during his first term (1891–1893) only four special messages were transmitted.[13] One contained census figures and requested reapportionment of the state; a second called for the appointment of a com-

---

[10] *Ibid.*, p. 182.

[11] *Addresses and State Papers of James Stephen Hogg*, ed. Robert C. Cotner, p. v.

[12] *Speeches and State Papers of James Stephen Hogg*, ed. C. W. Raines, p. 3.

[13] For the remainder of this chapter the term *special message* will be used to connote cases in which a message not specifically required by the Constitution or the statutes was sent to the legislative body (in regular session) to recommend a particular course of action. Excluded are vetoes, messages returning bills at the request of the Legislature, messages transmitting nominations, and inaugural messages. Special sessions have been dealt with elsewhere; therefore, the analyses in this chapter are confined to messages in regular sessions.

mittee to settle claims for enforcement of quarantine laws requested by the preceding administration; a third transmitted a resolution from the Kansas Legislature requesting Texas to participate in a conference of mining and agricultural states; and the fourth was a farewell message to the Legislature.[14] Likewise, there were few special messages during his second administration. The records show only three: one urging passage of a law to suppress mob violence (a direct result of a riot in Paris, Texas); another to grant the state university "a reasonable division of 4,393,835 acres of unappropriated domain to let it become the equal of any institution in the United States"; and a final, inclusive communication concerning railroad and corporation charters and receiverships, recommending that United States citizenship be redefined, and dealing with details of the appointment of certain judgeships.[15]

Since Governor Hogg made infrequent use of special messages, his main program was outlined in his messages at the start of legislative sessions. In his first communication he declared that it was the responsibility of the legislators to abide by the wishes of the people, as expressed in the Constitution and the party platform.

> Next [to the Constitution] are the pledges adopted by the ascendant political party in its platform—one of the most solemn means used by a majority of the people in uniting to declare their will to the lawmaking powers. If such demands and pledges are consistent with the Constitution, then it comports with duty and propriety for all those who have been elected on that platform to heed and redeem them.[16]

He then proceeded to sketch a six-point program to which he and a majority of the members were committed. In order of priority, he listed:

(1) Creating and providing for successful operation of a railway commission.

(2) Prohibiting corporate monopolies and perpetuities as to lands and titles thereto.

(3) Providing for support and maintenance of public schools for six months of each year.

(4) Providing for the proper endowment and maintenance of the university and other educational institutions.

---

[14] *House Journal*, Twenty-second Legislature, regular session, pp. 468, 624, 742, 907.

[15] *Ibid.*, Twenty-third Legislature, regular session, pp. 266–268, 412, 569–574.

[16] *Ibid.*, Twenty-second Legislature, regular session, p. 103.

(5) Establishing and supporting a home for disabled Confederate soldiers.
(6) Requiring railways in the State to provide separate coaches for their white and black passengers.[17]

By his own evaluation, the entire platform was redeemed except in providing for full maintenance of public schools and other educational institutions "to the constitutional standard." He expressed the belief that the most important bill passed was the one creating the Railroad Commission, an accomplishment which Hogg described as impressive, in view of the large, well-organized lobby against it.[18]

Hogg took his re-election in 1892 as an endorsement of his program, and by the time the Legislature convened he had ready a message to press for more reform legislation. Again he bluntly reminded the majority of its pledge of obedience to the Democratic platform. This time his speech was more detailed and included the following points:

(1) A pledge to support the railroad commission law unless the constitution be changed to make it an elective body.
(2) An agreement to submit to the people an amendment providing for chartering of state banks.
(3) A law to prevent issuance of fictitious and watered stocks and bonds by railway companies.
(4) A law that would curb issuance of bonds by local governments.
(5) A law to define perpetuities and prohibit further operation of land corporations in the state.
(6) An amendment to provide care for indigent ex-Confederates.
(7) Legislation to assure a six-months school term and proper endowment for the University and other institutions.
(8) A better lien law to protect material, men, artisans, mechanics and laborers.
(9) Opposition to hiring out or leasing of penal convicts to corporations and to individuals.
(10) A pledge of opposition to communism in any and all forms and of support for just and equitable protection of the interests of both capital and labor.[19]

Hogg carried the Legislature along with his plan to make the Railroad Commission positions elective for six-year terms, but because of political alliances in the House, the other amendments did not pass.[20] By and large, however, his suggestions on statutory meas-

---

[17] *Ibid.*
[18] *Ibid.*, p. 908.
[19] *Ibid.*, Twenty-third Legislature, regular session, pp. 13–33.
[20] Robert C. Cotner, *James Stephen Hogg, A Biography*, pp. 327–328.

ures were followed, as he pointed out in his end-of-term address. He
was especially proud, he said, of three laws enacted during that session: the statute regulating issuance of stocks and bonds, the act restricting issuance of municipal bonds, and the act defining perpetuities and "winding up" land corporations. He wrote, "No state in the
Union has better laws than these."[21] With the bulk of his reform legislation on the statute books, Hogg felt that he had accomplished his
purpose as Governor and was ready to retire to private life.[22]

MESSAGES OF THE FERGUSONS

Twenty years after the retirement of Hogg, a little-known, small-
town banker, James E. Ferguson, was elected to the high office of
Governor of Texas. Ferguson was destined to become one of the most
publicized executives Texas has ever had, and his impact on state
politics was to be felt for many years to come. Even after his impeachment he remained a potent force in Texas politics, exerting a strong
influence upon his governor-wife during her two terms of office.[23]
Professor Ralph Steen, a student of the Ferguson era, was led to
comment, "If he is not the great governor of Texas in the first half of
the Twentieth Century, then I do not know who would be given the
title."[24]

Following the example of Hogg, James E. Ferguson made little use
of the special-message device to communicate his ideas to the Legislature. In fact, the only special message during his entire first term
was one thanking the lawmakers for their cooperation during the
sixty-day session.[25] During the eight months he served of his second
term, he forwarded two special messages: one requesting the Legislature to urge Congress to locate a federal armor-plate plant in
Texas,[26] and one requesting a law to prevent railroads from confis-
cating coal which was needed by Texas citizens.[27]

Inasmuch as he was removed from office, Ferguson did not deliver
the customary farewell address; therefore, his use of the message
power was confined almost wholly to communications at the begin-

---

[21] *House Journal,* Twenty-third Legislature, regular session, p. 1212.
[22] Cotner, *James Stephen Hogg, A Biography,* p. 352.
[23] Interview with Ghent Sanderford, executive secretary to Governor Miriam
A. Ferguson, March 9, 1961, in Austin.
[24] Letter to Ghent Sanderford from R. W. Steen dated April 25, 1955, now
in possession of Mr. Sanderford.
[25] *House Journal,* Thirty-fourth Legislature, regular session, p. 1217.
[26] *Ibid.,* Thirty-fifth Legislature, regular session, p. 117.
[27] *Ibid.*

ning of each of his two terms. In his first message he urged loyalty to the Democratic Party state platform. Declaring that each of the planks had been fully discussed during the campaign and adding, "I take it that no one can now successfully insist that the platform, as adopted, does not represent the wishes of the people,"[28] Ferguson based his program on the platform. Carrying out his campaign promise and the Party platform, he asked for a law restricting the amount of rent charged tenant farmers. He proposed to void all contracts calling for rents higher than one-fourth the value of a cotton crop or one-third the value of a grain crop, if the tenant furnished everything but the land. He also requested a law to prohibit pools, combines, and trusts formed by persons or corporations from fixing farm prices. Other proposals included an act to prevent abuses to labor (both organized and unorganized), a law to allow the use of prisoners to build highways, reform of the court system, and abolition of the fee system for peace officers. He urged the protection of the public health through constructive legislation and promotion of the livestock industry. In the field of education he asked for liberal support for all educational institutions, especially those of rural districts; a revamping of the system of providing textbooks, so that "every school book used in Texas will be printed in Texas"; and placing of the government of The University of Texas and A. and M. College under a single board. To encourage industrialization, he suggested an amendment exempt manufacturers of cotton and woolen fabrics from taxation. Finally, he proposed what was to become a widely quoted slogan: "Bring together the landless man and the homeless land."[29]

Ferguson was highly successful in getting his program adopted, and upon adjournment of the Legislature "the press generally termed it the most constructive session on record."[30] The Governor's attention to the problems of the rural folk was to earn him untold political dividends in future years; in subsequent campaigns he could always count on the rural vote, which was at the time a substantial tally. One student of the era assesses the first Ferguson administration in these terms: "The Governor and the Legislature cooperated to the fullest extent. . . . Most of the Ferguson platform planks were enacted into law, and the veto was used to a very minor degree."[31]

[28] *Ibid.*, Thirty-fourth Legislature, regular session, p. 130.
[29] *Ibid.*, pp. 129–135.
[30] James A. Clark and Weldon Hart, *The Tactful Texan: A Biography of Governor Will Hobby*, p. 60.
[31] Ralph W. Steen, "The Political Career of James E. Ferguson, 1914–1917" (unpublished M.A. thesis), p. 51.

At the beginning of his second term Ferguson sent one of the shortest messages ever delivered by a governor to a new legislature, outlining the major accomplishments of his first term. First answering the question, "What has been done?" the Governor said that for the first time in history an administration had taken notice of tenant farmers and passed aid for country schools, that his Administration had put the penitentiary on a paying basis and had been "generous to a fault" to the cause of higher education.[32] The remainder of his message was devoted to answering the question, "What can be done?" As was his custom, he invited attention to the Democratic Party platform, saying every plank was worthy of careful consideration by the Legislature. He identified the planks by number, but was not always specific in his recommendations. The points covered included: itemized appropriations bills; farm legislation (although no precise proposal was included); labor legislation endorsing a "Buy-It-Made-in-Texas" slogan; a liberal policy toward "foreign" investors; building of a new asylum for the insane; a $2 million appropriation for country schools; creation of a Highway Commission;[33] judicial reform to relieve the Supreme Court of crowded dockets; and the fostering and encouragement of the livestock industry.

To these planks of the Party platform Ferguson added a few proposals of his own: a law to regulate carrying of a pistol ("The pistol-toter must go!"); an increase in the force of the Texas Rangers; provision for travelling men to vote absentee; creation of an industrial institution to train the adult blind; and Congressional redistricting. His concluding remark must have pleased the legislators when the governor wrote, "The people need us both to accomplish those things which represent their will."[34]

Some opposition to Ferguson had begun to build up, however, and he was less influential with the Legislature than he had been during his first term. There is some difference of opinion over the accomplishments of the Thirty-fifth Legislature, but it did enact at least four noteworthy laws: (1) creation of the Highway Commission, (2) judicial reform, (3) a liberal provision of funds for education, and (4) protection of the livestock industry through the establishment of a

---

[32] *House Journal*, Thirty-fifth Legislature, regular session, pp. 7–10.

[33] Tied to this proposal was an interesting idea calling upon the lawmakers to get rid of "speed maniacs" by making it a jail penalty to operate an automobile at a speed of more than ten miles per hour in an incorporated town or more than twenty-four miles per hour on country roads.

[34] *House Journal*, Thirty-fifth Legislature, regular session, p. 10.

tick-eradication program.[35] During this session Ferguson began to disagree with the administration of The University of Texas and ultimately used the item veto on appropriations for that institution. When he finally called a special session to deal with the matter, the Thirty-fifth Legislature removed him from office.

After an interlude of seven years, the Fergusons returned to the Governor's chair, this time in the person of Mrs. Miriam A. Ferguson. In keeping with family tradition, her first Administration (1925–1927) made limited use of the message power. Only the two required messages and one special message were sent to the Legislature, the latter to deliver an agreement executed between Mexico and Texas concerning division of water from the Pecos River.[36] In her first message Mrs. Ferguson alluded to the rigorous campaign of 1924 and reiterated that the state Democratic platform was the verdict of the people. She wrote: "I know that you gentlemen . . . will find pleasure in carrying out those platform demands in the fullest measure and it is a pleasure likewise to me to pledge my best efforts to aid you in this important undertaking."[37] Calling for economy and reform in government, she requested that appropriations be cut, that the Banking Department be investigated, that the duties of the Insurance Commission be clarified, and that laws concerning murder, robbery, and bootlegging be strengthened. She proposed a gasoline tax (to be spent for highways) and a tobacco tax (to be spent for education).

The effectiveness of this message was practically nil; the Legislature almost completely ignored the Governor's program. No laws of unusual interest were passed, no new taxes were voted, and no new bureaus were established. Although both the prison system and the highway system were investigated, no changes in them were made.[38]

Six years elapsed before Mrs. Ferguson again became chief executive (in 1933), but her opening message clung to the family tradition of earlier years by stressing economy and budget cutting. Her most striking proposal, no doubt, was the advocacy of a 3-per-cent sales tax—a measure favored by many members of the press but by few legislators.[39] Efforts to solve financial problems bogged down early in the session, forcing the Governor to deviate from the customary prac-

[35] Seth S. McKay, *Texas Politics 1906–1944*, p. 73.
[36] *House Journal*, Thirty-ninth Legislature, regular session, pp. 909–912.
[37] *Ibid.*, p. 94.
[38] McKay, *Texas Politics, 1906–1944*, p. 144.
[39] *Ibid.*, p. 247.

tice of other Ferguson Administrations and to make extensive use of special messages. During the remainder of the session she sent seventeen messages, concerned mostly with the financial crisis, the Depression, and relief programs.[40] A few of the more important proposals sent in these messages included a corporate income tax (forwarded in a thirty-nine-word message, one of the shortest on record); an intangible tax on corporations not paying the gross receipts tax; and a solution to the problem of bank failures—after she had assumed the authority to temporarily close banks of the state.[41] Another message gave the lawmakers a free hand to take up the question of raising revenue "in any way you see fit."[42]

Despite the Governor's many messages, however, her proposals were not followed to any appreciable extent, except in the matter of cutting appropriations, $13 million being eliminated. The only revenue-raising measure enacted during the session was an increase of the oil tax by two cents a barrel. Other major legislation included: congressional redistricting, adoption of a per capita pattern of appropriations for educational institutions, and a bill to legalize horse racing and prize fighting. In line with the Twenty-first Amendment to the national Constitution, the question of repeal of Prohibition in Texas was submitted to the electorate.[43]

Two prominent educators have evaluated the Ferguson era. Professor Frederick Eby gave credit to the Fergusons for fostering the development of country schools and increasing their terms from four months to nine. He defended Mrs. Ferguson's record by pointing out, "Although some have said that she was but a 'front' for her husband to continue in office, much of the legislation passed during her terms seems clearly to have come from a woman's heart and mind."[44]

After suggesting that during Mrs. Ferguson's first term "reform took a holiday,"[45] Rupert N. Richardson wrote:

It is difficult to evaluate Mrs. Ferguson's second administration. Relations between the legislature and the executive were not harmonious, and

---

[40] *House Journal,* Forty-third Legislature, regular session, *passim.*
[41] *Ibid.,* p. 645.
[42] *Senate Journal,* Forty-third Legislature, regular session, p. 1852.
[43] McKay, *Texas Politics, 1906–1944,* p. 251.
[44] *Austin American,* January 31, 1954.
[45] Rupert N. Richardson, *Texas, The Lone Star State* (2d ed.), p. 317. By permission of Prentice-Hall, Inc.

Richard Coke
January 15, 1874–December 1, 1876

Richard B. Hubbard
December 1, 1876–January 21, 1879

Oran M. Roberts
January 21, 1879–January 16, 1883

John Ireland
January 16, 1863–January 18, 1887

Lawrence S. (Sul) Ross
January 18, 1887–January 20, 1891

James S. Hogg
January 20, 1891–January 15, 1895

Charles A. Culberson
January 15, 1895–January 17, 1899

Joseph D. Sayers
January 17, 1899–January 20, 1903

S. W. T. Lanham
January 20, 1903–January 15, 1907

Thomas M. Campbell
January 15, 1907–January 19, 1911

Oscar B. Colquitt
January 19, 1911–January 19, 1915

James E. Ferguson
January 19, 1915–August 25, 1917

William P. Hobby
August 25, 1917–January 18, 1921

Pat M. Neff
January 18, 1921–January 20, 1925

Miriam A. Ferguson
January 20, 1925–January 17, 1927
January 17, 1933–January 15, 1935

Dan Moody
January 17, 1927–January 20, 1931

Ross S. Sterling
January 20, 1931–January 17, 1933

James V. Allred
January 15, 1935–January 17, 1939

W. Lee O'Daniel
January 17, 1939–August 4, 1941

Coke R. Stevenson
August 4, 1941–January 21, 1947

Beauford H. Jester
January 21, 1947–July 11, 1949

Allan Shivers
July 11, 1949–January 15, 1957

Price Daniel
January 15, 1957–January 15, 1963

John B. Connally
January 15, 1963–

All the foregoing portraits, unless otherwise indicated below, are from the Texas State Archives. Photographs of Governors Colquitt, Moody, Allred, Shivers, and Daniel were furnished by the Colquitt Family Collection, Mrs. Dan Moody, Mrs. James V. Allred, Mrs. Allan Shivers, Mrs. Price Daniel, respectively. The photograph of Mrs. Ferguson was furnished by the *Dallas Times-Herald;* the one of John Connally is an official United States Navy photograph.

Attorney General James Stephen Hogg campaigning for governor of Texas in Brownwood, May 1, 1890. In this picture Hogg has a beard, which in later years he did not wear.

Governor O. B. Colquitt campaigning for re-election to a second term in 1912. He is speaking in front of the high school at Sherman.

Governor James E. Ferguson (far left) and two aides look out a Capitol window at a crowd outside the Governor's Office, following his veto of the appropriation for The University of Texas in 1917.

University of Texas band and students march to the Capitol to protest Governor Ferguson's veto of the appropriation bill for the University in 1917.

Governor O. B. Colquitt, who was called "The Little Napoleon," is cartooned in the press for his stand on problems between the United States and Mexico in 1912 and 1913. The caption under the cartoon reads "Our War Governor."

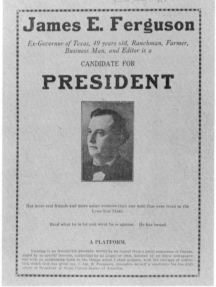

Campaign poster for Jim Ferguson in his race for President of the United States, May, 1920. The poster reads: "Has more real friends and more mean enemies than any man that ever lived in the Lone Star State," and declares, "Yielding to no irresistible pressure, moved by no appeal from a great concourse of friends, urged by no special interest, controlled by no clique or clan, boosted by no hired newspaper . . . I . . . announce myself a candidate for the high office of President of these United States of America."

Inauguration of Governor Dan Moody, January 17, 1927. On the rostrum, in the front row from the left, are former Governors Joseph D. Sayers, O. B. Colquitt, James E. Ferguson, William P. Hobby, and Pat M. Neff, all to the left of the podium, where Governor Moody is taking the oath

Mrs. James E. Ferguson in 1918, in a role in which she was seldom seen by the public. At this time Mrs. Ferguson had served as first lady of Texas while her husband was governor. Six years later she was herself elected to the governor's office to become the nation's first elected woman governor.

Governor-Elect Miriam A. Ferguson and her husband, former Governor James E. Ferguson, pictured in Dallas in December, 1932, shortly after Mrs. Ferguson's election to a second term.

Governor Miriam A. Ferguson addressing the Texas Legislature, January, 1925.

Governor James S. Hogg welcoming President Benjamin Harrison to Galveston, April 18, 1891, on board the Steamship *Lampasas*. To the President's left is General Thomas J. Rusk.

Attorney General Dan Moody and his bride, April 20, 1926, following their wedding breakfast, given by President and Mrs. Jefferson D. Sandefer of Simmons College, Abilene. On the same day Moody announced his candidacy for the governorship; he conducted a "honeymoon campaign" over the state, accompanied by his bride. In the picture are Mrs. Sandefer; Miss Helen Paxton, Mrs. Moody's sister who was maid of honor; Moody; Mrs. Moody; President Sandefer; and Ernest May, best man.

Among the activities of governors are the greeting and escorting of famous person-ages. *Top,* Governor James V. Allred introduces newly elected Congressman Lyndon B. Johnson to President Franklin D. Roosevelt, at Port Aransas, 1937. *Below, left,* former Governors Dan Moody (center) and Pat Neff (right) chat with the national chairman of the Democratic Party, Postmaster General James A. Farley, at Hillsboro, April 4, 1940. *Below, right,* Governor Coke Stevenson welcomes General of the Army Dwight D. Eisenhower to the Annual Muster at Texas A. and M. College, College Station, April 21, 1946.

Governors spend much time meeting their constituents, especially while campaigning for election. *Above, left,* Governor Allan Shivers, three weeks after becoming chief executive, makes his first formal appearance as governor before the State Convention of the American Legion, in Fort Worth, August 6, 1949. *Above, right,* Governor Coke Stevenson greets school children at the public school in Decatur, March 4, 1942. *Below, left,* Senator Price Daniel chats with voters at a Dallas barbecue stand during the gubernatorial campaign of 1956. *Below, right,* Governor Beauford Jester is introduced by Sam Rayburn to a delegate at the State Democratic Convention in Fort Worth, September 15, 1948.

Governor James V. Allred, performing a typical chore of Texas governors, wears western clothes and rides horseback to lead the parade at a rodeo in Stamford, 1940.

Governor Allan Shivers, in another familiar activity of Texas governors, helps publicize friendship between Texas and Mexico as he accepts a colorful sombrero from Raul Lopez Sanchez, Governor of Coahuila, Mexico, December 5, 1949.

Candidate W. Lee O'Daniel and his hillbilly band appear at a rally during his first campaign for governor, July, 1938. O'Daniel drew the largest crowds in the history of Texas politics, either before or since that time.

Crowds throng the tables at a barbecue held on the lawn of the Governor's Mansion at the second inauguration of Governor W. Lee O'Daniel, January 21, 1941. O'Daniel invited all the people of Texas to attend the barbecue and "talk with" him that day. An estimated twenty thousand who came were served barbecued beef, mutton, and buffalo.

Governor Beauford H. Jester chats with A. M. G. Swenson (seated) and W. G. Swenson at the Texas Cowboy Reunion in Stamford, July 4, 1948. A. M. G. Swenson was appointed by Jester to the Board of Regents of The University of Texas.

Governor-Nominee Price Daniel, Mrs. Daniel, and Daniel's brother, Bill, appear on the speakers' platform at the State Democratic Convention in Fort Worth, September 12, 1956. Daniel raises his hand in a plea for harmony at the faction-ridden meeting.

Courtesy Governor Connally's Office

Exercising the item veto, Governor John Connally red-lines $12 million in the General Appropriations Bill, June, 1963.

Courtesy *Dallas Times-Herald*

Gubernatorial Candidate John Connally speaks from the rear platform of his campaign train, April, 1962. Shown with him is Mrs. Connally.

the lawmakers distrusted the governor and her husband. . . . It must be said that the administration was economical and met with much greater approval than her first administration as governor.[46]

A thorough analysis of gubernatorial messages during the years 1923 to 1932 was made as a part of a broader study of governmental reporting by James L. McCamy in 1932. Cataloguing the topics discussed in executive messages of the period, McCamy found the following to occur with most frequency: prisons, taxation, administrative organization, fiscal needs, natural resources, education, coordination of work and increasing of efficiency in government. He concluded that the list indicated "a tendency to count first things first and to give the Legislature and the public information concerning the major functions and problems of government."[47]

Governor Pat M. Neff (1921–1925) probably made the most extensive use, up to his time, of the special message device. This practice undoubtedly reflected his outstanding ability as an expressive and fluent writer. From January 13 to January 20, 1923, Neff sent the House

eight comprehensive discussions of the need for a new constitution, the need for a means of evicting negligent elective peace officers, twelve specific recommendations for legislation on educational problems, a statement of the tax problem, a review of the work done by the Textbook Commission, a long survey of prison conditions with exhibits attached, a general discussion of highway matters, and a plea for the encouragement of factory buildings in Texas by lenient tax policies and providing Texas youth with training in textile engineering.[48]

The Legislature was not impressed by this free flow of words and took little action on the Governor's progressive program. In many respects, therefore, Governor Neff's accomplishments in office fell far short of his expectations and hopes. Among his unrealized proposals were the writing of a new constitution, enactment of a law providing for removal of negligent peace officers, elimination of unnecessary boards and bureaus, simplification of the judicial system, revamping

[46] *Ibid.,* p. 325. By permission of Prentice-Hall, Inc.
[47] McCamy, "Governmental Reporting in Texas" (unpublished M.A. thesis), pp. 187–189.
[48] *Ibid.,* p. 184.

of tax laws, and passage of legislation to attract industry to Texas.[49] Somewhat later, Neff wrote:

As I now look back on my four years in the Governor's office, it is difficult to know just how much worthwhile service was rendered. . . . Frequently a Governor is helpless to do the things that . . . should be done. Early in my administration I discovered that it was impossible to do the things I had dreamed I would do.[50]

Although the messages of Governor Dan Moody (1927–1931) were neither so flowery nor so frequent as Neff's had been, they reached a considerable volume. In his first message Moody called for a scientific system of taxation, reform of the judiciary and of court procedure, establishment of a civil service for state employees, a unified accounting system for state agencies, development of warehouse and marketing systems for Texas agriculture, laws against indiscriminate issuance of pardons, an increase in gasoline taxes, and adoption of liberal policies for developing public school facilities.[51]

As in the case of Governor Neff, Moody's program was too progressive to suit the Legislature and he hit a low score in trying to get it accepted: less than one-half of his recommendations were followed. Educational facilities and prison conditions were improved, and hundreds of miles of highways were built, but there was no constructive reform in the tax structure, no change in the judicial system, no merit system adopted, and no money voted to modernize the highway system.[52]

Moody's successor, Governor Ross Sterling (1931–1933) made limited use of the message power. At the outset he commended the state Democratic platform as his program, but once he had outlined his desires he made no demands for action. Sterling believed that the executive's role vis-à-vis the Legislature consisted only of advising it, not of attempting to dominate it.[53] Each branch of government, therefore, went its own way, and the lawmakers did little in the way of passing constructive legislation, earning for themselves the reputation of a "do-nothing legislature."[54] Sterling was denied a second term by the voters.

[49] Emma M. Shirley, *The Administration of Pat M. Neff, Governor of Texas 1921–1925,* p. 108.
[50] Pat M. Neff, *The Battles of Peace,* p. 241.
[51] *House Journal,* Fortieth Legislature, regular session, p. 99.
[52] McKay, *Texas Politics, 1906–1944,* p. 150.
[53] Warner E. Mills, Jr., "The Public Career of a Texas Conservative: A Biography of Ross Shaw Sterling" (unpublished Ph.D. dissertation), p. 138.
[54] McKay, *Texas Politics, 1906–1944,* p. 219.

MESSAGES OF JAMES V. ALLRED

The Governor of the state during the centennial celebration of Texas independence was James V. Allred (1935–1939), one of the youngest men to serve in the office, and described by a veteran political writer as one of "the best campaigners that Texas has ever known."[55] The young executive gained wide attention for promoting social-welfare legislation and became known as a protege of President Franklin D. Roosevelt. He has been called the most "liberal" governor the state has ever had.[56]

Following the pattern adopted by the progressive governors of the 1920's, Allred used the special-message device extensively in presenting his program. In his first message, on the "State of the State," he commended to the Legislature "for your careful study and action each plank in the State Democratic platform," a copy of which he inserted as an exhibit to his message. But he asked the legislators to consider only emergency subjects during the first month of the session because, in his words: "I doubt the wisdom of attempting to present to the Legislature at one time a complete and detailed program."[57] The emergency matters were: the "tremendous deficit," the disposition of $3½ million worth of bonds remaining unsold from an issue voted during the preceding administration, the establishment of a Planning Board to work in conjunction with the national recovery program, and the submission to the electorate of a Prohibition amendment to the state Constitution. He also called for a law to allow Texas citizens to take advantage of the federal housing program; for regulation of lobbies; and for a study of conservation laws, with a view to creating a conservation commission.[58]

Via the special-message device, he presented other proposals on ten different occasions before the end of the regular session. He sent messages concerning general appropriations, investigation of the handling of the Permanent School Fund, the creation of a state employment service, the repeal of race-track gambling, Texas' participation in the Interstate Oil Compact, state parks, the establishment of the Department of Public Safety, and the creation of special courts in Smith and Rusk Counties. To finance his program, Allred asked for the passage of a luxury tax and a chain-store tax, an increase in the

---

[55] *Austin American*, July 26, 1932.
[56] *Ibid.*, March 2, 1958.
[57] *House Journal*, Forty-fourth Legislature, regular session, p. 106.
[58] *Ibid.*, pp. 106–112.

rates of resources and inheritance taxes, and consideration of a state income tax.[59]

Allred had become tremendously popular with the public and with the press, but his popularity did not carry over to the Legislature. He was relatively successful in getting his nonfiscal measures through, but at the end of the session not a single revenue-producing tax had been enacted and three special sessions became necessary to care for the matter. The repeal of race-track gambling, a measure he had vigorously supported, was not voted.[60]

The beginning of his second term found Allred engulfed even deeper by fiscal problems than he had been two years previously, because almost every agency of government had expanded. Estimating the need for almost $7 million in additional revenue, the chief executive pointed to his messages of the last session and stated that his views remained the same as at that time. He suggested that taxes could be levied on "forty-five per cent of our state property now escaping" and advocated a "substantial increase" in severance taxes. This increase having been endorsed by the state platform of the Democratic Party, Allred asked why it should not be carried out by the lawmakers.[61] He recommended extension of social security to the blind and the crippled, and to dependent children; and he also asked for a driver's license law, increased salaries, and workmen's compensation for state employees, and provision for a teacher-retirement system.[62]

The use of the special message again figured prominently in the Governor's approach, with the number of messages more than doubled over that of the previous session. Some twenty-three messages[63] were used to deal with a diversity of subjects, including dog racing, narcotics, unemployment compensation, and establishment of a Board of Pardons and Paroles. One message threatened a special session unless an "aye" or "nay" vote was taken on repeal of race-track gambling. In spite of the repeated requests, however, the session ended as almost a repeat performance of two years before. Nonfiscal matters were approved, but nothing was done to solve fiscal problems, thus necessitating two extra sessions.

[59] *Ibid.*, pp. 119, 139, 158, 194, 254, 266, 268, 338, 351.
[60] Robert R. Martindale, "James V. Allred, The Centennial Governor of Texas" (unpublished M.A. thesis), p. 78.
[61] *House Journal,* Forty-fifth Legislature, regular session, pp. 33–53.
[62] *Ibid.*
[63] *Ibid., passim.*

An assessment of the Allred program cannot overlook the impressive array of social legislation passed at the governor's insistence, but his lack of success in handling fiscal matters must also be borne in mind. In his valedictory, the Governor seemed to be satisfied with the results he had obtained. He said, "On the whole, our efforts have been successful, and the 'condition of the State' is vastly improved. The past four years might well be termed the pioneer age in social security in Texas."[64] Almost all of Allred's special programs were presented to the Legislature through special messages!

MESSAGES OF ALLAN SHIVERS

Allan Shivers broke a long-standing Texas tradition by being elected to three terms. He broke with precedent also in endorsing a presidential candidate of a party other than his own. Not only did Shivers serve as Governor longer than has any other person, but on two occasions his support helped swing the state to a Republican President, Dwight D. Eisenhower.[65] To some, these two feats qualify Shivers as one of the strongest leaders ever to sit in Texas' executive office. A former member of the Texas House of Representatives has described him as "the most powerful Governor in Texas history, and the most controversial Texan since Sam Houston."[66]

Shivers made little use of special messages, especially during his first two terms, preferring instead to confine himself to outlining his program in the required messages at the beginning of a session. During his first full term Shivers sent only two messages concerning legislation; the first requested support for House Bill 6 (strengthening the election machinery by empowering the attorney general to investigate and prosecute violations of election laws) and asked for passage of certain uniform state acts to assist in extradition of criminals.[67] The second special message concerned the need for $57 million in additional revenue, which Shivers proposed to raise by continuation of an omnibus tax law and additional taxes on natural gas. He expressed also a desire for repeal of that portion of the law which froze funds for farm-to-market roads thereby requiring the Highway Department to spend at least $20 million yearly for such roads.[68]

---

[64] *Ibid.*, Forty-sixth Legislature, regular session, p. 22.
[65] See O. Douglas Weeks, *Texas Presidential Politics in 1952* and *Texas One-Party Politics in 1956*.
[66] D. B. Hardeman, "Shivers of Texas," *Harpers* (November, 1956), p. 51.
[67] *Senate Journal*, Fifty-second Legislature, regular session, p. 950.
[68] *Ibid.*, p. 1020.

Only two "emergency messages" appear in the legislative journals for his second full term: a request for the establishment of two additional tuberculosis hospitals,[69] and a request for authorization to accept federal funds for disaster relief to areas struck by tornadoes.[70] During his final term Shivers made his most frequent use of special messages, with a total of seven. He called for: addition of four district attorneys in Travis County to assist in clearing up the scandal-ridden land program, creation of a state building commission, establishment of a disaster fund for drought relief, special appropriations for agencies involved in investigation of irregularities in the land program, an appropriation of $14,000 to make recompense for animals killed in the program to stamp out the scrapie disease, an appropriation of $250,000 to supply Salk poliomyelitis vaccine to indigent and dependent children, and a law requiring the constitutional oath for appointive officers.[71]

The main program of each of his terms was embodied in the required messages on the State of the State. In his first message after election Shivers showed great concern for economy in government, suggesting that many needed improvements could be effected with little or no cost. Among these he enumerated: congressional and judicial redistricting; recodification of criminal, insurance, and water laws; increased traffic safety; research in the field of secondary recovery of oil (for which funds were already available); strengthened states' rights (including return to Texas of its tidelands); lengthening of terms of most state and local officials; and establishment of enforceable controls on the activities of the Communist Party. He also recommended that the Legislature cooperate with education groups to start work on a "realistic solution" to educational problems, that farm-to-market roads be continued as a part of the state highway program, and that agencies supported by fees be required to contribute a fixed percentage of such fees to the General Revenue Fund in exchange for services rendered to them by departments supported by that Fund. He urged the screening of "incidental expenditures" with a view toward effecting savings, and he advised a cost-of-living salary adjustment for state employees, based on a job-classification program. The only new service recommended was an adult-probation

[69] *Ibid.*, Fifty-third Legislature, regular session, p. 183.
[70] *Ibid.*, p. 1027.
[71] *Ibid.*, Fifty-fourth Legislature, regular session, p. 282, 283, 323, 392, 725, 749, 757.

program. The tenor of the whole program was in his closing remarks, in which he warned that all problems should be approached from the standpoint of "what we can *afford* to do rather than what we would *like* to do." He said that each item in each category should be tested by a simple formula: "1. Can we afford it? 2. Can we afford to do without it?"[72]

The Legislature responded to the Governor's propositions by enacting most of his program, except for job classification and salary increases, judicial redistricting, and "coordinating" the program of higher education. Shivers, therefore, included these items among the recommendations he made at the opening of the next regular session of the Legislature. A four-point program was also submitted, including requests for:

(1) Appropriations for cost-of-living increases.
(2) Funds for a TB hospital building program.
(3) Funds for teacher pay raises to be freed by changing the local contribution requirements to twenty-five per cent of cost by reallocating of certain tax revenues from the Available School Fund to the Omnibus Clearance Fund and then to the Minimum Foundation Fund.
(4) A minimum highway program (creating authority for toll roads, increasing the gasoline tax, and making no allocations except for construction and maintenance).

Shivers urged the members to dispose of general appropriations before taking up requests for specific items, and concluded, "We need to do two things that are politically unpopular: deny many sincere and worthy requests for expenditures, and at the same time vote additional taxes."[73]

For the second time the Shivers program fared well at the hands of the Legislature, except for the job classification plan and pay increases for state employees. Salaries were eventually raised by a special session which the Governor called the following year.[74]

In beginning his last State of the State Message, Governor Shivers said, "This Legislature faces more problems of major import than have confronted any other session during the twentieth century."[75] His message was the longest one he delivered and contained more specific recommendations than had his previous messages. Declaring

[72] *Ibid.*, Fifty-second Legislature, regular session, pp. 18–21.
[73] *Ibid.*
[74] See Chapter 9.
[75] *Senate Journal*, Fifty-fourth Legislature, regular session, p. 18.

that the state's number one problem was water, he asked for reorganization of the Board of Water Engineers and creation of a statewide water authority. Among his other proposals were: a capital-improvements program of $2 billion, to be spent over the next ten years for highways; better staffing for tuberculosis hospitals; more probation and parole officers; an increase of personnel in the Highway Patrol; and establishment of a professional school for law-enforcement officers. He also urged changes in insurance laws "with more attention to solvency than to competition," continuation of the land program for veterans, and amendment of unemployment laws to coincide with changes in the national program. He asked for laws to control striking and picketing, to increase old-age pensions, and to make congressional and judicial redistricting automatic. He sought a constitutional amendment to legalize advertising of the state.

To help finance this extensive program, Shivers requested increased tuition at state schools and an increase in both gasoline and cigarette taxes; he also pointed out that a change in the school law to base state aid on average daily attendance rather than on the school census would save the state $7 million annually.[76]

For the most part, relations between the chief executive and the Legislature remained cordial and his program had smooth sailing in both chambers. The esteem in which the Legislature held the Governor was attested by a resolution adopted near the end of the session when some criticism developed in California over Shivers' acceptance of an invitation to make the commencement address at the University of Southern California. The legislative resolution commended the Governor for "his character, leadership, intelligence, tolerance, patience, honesty and courage, and for the high honor paid him by the University of Southern California . . ."[77] In return, Shivers said the Legislature had completed "one of the best and most constructive sessions in recent history," and had accomplished 85 per cent of the job before it, the "big misses" being the problems of water, and adult probation and parole.[78]

In his farewell message Shivers again spoke of the close cooperation between the legislative and executive branches during his administration. He said that no one could ever take full credit for accomplishments in office because government was a "team game."

[76] *Ibid.*, pp. 18–23.
[77] *Ibid.*, p. 3495.
[78] *Austin Report*, Vol. 7, No. 31, June 12, 1955.

He summarized his years in the Governor's Office in these terms: "We have done our best to meet the emergency requirements of an expanding state economy and a rapidly growing population, while at the same time making plans for the future that will solve problems before they become emergencies."[79] He cited the handling of the problems of state hospitals as an example of both the emergency and long-range approach. As accomplishments of his Administration he claimed progress in matters of education, highways (the mileage of highways had doubled under his Administration), and the prison system. He pointed with pride to the salary increases given teachers and state employees and said that scandals in the veterans' land program and the insurance business had been "cleared up." He was gratified with the rebuilding of the School for the Deaf. Ending his message in a jocular vein, he said, "This administration has failed signally in at least one respect: we haven't been able to make it rain."[80] He added, however, that over $40 million had been spent on drought relief and that a water-conservation program had come close to being enacted in 1955.[81] As other matters he had suggested but which had not been carried out, he listed job classification for state employees, congressional and judicial redistricting, removal of restrictions on advertising the state, revision of the election code, and creation of a special court in Travis County to hear state cases.[82]

One former legislator wrote that even Shivers' enemies conceded that he was a skillful governor.

He was more successful in dealing with the legislature than any previous governor. When the legislature met, he would outline his program, then sit back until late in the session. After many disputes were settled and the legislators weary, he moved like a fresh fullback in the fourth quarter to force his program through.[83]

This observer reported that Shivers himself believes that his major accomplishments were alerting Texans to the dangers of federal encroachments, teaching Texans the need for independence in presidential elections, and participation in the successful fight for return of the tidelands to state ownership.[84]

[79] *Senate Journal*, Fifty-fifth Legislature, regular session, p. 40.
[80] *Ibid.*, p. 42.
[81] For an analysis of the legislative struggle on water problems, see John T. Thompson, *Public Administration of Water Resources in Texas*, pp. 97–99.
[82] *Senate Journal*, Fifty-fifth Legislature, regular session, p. 42.
[83] Hardeman, "Shivers of Texas," *Harpers* (November, 1956), p. 51.
[84] *Ibid.*, p. 52.

A few examples will indicate the importance of the message power in other recent administrations. Frequency of use of the message hit a peak during the two terms of W. Lee O'Daniel (1939–1941). A flour salesman lacking in political acumen, O'Daniel had advertised his products over the radio for many years, and continued to use that medium to advertise his gubernatorial program. His major campaign promise was to increase pensions for the aged, and he proposed in his first formal address to the Legislature to finance his program with a "transactions tax." This proposal precipitated one of the bitterest Texas legislative struggles of modern times, and a group—known as the "Immortal Fifty-Six"—was successful in blocking the tax.[85] (One of the leaders of the group was Representative Price Daniel of Liberty County.) During his first term Governor O'Daniel employed the special message nine times to send proposals to the Legislature, the most publicized messages being one to amend the budget law[86] and another to abolish capital punishment.[87] The legislature adjourned, however, without providing the pensions O'Daniel had promised. As a consequence, O'Daniel extended the olive branch to the legislators in his second State of the State Message; its entire tone was conciliatory. Speaking editorially of the message, the *Dallas Morning News* described it as "friendly, dignified, and for the most part constructive. . . . Most of the recommendations made should be followed. If this were done, Texas would be far better off."[88]

The Governor's proposals included the realignment of staggered terms on state boards, legislative appointment of the state auditor, use of the merit system for state employees, changing of truck load limits on highways, and passage of a pay-as-you-go constitutional amendment.[89] During the course of the session, O'Daniel sent forty-two special messages urging various parts of his program, but with little success. A chronicler of the times says: "Of thirty-three major recommendations, only fifteen were substantially carried out. One journalist quipped that the Governor's batting average in the 'Legislative League' was about .500."[90]

[85] Interview with William J. Lawson, executive secretary to Governor O'Daniel, March 13, 1961, in Austin.

[86] *House Journal,* Forty-sixth Legislature, regular session, p. 177.

[87] *Ibid.,* p. 511.

[88] *Dallas Morning News,* January 18, 1941.

[89] *Ibid.*

[90] Seth S. McKay, *W. Lee O'Daniel and Texas Politics,* p. 404.

In striking contrast, O'Daniel's successor, Coke Stevenson, found little use for the special-message device during his two terms. The records indicate only five such messages during his first term[91] and six during his second term.[92] According to one newspaper account, however, the only two major recommendations which were unfulfilled during the Stevenson years were those pertaining to legislative re-districting and judicial redistricting.[93]

Death ended the career of Governor Beauford Jester six months after the beginning of his second term. During his relatively brief tenure, however, Jester appeared to work well with the lawmakers in pursuit of his "middle-of-the-road" policies, which he adopted in an effort to heal the breach that had occurred in his party. Shortly after the end of the regular session of 1947 the Governor noted in a radio broadcast that he and the Legislature worked harmoniously and usually were in essential agreement on subjects advanced in his messages.[94] In a later broadcast he reported: "The Legislature very graciously enacted into law 21 of the 27 recommendations I made in my first message, and the Senate was kind enough to approve every nomination which I submitted."[95]

Jester's use of special messages increased considerably during the short period he served of his second term. According to one of his staff members, this increase was to satisfy the presiding officer of one of the chambers, who thought that a special message covering a limited number of topics would focus the attention of the lawmakers and the public on a particular issue at a given time. The approach worked well under the circumstances of the day.[96]

Jester used his message power in a different way. To urge favorable consideration of the Gilmer-Aikin Bills (improvement of the system of public education) he sent a message to each member of the Legislature. According to one of the House sponsors of the legislation, these individual messages were "a major contribution . . . to force final action on the bills."[97]

---

[91] *House Journal,* Forty-eighth Legislature, regular session, *passim.*

[92] *Ibid.,* Forty-ninth Legislature, regular session, *passim.*

[93] *Beaumont Enterprise,* June 2, 1945.

[94] "Report to the People," July 1, 1947 (mimeographed script of Jester's radio broadcast). Copy in Jester Biographical File, Barker Texas History Center, The University of Texas.

[95] *Ibid.,* January 21, 1948.

[96] Interview with Weldon Hart, March 29, 1961, in Austin.

[97] Rae Files Still, *The Gilmer-Aikin Bills: A Study in the Legislative Process,* p. 113.

THE BUDGET MESSAGE

In recent years the process of budget making has been decidedly emphasized in both government and business. Described by Dean Paul H. Appleby as a "specialized way of looking at problems in decision making,"[98] the budget has come to be one of the valuable tools of modern management. Since most questions involving the expenditure of money ultimately resolve themselves into value judgments, the budgetary function strikes at the heart of policy making. Indeed, "the budget, because it is at the same time the most important instrument of legislative control and of executive management, is at the core of democratic government."[99]

All except seven states in the Union place responsibility for preparation and submission of the budget in the hands of the governor— a direct outcome of the Administrative Reorganization Movement. In one state of the seven the old-fashioned "legislative budget" is used, and boards or commissions prepare the state's financial plan in the other six.[100] The governor's budget message frequently is a useful vehicle to outline a program of action. In the long run, budget decisions are decisions on tax rates and tax policy and the general scale of governmental activity.

Prior to 1921 the state of Texas had only a legislative budget, but with the establishment of the Board of Control (a three-member group appointed by the governor with approval of the Senate, for six-year overlapping terms), that Board became the budgetary agency for Texas state government. The Board, however, was little more than a compiler of estimates and had no authority to refuse requisitions or to make periodic adjustments in budgetary expenditures for state agencies. Pursuant to the Uniform Budget Law of 1931 the governor was made the chief budget officer of the state. The Board of Control continued to prepare estimates, but the governor was authorized to secure additional information from the state auditor and other officials, and to hold public hearings. He was required to submit to the Legislature five itemized appropriations bills, ac-

---

[98] Paul H. Appleby, "The Role of the Budget Division," *Public Administration Review*, XVII (Summer, 1957), 156. Professor Appleby was dean of the Maxwell School of Citizenship, Syracuse University, Syracuse, New York.

[99] Harold D. Smith, "The Budget as an Instrument of Legislative Control and Executive Management," *Public Administration Review*, IV, 3 (Summer, 1944), 181.

[100] Jesse Burkhead, *Government Budgeting*, pp. 21–25.

companied by a budget message furnishing financial information.[101] Gubernatorial interest in budgeting varied from one administration to another, and at times the governor turned out to be only the "transmitter" of the Board of Control's budget. During these years budget messages were not of great import as most of the governor's recommendations lay in the message he sent at the opening of the Legislature. This situation prompted the authors of the Griffenhagen Report, prepared for a legislative committee on state government, to point out:

Apparently it is assumed that budgeting is limited to the compiling of estimates, the holding of hearings, and the preparation of a financial budget document and appropriations bills. This is not at all the case . . . The adoption of the budget presupposes, not only the drawing up of a financial plan, but actual budgetary control of expenditures. The budget law is decidedly weak in failing to specify clearly and positively how the budget is to be executed, and the limitations imposed upon the spending agencies in incurring obligations under appropriations.[102]

Until 1949 the situation remained essentially unchanged, but in that year a law created a Legislative Budget Board, composed of the presiding officer and four members from each house, and charged it with the responsibility of preparing a biennial budget. The position of the governor was unchanged.[103] Two years later the budgetary functions of the Board of Control were transferred to the governor, who was directed to present a budget within five days after the beginning of a legislative session.[104] As a consequence of these two laws, Texas has had two budgetary agencies and two budget documents, but the arrangement apparently has worked well.[105]

During the first dozen years of their existence the Legislative Budget Board and the Governor's Budget Office have come to cooperate in some phases of the preparation of the two budgets—on such matters for example, as issuing instructions to operating agencies, holding joint public hearings, and using matching page num-

[101] *General Laws*, Forty-second Legislature, regular session, pp. 339–349.

[102] Texas Legislature, Joint Committee on Organization and Economy, *The Government of the State of Texas*, Part II, pp. 67–88.

[103] *General and Special Laws of Texas*, Fifty-first Legislature, regular session, Ch. 487.

[104] *Vernon's Revised Civil Statutes*, Arts. 688–689.

[105] L. V. Howard and John H. Fenton, *State Governments in the South: Functions and Problems*, p. 28. Hereafter cited as Howard and Fenton, *State Governments in the South*.

bers in both documents. In the end, however, estimates are different, with the legislative budget ordinarily being lower and the executive budget more frequently including completely new spending programs. The legislative budget for the biennium 1962–1963 was $32 million less than the executive budget.[106]

The relationship existing between the two budget offices has been described by the director of the Legislative Budget Board in these terms:

> The Legislative Budget Board has become a well-traveled bridge between the legislative and executive branches of the government. Countless instances exist of greater cooperation between the two branches . . .
>
> Legislative budget examiners are under instructions, when they snag a budget problem to which executive policy may give solution, to furnish the facts and obtain the advice of the Governor. Prior to legislative sessions, [the governor] has actively sought the suggestions of legislative leadership, the budget staff, the State Auditor and the State Comptroller on the content of his messages to the Legislature.
>
> Executive heads of departments and agencies use the Legislative Budget Board as a point for advice and consultation on major issues of policy and operating problems that occur between sessions of the legislature. Such discussions have contributed immeasurably to better understanding of mutual problems by both the legislature and executive heads.[107]

Despite the cooperation, one feature of Texas financial administration has plagued both budget-making agencies. In action typical of most Southern states, Texas, by either constitutional or statutory provision, has earmarked some revenues for particular purposes, thus placing them beyond the control of the budgeters. As early as 1933 the Griffenhagen Report on reorganization of Texas government advised the abolition of all special funds as an aid to better budgeting;[108] but twenty years later the number of special funds had increased until 82 per cent of Texas revenues was being set aside out of the General Revenue Fund.[109] In a study of state finances in 1958 the Texas Legislative Council reported that of all departments and

---

[106] The Legislative Budget Board's estimates of expenditures totaled $2,458,920,946 for the biennium, as compared with executive budget estimates of $2,476,363,614.

[107] Vernon A. McGee, "A Legislative Approach to State Budgeting," *State Government*, XXVI (August, 1953), 204.

[108] Texas Legislature, Joint Committee on Organization and Economy, *The Government of the State of Texas*, Part II, p. 65.

[109] Howard and Fenton, *State Government in the South*, p. 29.

agencies, thirty maintain local funds outside the State Treasury, fourteen have funds both in and out of the State Treasury, and sixteen have little or no connection with the State Treasury.[110]

In his first budget message to the Legislature in March, 1963, Governor Connally pointed out that only about 15 cents of every dollar in the State Treasury was available for appropriation by the Legislature, as more than 85 cents had already been committed for special purposes in previous years. "This situation is caused by a fantastic system of 'Untouchable Funds' shielded by Constitutional restriction or by existing laws, literally tying the hands of those of us who are charged with handling the State's finances," said Connally.

As a result of the dual budgetary system and the widespread use of special funds, the budget message of Texas executives is far less meaningful than in states where the governor bears full responsibility for fiscal control. Governors' messages of the past decade have devoted much space to explaining why differences exist between estimates of the governor's budget and those of the Legislative Budget Board. In his first budget message Governor Price Daniel suggested the feasibility of combining the two sets of figures into one comprehensive document, but that recommendation has not been heeded as yet.[111]

When the development of the budgetary process in Texas is analyzed, one must conclude that the budget message in this state is of less importance than in many other states. Indeed the State of the State Message in Texas frequently includes recommendations which ordinarily would be expected to find their way into a budget message. There is no way to tell how much weight either of the recommended budgets carries with the lawmakers, who have final authority; but one can be certain that the budget prepared by their colleagues will not be treated lightly. Clearly, the budget message of the governor cannot exert the same degree of influence that it would if it were the only recommendation.

USEFULNESS OF THE MESSAGE POWER IN PRACTICE

Compared to other formal methods of gubernatorial control of policy, the message power may rank as the least effective, although

[110] Texas Legislative Council, *An Inventory of Special Funds Outside the State Treasury*, A Report to the Fifty-sixth Legislature, No. 55–8 (December, 1958), p. 10.

[111] "Budget Message to the 55th Legislature," by Price Daniel, p. 6.

the frequency with which it is used and the skill of the governor in using it affect its influence. Nevertheless, in the long run, the message has been a positive force in the formulation of legislative programs. Its importance to modern governors was emphasized by Governor Price Daniel in his initial message:

> The Governor is supposed to furnish leadership and assistance through messages of this nature in order that we may work and reason together in meeting our common obligation to the people of Texas and to the future progress and glory of our State.[112]

The record shows that Daniel's hope that "we may work and reason together" has not always been borne out by practice; but if it had not been for the governor's message power, far less would likely have been accomplished.

A few generalizations become evident. It appears that the executives achieving greatest acceptance of their recommendations—Hogg, Ferguson (in his first term), Stevenson, and Shivers—relied mainly on outlining their programs during the early days of a session, reserving special messages for occasions considered to be true emergencies. Governors who were less successful in achieving enactment of their proposals—Neff, Moody, and O'Daniel—repeatedly aimed a barrage of verbiage at the legislators upon the slightest provocation. Results would seem to indicate that the Legislature resents too frequent a display of "gubernatorial influence" through the exercise of the message power.

As might be expected, the style of the communications has varied considerably through the years. From the oratorical style of Hogg and Neff, the messages have run the gamut of literary form to the blunt, unadorned brevities of Sterling, the brief, businesslike statements of Shivers, and the folksy expressions of O'Daniel. Skilled or not in the use of language, however, every governor has found the message power useful to some degree; even the ones least successful have sometimes employed it to their advantage.

When messages have failed, what have been the causes? In the state of Alabama, Hallie Farmer found four general categories into which unaccepted recommendations of gubernatorial messages may fall. Her classifiaction is equally valid for Texas:

[112] *House Journal,* Fifty-fifth Legislature, regular session, p. 79.

1. Proposals meeting organized resistance because they are contrary to the interests of some powerful group or groups [e.g., the abolition of the fee system].

2. Proposals on which public opinion is strongly expressed and sharply divided [e.g., prohibition and pari-mutuel betting].

3. Proposals for which the public mind is not ready [e.g., constitutional revision].

4. Proposals made by the Governor in expectation (sometimes knowledge) that they will not be adopted. A tongue-in-cheek proposal [e.g., reapportionment].[113]

How useful is the message power in Texas? The answer lies primarily in the multiplicity of laws on the statute books today which originated in gubernatorial messages.

[113] Farmer, *The Legislative Process in Alabama*, p. 172.

9

The Governor and the Legislature:
Special Sessions

A major instrument of control over public policy which the governor may exercise is his ability to call the state's lawmaking body into extraordinary session when he deems such action feasible. In all except fourteen states this power lies exclusively with the chief executive, and in a majority of the states he is authorized to specify the subjects of legislation to be considered at the special session.[1] The special session, therefore, frequently becomes "the governor's session." Through the years legislatures in the several states have been convened on numerous occasions for a multiplicity of reasons, but four purposes have generally had the greatest significance: (1) to complete passage of necessary legislation which the regular session was unable to finish, (2) to cope with emergencies, (3) to begin the operation of a program more expeditiously, and (4) to break the gap between regular sessions.[2]

The nature of the special session supplies fertile soil for gubernatorial initiative. Issues are pinpointed because fewer matters must be considered than in regular sessions, and obviously, a chief executive is likely to be relatively sure of substantial support for his position before issuing the call. In a special session the governor is able to force consideration of his program by focusing public attention upon his recommendations. One writer has described the use of special sessions in American state legislatures as "distant kin to the Prime Minister's power of formulating a legislative program and allocating

[1] *The Book of the States*, 1960–1961, pp. 40–41.
[2] Hallie Farmer, *The Legislative Process in Alabama*, p. 174.

Parliamentary time."[3] Ordinarily, a major proportion of the requested legislation is enacted. Usually it is only when recommendations offend political tradition that they are rejected in called sessions.[4]

THE SPECIAL SESSION IN TEXAS

The Texas Constitution couches the power of executives over sessions of the Legislature in these terms:

The Governor may, on extraordinary occasions, convene the Legislature at the seat of Government, or at a different place, in case that should be in possession of the public enemy or in case of the prevalence of disease thereat. His proclamation therefore shall state specifically the purpose for which the Legislature is convened.[5]

This clause gives the governor of Texas his most important control over legislative sessions. Not only does he have the prerogative of calling the session but also he may specify what is to be considered and he may present additional subjects for consideration after the session is underway.[6] His control of the agenda is not, however, without general limitations. In the first place, the governor's control applies only to legislative acts and not to those which are executive or judicial in character, such as appointments and impeachments.[7] Second, the executive can control the subjects of legislation but not the details. Consequently, on some occasions it has become necessary for a governor to veto bills on matters he had specified for consideration because the version passed was radically different from his own thinking.

Notwithstanding the governor's theoretical control of subject matter, the custom has developed in Texas that legislation on other topics may be passed unless some member of the house in which the bill is being considered raises a point of order that is sustained by the presiding officer. If such bills are passed and signed by the governor, or filed by him with the secretary of state without his signature, they are considered valid.[8]

[3] Leslie Lipson, "Influence of the Governor Upon Legislation," *Annals of the American Academy of Political and Social Science,* 195 (January, 1938), 74.

[4] Farmer, *The Legislative Process in Alabama,* p. 174.

[5] Art. IV, Sec. 8.

[6] Usually this is done by including in the proclamation calling the session a provision that other subjects may be submitted by the governor during the called session.

[7] *Ferguson* v. *Maddox,* 263 S.W. 888 (1924).

[8] Stuart A. MacCorkle and Dick Smith, *Texas Government* (4th ed.), p. 95.

Despite these general limitations the special session has served as an effective instrument in molding public policy in Texas. From the adoption of the present Constitution in 1876 through 1963 the Texas Legislature had been called into extraordinary session sixty-seven times. The duration of the sessions was from a few minutes[9] to thirty days. The called session seems to be on the increase; it has taken a decided upturn during the present century. Of the twenty-four persons to occupy the executive office since 1876, only five have failed to utilize the prerogative at least once.[10] The first two incumbents, Coke and Hubbard, found it unnecessary to convene special sessions, but since their day only Governors O'Daniel, Jester, and Connally have failed to call a session.

Although O'Daniel was unsuccessful in getting the regular session to finance increased old-age pensions—his major campaign promise —he steadfastly refused, on the grounds of economy, to call emergency sessions. Subjected to much pressure to fulfill his promise, his stock answer, when he chose to answer, was: "If they could pass neither a statutory tax bill nor a constitutional amendment in 163 days at a cost of nearly a million dollars, why should they be called back for a special session?"[11] Had it not been for the fact that Governor Jester died a few days after the close of the regular session during his second term he probably would have called a session to consider his item veto of appropriations for state hospitals and special schools. That task fell to his successor, Allan Shivers.[12]

John Connally declined to call a special session soon after the regular session in 1963, saying one was not then necessary. Several months later, when a federal court ruled that Texas congressmen must run at large unless more equitable districts were created by the Legislature, Connally said he would try to postpone action until the United States Supreme Court had made a further ruling on reap-

[9] The shortest special session on record occurred during the Neff administration. When Governor Neff vetoed the appropriations bill he called a special session to begin the day following adjournment of the regular session. Some members resented the action, and others were incensed because they were not allowed enough time to return home and thus could not draw their mileage allowance. The session met in compliance with the proclamation but adjourned without transacting any business. Neff was forced to call another session within a few weeks. Interview with J. H. Johnson, secretary to Neff, March 17, 1961, in Austin.

[10] Data on frequency and dates of special sessions were compiled from records kept by the Legislative Reference Service, Texas State Library, made available by Miss Doris Connerly.

[11] *Austin American*, July 3, 1939.

[12] *House Journal*, Fifty-first Legislature, first called session, p. 1.

portionment. The Supreme Court's action, he said, might affect the lower court's ruling, and he would prefer to save the $400,000 which a special session would cost and leave the matter of reapportionment to be considered by the next regular legislative session.

PURPOSES OF SPECIAL SESSIONS

The majority of governors in this state have made effective use of special sessions. For the most part, the sessions have been necessitated by urgent financial problems or by emergency conditions. Some of them have extended the length of regular sessions; others have resulted from wartime situations or economic depressions. Governors' proclamations calling special sessions in the years between 1876 and 1964 listed 231 subjects for consideration.[13] By far the most compelling reason given was the need for appropriations. More than one-third of the sessions, twenty-five of the sixty-seven, were called upon to appropriate money for some specific function of the state government. The second most important item of consideration has been taxation. Five chief executives specified "to provide additional revenue to help erase the State's deficit," and ten others specifically referred to taxes. Unlike their successors, three early governors asked for a reduction in tax rates. Six others, however, requested new taxes, and one suggested a complete overhaul of the tax structure.

On fourteen occasions some phase of education was specified for consideration. Other items found most frequently on the agenda are shown in the tabulation below.

Subject Matter	Number of Sessions at which Considered
Prohibition	8
Social welfare	6
Railroads	6
Prisons	5
Highways	5
Reapportionment of state districts	5
Eleemosynary institutions	3
Quarantine against disease	3
Public buildings	3
Banks	3
Bonds	3

[13] The proclamations of governors convening extraordinary sessions are found at the beginning of both the *House Journal* and the *Senate Journal* of such called sessions. Data included here were compiled therefrom.

Many other subjects were submitted at least once, including such diverse matters as regulation of prize fighting; outlawing of pari-mutuel betting; regulation of lobbies; request for state civil service; request for laws to prevent fence destruction; distribution of the state's surplus monies; provision of bonded warehouses by the state; revision of the fee system of compensation for various officials; and election of a United States senator. Some governors yield to the entreaties of members to submit legislators' "pet measures" which have been unsuccessful in the regular session.[14] This tactic may be used to gain support for the governor's own measures; it was employed frequently during the Ferguson administrations.

SOME REPRESENTATIVE SPECIAL SESSIONS

The period of World War I and immediately thereafter witnessed a surge in the frequency of special sessions in Texas. During the biennium of 1918–1920, Governor William P. Hobby called extra sessions to deal with protection of the rights of servicemen, drought relief, and woman suffrage. One of the sessions was "ordered" by federal authorities to enact legislation to control the pink bollworm problem, under the threat that the federal government would quarantine Texas cotton unless the state acted to stamp out the bollworm. Hobby's executive secretary of that period terms this incident the first direct intervention of the national government in internal affairs of the state.[15]

In the early twenties Governor Pat M. Neff ran into difficulties with the Legislature on money matters, and during his two terms a total of five extra sessions were necessary to pass appropriations for the operation of the government. The use of the special session in Texas, however, hit its zenith during the Depression years. Within an eight-year interval (1929 to 1937), four governors called nine-

[14] For example, see *House Journal*, Thirty-fourth Legislature, first called session, *passim*. Governor J. E. Ferguson submitted a total of seventy-one additional matters, most of which were requested by individual members. A later governor, James V. Allred, refused to do so. In declining the request of the county judge of El Paso County to submit a measure, Allred wrote: "The special session has for its primary purpose consideration of revenue measures. . . . It lasts only thirty days, and I find I cannot be too cautious about submitting subjects other than the main program to the Legislature as it is easy to jam the calendar to where little, if anything, will be accomplished, particularly on the subject for which the session was called." Letter to Joseph McGill, dated October 7, 1937. Papers of Allred Administration, Box T–1953, Texas State Archives.

[15] Interview of the writer with Raymond Brooks, March 4, 1961, in Austin.

teen sessions. Governor Dan Moody set an all-time record with five sessions during the second term of his administration. A devotee of the balanced budget, Moody steadfastly refused to sign appropriations bills enlarging the state's deficit, and so adamant was he that he openly threatened to keep on vetoing bills until the lawmakers found a solution.[16] In the end he was able to get appropriations bills acceptable to him, although his pleas for enactment of civil-service laws for the state went unheeded.

Moody's successor, Governor Ross Sterling, was in office only one term (1931–1933), but his Administration was beset with many economic crises.[17] Oil was selling for ten cents a barrel and cotton for five cents a pound, and the Governor called four special sessions to try to ease the crises. Ill-prepared to offer any constructive solution, Sterling proved his ineptitude as a political leader; to cope with desperate Depression problems he suggested with reluctance that salaries of state employees might be reduced; to assist in averting unemployment he said that some citizens might pick cotton. His proposals for the Depression years added up to keeping the state on an even keel financially and leaving as much money in private hands as possible.[18]

Governor Miriam A. Ferguson's second administration (1933–1935) likewise was the setting for four special sessions to deal with Depression problems, including state compliance with the National Industrial Recovery Act sponsored by the New Deal of President Franklin D. Roosevelt. Although she suggested to the regular session a 3-per-cent sales tax to finance state activities, no action was taken; Mrs. Ferguson then proposed to a called session the issuance of $20 million worth of bonds—which came to be known as "bread bonds" —to aid in a program of public assistance. The Governor attached proposed bills as exhibits to her message[19]—an indication of the urgency of the situation—and the lawmakers quickly complied with her wishes.

Taxation and the need for economic relief were also the principal

[16] See Chapter 7.

[17] Beginning with the Sterling administration in 1931, the length of regular sessions of the Legislature was increased to 120 days. Regular sessions had been 60 days before that time. Despite the longer session four special sessions were called during that biennium.

[18] Warner E. Mills, Jr., "The Public Career of a Texas Conservative: A Biography of Ross Shaw Sterling" (unpublished Ph.D. dissertation), pp. 151–161.

[19] *House Journal*, Forty-third Legislature, first called session, pp. 8–17.

problems recognized by Governor James V. Allred when he was inaugurated in 1935. The Governor proposed a state income tax, which
was not accepted, and following in the paths of his predecessors, he
was forced to call special sessions to deal with the matter of finances.
The pattern of the past had become so obvious that a leading newspaper commented at the end of the regular session: "*Sine die* adjournment of the Texas Legislature Saturday concluded a session *very true
to form of recent years* in the amount of necessary legislation left
pending and compelling a special session" [Italics mine].[20] Allred had
to convene three special sessions before selective taxes on oil, gas,
sulphur, carbon black, liquor, and other items were passed. The
state's financial situation had become so precarious that the pension
law had to be "deliberalized" by eliminating assistance except to
the very needy.[21] Congress, in the meantime, had passed the national
Social Security Act, extending grants-in-aid to the states, and two
special sessions were needed during the second Allred administration
to pass legislation enabling Texas to qualify for these benefits.

After reaching a peak during the Depression decade, the number
of extra sessions declined. Shortage of funds for appropriations and
the need for additional taxes had been the chief reasons for special
sessions, but now prosperity resulting from World War II had eased
the financial situation of the state to the extent that Texas had a
surplus. The two governors who, up to 1961, had served longer in
office than any other incumbent called few special sessions. Both
these governors, Stevenson and Shivers, succeeded to the office from
the lieutenant governor's post, and each was forced to call a session
shortly after his accession because of a situation inherited from his
predecessor. Governor Stevenson, within one month after assuming
office, called a session to deal with a highway-financing bill which
Governor O'Daniel had been unable to get through the longest regular session on record up to that date. Stevenson takes some pride in
the fact that the session he called was able to get the same bill passed
in eleven days; he attributes this success to his close personal contacts with members of both houses—and to a number of conferences
with legislators.

Stevenson has expressed a dislike for extra sessions, primarily on

[20] *Dallas Morning News,* May 12, 1935.
[21] *House Journal,* Forty-fourth Legislature, third called session, p. 607.

grounds of expense. "It is amazing how well we can get along without legislation when we have to,"[22] he says.

After the one session Stevenson stuck to his position of not calling others, even in the face of pressure from many legislators. In 1944 he received petitions from members of both houses asking for an extraordinary session to exempt soldiers from the payment of poll taxes. Believing such an exemption would be in violation of the constitutional provision on poll taxes, the Governor made it clear that he would not convene a session, as one newspaper commented, "to throw out a dragnet to find a valid act. The finished acceptable bill must be shown him before the call."[23] Accused by one senator of usurping the power of the judiciary by presuming to pass upon the constitutionality of the proposed action, and thus himself violating the Constitution, Stevenson retorted, "I certainly have not changed my mind and I am going to follow the Constitution."[24] His view prevailed, and there was no session.

Governor Shivers, a former senator and lieutenant governor, apparently shared Stevenson's position on called sessions, for in seven and one-half years, he called only two. Six months after his inauguration he convened the Legislature to consider the matter of appropriations for special schools and hospitals—an item vetoed by his predecessor, Governor Jester. In his opening address, he declared, "None of us like special sessions [but] an emergency exists."[25] After outlining the deplorable situation existing in many institutions, the Governor proposed a method of financing the improvements, and summarized his philosophy of the executive's role:

> I served in the Legislature a good many years. I believed then that when a Governor came before the Legislature with a problem, he should also stand ready to help find an answer. I still feel the same way. Having called this emergency session, I think I ought to have the courage to share with you the responsibility for resolving the emergency.[26]

He declined "in the interests of businesslike procedure" to submit additional subjects for consideration until after the hospital financing

---

[22] Interview with former Governor Coke Stevenson, February 27, 1961, at Junction, Texas.
[23] *Dallas Morning News,* January 21, 1944.
[24] *Ibid.*
[25] *House Journal,* Fifty-first Legislature, first called session, p. 13.
[26] *Ibid.,* p. 14.

had been accomplished. After that bill was passed, he presented thirty-two other items of less general importance.[27]

Four years later, in his other special session, the Governor followed the same practice of submitting only major subjects for consideration and not presenting additional topics until after his original program had been acted upon. At that session four items were listed in the proclamation: pay increases for public school teachers; salary adjustments for state employees; construction of needed buildings at state institutions; and outlawing of the Communist Party in Texas. The Governor explained that the matters were so pressing as not to allow waiting another year. He proposed as sources of income a "gathering" tax on natural gas and additional franchise and beer taxes. Again he expressed his view of legislative-executive relations:

> At this point it might be the discreet thing for me to say that money-raising is the prerogative of the Legislature—and that I don't want to infringe upon your prerogative. Perhaps because I served in the Legislature myself, I look at it a little differently. When the Governor recommends the spending of money, I think he ought to recommend the means of raising that money. When he puts you on the spot, I think he ought to have the courage to get on it with you.[28]

This approach apparently won the confidence of the legislators, for his program was, for the most part, enacted as he presented it.

In the mid-1950's the financial plight of the state worsened because of increasing inflation, and Governor Price Daniel used the special session more extensively than at any time since the Depression era. During his first term Daniel pushed, without success, legislation designed to regulate lobbying in the state in an attempt to "restore public confidence in state government,"[29] which had been shaken by scandals in the veterans' land program and the insurance business. The emergency session passed a law requiring lobbyists to register, but the bill was considerably "watered down" from the version the Governor had hoped for. The following year Daniel again called a special session, to which he presented an "Anti-Troop Bill," designed to maintain law and order in the operation of public schools without the use of military force, and to prevent violence in the racial integration of public schools.[30]

[27] *Ibid.*, p. 232.
[28] *Ibid.*, Fifty-third Legislature, first called session, p. 11.
[29] *Ibid.*, Fifty-fifth Legislature, regular session, p. 20.
[30] *Ibid.*, Fifty-fifth Legislature, second called session, p. 8.

Daniel was confronted with a huge deficit at the beginning of his second term in 1959, and the problem of taxation had again become the most urgent issue of the day. The Legislature recoiled from enacting the largest tax bill in the history of the state, and three special sessions were called before the impasse was resolved by increasing existing taxes on cigarettes, automobiles, radio and television sets, and levying new taxes on hotels, boats, air conditioners, and other items.[31] The deficit was even greater by 1961, and early in the regular session Daniel submitted a bill to allow the state to escheat unclaimed bank accounts. He sent along a brochure urging adoption of the proposal and saying he hoped a special session would not be necessary to get a law enacted.[32] A special session was necessary, however, in January, 1962.

TEXAS' MOST SPECTACULAR SPECIAL SESSION

Although most special sessions in Texas history have delved into problems of legislation, the enactment of laws has not been their sole function. The most publicized special session in the annals of Texas was that of 1917 in which the governor of the state was impeached. Controversy had developed between Governor James E. Ferguson and officials of The University of Texas over appropriations for that institution. In a session called immediately after the regular session, an appropriations bill was finally passed, but Ferguson item-vetoed the expenditures for the University because five faculty members had not been removed in accordance with his wishes. Several weeks passed, and the Governor called another special session to consider another appropriations bill. Immediately after the session convened, however, the speaker of the House, F. O. Fuller, presented articles of impeachment against the Governor. Most of the charges dealt with alleged misuse of state funds. Acting in its "judicial" capacity, the session which the Governor had called proceeded to pass certain of the articles and to sit as a high court of impeachment for him. A third called session (meeting under proclamation of Acting Governor Hobby) finally convicted and removed Ferguson.[33] These two special

[31] Institute of Public Affairs, The University of Texas, *The Fifty-sixth Legislature: A Review of Its Work*, pp. 3–9.
[32] *Austin Statesman*, February 15, 1961.
[33] A good account of the impeachment is given in Ralph W. Steen, "The Ferguson War on The University of Texas," *Southwestern Social Science Quarterly*, 35 (March, 1955).

sessions had far-reaching effects because the displacing of Ferguson subsequently resulted in his wife's election as chief executive, to become the nation's first elected woman governor. And for some two decades "Fergusonism" was a vibrant issue in most Texas elections. Probably the work of no other special session ever had such a long-lasting impact.

THE VALUE OF SPECIAL SESSIONS TO THE GOVERNOR

The mere recapitulation of subjects considered by special sessions of the Texas Legislature, and the frequency with which such sessions have been called, points up their importance as a formal instrument of gubernatorial control of public policy. The extraordinary sessions have frequently served as the forum for discussion of new revenue measures and have appropriated millions of dollars of the taxpayers' money. In addition, important public issues related to a variety of subjects have been debated. Table 9 summarizes the number of and reasons for special sessions from 1876 through 1963.

One can hypothesize a correlation between the frequency of special sessions and prevailing economic conditions. Certainly, in times of economic crises such as depressions or periods of extreme inflation, the special session has been useful in the compromising, if not the settling, of differences of opinion. Governors have been relatively successful in called sessions in pushing through the major parts of their proposals, especially in the matter of appropriations. No session yet has failed to work out some solution to provide essential services, possibly as a result of the publicity given the issues and the consequent crystallization of public opinion.

The extra session has proved to be a two-way street; while the governor may use it to push his proposals, the Legislature may use it as a "weapon" to keep the executive from going too far afield. Once convened, the assembly may proceed to nonlegislative matters, such as impeachment and confirmation of appointments. Because of the adoption in 1960 of the annual-salary plan for legislators, future governors of Texas may be less hesitant to convene extra sessions than has been the case in the past when legislators received extra pay for extra sessions. Governor Connally, however, gave the expense of a special session as his main reason for not calling one in 1963. Since the adoption of the Constitution of 1876, the sixty-seven special sessions of the Texas Legislature have played a vital part in the molding of public policy; such influence will undoubtedly continue.

TABLE 9

Frequency of Special Sessions of the Texas Legislature, 1876–1963

Governor	Biennium	Legis-lature	Number of Special Sessions	Major Items of Business
Coke	1876	15th	0	
Hubbard	1877–1878	15th	0	
Roberts	1879–1880	16th	1	Appropriations; sale of public land
Roberts	1881–1882	17th	1	Construction of public buildings; reduction of taxes
Ireland	1883–1884	18th	1	Taxation for schools
Ireland	1885–1886	19th	0	
Ross	1887–1888	20th	1	Taxation; distribution of surplus funds
Ross	1889–1890	21st	0	
Hogg	1891–1892	22nd	1	
Hogg	1893–1894	23rd	0	Legislation to control railroads
Culberson	1895–1896	24th	1	Legalization of prize-fighting; appropriations
Culberson	1897–1898	25th	1	Appropriations; revocation of fee system
Sayers	1899–1900	26th	1	Taxation
Sayers	1901–1902	27th	2	Appropriations
Lanham	1903–1904	28th	1	Appropriations; bond refunding
Lanham	1905–1906	29th	2	Appropriations; revision of election laws
Campbell	1907–1908	30th	1	Taxation; strengthening of corporation laws
Campbell	1909–1910	31st	4	Creation of bank; prison reform; insurance reform
Colquitt	1911–1912	32nd	1	Appropriations; reapportionment of congressional legislative, judicial districts
Colquitt	1913–1914	33rd	3	Appropriations; state-owned warehouses and bank supervision
J. E. Ferguson	1915–1916	34th	1	Appropriations; insurance laws
J. E. Ferguson	1917	35th[a]	2	Appropriations; uniform textbook law
Hobby	1917–1918	35th	2	Servicemen protection; impeachment of governor
Hobby	1919–1920	36th	4	Appropriations; bollworm quarantine; money for education

TABLE 9 (Continued)

Frequency of Special Sessions of the Texas Legislature, 1876–1963

Governor	Biennium	Legis-lature	Number of Special Sessions	Major Items of Business
Neff	1921–1922	37th	2	Appropriations; money for schools; reapportionment of congressional and legislative districts
Neff	1923–1924	38th	3	Appropriations; Prohibition enforcement
M. A. Ferguson	1925–1926	39th	1	Road bonds; investigation of state departments
Moody	1927–1928	40th	1	Appropriations; money for highways
Moody	1929–1930	41st	5	Prison reform; money for education; civil service for state employees
Sterling	1931–1932	42nd	4	Oil and gas conservation; money for highways
M. A. Ferguson	1933–1934	43rd	4	Relief bonds; public works
Allred	1935–1936	44th	3	Repeal of Prohibition; old-age pensions
Allred	1937–1938	45th	2	Social welfare measures; repeal of race-track gambling
O'Daniel	1939–1940	46th	0	
O'Daniel	1941	47th	0	
Stevenson	1941–1942	47th[b]	1	Highway financing
Stevenson	1943–1944	48th	0	
Stevenson	1945–1946	49th	0	
Jester	1947–1948	50th	0	
Jester	1949	51st[c]	0	
Shivers	1949–1950	51st	1	Building program for eleemosynary institutions
Shivers	1951–1952	52nd	0	
Shivers	1953–1954	53rd	1	Increase in teacher and state salaries; public buildings
Shivers	1955–1956	54th	0	
Daniel	1957–1958	55th	2	Regulation of lobbies; water conservation
Daniel	1959–1960	56th	3	Appropriations; state deficit
Daniel	1961–1962	57th	3	Taxation; teacher's pay scale; escheat legislation
Connally	1963–	58th	0	

[a] Two sessions called by Ferguson, and after his impeachment two called by Hobby.

[b] O'Daniel resigned to become U. S. Senator, and Stevenson called session.

[c] Jester died in office, and Shivers called session.

Source: Proclamations of governors convening special sessions found in *House Journal* of each session.

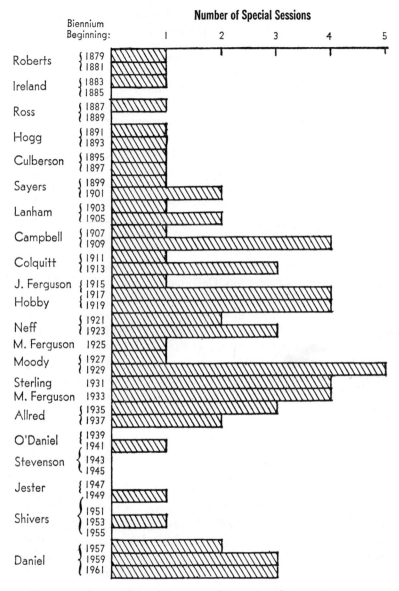

FIG. 6—Frequency of special sessions of Texas Legislature, 1879–1964.

RELATIVE IMPORTANCE OF THE LEGISLATIVE POWERS
OF THE GOVERNOR

The preceding three chapters, which present an analysis of executive-legislative relationships provided for in the Constitution of Texas, indicate the significant roles of the veto, the gubernatorial message, and the extraordinary session in the formation of the public policy of the state. Used individually, any one of these devices provides the governor with special influence, and when the three are employed together, the aggregate effect is considerable.

The relative importance of the three powers cannot be exactly assessed, but it would seem that the veto, coupled with the threat of veto, has been the most significant. The infrequency with which vetoes have been overridden since 1876 and the fact that no veto has been overridden for two decades attest to the strength of that power.

The ability to convene special sessions of the legislative body probably ranks closely behind the veto power for effectiveness in promoting a governor's program. Called sessions have loomed large in periods of war, depression, and financial crises, and most of the sixty-seven extraordinary meetings convened for a specific purpose have given the chief executives at least a portion of what they asked.

As it is used most often and as the skill of the governor in expressing himself is involved, the message power has yielded the poorest results of any of the three constitutional means of legislative leadership available to the executive. Nevertheless, Texas legislators appear more and more to expect the governor to outline his proposals for them to discuss, dissect and criticize.

The governor of Texas may not occupy the role of chief legislator in the same fashion as do his counterparts in many other states, but gubernatorial influence upon the legislative process in Texas has been decidedly increasing for some time.

Inasmuch as the relationship of the governor to the Legislature is largely personal rather than official, varying techniques of leadership, informal or extralegal in character, have been employed by governors to promote their programs. Among the more common of these are cultivation of individual contacts, "organization" of the Legislature, use of lobbyists and of citizens' study groups, and dispensation of patronage. The following chapter will investigate those informal techniques of leadership which supplement the formal relationships.

10

The Politics of Executive-Legislative Relationships

Anyone familiar with the realities of political life is aware that the "great game of politics" entails at one time or another varying degrees of cajolery, conniving, capitulation, cunning, and compromise. Nowhere is the give-and-take nature of politics more demonstrable than in the lawmaking process, and probably no better example of practical politics in operation can be cited than the techniques utilized by a chief executive in his dealings with the lawmakers. The informal methods employed to further a legislative program are as important, if not more important, than are the constitutional powers of delivering messages, calling special sessions, and exercising the veto. A common belief is that as many laws are "passed" in corridors, offices, downtown hotels, and social gatherings as are enacted in the legislative halls. The informal, extralegal techniques of politics are, therefore, of inestimable value to an executive in the promotion of his program.

One thorough exploration of executive-legislative relationships notes that the techniques used to promote legislative programs or to block measures inimical to such programs vary from state to state and even within the same state under succeeding governors. Nevertheless, many methods of influence merge to constitute what may be labelled a "cycle of influence" that affects each important piece of legislation.[1]

---

[1] Coleman B. Ransone, *The Office of Governor in the United States,* p. 202.

THE CYCLE OF INFLUENCE

The first step in the cycle occurs in the prelegislative sessions, i.e., the caucus of the majority party in a two-party state or informal meetings of various legislative factions in a one-party state. Decisions are reached in these conclaves as to who will be selected to fill important positions such as speaker of the House, president pro tempore of the Senate, and even, sometimes, the chairmen of important committees. The governor is vitally concerned about the occupants of these posts, for his program may be at their mercy while it is in the legislative process. The executive's participation in the selection of legislative leadership must be a matter of great delicacy inasmuch as legislators frequently are inclined to view any interference as an improper intrusion into their domain. "Yet, the governor has a very real interest in the selection of these important officers and must attempt to make his weight felt without giving offense to the legislature."[2]

The second step in the influence cycle develops with the presentation of the subject matter of proposed legislation as a part of the governor's message to the legislators.[3] Ordinarily the message receives widespread publicity, being discussed at length in the press and on radio and television, and consequently, it may carry considerable persuasive power. Representatives and senators know that their constituents are generally informed of the governor's program and that they may ask embarrassing questions about a failure to vote for the proposals, although, conversely, constituents may at times deluge legislators with requests to work against certain of the proposals. Since the governor's program probably has been publicized during the election campaign and since he has been elected by the people of the whole state, many of his requests may be approved without strong pressure and often with little or no effort on the part of the executive.

Sooner or later, however, a proposal will be viewed by some member of the Legislature as being obnoxious, or opposed to the best interests of his constituents, or unacceptable to his faction—a measure he cannot, for some reason, support. Here the influence cycle enters its third phase, which is based largely upon persuasion and cajolery and in which the governor must use every available technique to align the recalcitrant legislators on his side. The ways in

[2] *Ibid.,* p. 204.
[3] The message power is discussed in detail in Chapter 8.

which persuasion can be used were well summarized by Governor Walter Kohler of Wisconsin in explaining the "honorable" ways of influencing a legislature:

I have attended, when invited to do so, the caucuses of my party in the two houses and invited its members to support bills or resolutions which I deemed in the public interest. I have spoken, through members of my staff, at hearings when matters of this type were before the standing committees of the Legislature for consideration. I have met at regular intervals with the leaders of my party in both houses to discuss with them the legislative program before their houses and to receive the benefit of their advice and counsel on how best to solve problems of state concern. I have met with most members of the Legislature individually and urged upon them the importance of the measures which I have recommended. I have also received from them a great deal of helpful advice in discharging my responsibilities.[4]

Professor Coleman B. Ransone concludes that the first three steps in the influence cycle follow a general pattern in most states: (1) organization of the legislature, (2) introduction of the subject matter of proposed legislation by the governor's message, and (3) personal conferences with legislators by the governor to explain his program and to solicit support for his viewpoint. Ransone adds:

If these three steps fail, then the governor may resort to other methods and the steps in the cycle will not follow necessarily in any particular order since the influence must be tailored to the situation at hand. Among the more common methods used are the threat of veto and patronage. The latter may take the form of the appointment of a protege of the legislator to a government position or the promise of a future appointment to the bench or to some other position for the legislator himself. It also takes the form of awarding contracts to a firm in which the legislator is interested or paving of certain highways and even private roads in the legislator's district. Occasionally, the governor will use his pardoning power as a lever in influencing legislation.[5]

Although the control of patronage and a working liaison with the legislature are consistently the most important,[6] a wide variety of persuasive techniques are employed by governors to influence the legislators. Among the most common are direct appeal to the voters,

[4] Quoted in Ransone, *The Office of Governor in the United States*, pp. 206–207.
[5] *Ibid.*, pp. 208–209.
[6] Belle Zeller (ed.), *American State Legislatures*, p. 198.

social entertainments for the lawmakers, pleas from citizens' study groups, pressure from lobbyists, and individual conferences.

In the fourth and final phase, according to Professor Ransone, the influence cycle comes around to the most drastic step—use of the executive veto, or, in a few states, the executive amendment. While the veto power has been highly effective in practice, most chief executives prefer to use other means available to them.[7]

The Cycle of Influence in Texas

The executive-legislative relationships provided for in the Texas Constitution—the veto, the special session, and the message power—having been discussed in the preceding three chapters,[8] this chapter will be devoted to a consideration of the first and third steps of the influence cycle in Texas, namely, the presession activities and the persuasive devices. In the last analysis, these two steps are the informal extralegal techniques which are vitally important in the politics of legislation.

"Organization" of the Legislature

As the lieutenant governor of Texas, who is the ex-officio president of the Senate, is elected by the voters, the governor has little voice in the organization of the upper house. Of course, if he is a close friend of the lieutenant governor, he may offer counsel on the matter of committee appointments; but actions involving personal relationships between officials seldom become a matter of record, and the frequency and extent of a governor's suggestions are matters of conjecture. The presiding officer of the Senate has wide latitude in appointing standing committees of the Senate and their chairmen, as well as in referring bills to committee and in recognizing members desiring to speak. Many consider the office of lieutenant governor to be as powerful and important as the office of governor; some might maintain that it is even more important.[9] Because the lieutenant governor holds the key to success or failure of the legislative program, it would seem desirable for the governor to enlist his cooperation, or certainly to avoid open hostility toward him.

The "organization" of the House of Representatives is a different

[7] Ransone, *The Office of Governor in the United States,* pp. 212–213.
[8] Chapters 7, 8, and 9.
[9] Travis McBride, "The Office of Lieutenant Governor in Texas with Emphasis on Recent Administrations" (unpublished research paper), p. 24.

situation, as a new speaker is elected from the membership every two years, the contest sometimes becoming a bitter, hard-fought struggle. In such circumstances the chief executive has greater opportunity to make his influence felt. Because intervention is a delicate matter, a governor must proceed with caution, exercising a maximum of tact and diplomacy lest the members feel that he is attempting to dictate to them. But with finesse, the governor may be a major factor in the outcome of the speaker's race; conversely, he may become involved in bitter controversy. For this reason, most governors avoid open participation in the organization races, preferring to work through private, behind-the-scenes means. Whatever the approach, however, no governor can escape being interested in the organization of the House, for the presiding officer and his committees may spell the difference between life and death for the executive's program.

Although most governors of Texas remain nominally neutral in races for the speakership, some evidence exists of gubernatorial activity in the organization of the House of Representatives. An early incident, with far-reaching consequences, occurred in 1911, when Governor Oscar B. Colquitt supported Jeff Cox of Rockwall for presiding officer. In a letter to his friend Jake Wolters, Colquitt expressed his desire to see Cox elected and urged Wolters to work in Cox's behalf so there would be a House organization friendly to the Colquitt Administration.[10] The Texas Legislature was almost equally divided on the Prohibition issue, and Colquitt's intervention embroiled him in bitter quarrels with the lawmakers. His candidate lost the speakership to Sam Rayburn, of Fannin County, and Colquitt's program had difficulty throughout the session. The hostility engendered in this race carried over to the next session, in which Governor Colquitt sought unsuccessfully to get Speaker C. V. Terrell removed, declaring, "I have known for thirty days that the Speaker was a traitor to the administration, notwithstanding his previous profession of friendship."[11] Terrell retorted that the people resented the Governor's abuse of the Legislature and that public unrest over it was growing. Needless to say, these disputes did Colquitt's cause no good in the Legislature, and his program suffered.

[10] George P. Huckaby, "Oscar Branch Colquitt: A Political Biography" (unpublished Ph.D. dissertation), p. 236. The letter mentioned is among the Colquitt Papers in the Archives of The University of Texas.

[11] *Austin Statesman,* March 23, 1913. See also issues of March 24 and April 2, 1913.

Some years later, gubernatorial intervention in the speaker's race took a different turn. As related by Coke Stevenson, the following circumstances led to his election as speaker of the House during the second term of Governor Miriam A. Ferguson.[12] Representative A. P. Johnson of Edwards County, a staunch supporter of the retiring Governor, Ross Sterling, was conceded to have enough votes to be elected speaker in 1933, and on a Sunday following the election in the fall of 1932, several prominent attorneys sought an audience with Johnson to thrash out some legislative problems. When they telephoned for an appointment, Johnson, a devout churchman, informed them he would be happy to receive them but that it was against his principles to transact business on the Sabbath. Incensed at what they considered to be a "holier-than-thou" attitude, the lawyers told their friends of the "rebuff," and the matter soon came to the attention of the Governor-elect's husband, James E. Ferguson, who snorted, "If Johnson can't talk about legislation on Sundays *before* he becomes Speaker, what *will* he do when he gets elected?" In the view of Coke Stevenson, Johnson's attitude may have cost him the speakership, for shortly after the incident Ferguson contacted Stevenson to ascertain whether he would be interested in running for that position. Stevenson reminded Ferguson that he had not supported Mrs. Ferguson in the election, but her husband indicated that this oversight would make no difference if Stevenson would run for the office. "At least you don't have a son named for Ross Sterling," he said. (Johnson's son was named for Sterling.) All the "Ferguson men" in the House were advised to ditch Johnson in favor of Stevenson, who, with this assistance, won the speakership and went on to become lieutenant governor and governor of Texas.

PUBLIC ENDORSEMENT OF A CANDIDATE FOR SPEAKER

Two years later, in 1935, newly elected Governor James V. Allred took what was probably the most active role ever publicly assumed by a Texas executive in the organization of the House. Allred had held public office but had never been a member of the Legislature and possibly failed to comprehend fully the workings and the psy-

[12] The story of his election as speaker in 1933 was related by Coke Stevenson to the writer in an interview in Junction, Texas, February 27, 1961. Mr. Stevenson said that he did not believe that this account had been publicized before, but since almost thirty years had elapsed since it took place, he authorized the writer to quote him.

chology of the legislators. In youthful enthusiasm to push his social-welfare program through as rapidly as possible, he "stuck his foot in the legislative door and ended up with it in his mouth."[13] His shaky start with the solons came about principally because he openly favored J. B. Ford for the speakership. When it became apparent that Speaker Stevenson would seek an unprecedented second term as presiding officer, Allred was coaxed into shifting his support to Representative Robert W. Calvert of Hill County. Two of Allred's friends, who had contributed heavily to the campaign funds of several House members, wired from Galveston that the switch would be "in the best interests of the state."[14] Allred thus became deeply involved in a public controversy over the speakership. In the words of Dallas County Representative Sarah T. Hughes (now Federal District Judge Hughes), the question became whether to follow the leadership of the Governor or the leadership of the "sulphur company and oil interests."[15]

More than a quarter of a century later, the two principals reminisced about that 1935 race. Stevenson, who won, recalled that many of the original supporters of Ford were alienated by the Governor's action in switching his support to Calvert, but that an even greater number resented Allred's interference in the race at all. In language of a West Texas rancher, Stevenson commented that open gubernatorial intervention in the speaker's race is certainly the best way to "cut a gut."[16] On the other hand, Calvert, who later became chief justice of the Texas Supreme Court, expressed the opinion that Governor Allred had nothing to lose by entering the fight. A showdown between the opposing forces was inevitable, Calvert said, and the Governor might have won. Calvert also recalled that during the race one influential representative came to him asking for the chairmanship of a major committee in return for his support. When Calvert informed him that he was not yet in a position to make the assignment, the representative and several of his friends joined the Stevenson camp. In Calvert's opinion, the denial of this committee chairmanship probably swung the balance against him.[17] In any event, despite

[13] Robb K. Burlage, "James V. Allred—Texas' Liberal Governor" (unpublished research paper), p. 25.

[14] Interview with Chief Justice Robert W. Calvert, in Austin, March 25, 1961.

[15] *Dallas Morning News,* January 9, 1935.

[16] Interview with former Governor Coke Stevenson, in Junction, February 27, 1961.

[17] Interview with Chief Justice Robert W. Calvert, in Austin, March 25, 1961.

gubernatorial backing, Calvert lost to Stevenson by a vote of 68 to 80, but he rebounded to win the speakership two years later, this time with less open support from Allred.

Succeeding governors probably have profited from Allred's mistake, for since the Stevenson-Calvert contest no chief executive has openly taken part in the struggle for the speakership. Recent governors have preferred more subtle and less publicized tactics. During his own tenure in the top office, Stevenson let the legislators know whom he preferred for speaker, but he did so on an informal individual basis rather than by formally endorsing a candidate.[18] Allan Shivers disavowed any participation in the speaker's races during his incumbency. Saying that his long service in the Legislature had taught him that the lawmakers resented interference in internal matters, Shivers refused to be drawn into their squabbles.[19] Neither did Governor Price Daniel ever openly endorse a candidate for speaker during his three terms, although it was widely rumored in Austin that he favored Waggoner Carr in 1959 and James A .Turman in 1961, both of whom were elected. Asked if he thought the Governor worked in his behalf, Turman replied that there was a prevalent feeling that Daniel was in sympathy with his candidacy because the only other hopeful, Wade Spillman, had on previous occasions opposed some of the Governor's measures.[20] Turman said, however, that he knew of no specific instances in which the Governor had applied pressure in his behalf.

It would appear that governors of Texas have not been particularly successful in the first step of the influence cycle—"organizing" the House and the Senate. Certainly, if an executive is to participate, he would be well advised to do so through informal, individual contacts, for open, public endorsements seem to spell defeat for the endorsed candidate and consequently weaken the governor's influence with the Legislature.

THE CLEMENCY POWER AND THE LEGISLATIVE PROCESS

Prior to 1936 the practically unlimited power of the governor in matters of clemency often supplied a valuable tool with which support could be elicited for administration bills. Not infrequently, legis-

[18] Interview with former Governor Coke Stevenson, in Junction, February 27, 1961.
[19] Interview with former Governor Allan Shivers, in Austin, December 4, 1961.
[20] Interview with Speaker James A. Turman, in Austin, July 13, 1961.

lators called on the executive to grant pardons or reprieves to their clients or constituents; in return for such a favor the governor could pick up a vote in the Legislature. Citizens who had thus approached a legislator believed that his "influence" with the governor was responsible for the clemency and they were grateful to him as well as to the executive. Both governor and legislator gained position on this two-way street. In the opinion of two gubernatorial assistants of those days, the chief executive lost a valuable bargaining point for his legislative program when the constitutional amendment creating the Board of Pardons and Paroles relieved him of much of the responsibility for deciding on clemency matters.[21]

PATRONAGE

Another method open to the governor to influence legislation probably has declined in importance over the years. During the early part of this century the executive could use his extensive power of patronage to gain support for his proposals, but the gradual accretion of boards and commissions to perform state functions has whittled away some of this influence. Although the modern governor cannot require state agencies to employ his political proteges, as he could in times past, his power of patronage has not been dissipated completely, for he still makes hundreds of appointments to the board and commissions. Most of these appointments must be confirmed by the Senate,[22] and in numerous instances senators or representatives have friends or constituents whom they endorse for appointment. Occasionally a member may desire an appointment for himself. A case in point arose in the summer of 1961. While the Legislature was meeting in special session to tackle the problem of the sales tax, on which the regular session had reached an impasse, a vacancy occurred on the Railroad Commission. A large number of persons were interested in being appointed, and, according to one confidant of Governor Daniel, among them was Lieutenant Governor Ben Ramsey. The Governor, therefore, was able to use the bargaining power of the appointment to enlist the aid of the Senate's presiding officer in the legislative battle. Although Daniel was unable to get his position on the tax

[21] Interview with Ghent Sanderford, secretary to Governor Miriam A. Ferguson, in Austin, April 13, 1961, and with Pat Dougherty, secretary to Governors Dan Moody and Ross Sterling, in Austin, July 20, 1961.

[22] See Chapter 5.

accepted without compromise, quite possibly the Lieutenant Governor was more inclined to work with the chief executive in reaching the compromise than he would have been otherwise. As Ramsey had been in the chair for eleven years and had a large following among his colleagues, he could effectively "suggest" that they cooperate in the passage of tax legislation acceptable to the Governor. Whatever part he may have played, Lieutenant Governor Ramsey received the appointment some weeks after the special session had enacted legislation which was not completely repugnant to the Governor.

No one would claim that the power of patronage today is as potent a factor as it was in the 1920's and 1930's, but it cannot be disregarded even in the 1960's. Patronage remains an effective bargaining point, although a limited one now. The risk that a governor must run in making an appointment is that while winning some votes for his program he may simultaneously lose others by alienating the losing candidates and their supporters.

INDIVIDUAL CONFERENCES WITH MEMBERS OF THE LEGISLATURE

Undoubtedly, the method most consistently used through the years to influence legislation has been the individual conference between the chief executive and a legislator. Sometimes the governor may summon a member for discussion, or he may issue an open invitation for the lawmakers to come to him, as did Governor Pat Neff in one of his first messages:

> I covet an opportunity to make the personal acquaintance of every Senator and every member of the House. It is my desire that we confer freely touching all matters of interest to the people. I therefore most earnestly extend a cordial invitation to each of you to visit me at my office at any and all times. . . . If on coming you will be kind enough to make your presence known to my private secretary, you will be gladly and immediately received, prior to other callers.[23]

Reporting that Governor W. Lee O'Daniel frequently conferred with legislators during his term of office, Professor S. S. McKay wrote:

> Governor O'Daniel had been calling members of the House to his office in an almost steady stream during the first few days in March [1941]. He urged them to pass his plan to use the entire revenue of the general fund

[23] *Senate Journal*, Thirty-seventh Legislature, regular session, p. 120

to discharge the Social Security obligations. His efforts were interpreted as a purpose to create a condition from which there would be no escape from a general sales tax. . . . As one observer put it, the governor approached the legislators "with a lollipop in one hand and a club in the other as instruments of persuasion."[24]

In discussing the techniques used over the twenty years in which he served in the legislative and executive branches, Governor Price Daniel said he detects a trend toward much greater personal contact on the part of the executive. He noted that, as governor, he had attempted to have a conference with every member of both houses who cared to come for discussions of proposed bills. Usually the discussions were between him and one member, but on occasion he invited several members at one time to participate in the conferences.[25]

Governor Daniel also met with committees of the Legislature to present his views.[26] Speaker James A. Turman pointed out, for example, that during the first called session of the Fifty-seventh Legislature, a conference committee dealing with the sales tax called Governor Daniel one night near midnight to come to the Capitol to discuss how an impasse might be resolved. Although the Governor had already retired, he arose, went to the Capitol, and worked into the early morning hours with the committee to produce what ultimately was adopted as a compromise sales tax bill.[27]

The influence of such personal diplomacy is not calculable, but all chief executives have found conferences to be useful in effecting a better understanding of the positions of all parties. Without exception, governors, staff members, and legislators say they consider a conference to be one of the most successful and most frequently used techniques in the legislative process.

Legislative breakfasts. One particular type of conference has become especially useful in recent years. Governor Allan Shivers began the practice of inviting small groups of ten or twelve members to breakfast at the Executive Mansion, at which time he would promote his proposals and listen to the views of his guests.[28] In Shivers' judg-

---

[24] S. S. McKay, W. *Lee O'Daniel and Texas Politics, 1938–1942*, p. 380.

[25] Interview with Governor Price Daniel, in Austin, November 30, 1961.

[26] On March 15, 1961, this writer had an appoinment for an interview at 3:00 p.m. with Governor Daniel. Approximately thirty minutes before the time, the Governor's secretary called to cancel the appointment, saying that the House Committee on Revenue and Taxation had summoned the Governor to a meeting.

[27] Interview with Speaker James A. Turman, in Austin, July 13, 1961.

[28] Interview with former Governor Allan Shivers, in Austin, December 4, 1961.

ment, this maneuver was highly effective; it became so popular that it was continued by Price Daniel, who also rated it "very useful." During the Daniel administration, all of the 181 members dined with the Governor at some time during each regular session. At the meetings pending bills were brought up and discussed.

John Connally gave the hospitality technique a new twist in 1963. During the Fifty-eighth Legislature he instituted "nonpolitical," get-acquainted meals at the Mansion. Small, homogeneous groups of seven or eight members were invited for the purpose of getting better acquainted with the Governor. In attendance also, to mix with the legislators, were two staff members from the Governor's Office. Over the four-month period, practically all of the senators and about 95 per cent of the representatives dined at such a meal.[29] Despite the nonpolitical tag, such meetings no doubt were helpful in promoting the Governor's program. On the final evening of the session, Connally held open house in the Governor's Reception Room in the Capitol, where he served refreshments to the lawmakers and their families.

Visits in the homes of legislators. Governor W. Lee O'Daniel's approach to members of the Legislature was unusual, as were many aspects of his public career. Shortly after his re-election in 1940 O'Daniel announced plans to visit in the homes of as many members as possible, particularly those of the newly elected members, to "get better acquainted" prior to the legislative session. Having the governor of Texas drive up to his home naturally created favorable publicity in a legislator's locality, especially if he resided in a small town, and the plan met with the approval of both friends and foes of the Governor. The announced purpose of his visits was not to discuss legislative matters but to build good will by meeting families and seeing how the lawmakers lived. O'Daniel covered 7,000 miles in five weeks and visited 90 per cent of the members of the Legislature. Upon his return to Austin he revealed that results had been even more successful than he had hoped for.[30]

"WORKING THE FLOOR"

Governors have, from time to time, designated floor leaders in both houses, whose duty it was to operate somewhat in the same fashion

---

[29] Interview with Governor Daniel, in Austin, November 30, 1961. Interview with Frank Miskell, administrative assistant to Governor Connally, in Austin, August 14, 1963.

[30] McKay, W. *Lee O'Daniel and Texas Politics, 1938–1942*, pp. 343–344.

as do the majority leaders in the houses of Congress; but the use of this device has been sporadic and has had varying degrees of importance. Some executives have denounced the tactic, as did Governor Neff:

I shall have no one to represent me on the floor of either the House or the Senate. There shall be no administration bills from my office. Anything that I desire to communicate to this lawmaking body, I shall submit in writing or ask the high privilege of doing it in person. If the recommendations I see fit to make from time to time to this body have not enough merit in them to demand attention of some lawmaker, then that measure has not enough merit in it to be considered by this assembly, and if I should chance to recommend a meritorious matter, then I shall expect every man in the Senate and House, without regard to anything else in this world, to be the champion and defender of the recommendation.[31]

A similar view was expressed by Governor W. Lee O'Daniel some years later when he announced that he would not use floor leaders.[32]

Some other governors, however, have found it useful to have specifically designated lieutenants in the Legislature. For example, Governor James V. Allred whose inexperience in legislative matters and unwillingness to compromise and "whose [alleged] quick tongue and hot temper kept him in trouble with the two houses . . . could always count on some able floor leaders that kept his program moving."[33] According to the *Austin American-Statesman*, his "number one right hand men" in the House were Robert W. Calvert and Dero Cowley and in the Senate, Tom DeBerry and Ben O'Neal, a former law partner.[34] Despite strong opposition, these floor leaders were able to rally considerable support for Allred's programs, and the newspaper reported at the end of his term: "In retrospect, it must be said that Allred got more cooperation from the Legislature than have many of his predecessors."[35]

Governor Beauford H. Jester used the legislators from his home district, Senator James E. Taylor and Representative George Nokes, as Administration floor leaders in the respective houses, and Senator Ottis Locke was regarded as a spokesman for Governor Shivers, al-

[31] *House Journal,* Thirty-eighth Legislature, regular session, p. 57.
[32] McKay, *W. Lee O'Daniel and Texas Politics, 1938–1942,* p. 127.
[33] Burlage, "James V. Allred—Texas' Liberal Governor" (unpublished research paper), p. 26.
[34] December 25, 1938.
[35] *Ibid.*

though he was not officially designated.[36] During the Daniel administration, the practice was to shift floor leaders according to matters under consideration. For example, Senator A. M. Aikin, Jr., handled matters in the Senate relating to public education, though on one occasion he sponsored a tax bill approved by the Governor. Senator Crawford Martin and Representative Charles Hughes represented the Administration on the escheat law,[37] and Representative George Hinson assisted in sponsoring tax measures for the Governor in the House of Representatives. To promote his program in the Fifty-eighth Legislature Governor Connally chose not to use floor leaders, preferring other methods of contact.

Another development has been "working the floor" by representatives of the governor. Recent administrations have appointed a staff member to be the legislative liaison man. During the Jester administration, this role was filled by William L. McGill, executive secretary, and during the Shivers tenure, Weldon Hart, executive secretary, performed that duty. Governor Daniel assigned both his executive assistant, George Christian, and his administrative assistant, John Goldsum, to legislative relations. A long-time political observer, Allen Duckworth of the *Dallas Morning News,* likened the procedure, especially in the Shivers era, to that of a "well-trained army moving in."[38] Whenever a crucial vote was to be taken, the Governor's staff men would circulate among the members to ascertain their views, then "lobby" for support for the Governor's measures. Most of the work took place before and after daily sessions, but some gubernatorial secretaries have been known to go on the floor during sessions,[39] and persons in the galleries have at times been able to observe the governor himself on the floor mingling with the members, especially with the senators.

INFORMATION FROM THE GOVERNOR'S OFFICE

In the view of one official close to the legislative scene, a trend has been developing of legislators' looking to the governor's staff for information. Vernon McGee, director of the Legislative Budget Board,

[36] Interview with Vernon McGee, director of the Legislative Budget Board, in Austin, June 30, 1961.

[37] *Houston Chronicle,* May 27, 1962.

[38] Interview with Allen Duckworth, political editor of the *Dallas Morning News,* in Dallas, April 6, 1961.

[39] *Dallas Morning News,* March 18, 1941.

points out that staff members remain accessible in the Capitol corridors to supply data to the members of the two houses.[40] "Fact sheets" were prepared for several years by Governor Daniel's office for distribution to the lawmakers so that they might have brief, concise summaries of subjects under consideration. Polls have sometimes been conducted through questionnaires circulated to the members, with the results being collated and distributed in the two chambers. An example of one questionnaire used in the early days of the Fifty-seventh Legislature (1961) follows:[41]

1. Do you favor retiring deficit separate as an emergency matter? ——
2. Which of the following deficit proposals can you vote for?
    (1) Escheat enforcement bill ——
    (2) Two-factor formula on interstate corporations ——
    (3) One-year increase of 3% in gas production tax ——
    (4) Transfer of farm-to-market road financing from general fund to highway funds (keeping construction at present level) ——

Early in 1961, Governor Daniel wrote, personally paid for, and circulated to legislators, bankers, and district and county attorneys a printed brochure on his escheat bill. The booklet explained the bill, the reasons why the Governor thought it should be adopted, and the practices of other states under comparable legislation.[42] To each copy sent to the senators and representatives, the Governor attached a message stating that he hoped it would not be necessary for him to convene a special session to get the measure adopted. Notwithstanding this plea, a special session on the matter was necessary, but the publication undoubtedly helped educate the members to the need for escheat legislation.

APPEALS TO THE PUBLIC

With the expansion of the newer forms of communication, chief executives have been able to appeal directly to the public to support their programs. A survey made in June, 1961, found that governors

[40] Interview with Vernon McGee, director of the Legislative Budget Board, in Austin, June 30, 1961.

[41] Copy of the questionnaire furnished by George Christian, executive assistant to Governor Daniel. Mr. Christian discussed at length the techniques used to influence legislation during his period of service.

[42] Price Daniel, "Ten Reasons Why the Texas Escheat Law Needs Stronger Enforcement Provisions."

of all states used radio, and governors of forty-six states used television to communicate with their citizenry.[43] The famous "fireside chats" of President Franklin D. Roosevelt have been emulated by governors throughout the land. All recent governors of Texas have employed radio or television, but none has equalled the performance of Governor W. Lee O'Daniel, who relied on the use of radio, almost to the exclusion of all other forms of communication, in appeals to the public.

Skilled in the art of radio broadcasting because of his former connection with a daily program sponsored by his flour company, Governor O'Daniel went directly to the citizens every Sunday morning in his regularly scheduled broadcasts from the "front room" of the Governor's Mansion. In the broadcasts he discussed programs in which he was interested and "reported to the people" on the progress of the Legislature. In one such broadcast on May 28, 1939, O'Daniel bitterly attacked the minority in the Legislature which opposed his proposed sales tax amendment.[44] He read the names of those senators who had supported his program, labelling this list the "honor roll." He threatened to "take the stump" to oppose the re-election of those who worked against his program, and said he would read the "honor roll" of representatives after his proposal had been voted on. Even in the face of this threat, however, fifty-six members of the House killed the measure. In his next broadcast, O'Daniel implored at least six to change their positions so that the bill might pass. While this measure was being considered, O'Daniel was called "a Sabbath Caesar," "a ruthless demagogue," and "an ether egotist" for using the radio to "coerce" the House.[45] With alliteration befitting a poet laureate, O'Daniel replied:

> The speeches do not in any way reflect the opinion of the majority of the fifty-six. The vast majority . . . are too sensible to be swayed by the howlings of two or three wisecracking political proselyters polluting the place performing a personality piracy plot for the purpose of plucking personal publicity by the papers printing their prattle.[46]

[43] Council of State Governments, *The Governor and Public Information: Selected Methods Employed by Governors' Offices in Communicating With the Public,* pp. 2–3. Hereafter cited as Council of State Governments, *The Governor and Public Information.*

[44] *Dallas Morning News,* May 29, 1939.

[45] *Austin American,* June 9, 1939.

[46] *Ibid.,* June 12, 1939.

He was unable to budge a single member into changing his vote. However, several legislators whose names had been read on the broadcasts were defeated in the next primary.

A short time later, O'Daniel attacked Texas radio stations for "censoring" his speeches by requiring an advance copy of his text. Taking a cue from a predecessor, James E. Ferguson, who after his impeachment organized a newspaper known as the *Ferguson Forum* in which to voice his views, O'Daniel had his sons incorporate a newspaper in Fort Worth. Under the title *W. Lee O'Daniel News,* the publication was used as a weekly newsletter to inform the citizens on "matters of vital concern." O'Daniel said the newspaper was

the answer of the common citizens of Texas to the professional politicians of Texas who think they can control the radio stations and the newspapers. . . . The *W. Lee O'Daniel News* is going to be the means of getting facts and true facts to the great rank and file.[47]

The Governor encouraged his listeners to send twenty-five cents to cover the cost of a subscription for four months.

Since the heyday of radio in the O'Daniel era, all Texas governors have made use of that medium, though with less frequency and certainly with less color, to solicit support for their program. Governor Beauford H. Jester made periodic "reports to the people" in which he discussed the problems and progress of the state government and his proposals to the Legislature.[48] Governor Allan Shivers delivered radio "fireside chats" before he pioneered with television in Texas politics.[49] He was able to gain backing for many of his measures, and also was effective in urging Texas voters to bolt the Democratic ticket in the presidential races of 1952 and 1956.

Governor Price Daniel took to the air on several occasions to discuss legislative problems. He elicited an outstanding response in a broadcast on May 31, 1961, when he discussed the recently adjourned regular session of the Fifty-seventh Legislature and its failure to enact tax legislation. The Governor outlined his own position on the sales tax and invited citizens to make their wishes known to him prior

[47] Script of O'Daniel's broadcast of March 29, 1940, over Station XEAW, Monterrey, Mexico. Copy made available by William J. Lawson.

[48] Scripts of Jester's "Reports to the People" may be found in his Biographical File in Barker Texas History Center, The University of Texas.

[49] Governor Shivers, in an interview in Austin, December 4, 1961, said he believed the use of the mass media to be a very effective technique in marshalling public opinion in Texas.

to a called meeting of the Legislature in three weeks. He promptly received some 7,000 communications on the tax situation and was able to tell the Legislature, when it reconvened, that a substantial number of citizens supported his views.[50]

John Connally used television to great advantage in 1963. Following the adjournment of the Fifty-eighth Legislature, he addressed a statewide audience to explain that he was using the item veto to cut some $12.4 million from the appropriations bill passed during the session. He was laying that amount away, he said, to serve as a "nest egg" for the program of improvement in higher education which he had espoused. He added, "And you may rest assured that I plan to guard that nest egg like an old mother hen."[51] A month later, on July 19, Connally again took to television to outline his views on civil rights. Affirming a belief in a moderate approach, he said, "As I depart to represent the people of Texas [at a National Governors' Conference in Florida] . . . I want to ask *your* help in this vitally important matter. You, and only you can assure full civil rights for all."[52] Between that telecast and August 14, the Governor received 1,093 letters, approximately 95 per cent of which endorsed his stand.[53]

An older, and perhaps more universal, method of appealing to the public is through the press. According to a survey of the Council of State Governments in 1961, the gubernatorial press conference was used in every state, and thirty-four of the states (including Texas) employed a professional assistant for the governor's staff, primarily to handle public information.[54]

Reviewing forty years of experience as a Capitol reporter in Texas, Raymond Brooks of the *Austin American* declared that press relations of Texas governors came to be "formalized" and "conventionalized" only during the Shivers administration. He recalled that newsmen had easy access to the chief executives of the 1920's and 1930's,

---

[50] Interview with George Christian, executive assistant to Price Daniel, in Austin, November 21, 1961. Mr. Christian also indicated that the largest response to a telecast was received when Senator Daniel asked for opinions concerning his making the race for governor in 1956. Some 35,000 replies were received, the majority of them favorable.

[51] Script of telecast of statewide television address by Governor John Connally, Tuesday, June 11, 1963, p. 10.

[52] Script of telecast of statewide television speech by Governor John Connally, Friday, July 19, 1963, p. 13.

[53] Statistics furnished by George Christian, administrative assistant to Governor Connally, in interview, August 15, 1963.

[54] Council of State Governments, *The Governor and Public Information*, p. 1.

with individual correspondents being free to "drop in" on the governor as many as half a dozen times a day. The press conference was not begun until the administration of Governor James V. Allred, who held an informal meeting with newsmen each day—usually a "brief chatty affair."[55] Following this precedent, W. Lee O'Daniel began his term holding news conferences but quickly abandoned them when reporters badgered him with questions which brought out his unfamiliarity with government. He shifted to other media to inform the public.

Coke Stevenson used the Capitol news corps as a "kitchen cabinet," and his relations with the press probably were "the most personal of modern times." He talked over many state problems with the reporters, soliciting their advice and counsel. More formal procedures have been instituted since then, but gubernatorial press conferences today are still "easy-going give-and-take affairs and no questions are ruled out."[56] Connally's conferences are held intermittently, and on call of the Governor, and his press assistant prepares news releases as occasion demands. Perhaps the following observation, published while Shivers was governor, accurately describes recent trends in gubernatorial press relations:

Governor Shivers seems to recognize, more than those before him, that the interviewers are an impersonal group, trying most all of them, in an earnest and serious way, to portray in accurate perspective, the governor's attitude and commitments on legislation, state affairs, politics, and public policy.[57]

The effect of appeals to the public cannot be evaluated accurately, but such appeals do seem to play a vital role in educating the public concerning the executive's position on many important matters. The Council of State Governments has estimated that 80 per cent of Texas' population reside within the receiving area for broadcasts and telecasts and that an equally high percentage of the citizens have access to newspapers.[58]

USE OF LOBBYISTS BY THE GOVERNOR

Lobbyists, for which Texas is notorious, ordinarily represent particular pressure groups, but they also have been made use of by chief

[55] *Austin American,* January 5, 1955.
[56] *Ibid.*
[57] *Ibid.*
[58] Council of State Governments, *The Governor and Public Information,* p. 9.

executives. For example, when a bill taxing cigarettes originated in the Texas Senate in 1931, Governor Ross Sterling is reported to have conferred with "eight or nine lobbyists together with various members, and it was represented and understood that . . . no additional taxes would be necessary."[59] According to one legislator of that day, the agreement insured a "lot of support." However, immediately after passage of the bill, it was found that other sources of revenue would be needed after all.[60]

Undoubtedly the most effective use of lobbyists by a governor occurred during the Shivers administration. Shivers cultivated the friendship of many lobbyists, having breakfasts or luncheons with them and outlining his position on matters which concerned them as well as him. Sometimes the Governor would ask one of the lobbyists to arrange a meeting at which he could talk to thirty or forty of them; at other times he would invite a group of comparable or smaller size to the Executive Mansion. He would explain the immediate problem in which he was interested and would go over his suggested solution, saying, in effect, "This is what must be done in this situation. Now get to work on your legislators." Occasionally Shivers invited the employers of the lobbyists to similar meetings and discussed the same problems and solutions with them. He would then solicit their help in getting the lobbyists to deal with the legislators.[61] According to one former legislator, "Shivers was the first governor ever to call the lobbyists in, outline his demands, and tell them to get busy with the legislature."[62] In the view of one of the closest associates of Governor Shivers, all the people summoned to the meetings appreciated an explanation of the facts and "it worked like a charm."[63] On one occasion Shivers even had the lobbyists working to vote taxes on themselves!

CITIZENS' ADVISORY GROUPS

One of the new techniques of the past decade has been the appointment of citizens' advisory commissions to study a particular problem and then to make recommendations to the governor and the Legislature. The underlying idea is to appoint a cross section of the

[59] Byron C. Utecht, *The Legislature and the Texas People*, p. 171.
[60] *Ibid.*
[61] The tactics were explained to the writer by Weldon Hart in an interview, in Austin, March 29, 1961.
[62] D. B. Hardeman, "Shivers of Texas," *Harper's Magazine* (November, 1956), p. 51.
[63] Interview with Weldon Hart, in Austin, March 29, 1961.

citizenry, with a view to publicizing a problem in all sections of the state. Frequently the appointees become so engrossed in their work that they make speeches and "lobby" for the recommendations of the group. This approach gives the public a more immediate voice in the solving of state problems, and such recommendations cannot easily be overlooked by legislators.[64]

In 1953 Governor Shivers appointed a citizens' group to study the problem of pay for public school teachers in Texas and he also used the device on an informal basis for other matters.[65] Governor Daniel liked the study commission so much that he formalized organization of several groups to study problems such as water, taxation, education, the aged, oil imports, law enforcement, and revision of the Constitution. Two of the more publicized groups operating during the Daniel administration were the citizens' commission on water problems, whose report precipitated the reorganization of the State Board of Water Engineers (including renaming it the Texas Water Commission), and the study committee on public education (known as the Hale-Aikin Committee), whose recommendations resulted in the increase of the minimum salary for Texas teachers.[66] Upon his accession to office, John Connally continued to use the citizens' advisory group aproach. Declaring the quality of higher education to be one of the state's most pressing problems, he requested the Legislature to appropriate $50,000 for a Committee on Education beyond the High School. Although some legislators believed that the Legislature should be permitted to appoint some of the members of the Committee, eventually the Governor was authorized to name all twenty-five members, and the entire amount requested was appropriated. In the fall of 1963 the Committee had been organized under the chairmanship of H. B. Zachry of San Antonio and had begun its study on the problems of higher education in Texas; a research staff, which was to complete its work by the end of 1964, had been employed.

Evaluating the experience of a decade in the use of citizens' study groups, one official close to the legislative scene pronounced the

---

[64] David S. Brown, "The Public Advisory Board as an Instrument of Government," *Public Administration Review*, XV (Summer, 1955), pp. 196–204.

[65] Interview with Vernon McGee, director of the Legislative Budget Board, in Austin, June 30, 1961.

[66] Reports on the contributions of the Hale-Aikin Committee may be found in the monthly issues of the *Texas Outlook*, beginning in the issue of September, 1959.

technique very effective.[67] Its success to date may well portend its even greater use by future governors.

One of the floor leaders of the well-known Gilmer-Aikin Bills (which, in 1949, sought to revitalize public education in Texas) described the techniques used in securing passage of that important legislation:

In some cases, the Governor was asked to call members for conferences on the bills. The position of the Chief Executive of the State of Texas naturally carried with it a great deal of influence. To some legislators, the mere knowledge that the Governor was personally interested in his vote on a measure was persuasive. Often sponsors called personal friends, asking that they in turn call friends who might be influential. In fact, *every legitimate device that could be thought of* was used by the proponents of the bills until all three bills were finally passed by the House and Senate and signed by the Governor.[68] (Italics mine)

This assessment of legislative strategy could conceivably be extended to virtually any controversial bill, for the legislative process does entail the utilization of "every legitimate device that can be thought of" by the proponents of bills. The informal methods of persuasion that evolve into a cycle of influence are of incalculable value in the intricate and complex web of lawmaking. Without them, few laws would be spread upon the statute books.

[67] Interview with Vernon McGee, director of the Legislative Budget Board, in Austin, June 30, 1961.

[68] Rae Files Still, *The Gilmer-Aikin Bills: A Study in the Legislative Process*, p. 73.

PART FOUR

The Political Role of the Governor

11

The Nomination Process

Any enumeration of gubernatorial activities necessarily must include the role of the executive as a politician. Since politics is at the core of the democratic process, the typical governor, whether he desires it or not, is thrust into his state's political arena and more often than not becomes the leader of his party or faction. In some cases his political leadership is nominal; in many it is real. The degree of effectiveness with which he exercises his leadership depends upon the issues of the day, the traditions of the particular state, the general economic and political climate, and the energy and skill of the chief executive.[1]

THE GOVERNOR AS POLITICIAN

After serving several months as governor of Connecticut, Chester Bowles aptly described the political functions of the modern state executive:

I function as head of my political party, *as every Governor must*. I must be accessible at all times to my party's legislators, and my party's town chairmen and other state and local party officials, and help make political decisions. . . . *Every great American President, Senator, or Governor has been an able politician.* If he weren't, he would never have been elected or even nominated.[2] (Italics mine)

---

[1] Jewell L. Bellush, "Selected Case Studies of the Legislative Leadership of Governor Herbert H. Lehman" (unpublished Ph.D. dissertation), p. 354.

[2] "A Governor's Job as Seen by a Governor," *New York Times Magazine*, July 24, 1959, p. 8.

To evaluate the impact of a particular governor on a state, therefore, some attention must be focused upon his activities as a political leader.[3]

In addition to his own acumen, the opportunity of a governor to become the actual chief of his party or faction depends in important measure upon the political organization in his state. National policies may influence the form and behavior of state political systems, and the manner in which they strike different states contributes to the variations in the organization and conduct of state politics.[4] Apparently, however, the nature of a state's party system is decreed mainly by historical traditions and by the persistence of specific political issues over a long temporal span. According to Professor Cortez Ewing, that issue in the South has been the Negro problem, which has spawned what he calls "Southern unipartyism"—a development that appeared near the end of the nineteenth century.[5]

One result of this situation has been the dominance of the Democratic Party in the South, with some states, including Texas, seeing the appearance of distinct factionalism within the one-party framework. A second result has been the nomination and election to gubernatorial chairs of a host of colorful figures who, for good or evil, have left an indelible stamp on their states. Certainly, Southern states en bloc have produced their share of politicians who have attracted national attention.[6] Such names as Bilbo of Mississippi, Long of Louisiana, Talmadge of Georgia, and Wallace of Alabama are known throughout the land. Texas has also produced a goodly number of spectacular gubernatorial politicians in such persons as James S. Hogg, James E. and Miriam A. Ferguson, and W. Lee O'Daniel. The entrance of such characters onto the Texas political scene can be explained best by an analysis of the state's machinery for nomination and election of public officials.

NOMINATION BY CONVENTION, 1876 TO 1905

Prior to 1905 nominations for most state and local offices in Texas were made by party nominating conventions.[7] During much of that

[3] William C. Havard, *The Government of Louisiana*, p. 102.

[4] V. O. Key, Jr., *American State Politics: An Introduction*, p. 19. Hereafter cited as Key, *American State Politics*.

[5] Cortez A. M. Ewing, *Primary Elections in the South: A Study in Uniparty Politics*, pp. 3–5. Hereafter cited as Ewing, *Primary Elections in the South*.

[6] See Allan A. Michie and Frank Ryhlick, *Dixie Demagogues*.

[7] Several counties had adopted the "Crawford County System," the direct primary, by party rule, for nominating local officers and instructing delegates to

early time competition among political parties was relatively keen with several brief interludes of two-party politics within the state.[8] For example, in the election of 1882, John Ireland, the Democratic nominee polled 150,809 votes and G. W. Jones of the Greenback Party polled 102,501. A decade later James S. Hogg squeaked by his opponents to become a "minority governor" for his second term. As official nominee of the Democratic convention of 1892, he was opposed by George Clark, the candidate of a rump convention of "Jefferson Democrats," and T. L. Nugent, the standard bearer of the Populist Party. The vote was amazingly close, with Hogg receiving 190,486, Clark 133,395, and Nugent 108,483. Again in 1896, the Populists provided effective opposition with J. C. Kearby, who ran against Democratic Governor Charles A. Culberson for a second term. The vote: Culberson 298,258; Kearby 238,692.[9]

During this period of party competition, all gubernatorial candidates were nominated by party conventions—a method which came to be the subject of increasing criticism. Obviously, it did have its faults, and numerous instances could be cited of manipulations and behind-the-scenes deals. Sometimes unscrupulous party officials failed to give sufficient advance notice of the holding of conventions, and occasionally the conclaves were held at places impossible or impractical for the rank and file of voters to attend.[10] A great deal of power was wielded by corporation attorneys and other persons representing special interests, and the use of proxies was abused many times. For example, friends of certain candidates were known to visit roundups in the cattle country, persuade the cowboys and their foremen to constitute themselves as local conventions, and then carry away enough proxies to determine the outcome of state conventions.[11]

---

party conventions. Such procedure was authorized in 1895 by *General Laws of Texas*, Twenty-fourth Legislature, Chapter 34. In 1903 an amendment authorized primaries for local purposes on an optional basis. *General Laws of Texas*, Twenty-eighth Legislature, Chapter 101, Section 82–107.

[8] See Roscoe C. Martin, "The Farmers in Texas Politics, 1875–1900" (unpublished M.A. thesis).

[9] *Texas Almanac, 1961–1962*, p. 471.

[10] Allen Duckworth, political editor of the *Dallas Morning News*, told the writer that a story prevails to the effect that in the 1860's a state party convention was convened in Corsicana in a building once used to house animals. The site was infested so thoroughly with fleas that the delegates were unable to remain seated except for short periods. In Texas political lore the meeting came to be called "The Flea Convention." Although it is not known whether one group with unusual fortitude deliberately scheduled the meeting in that place in an attempt to make the opposition uncomfortable, such action was a distinct possibility.

[11] Rupert N. Richardson, *Texas, The Lone Star State* (2d ed.), p. 281.

Not infrequently, powerful personalities manipulated the nomination of hand-picked candidates. There is some evidence that incumbent governors felt it a part of their duties to participate in the choice of their successors; but during the last two decades of the convention era probably no individual Texan exerted as much influence in the choice of gubernatorial nominees as did Colonel Edward M. House of Austin, who might very well be labelled the "governor-maker" of the period. Not only was he well acquainted with every chief executive from Ross to Colquitt, but he was effective in the nomination of Hogg, Culberson, Sayers, and Lanham, and served as campaign manager for each of them. One historian reports that House greatly enjoyed manipulating conventions and that his rule of operation became, "My friends must be in command."[12] Extraordinary was the fact that he seldom attended a convention personally yet wielded such influence as always to get his candidate nominated, and "his influence was exercised so adroitly that even those affected did not understand it and the historian finds it impossible to delineate its course."[13] Notwithstanding his prominent role, however, House never became state "boss" in the usually accepted sense of that day, choosing rather to transfer his efforts to national politics (where he became the confidant of President Woodrow Wilson) after having dominated the Texas scene for approximately two decades.[14]

His biographer indicates that in many campaigns House ultimately had to oppose the man he had last made governor because the executive seemingly "always had plans calling for a successor whom Colonel House could not approve."[15] A custom had grown up in Texas that the attorney general had an unwritten right of succession to the governorship.

House thought that this was a wrong idea, a fallacious theory crippling the initiative of the voters and capable of being turned to bad account by unscrupulous politicians, who might secure control of the nominating machinery. He set his face firmly against it, and in the end destroyed it. . . . [His objection was that] a man who had not been Attorney General, no matter what his qualifications, could not be elected.[16]

[12] *Ibid.,* "Edward M. House and the Governors," *Southwestern Historical Quarterly,* LXI (July, 1957), 65.
[13] *Ibid.* See also Roy Sylvan Dunn, " 'New Deal': Made in Texas by a Texan," *Texas Parade* (April, 1961), 7–8.
[14] Arthur D. H. Smith, *Mr. House of Texas,* p. 30.
[15] *Ibid., The Real Colonel House,* p. 60.
[16] *Ibid.*

Because of this conviction, House blocked the nomination of Attorney General M. M. Crane, who was backed for the nomination in the Convention of 1898 by Governor Culberson. Alluding to Crane's good record in public office and saying he had no doubt Crane would make a good executive, Colonel House nevertheless said that the principle at stake was bigger than any question of individual fitness and that it was time to destroy the precedent which would dictate Crane's nomination. Later, House confided that he had ended the succession principle "because it savored too strongly of a semi-dynastic principle and had made possible the continued control of the executive office by any group of men who might saddle themselves upon the electorate."[17] No doubt this remark was aimed at the "Tyler gang," the group of East Texas politicians which had been able to produce many winning candidates since the days of O. M. Roberts in 1878.

THE "CAR BARN CONVENTION," 1892

Examination of a particular convention will give some insight into the nominating procedure of those days. One of the most famous of all gubernatorial nominating conventions in Texas history was the "Car Barn Convention" of 1892 in Houston. Taking its name from the site where it was held, that assembly turned into a wild melee among the Democrats and resulted in a bolt by the forces opposing Governor James S. Hogg's bid for a second term. The Governor had become a highly controversial figure because of his espousal of the establishment of the Railroad Commission, and the opposition had rallied to the support of Judge George Clark as the anti-Hogg candidate. For several months before the convention both Hogg and Clark conducted extensive speaking tours throughout the state to secure delegates who would be pledged to them for the September meeting. On at least two occasions, at Cameron and Cleburne, they engaged in public debates before thousands of people. Feelings ran so high that many fights broke out at the debates; heckling was rampant and so riotous that many could not hear what the candidates were saying; to add to the confusion during the second debate, the bleachers on which the spectators were seated gave way and twenty persons were injured.[18] After that misfortune the candidates cancelled all future

[17] *Ibid.*, p. 66.
[18] *Houston Daily Post*, May 5, 1892.

debates and stumped the state separately in search of convention support.

Hogg realized he faced formidable opposition. A typical letter he addressed to political workers throughout the state reads as follows:

Aug. 4, 1892

Hon. R. N. Stafford,
  Mineola, Texs.
Dear Sir:

I enclose you a list of names of gentlemen who want to go to the convention as delegates. I hope you can have them sent from Wood [County]. They are all good men; and if they are uninstructed in any particular I feel sure they will abide the wishes of the home delegates. Don't fail to put on Mark Elliston in any event, as we could not have a convention without him. It might be well to take in a few more from Dallas in the event that the Hogg delegation should not be seated at Houston.

Kindly advise me of the result with regard to the names given.

Yours truly,
J. S. Hogg[19]

Another letter was sent to John H. Jones of Quitman, Hogg's home town, enclosing the same list of delegates. The Governor wrote ". . . I hope you can get our friends to put them on from Wood."[20]

In the meantime, R. B. Levy, private secretary to Hogg, wrote to a friend in Huntsville:

The campaign committee fully realize the importance of activity and organization and are working systematically. Literature is being circulated to the full extent of the means at their command. Reports pouring in highly encouraging. The opposition however, are sleepless & tireless. Our people understand this & there will be no relaxation of effort in any quarter. Supposed that counties opposed to Gov. H two years ago will call *early* primaries for effect. At Wills Point the uprising of the *people* has astounded the opposition,—they came from all quarters,—the issues have been proclaimed,—the battle has begun, & something has been heard to drop from the cities & towns as well as from the "forks of the creek"— from now on—elbow will touch elbow all along the line—Hard work will go on all the same.[21]

By convention time, emotions were at fever pitch on the question of the Hogg reform programs, and the opposing camps were primed to make political capital of them.

[19] J. S. Hogg, Letters Written, Hogg Papers, X, 304, Archives of The University of Texas.
[20] *Ibid.*, X, 301.
[21] *Ibid.*, IX, 263.

The first big fight came on whether to elect the temporary chairman by roll call, a method supported by Hogg, or viva voce, as Clark desired. Both groups proceeded simultaneously to elect chairmen by their respective methods, and bedlam reigned supreme. At the end of the first day the Convention was hopelessly deadlocked, with two temporary chairmen claiming the right to preside. The Hogg group, determined to oust the Clark people, overnight built a huge fence around the Car Barn and deployed 300 assistant sergeants at arms in the area. The orders from the city marshal were, "If they force their way in, get your clubs and knock them down as fast as they come."[22] The popular conclusion, understandably, was that the Hogg supporters were in control.

Judging that they could not overcome such obstacles, the Clark followers retired to nearby Turner Hall to hold their own convention, which they called "the Democratic Convention of Texas." Each group emerged with a "Democratic" candidate and a platform. The major difference appeared to be whether the Railroad Commission would be appointive, a procedure advocated by Hogg, or elective, the Clark position. Despite a minority report, the Hogg platform repudiated the national Democratic platform on the coinage of silver, while the Clark platform supported it. Both groups appointed committees to "address" the people as to why the split had come about.[23] In the ensuing campaign the terms "Bolter-crats" and "Hoggocracy" became the common parlance of the opposing camps.

Clark was later endorsed by the Republican Party,[24] and Hogg won the election by only a plurality. Therefore, his second administration was concerned not only with pushing for more of his reforms but also with unifying the Democratic Party. In a harmony meeting in Dallas in March, 1894, the Governor appealed to all members to forget their differences of the past and to unite against the Republicans and Populists. He declared: "The Democratic party has a mission to perform. Republicanism means centralization, and Populism—what in thunder does that mean? The overthrow of law and order?"[25] He rousingly called on the "Democracy" to "get together and let the ac-

---

[22] William McCraw, *Professional Politicians*, p. 151. In this work the former Attorney General of Texas presents an excellent case study of Hogg as a political leader.

[23] A detailed account of the "Car Barn Convention" and the campaign of 1892 is given in Grady S. St. Clair, "The Hogg-Clark Campaign" (unpublished M.A. thesis), pp. 28–117.

[24] McCraw, *Professional Politicians*, p. 154.

[25] *Ibid.*, p. 163.

tion of this day be a guarantee that not a Populist shall hold an office in Texas, nor any Republican from Texas disgrace the halls of Congress. United we stand, not divided at all."[26]

EVALUATION OF THE CONVENTION METHOD AND ITS NOMINEES

Regardless of its vulnerability to manipulation, the convention system of nomination was not without advantages. Under that method the party itself was in charge and the mistakes made were its responsibility. Certainly the convention kept the state party leadership on its toes. Since the general election was the only chance to gain office, the political leaders in the "smoke-filled room" knew that they were obliged to submit to the electorate candidates who had some claim to competency as well as attractiveness as vote getters. The Greenbackers, Populists, and Republicans offered effective opposition to the Democrats for brief periods, and the people—not tired of going to the polls because of two primaries, as is often the case now— turned out in large numbers at the general election in November.[27] Such interest gives rise to speculation that a continuation of the convention form of nomination by all political parties might have resulted in the building of a two-party system in the state.[28]

Thirty years elapsed from the adoption of the Constitution of 1876 until the passage of the direct-primary law. During approximately the first half of that period the executive office was held by a succession of Confederate governors, conservative in thought and deed, but with standing in public and party affairs, and generally competent.[29] During the 1880's, with the growth of the Populist Party, repercussions were felt in the Democratic Party and the leadership was shifted to a younger group of non-veterans who appealed more to the wage-earning classes. The nomination of James S. Hogg in 1890 on a platform endorsing railroad regulation brought charges of a "revolution"

[26] *Ibid.*

[27] For election returns of all gubernatorial elections, see *Texas Almanac, 1961–1962*, pp. 471–473. In the general election of 1904, the last year in which conventions were used to nominate Democratic candidates, the total vote was 279,874 as compared with the general election of 1906, the first year of primary nominations, when the vote was 185,840.

[28] Allen Duckworth, "Democratic Dilemma in Texas," *Southwest Review,* XXXII (Winter, 1947), 35.

[29] "A Political History of Texas, 1900–1930," by Ralph W. Steen in F. C. Adams (ed.), *A Centennial History of Politics and Personalities of the Democratic Party—1836–1936*, p. 319. Hereafter cited as Adams (ed.), *Texas Democracy.*

in the Party. The *Galveston Daily News* commented editorially that it meant the overthrow of the older leaders and turning the Party over to the "kids," with the "biggest kid in Texas" heading the ticket.[30] Whether or not the revolution label was justifiable, a change in the philosophy of the leadership did occur; the matters which Hogg set forth as platform demands were either completely new or at least more definite than in previous years.[31]

When Hogg retired to private life his mantle of leadership fell upon another young man of similar political persuasion, Charles A. Culberson—a capable and astute politician, though he lacked the color of Hogg. Apparently Culberson was a fortunate choice because "he furnished strong leadership and had proven his right, as Hogg's successor, to lead the Democratic Party in Texas."[32]

By the end of the century prosperity, the lack of which had accounted for the agrarian movement, had largely returned; the middle class was again in control of Texas politics, and the Populist Party was moving rapidly into oblivion.[33] About the same time some Democrats tired of the domination of their Party by the "Tyler gang." With the assistance of Colonel House, they succeeded, for the last eight years prior to the installment of the primary, in returning the leadership of the Party to the older Confederate veterans of the same mold as those who had been dominant before the Hogg-Culberson interlude. A distinguished Texas political veteran recalls that two members of the national House of Representatives, Joseph D. Sayers and S. W. T. Lanham, were persuaded to return from Washington to Austin to serve as the state's chief executive.[34] During their adminis-

[30] *Galveston Daily News*, July 16, 1890.

[31] Mizell F. Kennedy, "A Study of James Stephen Hogg, Attorney General and Governor" (unpublished M.A. thesis), p. 118.

[32] Robert L. Wagner, "The Gubernatorial Career of Charles Allen Culberson" (unpublished M.A. thesis), p. 105.

[33] Steen, "A Political History of Texas 1900–1930," in Adams (ed.), *Texas Democracy*, p. 319.

[34] A member of the Texas Legislature at that time, John N. Garner, told the writer in Uvalde, Texas, on April 17, 1961, that the Democratic Party of Texas was badly split between the supporters of Hogg and those of Joseph W. Bailey. The schism caused a real threat to the future of the Party, and in the interests of harmony a group of interested Democrats met to decide upon a candidate for governor who would be acceptable to all sides. Congressman Sayers was selected as one whom "no one could really oppose." A delegation, including Mr. Garner, went to Washington to persuade Sayers to allow his name to be placed in nomination for governor at the state convention. At first unreceptive to the idea, Sayers was convinced finally that such a course of action would be advantageous not only to the Party but to the state, and that he would be rendering real service

trations the state was free of political strife, causing one political writer to label those years the "quiet era" of Texas politics.[35]

By and large, the governors nominated by conventions after the Reconstruction period were men of high caliber and well qualified by temperament and training to lead the state. They were more influential in Party circles than have been some of their successors nominated by primaries, because, if they wished to survive politically, they were compelled to avow loyalty to the Democratic Party and its platform; their futures depended upon it. Without exception, the nine incumbents from 1876 to 1906 urged the Legislature, in their initial messages, to enact into law the planks of the Democratic platforms upon which they were elected. Not infrequently, they used other means at their command to throw weight behind Party causes. Despite some intra-Party feuds that erupted, this was in the main an era of great Party loyalty and responsibility for the governors of Texas. That they met the tests before them is supported by the observation of one student of Texas politics who wrote:

> It has been contended with some truth that the primary system has brought forth no leaders to compare in ability and prolonged influence in the party and the state with Coke, Hubbard, Roberts, Ireland, Ross, Hogg, Culberson, Sayers, and Lanham.[36]

NOMINATION BY THE DIRECT PRIMARY

THE TERRELL ELECTION LAW, 1905

In the closing years of the nineteenth century the use of the direct primary for nominating public officials gained momentum, particularly in the South. According to Professor V. O. Key, this change occurred because one heritage of the Civil War in many states "was a party system unable to implement the doctrine of popular government by presenting the electorate with genuine alternatives." As a consequence the states turned to the direct primary, which "apparently constituted at bottom an escape from one-partyism."[37]

---

to both. In the judgment of Mr. Garner, himself later to become Vice President of the United States, the choice was most fortunate. Not only was the split in the Party healed, but Sayers proved to be "one of the best governors Texas has ever had."

[35] William M. Thornton in *Dallas Morning News*, December 21, 1934.

[36] "The Texas Direct Primary System," by O. Douglas Weeks in Adams (ed.), *Texas Democracy*, p. 534.

[37] Key, *American State Politics*, pp. 88–89.

Joining the nationwide trend, the Texas Legislature in 1905 enacted the Terrell Election Law, which instituted the primary as the method of nomination for most public officials in the state.[38] Under its terms, nominations were still made at conventions, but the vote of each county represented at the convention was prorated among the various candidates on the basis of the number of votes received by the candidate at the primary held within the county. If no one received a majority, the lowest candidate was dropped at the end of the ballot; the county would then prorate the released votes among other candidates selected by the county delegation.

In 1906 Governor Thomas M. Campbell became the first governor to be nominated in this fashion, but the procedure proved to be so cumbersome in the hands of men not skilled in mathematical computation that the next Legislature amended the law to provide for the nomination of the candidate who led in the primary, regardless of whether he had a majority of the votes cast.[39] Through this system of nomination by plurality, Campbell was chosen for a second term.

The adoption of the primary brought about a change in the complexion of party politics in Texas. Since nomination by the Democratic Party was tantamount to election, the attention of the public shifted from the general election to the primary, and, in effect, the "election" of most public officials took place in the Democratic Party primary. A fundamental change occurred. When there was no longer a conflict between parties, the situation deteriorated into a conflict between personalities or between more or less amorphous factions within the Democratic Party, and the number of candidates (qualified or not) increased greatly. During the first half of the twentieth century Texas averaged 7.38 candidates per contest in gubernatorial races, ranking third in the South among states having the largest number of aspirants for the office.[40]

The primary also weakened party leadership. No longer were candidates chosen by a convention of party stalwarts; anyone who could meet the minimum requirements could conceivably become the party's standard bearer. In practice, the choice of the voters was limited to virtually self-selected candidates—some of whom had no qualification but that of aspiring to public office.[41] The result has

[38] *General Laws of Texas,* Twenty-ninth Legislature, first called session, Chap. 11.

[39] *General Laws of Texas,* Thirtieth Legislature, regular session, Chap. 177.

[40] Ewing, *Primary Elections in the South,* p. 21.

[41] Key, *American State Politics,* p. 121.

been that many colorful candidates have campaigned and all kinds of tactics have been used to attract the attention of the public.

The primary inaugurated a period of much less party loyalty than in former days. According to the political editor of the *Dallas Morning News*, the Democratic Party became "a public utility with little power to govern itself and practically no control over the rank and file of voters who cast their ballots in the Democratic column."[42]

Referring to the changes in the nomination procedure that had taken place after the enactment of the Terrell Law, he continued:

The Democratic party took only fourteen years to change from an organization supporting certain philosophies of government to a semi-public function of the government itself. It succeeded in freezing out Republican opposition, but lost the right to prevent Republicans or those with Republican leanings from entering its primaries and becoming party officers.[43]

GUBERNATORIAL PRIMARIES, 1906 TO 1918

The first and only primary held under the original Terrell Election Law, providing for the system of convention balloting, was in 1906, when four candidates were in the race. On the basis of primary returns, the first prorated vote was as follows: Campbell, 213,345; Colquitt, 169,934; Bell, 163,367; Brooks, 156,318.[44] Brooks was dropped after that ballot, and Colquitt withdrew. The final vote in the state's first gubernatorial primary was Campbell, 418,656; Bell, 257,234.

The revision of the law in 1907, providing for plurality nomination in the primary, remained in effect for a decade. During this time Campbell won renomination for a second term, Colquitt was chosen for two terms, and James E. Ferguson won the nomination twice. Despite the fact that only a plurality was necessary for nomination, in just one case did the winner fail to get more than one-half of the votes cast: in 1910, from a field of five aspirants, O. B. Colquitt polled 146,526 votes out of a total of 357,380, approximately only 41 per cent.[45] Perhaps the most significant developments of this period were the injection of the Prohibition issue into Texas politics and the

[42] Duckworth, "Democratic Dilemma in Texas," *Southwest Review*, XXXII (Winter, 1947), 34.
[43] *Ibid.*, p. 35.
[44] Roy W. Stroud, "The Run-Off Primary" (unpublished M.A. thesis), p. 74.
[45] *Texas Almanac, 1961–1962*, p. 472.

nomination of a political unknown, James E. Ferguson, whose stormy career as a public official was halted abruptly by his impeachment in August, 1917.

THE RUNOFF PRIMARY

According to one political writer of the day, the runoff primary system was passed by the Texas Legislature to thwart James E. Ferguson's attempt at a political comeback in 1918.[46] Whatever the reasons, Texas was only following the practice that had been adopted at that time by seven other Southern states.[47] The statute provided for a second primary for state and district offices in those cases where no candidate received a clear majority of the votes cast in the first primary. The two highest candidates were required to meet each other in a runoff held four weeks after the first primary.[48] Although the law was in effect in 1918, only two candidates announced for governor—William P. Hobby and James E. Ferguson—and Hobby won easily.

In 1920, therefore, the first runoff primary was held in Texas. Four candidates were in the race: former Senator Joseph W. Bailey, who for many years had been a controversial figure in Texas politics, former Speaker of the Texas House of Representatives Pat M. Neff, the incumbent Speaker of the Texas House Robert E. Thomason, and former Attorney General B. F. Looney. Since all of the entrants were men with political know-how, the race was a torrid one. Bailey led the ticket but was forced into a runoff by Neff, who had campaigned in "thirty-seven counties in which there had never been a Governor or a candidate for Governor in the history of Texas."[49] In the runoff, in which only 1,333 fewer votes were cast than in the first primary, Neff won by a vote of 264,075 to 184,702.[50]

In the years since Neff won the first runoff, twenty-one Democratic

[46] Tom Finty, Jr., in *Dallas Morning News*, November 21, 1922. In a series of fifteen articles beginning on November 19, 1922, Mr. Finty gave a critique of the direct primary in Texas.

[47] Stroud, "The Run-Off Primary" (unpublished M.A. thesis), p. 16.

[48] *General and Special Laws of Texas,* Thirty-fifth Legislature, fourth called session, Chap. 90.

[49] Pat M. Neff, *The Battles of Peace,* p. 8.

[50] *Texas Almanac, 1961–1962,* p. 472. Raymond Brooks, who in 1920 was secretary to Governor Hobby, told the writer in Austin, March 4, 1961, that it was generally believed that Speaker Thomason would have been in the runoff had it not been that he had to preside over a special session called by Hobby during the course of the campaign. Consequently he was unable to make as complete a canvass as were the other candidates.

primaries and six Republican primaries have been held to nominate candidates for the state's highest office.[51] Runoffs have been necessary in ten instances, only three of which involved incumbents (Mrs. Ferguson, Sterling, Shivers) seeking another term.[52] Interestingly enough, the persons who placed second in the initial primary bested their opponents in the runoff in the years 1920, 1924, and 1930 (Neff, Mrs. Ferguson, Sterling). Since then, however, the leader in the first primary always has emerged as the victor in the runoff.

Only one nonincumbent seeking a first elective term has been able to win the Democratic nomination by majority vote in the first primary. After a sensational campaign in 1938, W. Lee O'Daniel, although without previous political experience, shattered precedent by polling a total of 573,166 votes out of 1,114,885, to win the nomination over twelve opponents.[53] Two years later he was again nominated by majority vote in the first primary.

O'Daniel's successor, Coke Stevenson, also was able to avoid a second primary campaign, at the same time breaking the no-third-term tradition that had been built up over many years. O'Daniel and Stevenson, therefore, remain the only two executives to be nominated without a runoff since 1920. Four other governors to serve subsequently—Jester, Shivers, Daniel, and Connally—each have been required to face an opponent in a second primary on at least one occasion, although Shivers' experience was the reverse of the usual case. He faced a runoff while seeking a third elective term in 1954, after having escaped one in each of his two earlier terms.

The runoff has denied incumbent governors a second term on only two occasions. Following a bitter campaign in 1926, Mrs. Miriam A. Ferguson was unseated by Attorney General Dan Moody. Six years later she returned to defeat Moody's protege, Ross Sterling, who was trying for a second term.

Since the adoption of the runoff law the number of persons seeking the office of governor has ranged from two to fourteen in the

[51] Originally, the law provided that all parties polling 100,000 votes in the last gubernatorial election must nominate by primary, with other parties being authorized to nominate by convention if they so chose. In 1945, with backing from the Republican Party, the number was raised to 200,000, which today is in effect. Texas Republicans have been required to nominate by primary in 1926, 1930, 1934, 1954, 1958, and 1962.

[52] Runoff primaries were held by the Democratic Party in 1920, 1924, 1926, 1930, 1932, 1934, 1946, 1954, 1956, and 1962. *Texas Almanac, 1961–1962*, pp. 472–473.

[53] *Ibid.*, p. 473.

various elections. Experience has shown that there are usually two, three, or four leading candidates who split most of the votes. Table 10 illustrates this point.

TABLE 10

Gubernatorial Candidates in Texas Democratic Primaries, 1918–1962

Year	Total Number of Candidates	Number Receiving 5% or More of Vote
1918	2	2
1920*	4	4
1922	4	3
1924*	9	4
1926**	6	3
1928	4	2
1930*	11	7
1932**	9	3
1934*	7	6
1936	5	4
1938	13	4
1940	7	5
1942	6	2
1944	10	2
1946*	14	5
1948	8	3
1950	7	2
1952	3	2
1954**	4	2
1956*	5	3
1958	4	3
1960	2	2
1962*	6	6

* Runoff held this year.
** Incumbent involved in runoff.
Source: Compiled from *Texas Almanac, 1961–62,* pp. 472–473.

Several generalizations can be drawn from an analysis of the state's experience under the double-primary system. Ordinarily, governors who sought the office for the first time have had to go into a runoff, while in a majority of cases incumbents have won another term without a second primary. Since Stevenson broke the two-term tradition in 1944, there appears to be a trend toward longer tenure in office.[54] Both Allan Shivers and Price Daniel won third elective terms,

[54] Stevenson succeeded to office when O'Daniel resigned to become U. S. Senator in August, 1941. He served approximately five and one-half years. Shivers became Governor in July, 1949, (when Governor Jester died early in his second term) and served approximately seven and one-half years.

and in 1962, Daniel announced for, but did not win, an unprecedented fourth term.[55] It would seem that Texas voters have joined in the nationwide trend toward lengthening the term of the executive; however, Texas uses its own approach—the ballot box rather than constitutional revision.

The primary system has not only increased the number of aspirants but also the costs of conducting a campaign for office. Whether a candidate travels the considerable length and breadth of Texas or whether he employs some of the more expensive mass media of communications, he must bid for the votes of more than two million individuals.[56] In any case, serious participation in a primary is quite costly.

THE COSTS OF CAMPAIGNING FOR GOVERNOR

The financing of political campaigns was long ago called American democracy's greatest unresolved problem. In practice, even the more stringent attempts at regulation have been relatively unsuccessful.[57] Any effort to estimate the amounts spent in political campaigns can be only speculation as it would be impossible to total the sums spent by all who may be interested in furthering the cause of a particular candidate. In fact, many dollars are spent without the knowledge of the candidate. The switch to the primary system of nomination logically brought about the expenditure of considerably more money by the candidates. One thing is certain: the public became more conscious of the problem of campaign finance once they began to witness the far-ranging travel of candidates in making personal appeals for votes.

Before World War I the amounts spent on campaigns in Texas attracted little interest. One newspaper account of the expenses of the first nominee of the primary system apparently caused little public concern. It read:

It cost Governor Campbell over $16,000 to be governor of Texas and $2,000 to be elected to the second term. From the vigor of the present campaign [1910] no candidate will get out of the race without tremendous expense, one or two of them possibly exceeding the expenses of Gov. Campbell.[58]

[55] *Austin American*, February 3, 1962.
[56] *Texas Almanac, 1961–1962* shows a total of 2,239,189 poll taxes in 1960. P. 476.
[57] Alexander Heard, *Money and Politics*, p. 1.
[58] Newspaper clipping in the Thomas M. Campbell Biographical File, Barker Texas History Center, The University of Texas. The name and date of the publication are not identified.

The daughter of James E. Ferguson reported that he spent $30,000 in his first bid for the nomination in 1914.[59] A few years later Governor William P. Hobby attempted a sort of self-regulation of campaign finances by taking the unprecedented step of furnishing the press with a complete list of contributors to his campaign. Alluding to the fact that the largest contribution outside his family was in the amount of $2,000, Hobby made this statement:

More liberal contributions were perhaps made than is ordinarily the case, but that is accounted for by the fear felt by many citizens that in view of the unusual political conditions in Texas it was not a time to spare money or effort to bring about victory for good government. *The cost of the campaign* [estimated to be above $80,000], *however, in my judgment is less than any other successful one in very recent years in this state.*[60] (Italics mine).

REGULATION OF EXPENDITURES: $10,000 MAXIMUM

The year after the adoption of the runoff system, a statute was passed setting a limit of $10,000 to be spent by candidates for governor and United States senator in Texas.[61] Apparently believing the amount to be unrealistic, the Legislature left a number of loopholes, the most important of which provided that the limit would be confined to those expenditures actually made by the candidates themselves or their campaign headquarters; the limit would not include money spent for the candidate by friends, by state, district, or local committees, or by other interested groups. With such leeway, it was not difficult for the candidates to stay within the statutory maximum while unlimited sums were spent in their behalf.

One of the few written accounts of the costs of campaigning for governor of Texas was penned by Pat Neff shortly after his retirement from office. Stating that the occupant of the Executive Mansion "pays a high price for the privilege of so serving," the former Governor told of the nonmonetary costs, such as the slanderous attacks upon a person in office, the lack of time to devote to family and friends, and the physical strain. He estimated that it took about one year to campaign and to be oriented for service. In his own case, he estimated that his income as an attorney for the five years spent in campaigning and holding office would have been $50,000. He spent $14,000 in his campaign, he said, plus about $8,000 over his aggre-

[59] Ouida Ferguson Nalle, *The Fergusons of Texas,* p. 74.
[60] *San Antonio Express,* November 10, 1918.
[61] *Acts of 1919,* Thirty-sixth Legislature, regular session, p. 143.

gate salary during his terms in office. He concluded that it had cost him at least $56,000 more than his salary, considering what he would have made practicing law, to serve the state.[62]

The faulty operation of the maximum expenditure law may be illustrated by two accounts of the costs of campaigning in the first bid of Miriam A. Ferguson for the governorship. The report filed with the secretary of state showed her expenditures in the 1924 race to be $3,498.57, which was generally believed to be the smallest amount spent by any candidate for the office that year.[63] A newspaper reported that her opponent in the runoff, Felix D. Robertson, "spent over $8,000 to get defeated."[64]

An entirely different version of the costs was told in a national magazine in 1925 by a columnist who interviewed the state's only woman governor. He wrote:

A writer who goes to Austin to obtain an article about the governor of Texas for a national magazine asks to see the governor, and sees, first, Governor Jim, who asks what the magazine is willing to pay. . . . "It cost us $400,000 and many tears to *git* here, and we ain't giving nothing away."[65]

The comparison of these two accounts emphasizes the problem of obtaining accurate reporting of campaign expenditures.

A later governor, Ross Sterling, who was a millionaire oilman, certified that he spent $3,920.40 in his campaign of 1930, listing $67.55 for "travel" and $100.84 for "oil and gas."[66] Obviously, both items must have been far below actual expenditures for those purposes, but undoubtedly some interested campaign workers were able to furnish the candidate with transportation.

One of the many innovations which W. Lee O'Daniel brought into the Texas political picture in 1938 concerned the matter of campaign finance. Calling on "the common people" to help provide funds for their fight against "professional politicians," his favorite fund-raising technique was to have his teen-age daughter, Molly, circulate among the crowds carrying a small barrel labelled "Flour Not Pork" and requesting "dimes, quarters, and dollars."[67] According to official re-

[62] Neff, *The Battles of Peace*, p. 261.

[63] *Austin American,* September 5, 1926.

[64] *Ibid.*

[65] Willson Whitman, "Can a Wife Be Governor?" *Colliers,* 76 (September 5, 1925), 6.

[66] *Dallas Morning News,* July 19, 1930.

[67] *Fort Worth Star-Telegram,* June 22, 1938.

ports, the plan netted a profit. O'Daniel listed expenses of $5,789 and contributions of $6,586. Later he presented a check to the American Red Cross for the difference above "the amount the people donated above my expenses in the race for governor."[68]

REVISION OF THE TEXAS ELECTION CODE

Public criticism of obviously watered-down figures which were reported, use of new and more expensive campaign methods, the inflation of the war period, and his own campaign experience probably combined to cause Governor Jester in 1948 to appoint a Commission To Study Election Law Reform. After hearing a number of witnesses, the group called Secretary of State Paul H. Brown, who candidly told them, "Candidates' expense accounts are a joke."[69] The results of the inquiry led to the revision of the Texas Election Code in 1951; the Legislature removed all limits upon the amount that could be spent but tightened requirements for reporting both expenditures and contributions. Not only was the candidate to continue filing reports with the secretary of state on campaign finances, but contributors also were given responsibility for reporting. Both civil and criminal liability were imposed.[70] But the law still covered only those funds spent by the candidate through his headquarters.

Since 1951 a more realistic picture of campaign outlays has been available, and the tremendous costs of conducting an intensive campaign for a job paying only $25,000 annually are most impressive.

NEEDED: HALF A MILLION DOLLARS

An analysis of campaign expenditure reports filed by the candidates with the secretary of state in the gubernatorial races between 1954 and 1962 reveals that staggering sums are spent in some of the heated races. The amounts reported in 1954, 1956, and 1962, the years in which runoffs were held during that period, contrast vividly with totals spent in other years. Table 11 points up the differences.

Although these figures reflect the enormous size of the outlays and contributions in recent canvasses, even they are not the whole amount.[71] They do not account for sums spent by every friend, com-

---

[68] *San Antonio Express*, August 9, 1938.
[69] *Dallas Morning News*, December 9, 1948.
[70] *Acts of 1951*, Fifty-second Legislature, Chapter 492. See also *Texas Election Code*, Art. 14.08.
[71] The gubernatorial campaign is not always the most expensive statewide race.

TABLE 11

Reported Expenditures of Major Candidates in
Gubernatorial Races, 1954–1962

Year	Candidate	Amount Spent	Contributions	Debts (including loans)
1954	Shivers	$285,121	$242,087	None
	R. Yarborough	279,722	245,394	$ 35,258
1956	Daniel	$389,496	$367,470	$ 23,365
	R. Yarborough	176,574	168,877	71,472
	O'Daniel	138,456	8,905	Not reported
1958	Daniel	$ 91,114	$100,398	$ 12,494
	Gonzalez	17,076	20,073	4,740
	O'Daniel	14,896	12,578	216
1960	Daniel	$ 22,103	$ 38,860	$ 19,804
	Cox	129,021	129,757	26,631
1962	Daniel	$126,484	$102,404	$ 81,292
	D. Yarborough	231,863	197,503	90,707
	Connally	699,102	411,974	162,017
	Cox	231,476	232,497	29,596

Source: Expenditure Records in the office of secretary of state, supplemented
by reports in *Dallas Morning News*, September 9, 1954; October 31,
1956; August 5, 1958; *Houston Post*, March 19, 1962; *Dallas Morning
News*, June 13, 14, November 20, 1962.

mittee, or organization that may be working for a particular candidate. Consequently, the actual cost of becoming governor today remains almost as speculative a matter as it was in the 1920's. In 1956
Senator Price Daniel reported that $389,496 was spent through his
headquarters in his bid for a first gubernatorial term.[72] The all-time
record was probably set in 1962 when John Connally's campaign was
generally said to have cost not less than $675,000. It should be noted,
however, that whereas earlier candidates had to conduct serious campaigns in only the Democratic primaries, Connally had vigorous Republican opposition as well. His race, therefore, actually encom-

---

Ben Ramsey, seeking a sixth term as lieutenant governor in 1960, reported expenditures of $61,724, contributions of $68,316, and debts of $14,964; his op-
ponent, Don Yarborough, reported expenses of $27,447, gifts of $29,761, and
debts of $10,848. *Houston Post*, March 19, 1962. In the 1962 campaign for
Lieutenant Governor, Senator Preston Smith (who won) listed expenditures,
$91,298; amounts received, $83,861. Speaker of the House James A. Turman,
Smith's opponent in the runoff, reported expenditures, $71,616; debts, $15,664;
loan, $5,000; contributions, $37,835. *Dallas Morning News*, June 13, 1962.
  [72] *Dallas Morning News*, October 31, 1956.

passed three hot campaigns—the first primary in May, the runoff in June, and the general election in November.

One writer estimated in 1949 that at least $100,000 was needed at that time to make even a modest race for the governorship of Texas and that it was "generally agreed that a minimum of $300,000 is necessary to assure election."[73] He hypothesized that few candidates not backed by oil interests have a chance.

Since that estimate was made, living costs have mounted and campaign techniques have become more expensive, due largely to the introduction of statewide television and professional public relations firms into the gubernatorial races. If the experience of the 1950's and 1960's can be used as a yardstick, costs of a hard-fought contest will continue to rise.[74] Any figure in the neighborhood of half a million dollars is about as accurate an estimate as can be made today.[75]

[73] Hart Stilwell, "Texas: Owned by Oil and Interlocking Directorates," in Robert S. Allen (ed.), *Our Sovereign State,* p. 315.

[74] J. J. Pickle, who at the time was a member of an advertising firm handling much of the Shivers campaign of 1954, told the writer in an interview on July 18, 1961, in Austin, that his "rough estimate" of the total amount spent in behalf of the candidate would be approximately $450,000. He pointed out that a $300 advertisement in a newspaper could be paid for by some twenty persons each contributing $15.00. Such an expenditure would not have to be reported under the law.

[75] Alexander Heard estimated that between $500,000 and $1,000,000 (including subventions to local organizations) might have been spent by all candidates in a Texas statewide primary in 1956, which he figured cost 33 cents to 66 cents per vote cast. In an excellent series entitled "The Costly Campaigns," appearing in the *Houston Post,* March 18–22, 1962, William H. Gardner, chief of the Austin Bureau of the *Post,* estimated that a race should not be undertaken by a first-time candidate unless he had a *minimum* fund of $200,000.

12

The Gubernatorial Campaign

Cognizant of the high costs of conducting a canvass for public office, a contemporary author has declared that the character of political campaigns in the United States has been for a long time a continuing source of dissatisfaction to friendly students of American political life. At the turn of the century, indignation with current electioneering and campaign methods was an important feature of reform movements.

The long list of proscribed practices written into the state election codes at that time—including vote buying, treating, bribery of editors, repeat voting or intimidation—record some of the least savory tactics used by campaigners as well as the success of reformers in arousing the public.[1]

About the same time these abuses were most prevalent, a majority of the states were exploring the adoption of the direct primary, which, according to Professor Key, was designed to break the party organization's monopoly of the function of developing, grooming, and promoting candidates for statewide office. The primary made it difficult for the party organization to play an effective role in the nominating process, and the promotion of candidates went by default to others.[2] The primary has produced "almost unbelievable sorts of nominations" in numerous cases,[3] says Professor Key.

It naturally followed that the change from nomination by convention to nomination by primary would revolutionize techniques of campaigning. Before, candidates had concentrated on an organiztion designed to control convention delegations, now they were re-

[1] Stanley Kelley, Jr., *Political Campaigning*, p. 1.
[2] V. O. Key, Jr., *American State Politics*, p. 271.
[3] *Ibid.*, p. 288.

quired to pitch their appeals to the masses. Inevitably, campaigns began to center more upon personalities than upon issues. Also, the leading figures changed more rapidly since the hold of leaders under a primary system is generally of short duration and since publicity and lucky breaks count for much in bringing figures rapidly to the center of the public stage.[4] The coming of the primary also brought unprecedented displays of showmanship in appeals for votes. In this respect Texas has ranked among the most spectacular.

CAMPAIGNS OF PREPRIMARY DAYS

Prior to adoption of the primary system a candidate had to travel over the state seeking the support of delegates to nominating conventions. To elicit a following he went to the far corners of Texas, traveling by train, to speak to hundreds of people on issues that were likely to draw the battle lines in the convention hall, and to seek delegations favorable to his point of view and his candidacy.

Governor James S. Hogg's campaigns were typical of the period. His basic technique was described by one of his cohorts, M. M. Crane, a former attorney general and a formidable candidate for governor in 1898, as follows:

> In all of his campaigns he never sought mere personal vindication, but always coupled his campaigns with contentions for the benefit of the masses, behind which contentions he seemed to seek to hide his personality but in reality most effectively exhibited it. . . . Hogg was always too wise to risk a battle on his own mere personality, but always linked himself to some question that was stronger than any man. In that way he led the masses to believe that he was their friend and champion, and not a self-seeking politician.[5]

Hogg's first campaign in 1890 was opened at Rusk, his birthplace in East Texas. He arrived by train, accompanied by many friends, and found 3,000 people gathered for the occasion. After a welcome by brass bands in full regalia, he went to the home of a friend to rest before his speech. The crowd was so large at the afternoon rally that some had to climb trees to hear the introduction, but Hogg's strong voice carried to the most distant as he began with a summary of his record and a demand that all candidates outline fully their po-

---

[4] "The Texas Direct Primary System," by O. Douglas Weeks in Adams (ed.), *Texas Democracy*, p. 534.

[5] Mizell F. Kennedy, "A Study of James Stephen Hogg, Attorney General and Governor" (unpublished M.A. thesis), p. 169.

sitions on the new issues prior to the convention. Then he introduced what was to become the major issue of the campaign—his advocacy of railroad regulation. For almost three hours he held the attention of the giant rally.[6] Hogg's oratory and his personality could always command the undivided attention of an audience.

In 1892 a new technique was injected briefly into the campaign.[7] In tactics reminiscent of the Lincoln-Douglas debates Governor Hogg engaged in two public debates with his chief opponent, Judge George Clark, who was supported by the anti-Hogg Democrats. The discussion centered on the Railroad Commission, which had been established during Hogg's first administration. When questioning from the audience began, the opposing sides became unruly and had to be quieted by an appeal from Hogg. The following day more disorder prevailed, and the candidates decided to go their separate ways. The issues were so potent, however, that the individual candidates continued to attract huge crowds.

Political rallies were big events in the preprimary days. A community and the surrounding countryside turned out en masse to hear the candidates' orations, which usually lasted for several hours, and there was considerable public registration of approval or disapproval of a stand, with heckling being commonplace. An important difference between campaigns then and later was that issues subordinated personalities, and entertainment was furnished the candidates by the townspeople rather than vice versa. It was a period when the voters thirsted for information rather than a show.

CAMPAIGNS UNDER THE PRIMARY SYSTEM

Governor Campbell was the first nominee of the party primary, but the convention selected the candidate on a complicated pro rata system based on votes previously cast in the primary. Since Campbell found it necessary to run in both the primary and the convention, the campaign of 1906 was not greatly different from those of previous years. Under a new plurality system Campbell sought a second term in 1908, but he had only one opponent and made only a token race. The year 1910, therefore, could be said to mark the departure from the older methods of campaigning which had been used to garner support from convention delegates. The transition was not sudden

[6] Robert C. Cotner, *James Stephen Hogg, A Biography*, pp. 193–199.
[7] *Ibid.*, pp. 284–293.

(such issues as Prohibition, "Baileyism," and the Ku Klux Klan were to be prominent for several years to come), but certain aspects of the 1910 campaign are discernible as precursors of campaign techniques to come. Personalities began to figure more prominently, showmanship tactics were introduced, and a larger number of candidates entered the race.

The evolution of gubernatorial campaigning since 1910 falls conveniently into three periods: the Age of the Platform Speech, the Age of Radio Campaigning, and the Age of Television.

The Age of the Platform Speech

For approximately the first quarter-century after 1910, the stump-speaking tour, in which the candidates mounted the hustings for face-to-face meetings with the electorate, was the most significant method of campaigning in Texas. It produced the state's most famous orators in such figures as O. B. Colquitt, James E. Ferguson, Pat Neff, and Dan Moody, each of whom travelled to speak in distant parts of the state from bunting-covered platforms, from beds of wagons, from courthouse steps, or at street corners.[8]

OSCAR B. COLQUITT—PIONEERING IN SHOWMANSHIP

O. B. Colquitt, in 1910, was one of the first to use showmanship in a campaign in Texas. Discussing the need for prison reform and deploring methods of operation in the state's penitentiary, Colquitt would display a blood-stained whip and announce it had been used to discipline prison inmates. The scene has been described as follows:

Although only 5'6", he was powerfully built and weighed 180 pounds, yet it was all he could do to wield this whip in giving a demonstration of how it was used on a convict's back. Colquitt was a superb showman, and he had worked out this part of his speech until the effect upon his audiences was tremendous.[9]

JAMES E. FERGUSON—APPEAL TO RURAL AREAS

Colorful as he was, Colquitt was hardly the equal of James E. Ferguson. Almost by accident, Ferguson hit upon a campaign tech-

[8] Newspaper clippings of each campaign appear in the biographical files of individual governors in Barker Texas History Center, The University of Texas. Much of the information used in this section came from these files.

[9] George P. Huckaby, "Oscar Branch Colquitt: A Political Biography" (unpublished Ph.D. dissertation), p. 226.

nique that in later years was to pay untold dividends in its uncanny appeal to rural voters. Upon entering the primary of 1914, Ferguson challenged his opponent Thomas H. Ball to a public debate in Waco as the opening feature of the campaign. Apparently he had in mind the same kind of meeting that had taken place in the Hogg-Clark campaign of 1892. Fortunately for him, Ball declined, whereupon Ferguson reversed his plan of opening in a city, reasoning that it would be better to have a big crowd in a small town than no crowd in a big town.[10]

After a careful search, Ferguson chose to open at Blum, Hill County. The choice was a good one: about 700 turned out in the small community, making it a gala affair. In his speech the candidate proposed that a tenant farmer should receive an income of a fixed-minimum percentage of the revenue of the farm on which he worked —a proposal which made Ferguson the idol of the "dirt farmers" and other rural voters. He came to be known as "Farmer Jim," and in practically all subsequent elections in which he or his wife stood for office they could count on the rural vote. To appeal to this unsophisticated group of the electorate, Ferguson adopted a style of speaking which became his trademark. Frequently criticizing the "city-slickers" and the "educated fools," he purposely used bad grammar and expressions which he thought would appeal to the country folks. In a typical speech in Galveston he said he "warn't no college dude, and durned glad of it," and that he didn't have to have "no edgecashun to be smarter than the durned fool Ball crowd."[11]

Evaluating the anti-intellectual technique of this rural demagogue, one writer has said, "Ferguson stood out unique. His style was wonderful if worthless. It was not original, but purely imitative. It was not even new. It was just a little different in Texas politics."[12]

MIRIAM A. FERGUSON—A FRESH APPROACH

The introduction of his wife into his political career in 1924 changed James E. Ferguson's style of campaigning but little. His

[10] Don H. Biggers, *Our Sacred Monkeys or 20 Years of Jim: A Thousand Chuckles and A Thousand Facts Showing the Amusing Humbuggery of the Whole Business Particularly Since Jim Broke Into the Game in 1914*, p. 19. Hereafter cited as *Our Sacred Monkeys.*

[11] *Ibid.*, p. 22. Several persons who were acquainted with Mr. Ferguson told the writer that in private conversations he spoke polished English. Ghent Sanderford, long-time assistant to the Fergusons, said that Mr. Ferguson was well-read in the classics and was a well-educated man despite his lack of a college degree.

[12] Biggers, *Our Sacred Monkeys*, p. 24.

stump speech, with its bad grammar and its assaults upon the educated, continued to be effective. Mrs. Ferguson adopted a fresh approach by directing her remarks toward the recently enfranchised women. During that campaign she acquired the title of "Ma" Ferguson, a name she loathed but was never able to overcome.[13] Mr. Ferguson automatically became "Pa."

As to new techniques introduced into that campaign, Mrs. Ouida Ferguson Nalle, the elder daughter of the two governors, who toured the state with them, reported:

During most of the first part of that campaign [1924] they traveled together. Mama would speak first, and in her own way ask the mothers, sisters and wives of Texas to help her clear her family's name. That was her trump card and she played it with finesse. Had she been a militant suffragist all her life her appeal would not have had half the force it had coming from a quiet, home-loving wife, mother and grandmother. In the name of her children and her grandson, not in her own, she would plead and would end with: "A vote for me is a vote of confidence for my husband, who cannot be a candidate because his enemies have suceeded in barring him from holding public office."

This entreaty of a gentle woman was becoming a problem to the professional politicians; they didn't know how to meet the attack, so simple and unprecedented. It had never occurred before in American politics.[14]

After this brief introductory appeal, Mrs. Ferguson would step aside to turn the platform over to her husband, and he would outline the Ferguson platform before blasting away at the opposition. Always he ended on the theme that Texas would have "two governors for the price of one."[15] The campaign slogan was "Me for Ma." Some automobile stickers added: "And ain't got a durned thing against Pa."

In later campaigns the Ferguson combination proved to be still a

---

[13] Apparently the name "Ma" was inadvertently originated by a Scripps-Howard newspaperman, Frank Gibler, who claims that he was not trying to arouse the ire of Mrs. Ferguson but was simply trying to make a headline fit. The following account was reported by Gibler in an interview in 1961. One night during the 1924 campaign, he was trying to work out a headline for his newspaper, the *Houston Press*. Counting the letters in "Ferguson," he asked someone in the newsroom, "What's her first name?" The answer was "Miriam Amanda." Gibler replied, "M. A. Great! We'll call her 'Ma.' It's the only thing that fits the head count." So Mrs. Ferguson, the housewife soon to be Governor of Texas, became a symbol of folksy politics to a nation. For this, however, she never forgave Gibler. *Austin Statesman,* September 22, 1961.

[14] Ouida Ferguson Nalle, *The Fergusons of Texas,* p. 169.

[15] *Ibid.,* p. 170.

vote-getter of no mean ability. In 1926 Mrs. Ferguson introduced to
Texas politics the use of the public-address system, and, although she
lost the race, this instrument was soon standard equipment on the
hustings.[16] In 1930, after the report of an assassination plot, the two
Fergusons went their separate ways on the campaign trail for the
only time in their careers.[17] Mrs. Ferguson was again defeated, but in
1932 they reunited on the platform to make their customary combined appeal for votes, and Mrs. Ferguson was elected governor. In
their last campaign (1940) they were defeated. Much of the old fire
was missing. Their daughter believed the race "was too dignified to
attract the public," although during the closing days, she noted, her
father "turned loose his guns."[18] The radio had become an integral
part of political campaigning by that time, and the Fergusons were
far less adept with that medium than with the traditional face-to-
face, personal appeal which had been their forte.

PAT M. NEFF—EMPHASIS ON HANDSHAKING

Few governors of Texas have recorded their own observations on
running for office, but Pat Neff, a skilled writer, meticulously described his experiences and set forth some of his philosophy on the
process. Without a campaign manager or headquarters, Neff took his
candidacy "in person to the hearts and homes of the people."[19] Find-
ing it "a liberal education to campaign for Governor of Texas," he
began in the sparsely settled areas, where he spoke three to seven
times a day. During the campaign he used "every means of transportation from a mule to a flying machine."[20] He drove his own car 6,000
miles, patched his own blowouts, and pumped up his own tubes. In
Neff's opinion, handshaking was the best political technique:

> When I campaigned in a small town without a speaking date, as I
> frequently did, I made it a practice to shake hands with every person I
> could find, never skipping the man handling bacon in the back of a store,
> or the carpenter building a shack in the alley. This association was one of
> the most interesting phases and one of the most important factors of my
> campaign. I found meeting people face to face to be good campaign psy-
> chology. . . . It is the personal touch that counts.[21]

[16] *Ibid.*, p. 201.
[17] *Ibid.*, p. 208.
[18] *Ibid.*, p. 249.
[19] Pat M. Neff, *The Battles of Peace*, p. 7.
[20] *Ibid.*, p. 8.
[21] *Ibid.*

Neff estimated that he spoke 850 times during the campaign, setting a record of twenty-one speeches within three days in Dallas and Tarrant counties. After each speech he proceeded to shake hands "with everyone who would permit it."[22] He spoke particularly to the old friends he had made during his school days and called them his most valuable asset.

Contrasting the campaigns of the first primary and the runoff, Neff said the former was a singlehanded battle except for his friends but that during the runoff a number of organizations had to be established. His candidacy had ceased to be a personal matter and had become a symbol of opposition to "Baileyism" (Joe Bailey was a powerful figure in Texas politics at the time). People gathered by the thousands at the rallies, and bands, badges, and banners were everywhere.[23]

Throughout the campaign Neff refused to employ a campaign manager, and his headquarters were wherever he went. In his words:

A campaign manager is chiefly some one who makes promises to special interests before the election and then tells the Governor what he must do after the election. Political headquarters is the place where buttons are touched before the election that ring in the Governor's office after the election.[24]

DAN MOODY—HONEYMOON ON THE CAMPAIGN TRAIL

Dan Moody, elected attorney general at the age of thirty, served during the first administration of Mrs. Ferguson. He became one of the severest critics of the Fergusons and soon became a leader of the anti-Ferguson faction in Texas. The gubernatorial campaign of 1926 between Mrs. Ferguson and Moody was bitter, and probably contained more verbal exchanges between personalities than had any previous campaign. Both Ferguson and Moody stumped the state, and Moody added romance by getting married just before the campaign opened. His honeymoon was spent on the campaign trail, prompting Ferguson to comment that Moody was a candidate "with nothing to recommend him save a lipstick, a new wife, and a big head."[25] Moody replied by referring to Ferguson's impeachment and declaring that the only real issue was "Fergusonism." Ferguson la-

---

[22] *Ibid.*, p. 9.
[23] *Ibid.*, p. 11.
[24] *Ibid.*, pp. 11–12.
[25] S. S. McKay, *Texas Politics, 1906–1944*, p. 149.

belled Moody "an upstart," a "young spud," and a "contemptible demagogue." Moody replied that "Jim exercises the power of governor without being responsible to the people for any of his actions." He insisted that the Ferguson Administration had been "utterly barren of achievements and cluttered with the bones of unfilled pledges."[26]

One interesting sidelight of the campaign was Mrs. Ferguson's challenge to Moody. In Sulphur Springs, two months before the first primary, she told a crowd of 7,000, "I will agree that if he leads me one vote in the primary, I will immediately resign . . . if he will agree that if I lead him 25,000 in the primary on July 24, he will immediately resign."[27] Moody accepted the wager, thereby causing a mild furor. Mrs. Ferguson failed to follow through when she was bested in the first primary.

Moody's prowess as a campaigner carried over into the races of his successor, Ross Sterling, for whom he also stumped the state. His assistance was valuable, no doubt, because Sterling lacked color and campaigning ability.[28]

JAMES V. ALLRED—WHIRLWIND CAMPAIGN

The campaign of James V. Allred was reminiscent of that of Moody. Both had been elected attorney general in their early thirties, and both were capable public speakers. Allred had variety and originality, and he traveled widely and swiftly. One political writer of the time said that he had talents as an actor and as an evangelist, along with oratorical ability.[29]

The Allred technique in politics is peculiarly individualistic and a little paradoxical. His very presence exudes the spirit of friendliness and yet he probably is as reserved in his intimate fellowship with men as was Pat M. Neff. . . . It has been observed that in the gubernatorial campaign, Allred has found his way into more offices to call men by their names, assure them of his appreciation of their suffrage, and be on his way than any other candidate.[30]

THE AGE OF RADIO

Radio was introduced into national campaigns during the Hoover-Smith presidential election of 1928, but it was used only sporadically

[26] *Ibid.*, pp. 149–150.
[27] *San Antonio Express*, May 23, 1926.
[28] McKay, *Texas Politics, 1906–1944*, pp. 203–205; 228–230.
[29] Harry Crozier in *Dallas Morning News*, July 14, 1934.
[30] *Ibid.*

in the next several campaigns in Texas until its full-blown appearance in the campaign of 1938—which one historian enthusiastically describes as "one of the most outstanding campaigns in history."[31]

W. LEE O'DANIEL—LANDSLIDE IN THE FIRST PRIMARY

Impetus was given to the use of radio in 1938 because Candidate W. Lee O'Daniel was already a radio personality, having conducted a daily program of hillbilly music and homey advice for several years to advertise the products of a flour mill. The other candidates found it necessary to use radio extensively in an attempt to offset the advantage which O'Daniel carried into the campaign.

Thirteen candidates, a record number, entered the race, among them Railroad Commissioner Ernest O. Thompson, Attorney General William McCraw, Tom F. Hunter, who had previously been in a runoff against Allred, and O'Daniel. The race became a free-for-all with each candidate vying to put on a better show than his opponents. Showmanship and the sound truck were extremely successful at rallies and joined the radio as being the principal techniques used by the candidates. Thompson hired tap dancers, and Hunter carried a troupe of nightclub entertainers, who topped off their show with a mind-reading act. O'Daniel, of course, already had his own hillbilly band.[32] McCraw was the only major candidate who did not engage entertainers to accompany him, and even he would begin his remarks by apologizing that he had not brought along his banjo.

Had it not been for the radio, W. Lee O'Daniel, who came to be called "Pappy," probably never would have become governor of Texas, for it was on one of his daily broadcasts that he broached the subject of his candidacy to the public. Within a few days, he claimed to have received 54,499 replies from persons urging him to run and only four replies opposing him.[33] He pledged that he would rid the state government of "professional politicians," "clean out the bureaucrats" in Austin, and give the state a "businesslike" administration. Blessed with a mellifluous voice, he was able to convince a large number of his listeners of his sincerity and his devotion to these objectives.

During the initial stages of the campaign he used the radio ex-

[31] Rupert N. Richardson, *Texas, the Lone Star State* (2d ed.), p. 333. By permission of Prentice-Hall, Inc.

[32] C. L. Douglas and Francis Miller, *The Life Story of W. Lee O'Daniel*, p. 112.

[33] "O'Daniel's Own Life Story" in *Dallas Morning News*, September 27, 1938.

clusively, applying the same tactics to politics that he had been using to promote flour sales for many years: popular music interspersed with neighborly comments and an occasional short, informal sales speech. As the campaign progressed he decided to take to the stump to supplement his broadcasts. Wherever he went he attracted some of the largest crowds in the state's political history. In Austin, his crowd in Wooldridge Park was estimated to be between 35,000 and 40,000; in Sherman he drew 10,000, and in San Angelo 8,000.[34] In Houston he had the largest political turnout in the history of the city.[35]

O'Daniel injected a religious theme into the campaign by running on a platform of the Ten Commandments and the Golden Rule. His rallies were reminiscent of an old-fashioned camp meeting, and they "appealed to the same deep human instincts and provided the same emotional outlets which the camp meetings formerly afforded."[36] Another novelty was the taking of a collection at the rally to finance his campaign—a practice which apparently "impressed the people that his fight was their fight and that no large hidden interests were supporting or controlling their leader."[37]

Accompanying O'Daniel on his swing around the state were his attractive wife and three handsome teen-age children—perfectly named Pat, Mike, and Molly—as well as his band, "The Light Crust Dough Boys," already known to thousands of radio fans. To avoid the stigma of being connected with any local political element, O'Daniel departed from campaign tradition by introducing himself to his audiences. Afterward, he would have the band play several tunes, usually including his own composition, "Beautiful Texas," and would then proceed to speak. Ordinarily he closed the meeting with a song which he had composed for the campaign, "Them Hillbillies Are Politicians Now":[38]

> Been hangin' round the mountains all these years
> Singin' songs about the train-wrecked engineers
> They've been pavin' all the cities
> With their pretty corn-fed ditties,
> And they've got the politicians all in tears.
> They come to town with their guitars

[34] S. S. McKay, *W. Lee O'Daniel and Texas Politics, 1938–1942*, pp. 34–35.
[35] Douglas and Miller, *The Life Story of W. Lee O'Daniel*, p. 126.
[36] Frank Goodwyn, *Lone-Star Land: Twentieth-Century Texas in Perspective*, p. 258.
[37] *Ibid.*, p. 259.
[38] Douglas and Miller, *The Life Story of W. Lee O'Daniel*, p. 112.

> And now they're smokin' big cigars—
> Them Hillbillies are politicians now.

To say that the O'Daniel methods were unorthodox would be a gross understatement, but obviously, the voters of that time liked the change. Many politicians since have tried to imitate him, but no one has seemed to handle his approach so well as he.[39] In a comeback try in 1956, however, O'Daniel found that the temper of the times was no longer suited to his brand of showmanship. Travelling in a red fire engine, he again carried a string band and again declared that he would "clean out" the State Capitol. But his loss of voter appeal was such that he was defeated in the first primary and only $160 was netted from the "free-will contributions" at his political rallies.[40] Despite his decline, O'Daniel holds a place as one of the most colorful and effective campaigners Texas has ever known.

COKE STEVENSON—TOKEN CAMPAIGN

The campaign of 1940, when O'Daniel was re-elected, was in many ways a continuation or repetition of the sensational race of two years earlier.[41] These two campaigns stand out in bold contrast to the two campaigns which followed them. After serving only seven months of his second gubernatorial term, O'Daniel ran for a vacancy in the United States Senate. Upon his election, Lieutenant Governor Coke Stevenson became governor of Texas. Four months later the United States entered World War II, and attention shifted to the international scene. Stevenson, the wartime governor, won renomination to a full elective term in 1942 and again in 1944, thereby shattering the no-third-term tradition in Texas. No doubt the war situation created a lack of interest in the state races, but, also, Stevenson had many friends as the result of a long legislative career. The two factors combined to prevent any formidable competition in either of his races,[42] and he conducted only token campaigns, consisting of several

[39] One of his opponents tried what newspapers called "a new wrinkle." Supporters of Attorney General McCraw chartered a train to carry the public to Arlington for his opening speech. Announcing the trip, the papers advertised a free ride for everyone, with no conductors to collect fares. All who could crowd aboard were welcomed to the "Bill McCraw Special." *Dallas Morning News,* April 23, 1938.

[40] From sworn statement of Mrs. W. Lee O'Daniel, campaign manager, on file in office of secretary of state.

[41] McKay, *W. Lee O'Daniel and Texas Politics, 1938–1942,* p. 215.

[42] McKay, *Texas Politics, 1906–1944,* p. 293.

radio speeches and occasional appearances at public gatherings. Perhaps no other product of the primary system ever has won, or for that matter, ever again will win, the Democratic nomination with such a minimum of campaigning as did Stevenson.

The end of the war signalled a revival of interest in gubernatorial politics, and the first postwar campaign unfolded in a manner reminiscent of preprimary days, when philosophies of government constituted the major basis of political discussion. In 1946 fourteen candidates, espousing practically every shade of politics, announced. Three were incumbent officeholders: Lieutenant Governor John Lee Smith, Railroad Commissioner Beauford Jester, and Attorney General Grover Sellers. Two others were well known: Dr. Homer P. Rainey, former president of The University of Texas, and Jerry Sadler, who had resigned from the Railroad Commission to enter the military service.

The candidates did not engage in excessive showmanship, and the whole tone of the campaign was more sophisticated than that of the last hard-fought race, concentrating in the main upon political ideologies. The liberal-conservative schism which had been smoldering for the past several years suddenly burst into open flame again; and the election was fought on the supposed superliberalism of Dr. Rainey.[43] Ousted in 1944 as president of the state university because of differences with the Board of Regents, Rainey ran as a martyr, espousing conventional New Deal views. Naturally he was popular with the pro-Roosevelt faction, and he appealed strongly also to two groups which had not theretofore been potent forces in politics in Texas: the newly enfranchised Negro Democrats and the elements of organized labor which had migrated to the state with the industrialization accompanying the war.[44]

To counteract extremism on both sides, Beauford Jester came forward with a moderate approach designed to weld a coalition to follow what he called "the peoples' path." Dwelling lightly upon Rainey's dismissal, Jester took hefty swings at both ultraconservatives and ultraliberals. He castigated certain labor leaders and urged the "up-

[43] V. O. Key, Jr., *Southern Politics in State and Nation*, p. 257. Hereafter cited as Key, *Southern Politics*.

[44] In 1944 the "white primary law" of Texas was declared unconstitutional. *Smith* v. *Allwright*, 321 U.S. 649.

holding of states' rights and the rejection of federal grants."[45] Not only did his middle-of-the-road approach win the election for him, but it came to be a popular political stance in subsequent years and is the one assumed by Governor John Connally today.

THE AGE OF TELEVISION

Perhaps more than any other single decade, the 1950's witnessed revolutionary developments in political campaigning. The introduction of television multiplied costs and also demanded more efficient planning and management, better organization, and a higher degree of specialization.[46] The inevitable result was that the traditional campaign organization found itself unable to cope with the complexities of the new mass medium and was forced to seek assistance from professional public relations firms in conducting campaigns.

Throughout the country a number of firms have begun to specialize in the conduct of political campaigns, with more than half of the total number being concentrated in California, New York, and Texas. Such firms run virtually every aspect of a campaign for a candidate. They raise money, help determine issues, write speeches, handle press releases, prepare advertising copy and radio and television shows, and develop whatever other publicity techniques are necessary for a particular race.[47] Professor Alexander Heard quotes the head of a Texas firm as suggesting that Texas is so large, and its politics so heterogeneous, that really six or seven campaigns must be run at once to get statewide coverage.[48] Such an undertaking requires *savoir faire*. One Texas firm divides its activities into three phases: helping decide the "pitch" of the campaign, providing the "ammunition," and managing the field campaign through county and district organizations. Frequently, one firm handling the statewide campaign will engage other firms in leading cities to expedite the work in those specific areas.[49]

[45] *Port Arthur News*, May 5, 1946.

[46] Alexander Heard, *The Costs of Democracy*, pp. 410–411.

[47] Robert J. Pitchell, "The Influence of Professional Campaign Management Firms in Partisan Elections in California," *Western Political Quarterly*, XI (June, 1958), 278.

[48] Heard, *The Costs of Democracy*, p. 418.

[49] *Ibid.*, pp. 420–421. Among the names of public relations firms appearing in candidates' expense accounts on file with the secretary of state are Read, Petty, and Poland of Fort Worth, Ben Kaplan Agency of Houston, and Nichols and Associates of Pecos. Professor Heard mentions J. J. Pickle and John Van Cronkhite of Austin as two of the most prominent individuals in the field at that time.

Only three individuals—Allan Shivers, Price Daniel, and John Connally—have been elected governor since the entrance of television onto the Texas political scene. Both Shivers and Daniel conducted extensive races against a common opponent, Ralph W. Yarborough, and as both employed some of the same professional advertising people to assist them, their campaigns were similarly organized and conducted.

Texas electioneering history was made on July 6, 1954, by Allan Shivers, who, as the state's first aspirant for three elective terms, appeared simultaneously on a statewide hookup of eleven television and thirty-nine radio stations.[50] This telecast truly opened up "a new era of political campaigning in Texas."[51]

During the course of this campaign Shivers appeared on statewide television on two other occasions and supplemented his telecasts with numerous radio broadcasts. Undoubtedly the use of these media lessened the need for as extensive a series of public appearances as had been customary in prior campaigns, and the Governor was able to reach more people with less travel. His itinerary for the campaign of 1954 lists only twenty-nine formal speeches in some eighteen different locations. His full campaign schedule for the two primaries is set forth in Table 12.

Probably one of the best-organized political campaigns in Texas history was conducted by John Connally in 1962. Opposed by five well-known candidates, including the incumbent Governor Price Daniel, Connally relied heavily on the assistance of a public relations firm in running the campaign. As explained by a member of the firm, Connally's campaign was really three campaigns: (1) the first primary, in which the major emphasis was upon the introduction of Candidate Connally to the people of Texas; (2) the runoff, in which a border-to-border train trip was featured to carry the candidate over the state for personal contact with voters; and (3) the fall campaign, in which a novel technique—a "campaignathon"—was employed to attract maximum attention to the Nominee.[52]

The official opening of the Connally campaign was at a mammoth

---

[50] Harold J. Marburger, *Texas Elections, 1918–1954*, p. 148.

[51] Interview with Clyde Johnson, executive director, State Democratic Executive Committee, in Austin, July 19, 1961.

[52] Interview with Julian Read, of Read and Poland, Inc., Fort Worth, August 14, 1963.

TABLE 12

Itinerary of Allan Shivers in the Democratic Primaries of 1954*

Date	Place	
June 21	Lufkin	Opening speech
June 26	Kerrville	Chamber of Commerce banquet
June 30	San Antonio	Radio
July 1	San Antonio	State Bar Association
July 3	North Fort Hood	Governor's Day Review, 49th Div.
July 6	Dallas	Television and Radio (statewide)
July 9	Beaumont	Radio
July 15	Tyler	Radio
July 15	Palestine	Radio
July 16	Dallas	Television
July 19	McAllen	Radio
July 21	Denison	Radio
July 22	Dallas	Radio
July 23	Woodville	Radio
August 3	Austin	Radio
August 6	Austin	Radio
August 10	Dallas	Radio
August 11	Port Arthur	Radio
August 13	Austin	Women's rally
August 17	Austin	Radio
August 18	Wichita Falls	Radio
August 19	Austin	Public rally
August 19	Austin	Television
August 20	Texas City	Public rally
August 20	Galveston	Public rally
August 23	San Antonio	Alamo rally
August 26	Henderson	Radio
August 27	Houston	Radio
August 27		Radio (statewide)

* First primary, July 24, 1954; runoff primary, August 28, 1954.
Source: Derived from the Governor's appointment book, 1954. Made available
 to the writer by Weldon Hart, executive secretary to Governor Shivers.

barbecue on his ranch near Floresville, Wilson County, the objective being to promote the image of a "hometown boy" that the "home-folks" were solidly behind. Well covered by the press and television, the crowd was estimated at 10,000, with some well-known political figures among the ordinary voters. To complete the task of introducing Candidate Connally, during succeeding weeks a series of "Coffee With Connally" programs were carried each morning between 7 and 8 o'clock on television stations in every section of Texas. Each five-minute, taped program was confined to one particular issue, such as education, fiscal responsibility of the state, relations between state and nation, and the like. Through these capsule programs thousands of Texans became acquainted with their future governor.

After Connally led the ticket in the first primary, he entered a runoff with Don Yarborough, regarded as the most liberal Democrat in the race. To enliven the campaign, an old technique, successfully employed by Harry S. Truman in the presidential race of 1948, was decided upon. A campaign train, the "John Connally Victory Special," embarked early one morning with an enthusiastic send-off from Texarkana and traveled to El Paso—almost 900 miles away—stopping at practically every station en route for remarks by Connally and handshaking with the voters. The trip is given considerable credit for helping him win the Democratic nomination.

Faced with the strongest threat in decades from the Republican Party, which had in 1961 unexpectedly won a Texas race for United States senator, Connally entered what was to be the most vigorous general election campaign in the history of Texas up to that time. His opponent was Jack Cox, who two years before had run against Price Daniel in the Democratic primary, but who had later defected to the Republican Party and, as the Republican candidate, was campaigning actively and widely. Planners of the Connally campaign now sought something unique to promote the Democratic candidate. They designed the "Campaignathon," a last-minute airplane tour all over the state. For forty-eight hours around the clock, the candidate travelled, spoke, and greeted voters. Never before had political rallies been held at 3:00 A.M. in Texas, but the novelty of the idea was enough to attract the desired attention. Departing from San Antonio at 6:30 P.M. on Thursday, November 1, the "Campaignathon" followed a strict schedule, winding up in Corpus Christi on Saturday, November 3, at 7:15 P.M., two days before the election, having covered 3,618 miles and made thirty stops. A complete schedule appears in Table 13. Although earlier candidates may have travelled the length and breadth of Texas to appeal for votes, none had ever before engaged in such an intensive effort. At the polls, Connally was elected Governor, approximately eleven months after he had announced for the office.

TABLE 13

John Connally's Forty-Eight-Hour "Campaignathon," 1962

	City	Arrival Time	Elapsed Time	Miles Traveled
1.	San Antonio	6:30 P.M.		
2.	Harlingen	9:35 P.M.	3 hrs. 5 min.	252
3.	McAllen	10:25 P.M.	3 hrs. 55 min.	292
4.	Del Rio	12:45 A.M.	6 hrs. 15 min.	592
5.	Fort Stockton	2:15 A.M.	7 hrs. 45 min.	772
6.	El Paso	3:10 A.M. (MST)	9 hrs. 45 min.	1,017
7.	Big Spring	7:10 A.M. (CST)	12 hrs. 40 min.	1,332
8.	Sweetwater	8:10 A.M.	13 hrs. 40 min.	1,400
9.	Brownwood	9:20 A.M.	14 hrs. 50 min.	1,505
10.	Austin	10:45 A.M.	16 hrs. 15 min.	1,640
11.	Temple	2:30 P.M.	20 hrs.	1,708
12.	Waco	3:20 P.M.	20 hrs. 50 min.	1,745
13.	Stephenville	4:25 P.M.	21 hrs. 55 min.	1,835
14.	Wichita Falls	5:45 P.M.	23 hrs. 15 min.	1,962
15.	Gainesville	6:50 P.M.	24 hrs. 20 min.	2,052
16.	Dallas	7:50 P.M.	25 hrs. 20 min.	2,127
17.	Fort Worth	9:50 P.M.	27 hrs. 20 min.	2,164
18.	Sherman	10:50 P.M.	28 hrs. 20 min.	2,239
19.	Paris	11:45 P.M.	29 hrs. 15 min.	2,306
20.	Sulphur Springs	12:25 A.M.	30 hrs. 5 min.	2,351
21.	Texarkana	1:30 A.M.	31 hrs.	2,456
22.	Palestine	3:30 A.M.	33 hrs.	2,614
23.	Nacogdoches	4:25 A.M.	33 hrs. 55 min.	2,674
24.	Lufkin	5:10 A.M.	34 hrs. 40 min.	2,696
25.	Beaumont	6:20 A.M.	35 hrs. 50 min.	2,801
26.	Conroe	9:10 A.M.	38 hrs. 40 min.	2,906
27.	Beeville	10:55 A.M.	40 hrs. 25 min.	3,116
28.	Bryan	3:35 P.M.	45 hrs. 5 min.	3,303
29.	Houston	4:45 P.M.	46 hrs. 15 min.	3,408
30.	Corpus Christi	7:15 P.M.	48 hrs. 45 min.	3,618

Source: Governor Connally's office.

CHANGES EFFECTED BY TELEVISION

Since the advent of television, giant political rallies in Texas seemingly are a thing of the past. In the opinion of one veteran campaign worker in both Shivers and Daniel races, the change has come about, at least in part, because of the changing habits of voters.[53] No longer are they willing to leave the television set and the comfort of an air-conditioned room to attend an outside rally on the courthouse steps, as they did thirty years ago. Now they prefer to scrutinize candidates on camera, where they may feel they can get a closer look and more accurately evaluate personalities. But the day of face-to-face campaigning is not gone. Instead of the large crowds before which Hogg, the Fergusons, and O'Daniel appeared, the candidates of the sixties have found personal contact with smaller groups to be desirable. Appearances at small gatherings at civic clubs, teas and coffees, open houses, and suburban shopping centers have proved useful to supplement TV coverage. Connally, a newcomer to state politics, found it necessary to make personal appearances all over Texas to introduce himself to the voters.

Candidates may not be content, either, to abandon the old tactics completely. In the heated race of 1956, "candidates in the Texas governor's race herded their assemblages of hillbilly bands, fire trucks, movie stars, and donkeys into the big cities . . . in hopes of corralling the metropolitan voter."[54] Price Daniel's introduction on statewide television by Fess Parker, "the Davy Crockett of Hollywood," was apparently successful enough to draw the fire of one of his opponents, who accused him of becoming a theatrical producer.[55]

Television has worked both to the advantage and to the detriment of candidates. While they can become better known to more people within a shorter period, they must now be better speakers and have pleasing television personalities. Speeches must be more polished and less repetitious. Perhaps this requirement has led to a more dignified type of campaign by eliminating some of the excessive showmanship, name-calling, and mudslinging so common in former years. One feature, however, is noticeably absent from the television speech, and its lack is deplored by a nationally known columnist, who regrets that there is no opportunity for questioning or heckling and that the candidate cannot sense the reaction of his listeners.[56]

[53] Interview with J. J. Pickle, in Austin, July 18, 1961. As a member of an Austin public relations firm, Pickle actively participated in campaigns of Shivers and Daniel.

[54] *Austin American,* July 24, 1956.

[55] *Ibid.*

[56] James Reston, "Our Campaign Techniques Re-examined," *New York Times Magazine,* November 9, 1952, p. 62; see also Robert Bendiner, "How Much Has TV Changed Campaigning?" in *ibid.,* November 2, 1952, p. 71.

A PROCESS OF DISPLACEMENT

Throughout the history of campaigning a process of displacement has gone on. As new forms of campaigning develop, they push aside older ones.[57] Nowhere is the displacement principle more vividly illustrated than in Texas politics, which have produced a multiplicity of vote-getting tactics during the past three-quarters of a century. A brief editorial in the *Dallas Morning News* entitled "New Campaign Tactics" succinctly summarizes the changes:

Only oldsters can remember the political torchlight parade and the excitement it stirred. It disappeared long ago in the interest of safety. Then went the special train. Even the sound truck appears to be on the way out. It had become a major nuisance and its operation in many cities was in violation of anti-noise ordinances.

Radio and television are taking over as the principal means by which candidates reach voters. They are expensive, but they carry the candidates' voice and message to more people than did any of the earlier means.

Candidates are supplementing them with extensive handshaking tours and occasional barbecues. This year's [1958] political winners are likely to be those who can make the best showing on television.[58]

Between 1876 and 1963, residents of Texas witnessed forty-four gubernatorial campaigns from which twenty-four individuals emerged as victors. Nine were nominees of state conventions, three were chosen by the plurality system, and twelve were products of the double primary. Invariably, students of government are questioned as to which method of nomination produced the best candidates, but an answer is not readily ascertainable. One historian claims that there is no definite way of telling and declares that such speculation "would be a needless entrance into political controversy, and, at best, would be nothing more than a personal opinion."[59]

In assessing the forty-four campaigns, which have been conducted with such a diversity of techniques, one can surely find that each method of nomination has produced both good and bad candidates—depending largely upon the individual's point of view. But it cannot be denied that the direct primary has occasionally afforded opportunity for an unlikely candidate to win the nomination if he hap-

---

[57] Heard, *The Costs of Democracy*, p. 408.
[58] *Dallas Morning News*, July 5, 1958.
[59] Ralph W. Steen, *Twentieth-Century Texas: An Economic and Social History*, p. 333.

pened to appear at a propitious moment with a unique method of voter appeal. The change from nomination by convention to nomination by primary, with the accompanying changes in electioneering tactics, has undoubtedly produced somewhat more colorful and exciting gubernatorial races; but many potentially qualified candidates probably have been discouraged from entering politics in Texas because of unwillingness to subject themselves to the abuses and invective which sometimes are heaped upon those who canvass for the high office.

13

The Governor as Political Leader

The introduction of the party primary heralded the decline, but not the demise, of the party convention in Texas. Under the provisions of the Terrell Election Law, the rank and file of members of a political party hold a convention in each voting precinct on the day of the primary. That assemblage chooses delegates to a county convention, which, in turn, selects delegates to a state convention. Meeting in September of even-numbered years, some weeks following the primary, the convention's principal activities are the certification of party candidates, the drafting of a platform, and the election of a state executive committee of the party.[1]

Traditionally, the September convention has been dubbed the "Governor's Convention," as it provides a ready-made opportunity for the governor-nominate to secure control of the party machinery and to incorporate his campaign promises into the state platform. Describing the convention, one Associated Press writer many years ago said, "It is customary to let the nominee for governor have his way in nearly everything because he is head of the state party and its mouthpiece."[2]

State conventions prior to 1906 were the center of public attention because they nominated candidates for statewide offices and provided a forum for discussing the principal issues of the day. The

[1] In years in which presidential elections are held, an extra series of conventions is called to choose delegates to the national convention and presidential electors. Before 1944 governors were not particularly active in these conventions held in the spring. Beginning in 1960, the same slate of delegates chosen for the presidential convention also attended the regular biennial convention. In this chapter the September convention is emphasized because it provides the setting for the governor to exercise leadership in party organization and operation.

[2] *Fort Worth Star-Telegram*, August 22, 1938.

shifting of the nominating machinery away from the convention naturally resulted in lagging interest in the party conclaves. For many years they were poorly attended, and frequently the delegates were totally unrepresentative of the sentiments of a majority of the members of the party.[3] For over thirty years the biennial meeting was little more than a token of compliance with the law, and on occasions even governors brushed aside the meetings as being of no great consequence in furthering their programs. Little importance was attached to party platforms in those years, although invariably the executives paid lip service to them by urging the Legislature to enact their planks into law.[4]

Some specific examples will illustrate the difference in approaches used by various governors in their dealings with the party organization. Just as they reflect practically every kind of political philosophy, the annals of Texas politics record all kinds of political leadership from complete domination to total abstinence from party affairs.

Before 1944: An Inactive Political Role

PAT M. NEFF—THE OPEN CONVENTION

The first major deviation from the accustomed pattern in the relationship of the governor to the party organization was introduced by Pat M. Neff in 1920. Neff, who had been speaker of the House of Representatives some years previously, amazed the politicians by defeating the well-known Joseph W. Bailey in the state's first runoff. Equally astonishing was his announcement that he would allow the Governor's Convention a free hand in formulating a platform and in selecting the state executive committee. In reporting the convention, Clarence DuBose of the *Dallas Morning News* wrote:

> Today's Democratic convention contrasts strangely with the campaign of which it is the finale. Just as that campaign established, probably, a record for noise and turmoil and violent emotion and expression, so today's convention went in inverse ratio to the opposite extreme. Perhaps there has never been in Texas a state political gathering so calm and quiet and complacent, so unruffled and unexcited and unexciting, so mild and perfunctory as that of today. Nor has any convention in recent years been attended by so few persons. [An actual count of the gallery showed 427]

---

[3] Allen Duckworth, "Democratic Dilemma in Texas," *Southwest Review*, XXXII (Winter, 1947), 35.
[4] See Chapter 8, on the "Message Power."

. . . and there were not more than 500 delegates with many absent at times.[5]

Upon assuming office, Governor Neff called upon the Legislature to redeem the pledges made in the platform, a copy of which he submitted as "our confession of political faith." Urging the lawmakers to write into the statutes every concrete proposal of the platform, he spoke of his "open convention" approach:

For the first time, perhaps, in more than a quarter of a century, the platform was not dictated by the nominee for Governor. The nominee in the recent election declined to take any part in the drafting of the party platform. It was drawn by and represents the crystallized thought of representatives fresh from the people.[6]

Neff was only moderately successful in securing the passage of his proposals, it being necessary for him to call special sessions during both of his terms.[7] Possibly his "hands-off" attitude in party affairs compounded his legislative difficulties.

DAN MOODY—ACCENT ON HARMONY

Dan Moody, at the age of thirty-three, became the state's youngest executive. The victory came in 1926 after a hard-fought campaign through two primaries, in which Moody unseated the incumbent, Miriam A. Ferguson—the first time in the twentieth century that a Texas governor had been denied a second term. His meteoric rise gave Moody a significant role in the National Democratic Convention which met in Houston in 1928, and he was mentioned prominently as a candidate for Vice President of the United States. Moody campaigned for the Democratic national ticket in many states,[8] but in the election, Texas supported the Republican nominee, Herbert Hoover. The next session of the Legislature, therefore, undertook to castigate the Democratic Party bolters by amending the election code. As passed, the bill would have given political parties the power to prescribe qualifications of their members and to determine who

[5] September 8, 1920. An interesting sidelight was that there were also no "smoke-filled rooms." The entire convention abstained from the use of tobacco, causing DuBose to report, "This nicotineless novelty also sets a new standard in Texas politics." Some attributed the abstention to the presence of ladies, others to the fact that the meeting was held in the First Baptist Church.

[6] *House Journal*, Thirty-seventh Legislature, regular session, p. 157.

[7] See Chapter 8.

[8] Interview with former Governor Dan Moody, March 15, 1961, in Austin.

could vote in future primaries,[9] and would have negated the then-existing provision that "no person shall ever be denied the right to participate in a primary because of former political views or affiliations or because of membership or nonmembership in organizations other than the party."[10]

Moody's philosophy of political leadership was exemplified in the veto message which he penned on Senate Bill 504:

> The purpose of this bill is to give powers mentioned to the Democratic State Executive Committee, and it may as well be discussed from its effect upon the Democratic Party and thereby its effect upon the State at large, in view of the fact that the Democratic Party has been, is now, and I hope in the interest of general welfare will continue to be the predominant political party of this State.
>
> I have nothing to say about parties controlling their own destines as voluntary organizations. Under ordinary circumstances, a Bill of this kind would excite little interest and it would have my approval. However, the Bill comes at this time as one of the indirect results of the division which occurred in the Democratic Party in the campaign preceding the recent General Election. It appears evident to me that if the Bill becomes law it will prolong the bitterness which that campaign aroused and will continue and widen the breach in the Democratic Party. I am of the opinion that the welfare of the Party and the welfare of the State are to be advanced by promoting harmony among those whose views are in accord with the principles of the Democratic Party.[11]

ROSS STERLING—POLICY OF NON-INTERVENTION

A successful business man and a devotee of *laissez faire*, Ross Sterling attempted to transport his business philosophy into government. He reasoned that he was a leader of the whole people, not of special groups (not even his own Democratic Party), and that his job as chief executive was a full-time one. Somewhat to his consternation, however, he soon found that being the head of the executive branch of the government was a political liability as well as an asset and that no governor could escape criticism. Abandoning his original intention of lofty disengagement from politics, he vowed to clash "head-on" with his chief antagonist, James E. Ferguson. After about a year in office, Sterling began to appear at political meetings and to ex-

[9] Senate Bill 504, Forty-first Legislature, regular session.
[10] *Revised Civil Statutes of Texas*, Art. 3107.
[11] Vetoed Bills, Forty-first Legislature, on file in the office of the secretary of state.

change verbal blows with Ferguson. The turnabout apparently came too late for him to redeem himself with Party stalwarts, and, handicapped by his innate lack of political ability, he lost out to his critic. In the campaign for re-election in 1932, Sterling was embittered by reports of fraudulent voting in Nacogdoches and Longview; he became convinced that he was rightful nominee despite Mrs. Ferguson's apparent majority of 3,300 votes.[12]

To recapture control of the Democratic Party, the Sterling followers conceived of two plans: legal proceedings against Mrs. Ferguson, contesting her right to the nomination; and a political fight to secure control of the Legislature (which was just convening for a third called session), of the State Democratic Executive Committee, and of the state convention scheduled to meet in September. In every maneuver, however, the Sterling camp was unsuccessful. They could not persuade the Legislature to create an investigating committee to look into the alleged fraud in the election,[13] and they lost their case in the Supreme Court on the grounds that the suit was moot for lack of time in which the case could be heard and adjudicated.[14] Perhaps most important, they were defeated in the state convention because of their failure to move swiftly enough to seize control of that body.[15]

While Sterling sat in his hotel room the Fergusons were active among the delegates pleading their cause and were highly successful in organizing the convention. The newspaper report of the meeting was something of a tribute to their efforts, which completely squelched the hopes of Sterling for the second term which he believed to be rightfully his:

James E. Ferguson so completely controlled the State Convention which on Tuesday nominated his wife for Governor of Texas on the Democratic ticket that not even a breath of opposition dared manifest itself on the floor. . . . at every opportunity the great crowd shouted for the Fergusons. Every convention activity was under Ferguson domination. . . . Only a few anti-Ferguson men were named members of the state committee.

[12] A thorough analysis of Sterling as party chieftain is given in Warner E. Mills, Jr., "The Public Career of a Texas Conservative: A Biography of Ross Shaw Sterling (unpublished Ph.D. dissertation), Chapter V. Hereafter cited as Mills, "A Biography of Ross Shaw Sterling."
[13] *Senate Journal*, Forty-second Legislature, third called session, pp. 29–30, 39–42, 54–55.
[14] *Ferguson* v. *McCallum, Secretary of State; Sterling* v. *Ferguson*, 53 S.W. (2d) 753 (1932), *per curiam.*
[15] Mills, "A Biography of Ross Shaw Sterling," (unpublished Ph.D. dissertation), p. 213.

Last was the adoption of the platform and it caused no fight, which was an innovation when other conventions are recalled. . . . Record speed was made throughout the meeting.[16]

Again, the hands-off policy of a governor had not reaped dividends in party circles.

W. LEE O'DANIEL—ABDICATION OF THE POLITICAL ROLE

Of all the governors elected by the voters of Texas, one of the most politically naive was W. Lee O'Daniel, the flour salesman who was himself not qualified to vote.[17] Within a matter of weeks he was catapulted from political anonymity to the state's highest office in one of the most sensational campaigns in the history of Texas. Although he was a popular radio personality, few took his candidacy seriously when he first announced. Shortly afterwards, however, using unorthodox campaign methods, he had started a bandwagon rolling and was able to capture the nomination without a runoff.

To an even greater extent than Neff and Sterling, O'Daniel adopted a policy of indifference to party affairs—a position which could be described as one of complete aloofness to the Democratic Party. Immediately after his win he took the unprecedented step of publicly endorsing the candidacy of six persons in the runoff for state office.[18] He also announced that he had no interest in the upcoming county conventions, saying confidently that he would rely on his friends to take care of his interests. From that time until about two weeks before the state convention, he maintained utter silence on party mat-

---

[16] *Dallas Morning News*, September 14, 1932.

[17] While most public officials are required by law to be qualified voters, the governor does not have to be a poll-tax holder. Constitution of Texas, Art. IV, Sec. 4.

[18] S. S. McKay, *W. Lee O'Daniel and Texas Politics, 1938–1942*, p. 73. Candidates whom he endorsed were Coke Stevenson for Lieutenant Governor; Walter Woodul for Attorney General; C. V. Terrell for railroad commissioner; Bascom Giles for commissioner of the General Land Office; H. N. Graves for the Court of Criminal Appeals; and Richard Critz for associate justice of the Supreme Court. Stevenson, Giles, Graves, and Critz won.

In an interview at Junction, Texas, on February 27, 1961, Coke Stevenson told the writer that he did not solicit O'Daniel's endorsement and felt that it hurt his race because of general resentment against the intervention. He speculated that it may have cost him 50,000 votes, and said he was beseiged with calls from throughout the state demanding to know the meaning of the Governor's move. Considerable "smoothing over" was needed to repair the damage caused by the endorsement, he said. Stevenson also said that many thought O'Daniel's endorsement caused Walter Woodul to be defeated for Attorney General.

ters, coming forth then only to blast at his enemies, charging that they were planning "to throw the convention at Beaumont into confusion," and were seeking to defeat those whom he had endorsed. He stated that he would attend the convention but had no plans to try to run it.[19]

A few days before the convention was to open, O'Daniel supporters released a list of their choices for temporary and permanent convention officials. The nominee, meanwhile, remained aloof. At a Houston banquet which he attended en route, he reiterated that he was "not figuring on insisting on anything" at the conclave because "the Beaumont meeting is not my convention."[20] He refused to be drawn out on several controversial matters of the day, declaring that they would not be issues until they came up in the Legislature.

The September convention in 1938 had the largest attendance of any Texas state party convention up to that date, and the O'Daniel nominees for convention posts won handily. During the early hours of the meeting, harmony reigned while the Gubernatorial Nominee addressed the gathering in the platitudes he had made so popular during the preceding campaign. After referring to his campaign platform —the Ten Commandments and the Golden Rule—and his campaign slogan—"More smokestacks and businessmen; less Johnson grass and politicians,"—O'Daniel urged the necessity of industrializing Texas, of caring for the unfortunate, and of paying larger old-age pensions. He also made a fervent plea for the repeal of the poll tax and the abolition of unnecessary governmental expenditures.[21]

Before the day was over, however, the convention became embroiled in a fight over the platform, causing a number of tempers to flare. Late in the evening, when O'Daniel returned to the hall during a roll-call vote and attempted to speak on his old-age-pension plan, he was howled down by the delegates. Asked to return a second time (in a misguided attempt by convention officials to bring harmony to the disgruntled delegates), the Nominee was booed so loudly that he left the meeting in despair. According to one of his closest associates, the incident permanently ended his participation in Party meetings, and during his administration, he had practically no contact with Party officials.[22] Recommendations from members of the State Democratic Executive Committee for individuals desiring government jobs

[19] McKay, W. *Lee O'Daniel and Texas Politics, 1938–1942*, p. 74.
[20] *Houston Post*, September 12, 1938.
[21] *Beaumont Enterprise*, September 14, 1938.
[22] Interview with William J. Lawson, executive secretary to Governor O'Daniel, in Austin, March 13, 1961.

were virtually ignored and frequently became the "kiss of death" for an application.

A leading newspaper attributed O'Daniel's misfortune at the convention to the absence of aggressive leadership, due in part to his lack of political experience. It reported that throughout the proceedings the Nominee pursued a course of conciliation, opposing no one and refusing to fight back even when he could have done so. Perversely, the convention loudly applauded Gerald Mann, nominee for attorney general, who had not received O'Daniel's blessing in the runoff. According to the newspaper, O'Daniel's intervention in other races had generated a "near theme of hate," which lay at the bottom of his difficulties in the convention. It added:

> The howling down of the party choice a few hours after his nomination was the first instance of its kind in the history of Texas politics and has caused a near sensation in capital circles. Those who knew the past could hardly believe the Beaumont reports. . . . O'Daniel was a pathetic figure at the height of the tumult as he looked on bewildered.
>
> He appeared unable to comprehend the wild scenes that were enacted nor to understand the boos and vituperations hurled at him by the same convention that had nominated him and cheered his speech of acceptance.[23]

The editorial predicted, furthermore, that unless a popular wave of resentment swept the state at the way the convention had treated its candidate, O'Daniel would "have a hard row to hoe" with the Legislature. These were prophetic words, to be substantiated later by the Governor's poor record in getting his proposals enacted. He became the governor whose veto was overridden more frequently than that of any other Texas chief executive of the twentieth century.[24]

O'Daniel's conception of his relationship to the Party organization was illustrated in a telegram which he sent to E. B. Germany, chairman of the State Democratic Executive Committee, on March 9, 1940. Sending "greetings and best wishes" to all members attending the Committee meeting at Hillsboro, the Governor said:

> There seems to be some sort of impression existing with some people outside of the Committee Members and stated in many press reports that the State Democratic Committee is considered to be a tool of the Governor and for the purpose of performing certain tasks which the Governor wishes. I do not know what has caused this impression unless it has been

---

[23] *Dallas Morning News*, September 15, 1938.
[24] See Chapter 7.

the actions of some of the committees during former administrations, and I want to make it distinctly understood that such condition does not exist now. I have absolutely no desires or wishes to express regarding anything which your committee does. I consider each and every member free to act as they think best on all matters for consideration and I do not in any way want to receive praise for anything good they do, nor blame for anything bad they do. I do not consider the committee connected in any way, shape, manner or form with the Governor's Office and hope that each member will consider their duty and responsibility is to serve the citizens of their respective districts.[25]

Throughout his tenure O'Daniel maintained the view that he was divorced from the Party structure. Although he was supposedly titular head of the Democratic Party, he never made any overt effort to exploit the potentialities of that ex-officio position as an avenue of leadership. After his nomination for a second term, he wrote to the chairman of the State Democratic Executive Committee that he did not wish to participate in the shaping of the Party platform of 1940. He added:

I expect to attend the convention, but for the purpose of meeting my many friends throughout Texas, and visiting with them and not for the purpose of seeking either directly or indirectly to influence the judgment of the convention on other matters.[26]

Despite his indifference to the political role, O'Daniel apparently came to realize that no governor of Texas can separate himself completely from political processes. Profiting from his experience of two years before, he issued a statement that he was not endorsing any candidate for office, but he urged the voters to weigh the records of all aspirants to be sure that they were voting for those who "would work with your Governor."[27]

COKE STEVENSON—ATTEMPTS AT APPEASEMENT

The New Deal of Franklin D. Roosevelt had a tremendous impact upon the Texas political situation. For several years, intra-Party tensions had been mounting among Texas Democrats, leading V. O.

[25] William J. Lawson, executive secretary to O'Daniel, made available to the writer his files containing carbon copies of press releases during the O'Daniel administration. Text of this telegram, dated March 9, 1940, appears there.

[26] Letter from O'Daniel to E. B. Germany, dated August 27, 1940, in Lawson files.

[27] Text of a message to the press from Governor O'Daniel, dated August 22, 1940, copy of which is in Lawson files.

Key to conclude that of all Southern states, Texas had the bitterest struggle along New Deal and anti–New Deal lines. Detecting "the vague outlines of a politics . . . in which irrelevancies are pushed into the background and people divide broadly along conservative and liberal lines,"[28] he suggested that Texas was experiencing a politics of economics, which was evolving because of the personal insecurity of the *nouveaux riches* who were fearful of losing their wealth. Although such an alignment has not appeared consistently, it has been demonstrated in about as sharp a form as is possible under a one-party system.[29]

The political factionalism thus evolving within the past quarter of a century has been nebulous and subject to constant change. It has been confined largely to presidential and gubernatorial campaigns, playing an insignificant part in elections for Congress, statewide offices other than the governorship, legislative seats, and district or local offices. No consistent division in the Legislature has been created because of it.[30]

Although it probably began during the mid- or late-1930's, the first open indication of the present Democratic cleavage in Texas occurred at the Party convention held in May of 1944 to select delegates to the Democratic National Convention.[31] At that time a serious rift developed over whether to send an instructed or uninstructed delegation and also whether to instruct the electors chosen for the November election. The result was that the "regular" Party convention (composed of the anti-Roosevelt faction and calling themselves the "Texas Regulars") nominated a slate of uninstructed delegates and electors, and the bolting liberals (made up of Roosevelt supporters) nominated a delegation instructed to support the President for a fourth term. The Texas Regulars marked the first significant organized revolt of Southern Democrats against the national Party.[32] In a spirit of compromise, the credentials committee of the National Convention

[28] Key, *Southern Politics*, p. 255.

[29] *Ibid.*

[30] O. Douglas Weeks and Wilfred D. Webb, in Texas section of *A Survey Report on the Impact of Federal Grants-in-Aid on the Structure and Functions of State and Local Governments*, p. 413.

[31] Interview with Allen Duckworth, political editor of the *Dallas Morning News*, in Dallas, Texas, April 6, 1961.

[32] Alexander Heard and D. S. Strong, *Southern Primaries and Elections, 1920–1949*, p. 132.

seated both delegations from Texas and divided the state's vote between them.[33] Frequent clashes occurred at the National Convention between the Regulars, headed by former Governor Dan Moody, and the delegation of liberals, headed by former Governor James V. Allred. While at the National Convention, Allred promoted a plan for his group to gain control of the state Party machinery by active participation in the upcoming precinct conventions; accordingly, the pro-Roosevelt faction got to work in the ensuing weeks. On the day of the first primary a number of tumultuous precinct conventions were held, and fist fights, walkouts, and rump conventions were prevalent in many parts of the state, but the Allred group triumphed and prepared to take over the September state convention.[34]

Rather than assume an active part in the campaign to control the precinct conventions, Governor Stevenson set himself to trying to restore some measure of Party unity. Reportedly, he flew to Washington and received President Roosevelt's tacit approval to place two slates of electors on the November ticket—one, an uninstructed slate, to appease the Texas Regulars, and another, with instructions to support the national nominees, to appease the liberals.[35]

His efforts notwithstanding, the "Governor's Convention" in Dallas in 1944 was destined to make real history. The Convention was expected to make a statement concerning Negro voting as well as settling the matter of seating contesting delegations and deciding on Stevenson's plan. However, the issue of the two slates of electors became so involved that no preliminary action was taken toward drafting a platform. An open fight developed on whether to follow the Governor's plan for two slates (a position in which Stevenson drew support from both factions, but more heavily from the Texas Regulars) or whether to "steam-roller" the Regulars and seize control of the Party machinery (an action favored by Allred, Herman Jones of Austin, and other prominent liberals).[36]

The Governor arrived before opening time, prepared to present his compromise plan, but the Convention's first action was to try to decide which of the two Dallas County delegations would be seated. The fight on the floor over this question dragged on for several hours,

[33] O. Douglas Weeks, *Texas Presidential Politics in 1952*, p. 7.
[34] McKay, *Texas Politics, 1906–1944*, p. 446.
[35] Interview with Allen Duckworth in Dallas, April 6, 1961.
[36] *Dallas Morning News*, September 10, 1944.

and the Governor left without having had an opportunity to speak.[37] Challenges, heckling, boos, insults, and intermittent fisticuffs were the order of the day. Finally, former Governor James V. Allred was elected chairman of the Convention and announced that the pro-Roosevelt delegates had won control by a vote of 799 to 769, thus removing the Governor of Texas from control of his Party.[38]

The following day the work of the May convention was undone through a purge of all presidential electors who would not agree to support the national nominees. The list of Party officials changed almost completely, with fifty of the sixty-two members of the State Executive Committee being displaced, along with fifteen of the twenty-three electors. Sidney Latham, the secretary of state, refused to certify the newly chosen electors, only to have his action reversed by the Supreme Court of Texas.[39] Shortly thereafter the Texas Regulars took steps to officially organize a new political party; included among the membership were at least two former governors—Dan Moody and W. Lee O'Daniel.[40]

The action of the September convention in upsetting the work of the May convention was without precedent, but the judicial sanction opened the way for such a course of action in the future.[41] For the first time in many years a governor-nominate had lost control of the Party machiney,[42] signalling the solidification of two distinct groups of leaders among Texas Democrats: the governmental officers elected

---

[37] During the convention a rumor persisted that leaders of the pro-Roosevelt group feared that Stevenson's plan for two sets of electors would be adopted if it were allowed to reach the floor of the convention, and they resorted to dilatory tactics. Another general rumor was that a prominent political leader, who was in a position to swing a large bloc of votes, was pressured into abandoning his support of Stevenson's plan. He was told that influence would be used to prevent the granting of a federal pardon in which he was interested unless he changed his stand. Interview with Allen Duckworth (who attended the convention) in Dallas, April 6, 1961.

[38] McKay, *Texas Politics, 1906–1944*, p. 461.

[39] *Seay* v. *Latham*, 182 S.W. (2d) 251 (1944).

[40] McKay, *Texas Politics, 1906–1944*, p. 471.

[41] Weeks, *Texas Presidential Politics in 1952*, p. 7.

[42] In an interview at Junction, February 27, 1961, former Governor Stevenson told the writer that he considered the chief executive's role in his party to be of minor importance. He alluded to the fact that it was of much greater consequence to cultivate friends in the Legislature, where programs are acted upon. One prominent official of the Democratic Party, who asked not to be quoted, took issue with this position, and surmised that Stevenson might have defeated Lyndon Johnson for United States Senator in 1948 if he had maintained friendlier relations with party workers.

by popular vote and the Party officers selected by the convention. In the ensuing months these two leaderships were frequently at odds. Certain liberal Party officials clashed openly with Governor Stevenson, and on several occasions, the leadership of the Party lobbied against his appointments. There is no record that Stevenson ever received a copy of the platform finally drawn by the Convention.[43] The liberals remained in control of the Party machinery, and the Texas Regulars Party was dissolved in 1945.[44]

SINCE 1944: A REVITALIZED PARTY LEADER

Stevenson's defeat, however, may have heralded a renaissance of the role of the governor of Texas within the Democratic Party. The events of 1944 seem to have alerted succeeding governors to the potentialities as well as the dangers of their political role. From a low of participation in party affairs during the O'Daniel-Stevenson era, the pendulum seems to have swung toward more active political leadership on the part of the governor, and every indication points to a continuance of the trend. Certainly no future executive can afford to overlook the importance of the precinct convention as a device to control party machinery. Neither can he neglect the role the party can play in furthering his announced program.

BEAUFORD JESTER—COALITION POLITICS

A spirited primary campaign in 1946 demonstrated that the liberal wing of the Democratic Party remained substantially intact but that, although the Texas Regulars had disbanded, the conservatives retained formidable strength. The nominee, Beauford H. Jester, was inspired to announce a political philosophy of moderation, introducing the middle-of-the-road approach into Texas politics. He was successful in welding a coalition of conservative liberals and liberal conservatives to support his position and his election.[45] In succeeding years this position of Jester's has sometimes served as a useful point of reference, or measuring stick, by which to judge whether a governor is liberal or conservative.[46]

[43] Duckworth, "Democratic Dilemma in Texas," *Southwest Review*, XXXII (Winter, 1947), 39.
[44] Harold J. Marburger, *Texas Elections, 1918–1954*, pp. 212–213.
[45] Interview with Allen Duckworth in Dallas, April 6, 1961.
[46] Raymond Brooks, "Middle of the Road," *Austin American-Statesman*, March 2, 1958, p. B–2.

One veteran participant in Democratic affairs in Texas dates the present status of governor-party relationships from the Jester Administration.[47] In his view, Jester was able, because of his coalition, to exercise more control over the Party convention than had been the case for a number of years. In 1948, when the Party organization was threatened by the "States' Rights Democrats" (commonly called the Dixiecrats), Governor Jester was able, through his "harmony" strategy, to recruit enough moderates and liberals to permit him to retain control of the Party machinery and to bar the Dixiecrats from certifying as "Democrats" their nominees for President and Vice President.

ALLAN SHIVERS—PURGE OF THE STATE EXECUTIVE COMMITTEE

Allan Shivers gave added impetus to the political role of the governor. Realizing that the chief executive would be judged more on the program he accomplished than on his intentions, Shivers saw the Party organization as a useful tool for implementing his goals. He seemed to regard the State Democratic Executive Committee as a "board of directors" to assist him, and accordingly felt it imperative that the Committee be composed of individuals friendly to the governor and sympathetic toward his objectives.[48]

Since his retirement from public life, Shivers has summarized his views on the techniques of political leadership. In answer to the question, "How does the governor make himself felt in national and state party affairs?", he listed the following avenues of influence:

Through his controlling influence with the State Democratic (or Republican) Executive Committee, and with the National Committeeman and/or Committeewoman.

Through personal friendship with national leaders (other Governors, U.S. Senators, etc.) on the national level, and with local leaders.

Through controlling precinct, county, and state conventions.

Through public speeches and statements; sometimes through advocacy of or opposition to certain candidates.[49]

---

[47] Interview with J. J. Pickle in Austin, March 30, 1961. Mr. Pickle has been active in affairs of the Democratic Party in Texas for many years, and from 1957 to 1961 served as the first executive director of the State Democratic Executive Committee. He was elected to Congress in 1963 to serve out the unexpired term of Homer Thornberry, who had received an appointment as a federal district judge.

[48] *Ibid.* Mr. Pickle assisted Governor Shivers in organizing the state convention of 1950.

[49] Copy of a script of a television interview with former Governor Shivers at the University of Houston, April 1, 1960. Copy of script furnished the writer by Weldon Hart, former executive secretary to Shivers.

To implement his philosophy of party organization, Shivers and his lieutenants undertook a purge of the State Democratic Executive Committee in 1950, the first year in which Shivers was elected governor (although he had earlier succeeded to the office upon Jester's death). The selection of the Committee had been left in the past to the caucuses of the individual senatorial districts, with the ratification of the group *in toto* by the convention being largely a matter of routine.[50] Under such a procedure some members would not be in sympathy with the governor, but it was usually felt that their presence on the Committee was relatively inconsequential. Shivers did not accept this view; in his judgment it was undesirable to have *any* member of the State Executive Committee unfriendly to the governor. To achieve his desires, a process of screening nominees from the various district caucuses was undertaken. In the words of one of Shivers' political allies, the 1950 convention could be described as the first "scientifically organized" convention in Texas political history.[51]

To insure a Committee completely acceptable to the executive, the nominees for committeeman and committeewoman from each of the thirty-one senatorial districts were scrutinized carefully by the convention's "Committee to Nominate Party Officers"—a group composed of Shivers' followers. The names of eight people nominated by the caucuses were stricken from the list which was to be submitted on the floor of the convention. In reporting the purge, the *Austin American* stated:

The State Democratic Convention Tuesday night gave Governor Allan Shivers firm control of all party affairs. . . . By voice vote it approved a State Executive Committee dominated by Shivers' supporters. Earlier he

[50] Article 13.38, Texas Election Code, provides: "Said convention shall elect a chairman and vice-chairman of the Executive Committee, one (1) of whom shall be a man and the other a woman, and sixty-two (62) members thereof, two (2) from each senatorial district of the State, one (1) of whom shall be a woman and the other a man, the members of said committee to be those who shall be recommended by the delegates representing the counties composing the senatorial districts respectively, each county voting its convention strength, each of whom shall hold said office until his successor is elected."

In interpreting this section, the Supreme Court of Texas ruled:

"Except to the extent that jurisdiction is conferred by statute or the subject has been regulated by statute, courts have no power to interfere with the judgments of constituted authorities of established political parties in matters involving party government and discipline, to determine disputes within a party as to the regularity of election of its executive officers, or their removal, or to determine contests for positions of party committeemen or convention delegates." *Carter* v. *Tomlinson*, 227 S.W. (2d) 795 (1950).

[51] Interview with J. J. Pickle in Austin, March 30, 1961.

had overwhelmingly beaten down all opposition and had his platform adopted without a murmur of protest. It turned out to be a Shivers convention all the way, just as he wanted it.[52]

As a consequence of the purge of non-Shivers personnel, the machinery of the Party remained in the hands of the Governor's political cohorts for the next two years, although there was some indication of strong opposition from his political enemies. By 1952 the major political question in Texas concerned the support of the national Democratic nominees, Adlai Stevenson and John Sparkman. After Stevenson announced his concurrence in the decision of the United States Supreme Court ceding the Texas tidelands to the national government, Governor Shivers retaliated by declaring that he would not support the Democratic ticket in the general election; he was joined in the bolt by Attorney General Price Daniel. Shivers retained control of the Party machinery, and in his keynote address to the September convention of 1952 he stated that the Democratic Party standing of anyone in Texas would not be impaired by support of the Republican national ticket along with the state Democratic candidates. So strong was Shivers' following that the convention adopted a resolution urging "all Democrats who have pledged support to Stevenson and Sparkman to reconsider their action and actively support Eisenhower and Nixon."[53] The Shivers-dominated platform which was adopted was replete with condemnation of Stevenson's stand on the tidelands, the "political exploitation of minority groups," and the "centralizing tendencies of the Truman administration."[54]

The Republicans—victorious in Texas for the first time since it had fallen into the Hoover column in 1928—carried the state with 53.13 per cent of the total vote.[55] Several reasons can be given for this change in the traditional voting habits of many Texans: Eisenhower was a national war hero; he was a native Texan; the tidelands issue was an emotional one for Texans. But the leadership of important state Democratic officials was also extremely influential among the voters, and, in the words of one commentator, there could "be no doubt that the presidential election of 1952 left the machinery of the Democratic party in the state more firmly in the hands of a conserva-

[52] September 13, 1950.
[53] *Amarillo Globe-Times*, September 10, 1952.
[54] *Ibid*.
[55] Weeks, *Texas Presidential Politics in 1952*, p. 97.

tive-moderate majority than it had been for some time."[56] The vote was undoubtedly a tribute to Shivers' political leadership.

But the popularity of Governor Shivers and his strength within the Party were not to last forever. By 1954 there was evidence that the "Shivercrat" coalition (as it had come to be called by Shivers' opponents) had begun to lose many of its former supporters to the liberal groups. Perhaps the best evidence of the changing political complexion was the fact that the Governor was for the first time forced into a runoff by his opponent, Judge Ralph Yarborough, who had unceasingly denounced the bolt from the national Democratic Party. Despite losses, Shivers was able to remain in firm control of the convention of 1954, in which his forces won four of the big-city delegations and his demand for a friendly Executive Committee was met.[57] Nevertheless, the Governor's influence was waning. Professor O. Douglas Weeks attributes his loss of strength to a complex of factors: (1) the Governor had been elected to a fourth term in violation of the strong two-term tradition; (2) 1954 was not a presidential election year and the alignment of factions attendant upon such an election was absent; (3) the tidelands issue had been settled; (4) the Veterans' Land Board scandals, which had occurred earlier in the year, had injured Shivers' prestige; and (5) possibly his strong stand against racial integration had lost him some supporters.[58]

By the middle of his last term Shivers was still a potent personality in Texas politics, but the Democratic Party, of which he was the titular head, was far from united. The situation in Texas in 1955 was compared to the multiparty politics of France by one columnist, who suggested that there were at least four Texas factions of importance: "Brass-Collar Democrats"; Liberal-Loyalists; Shivercrats; and "Wright Morrowcrats."[59]

As time passed, the multiparty situation continued to prevail among the Democrats, and the influence of Governor Shivers in Party circles continued to wane. By 1956 it had become obvious that whoever was to gain control of the Party machinery would have to

---

[56] *Ibid.*, p. 110.

[57] *Austin American*, September 13, 14, 15, 1954.

[58] O. Douglas Weeks, *Texas One-Party Politics in 1956*, pp. 7–8.

[59] Douglass Cater, "The Trouble in Lyndon Johnson's Back Yard," *The Reporter*, December 1, 1955, p. 32. Another writer, George Fuermann (in *Reluctant Empire*, p. 56) labelled the Shivercrats as "Donkephants." Wright Morrow was a Texas Democratic national committeeman who had expressed sympathy with Democratic Party bolters.

weld a coalition of even more divergent elements than Governor Jester had recruited a decade previously. It was a presidential year, and interest in politics ran high. Additional excitement was injected into the situation by the proposal of Sam Rayburn (now powerful speaker of the United States House of Representatives) that the Texas delegation to the National Convention should sponsor the candidacy of United States Senator Lyndon Johnson as a favorite son for the Presidency.[60] Rayburn also suggested that Johnson should be designated chairman of the delegation—a spot usually reserved for the governor, if he wanted it.

Incensed by the suggestion that the Governor be displaced from that position, supporters of Shivers publicly opposed the Rayburn proposal, and in the spring of 1956 a cataclysmic intra-Party struggle erupted between the Shivers camp and the Johnson-Rayburn camp. The latter were victorious in the precinct conventions and ultimately controlled the May state convention. One significant action of that meeting was the creation of a Democratic Campaign Committee, designed to bypass the Shivers-dominated State Executive Committee in conducting the presidential campaign. After completing its business, the state convention adopted a motion to recess rather than to adjourn *sine die*. The maneuver permitted the group to reconvene at any time it might wish to override a State Executive Committee action of which it disapproved.[61]

PRICE DANIEL—INSTITUTIONALIZATION OF PARTY HEADQUARTERS

Although Johnson did not win the presidential nomination, and Texas was again to depart from the national Democratic ticket and help re-elect Republican President Eisenhower, the liberal-loyalist faction of the state Democrats continued to gain adherents. In the summer of 1956 that group hit a peak of strength.[62] Following a rigorous primary campaign, United States Senator Price Daniel, a moderate, won the gubernatorial nomination by only a paper-thin margin over Ralph Yarborough, a liberal. At that time three predominant groups had to be reckoned with politically in Texas: (1) the Shivercrat right wing, (2) the liberal left wing, and (3) the large, but constantly shifting, moderate center.[63] The fluid state of affairs was at-

---

[60] Weeks, *Texas One-Party Politics in 1956*, pp. 18–25.
[61] *Ibid.*, p. 27.
[62] Interview with J. J. Pickle in Austin, March 30, 1961.
[63] Weeks, *Texas One-Party Politics in 1956*, p. 39.

tested by a headline in a Fort Worth newspaper the day before the opening of the September convention: "DANIEL'S CHANCES TO CONTROL CONVENTION APPEAR SHAKY."[64] The paper indicated that the loyalists were plotting strategy to gain control of the conclave by seizing four hundred contested seats. As it unfolded, the convention proved to be a turbulent one. After getting off to a late start, it became "one of the hardest fought in political history, with the determination of control not coming until twelve hours after the opening."[65] Both sides stalled for time, hoping to pick up strength. When Nominee Daniel attempted to speak he was booed frequently, and several persons were forcefully ejected from the hall. Had not Sam Rayburn and Lyndon Johnson come to his rescue, the Governor-nominate probably would not have gained control. At the propitious moment, however, the two Texas members of Congress made a plea for Party harmony, and a coalition of their supporters and those of Daniel was able to muster a vote of 1,006 to 869. With this alignment, the platform advocated by the liberals was rejected, although a resolution was adopted supporting the national nominees. Finally, the convention "gave Daniel just about everything he asked in the way of a platform" and he was allowed to replace four members of the State Executive Committee whom he considered objectionable, leaving him a majority of about two-to-one in that body.[66]

Battlewise from his traumatic convention experience, Governor Daniel apparently realized the value of a closer liaison between the Executive Office and Democratic Party officials. He fostered the idea of "institutionalizing" the State Executive Committee through the creation of a staff headquarters in Austin. The 1952 convention had authorized a Party office to be opened in the capital, but that office had served only as a record-keeping establishment. With insufficient funds, it was unable to assist Party members at the local level.[67] Believing that the central office should be more active, Daniel promoted the idea of enlarging the staff to undertake research, to assist in organizing at the grass-roots level, and to serve as a kind of educational

---

[64] *Fort Worth Star-Telegram,* September 11, 1956.
[65] *Ibid.,* September 12, 1956.
[66] *Ibid.*
[67] Stuart Long, former member of the State Democratic Executive Committee, told the writer in Austin, June 28, 1961, that he sponsored the resolution calling for a Party office. Weldon Hart, at that time secretary of the Committee, said that the office for several years employed only one full-time secretary whose function it was to keep Party records. Interview in Austin July 26, 1961.

agency to train Party workers. More important to the Governor, the headquarters was organized to serve as his "unofficial right arm" in political and legislative matters by providing a clearinghouse of information for Party affairs, including appointments to political jobs. Under this arrangement, the Governor, as chief of the Party (or perhaps one should say, as chief of the controlling faction of the Party), was to make recommendations for actions to be taken by the organization and to serve as official spokesman for the Democratic organization in the state. During its short lifetime this headquarters office has already become an integral part of Democratic political machinery.[68] It has brought about a closer working relationship between the governor and top Party officials and has assisted the executive in his role as a leader.[69]

About the time the state headquarters was being enlarged, the liberal elements of the Party were forming their own organization (called the "Democrats of Texas" and shortened to DOT) with which they hoped to capture the conventions of 1958 and to make a good showing in the primaries. However, the July primary seemed to prove that the voters paid little attention to conservative or liberal labels, as Governor Daniel, a moderate, roundly defeated Henry Gonzalez, a liberal, at the same time that a liberal candidate for United States Senator, Ralph Yarborough, won renomination over a conservative, William Blakely.

In the simultaneously held precinct conventions the moderates won generally, ruling out both pronounced conservatives and liberals and thus ensuring Daniel's control of most of the county conventions and the State Convention. The September State Convention was largely in Daniel's hands. His choice for temporary chairman was named, and he vetoed the selection of two liberals nominated by state senatorial district caucuses for places on the State Executive Committee.[70]

Both Speaker Rayburn and Senator Johnson reportedly were un-

---

[68] Interview with J. J. Pickle in Austin, March 30, 1961. Mr. Pickle served as executive director of the SDEC from 1957 to 1961. The headquarters office, located at 1010 Lavaca Street in Austin, supplies educational materials to the public and to Committee members. One such publication is *Texas Political Calendar, 1960*, distributed to remind the public of important dates and events. Mimeographed material about the Party is available also.

[69] Interview with George E. Christian, executive assistant to Governor Daniel, in Austin, July 19, 1961.

[70] O. Douglas Weeks, "The Presidential Election of 1960," a paper read to the Southwestern Social Science Association in Dallas, Texas, March 31, 1961, pp. 5–6.

happy because Daniel "bumped" the two committeemen, but the Governor is supposed to have retorted that the committeemen would not support the Committee's program and should not be elected.[71] The displacement of these two caused almost unprecedented noise-making even for a usually rowdy Democratic convention.

A thousand outraged members of liberal delegations milled around the auditorium for forty-five minutes shouting, chanting, and walloping the floor with placard poles after they were refused a roll call vote on replacement of the nominees.[72]

The governor was reported to have become worried about the safety of his family in the tense atmosphere. Except for the purge of Committee members, the convention program seemed to suit even Daniel's critics fairly well.

This defeat of the liberals presaged a decline of influence for that faction, for in the precinct and county conventions of 1960 liberal strength was decidedly weak, and in the state convention of June, 1960 (to name delegates to the presidential convention), the liberals were almost obliterated by a vote of 2,252 to 40. A walkout led by their former darling, Mrs. Frankie Randolph, attracted only a handful of followers.[73] Even the organized labor groups, in the past so faithful, deserted to join conservative moderates in endorsing Lyndon Johnson for the Presidency of the United States. By the time of the September convention, Governor Daniel was in complete control. For the first time, the same slate of delegates to the June convention returned as delegates to the "Governor's Convention."

The Harris County delegation which had in no uncertain terms repudiated the national platform was kept out of the convention until nearly the end because the credentials committee had questioned its loyalty—thus a chief source of possible upheaval was eliminated. . . . Governor Daniel pushed through a conservative platform but beat down all attempts to repudiate the national platform openly. . . . The state platform differed with the national one at many points. It supported the oil depletion allowance, condemned sit-ins, supported the Texas right-to-work law and advocated states' rights generally. It made no mention, however, of the national platform or presidential ticket. No roll call vote was taken on anything. The two presidential electors were replaced who had said they would not cast their votes for Senator Kennedy [who had been nominated for the Presi-

---

[71] *Dallas Morning News*, September 26, 1958.
[72] *San Antonio Express*, September 10, 1958.
[73] *Austin American*, June 15, 1960.

dency]. Thus, the convention remained loyal to the national ticket but in effect repudiated the national platform without specifically saying so.[74]

For the first time since he became governor, Daniel did not purge any members from the State Executive Committee, and the 1960 convention turned out to be the most peaceable convention of his tenure.

The 1962 convention was largely a *pro forma* one, with no fireworks. Democratic nominee John Connally's organization was in control, and observers were almost inclined to call the proceedings "dull" and "uninteresting." Daniel, although he had been Connally's opponent in the primary, joined in a display of harmony.

Daniel's views on his role as leader in the Democratic Party were summarized in an interview in 1961. When questioned about the importance of the position of the governor as a party leader, he replied:

Of course the leadership of the governor as titular head of his party is not as important as it is in a two-party state. On the other hand, here in our state with our division that we have within our Democratic Party it is very important that the governor exercise his power as titular head of the Democratic Party and that he have that power through the conventions because there are many influences through our state Democratic Executive Committee and our precinct conventions that are important in the life and government of our state. And if the governor is not the titular head of his party, of course, he does not have the power of persuasion to get over his program that he would have if he had the party leadership.[75]

Some months later, Governor Daniel reaffirmed this position, declaring that during 1961 the State Democratic Executive Committee had assisted him in pushing his program, which had been embodied in the state platform by the September convention in 1960.[76]

POLITICAL PHILOSOPHIES OF THE LEADERS

Just as the effectiveness of the leadership role of governors has fluctuated within the Democratic Party from time to time, so have the political philosophies espoused by the executives varied. The

[74] O. Douglas Weeks, *Texas in the 1960 Presidential Election*, p. 49.

[75] Interview of Governor Daniel with Miss Pauline Yelderman of the University of Houston, April 5, 1960. The interview was used in the University's educational television program, and the script was made available to the writer by the University of Houston.

[76] Interview of the writer with Governor Price Daniel in the Executive Office in Austin, November 30, 1961.

majority of Texas governors in the twentieth century have definitely been inclined toward the right of center, but those chosen through the direct primary since 1906 have completely spanned the political spectrum from left to right. Changing public opinion has been thus reflected, at times bearing no small correlation to the political ideologies of those occupying the Presidency of the United States. The most liberal occupants of the Executive Mansion in Austin were there during the White House tenures of Theodore Roosevelt, Woodrow Wilson, and Franklin D. Roosevelt; but over the long range, many political ideologies have been exemplified in Texas governors.

Any attempt to classify the political inclinations of Texas chief executives immediately encounters the thorny problem of defining terms, with the added complication that meanings of terms change from time to time. If the political role of the governor is to be considered in detail, an attempt must be made to categorize the political leanings of the men who have held the position. One of the best classifications of gubernatorial politics in Texas was made in 1958 by a veteran Capitol correspondent.[77] Raymond Brooks, secretary to Governor William P. Hobby during World War I, has been personally acquainted with every occupant of the Governor's Office since 1915. Either as staff member or as newspaperman, he has been associated with each executive since James E. Ferguson, and on the basis of his long-time personal observation is perhaps as well qualified as anyone to evaluate the political philosophies of governors of Texas.

Mr. Brooks took as a point of reference, or measuring post, the middle-of-the-road philosophy proposed in 1946 by Governor Beauford Jester in his attempt to bridge the intra-Party schism that had developed during the O'Daniel-Stevenson period. Adopting the device of a price index, in which a given period of time is equated with 100, Brooks assigned Jester's "middle" position to 100 and evaluated the political positions of governors before and after Jester's time, despite changing terminology, against that "norm." In his classification, two categories—liberal and moderate leftist—were placed to the left of center, and two categories—moderate rightist and conservative—to the right of center.

Explaining his terms, Mr. Brooks wrote:

Inadequately defined, liberalism is taken to connote sharing the wealth by government action, government regulations and controls, government

[77] Raymond Brooks, "Middle of the Road," *Austin American-Statesman*, March 2, 1958, p. B–2.

ownership, public spending. Conservatism objects to government meddling with private enterprise; opposes government ownership, and is particularly hostile to the extension of centralized government and federal
meddling with state and local affairs.[78]

Using his middle-of-the-road index, Brooks found that, in the
main, Texas governors have been on the conservative side—even
when liberals controlled the state conventions. Pointing out that
Texas moved away from the New Deal ideology sooner than did the
nation as a whole, he indicated that by 1958 the political pendulum
had begun to swing somewhat to the left again.[79] Among the governors since 1915, Mr. Brooks would categorize only the Fergusons
and Allred as liberals. Translated into years of service, this would
mean that governors with conservative leanings have held the office
more than three times as long as have those of a liberal bent. Excluding Jester, whom Brooks assesses as completely middle-of-the-road,
eight incumbents of conservative persuasion served a total of more
than thirty-three years, whereas the three liberals served a combined
total of only ten years and eight months. Brooks' estimation can give
some indication of the general complexion of Texas politics for almost half a century.

As the election of a liberal to the governorship of Texas appears to
be an exception, a more careful scrutiny of this classification with
reference to the three liberals might be in order. One of the principal
lieutenants of the Governors Ferguson wrote:

> The two governors were people of liberal minds. This is evident through
> official acts and public utterances over a long period of years. [Mr. Fergu-
> son's] last political speeches were for the re-election of President Roosevelt
> for a third term.[80]

Apparently, Governor Miriam A. Ferguson liked to consider the
team as liberals. In preparing a summary of achievements during the
four terms of her husband and herself, she demonstrated pride in

[78] *Ibid.*
[79] It should be noted that in 1960 the Democratic candidates for presidential
electors and other statewide offices carried the state. In 1961, however, the two
top contenders in a special election for United States Senator, to fill the seat
vacated by Vice President Lyndon B. Johnson, were both regarded as staunch
conservatives. Whether the election of a Republican indicates a swing back
toward conservatism is still a matter of intense speculation in Texas.
[80] Ghent Sanderford, "The Ferguson Era—1914 to 1944" (unpublished ms.),
p. 8.

some liberal accomplishments. Among others, she considered the following to be important:

Fifty-four hour law for protection of women workers.
Semi-monthly pay day law.
Creation of Industrial Accident Board.
Eight Hour Law.
Organized Texas Relief Commission enabling Texas to receive more than $50 million to feed the hungry and unemployed.
Sponsored adoption of Constitutional Amendment providing for $20 million in bread bonds, which amount was more than matched by the Federal Government.
Creating of Lower Colorado and Brazos River Authorities, thereby beginning projects that have and will continue to mean many millions of dollars for Texas people.[81]

Professor V. O. Key agrees that the Fergusons were the liberals of the 1920's, "at least in Texas."[82]

There can be little doubt that the title of Texas' most liberal governor must be accorded James V. Allred. One thorough study of his administration concluded:

It is difficult to simply summarize Allred's terms. He was "liberal" in social welfare and labor legislation but "conservative" in fighting for state's rights against federal oil control—and against alcohol and gambling. However, he pioneered in toe-to-toe cooperation with the federal government in relief programs, unemployment compensation, etc.[83]

Citing the Brooks study, the foregoing writer agrees that Allred's philosophy extended "into the category of moderate liberal in other than state-federal relations." He reports an interview with the former Governor shortly before Allred's death, in which Allred scoffed at attempts to sum him up and declared, "I'm proud to be in a class by myself." The Allred administration, he concludes,

was perhaps the greatest period of expansion and reform in Texas history. Politically it was just about the only time the "liberals" have had a man they could honestly call their own as governor since the bygone days

[81] "A Partial List of Outstanding Achievements of the Ferguson Administration," prepared by Miriam A. Ferguson. (Mimeographed.) Copy furnished the writer by Governor Ferguson in April, 1961.
[82] Key, *Southern Politics*, p. 264.
[83] Robb K. Burlage, "James V. Allred—Texas' Liberal Governor" (research paper), pp. 145–146.

around the turn of the century when the revolutionary farm boy, Jim
Hogg, started State government into its modern period of growth.[84]

Using the framework of the Brooks classification system, this writer
has evaluated three governors nominated by primaries but not included in the Brooks study. As can be seen in Figure 7, Thomas M.
Campbell (1907) was placed to the left and his successor, Oscar B.
Colquitt (1911), to the right. Although the record of John Connally's
service in the gubernatorial office is not yet complete, this writer has
tentatively placed the incumbent Governor a bit to the right of his
predecessor, Price Daniel. This tentative placement was discussed
with the originator of the yardstick, Raymond Brooks, who concurred in the assessment.

The development of Campbell as a liberal is not difficult to understand. He had been a lifelong friend of James S. Hogg, who was the
apostle of liberalism during the last decade of the nineteenth century.
They were reared as neighbors in East Texas, and the long association was apparently reflected in their comparable political
philosophies. After the Hogg-Culberson era during the 1890's, Texas
experienced an interlude of eight conservative years under the administrations of Governors Sayers and Lanham;[85] but the followers of
Hogg had not died out, and it was logical that Campbell should take
up the gauntlet when public opinion swung back to more liberal
politics. By 1906 the people seemed to want a return to the progressivism of the Hogg days—or they were falling under the spell of the
progressive movement which was then gaining momentum for a
sweep of the country in 1912. One Texas historian reports:

As the campaign of 1906 approached, public sentiment swung definitely
away from conservatism. . . . All candidates favored a war on the trusts, an
anti-lobby law, tax reform, and generous support of the state's institutions.
Campbell had the endorsement of ex-Governor Hogg, who had voiced repeatedly his dissatisfaction with the attitude of Sayers and Lanham toward
big business. . . . [Campbell's] program of tax reform and more effective
regulation of business provoked opposition; in 1908 he was opposed for
renomination by R. R. Williams on a platform calling for justice to corporations. Campbell was again nominated by an overwhelming vote and

84 *Ibid.*, pp. 146–147.
85 Key, *Southern Politics*, p. 262.

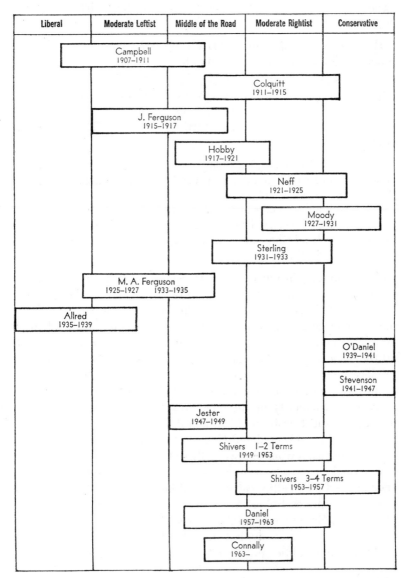

Fig. 7—A political classification of governors of Texas who were nominated by Democratic Party primaries. (Taken from *Austin American-Statesman* of March 2, 1958, with additions by this writer.)

again was elected. . . . The legislature was in sympathy with the governor's progressive ideas.[86]

If the premise that Campbell is appropriately classified as a liberal is accepted, then the classification of his successor, Oscar B. Colquitt, as a conservative is logical. A biographer of Colquitt notes that he opposed Campbell on nearly every issue and claims that consequently he was "forced" to take a more conservative view on practically every matter that his personal convictions warranted. The biographer adds:

> . . . there can be no doubt that Colquitt was more liberal than many of his most powerful backers, and that fact was destined to make his administration a stormy one. This also caused Colquitt's reputation to suffer at the hands of both liberals and conservatives. The liberals mistrusted and castigated him for the company he kept and for his opposition to Campbell. . . . On the other hand, the conservatives came in time to regard him as a traitor to his friends.[87]

As he continued in office, Colquitt veered steadily to the right—a position perhaps unwillingly assumed because of political exigencies. He opposed Woodrow Wilson, and in the opposing became "champion of men and of measures that were more conservative than he himself would have preferred."[88] Regardless of his reasons for his attitudes, he must be classified as more conservative than either his predecessor or his successor, who was James E. Ferguson.

Since Colquitt's administration the shades of conservatism espoused by a majority of the governors have varied from the mild moderate-rightist position of William P. Hobby to the ultraconservatism of W. Lee O'Daniel and Coke R. Stevenson, with other incumbents falling somewhere between these two extremes. The conservative outlook of most governors is credited by some to the vast influence exerted by wealthy cattle and oil interests upon Texas politics. One writer quotes Robert W. Calvert, then chairman of the State Democratic Executive Committee, as saying in 1947, "It may not be a wholesome thing to say, but the oil industry today is in complete control of State politics and State Government."[89]

---

[86] Rupert N. Richardson, *Texas, The Lone Star State* (2d ed.), p. 276. By permission of Prentice-Hall, Inc.

[87] George P. Huckaby, "Oscar Branch Colquitt: A Political Biography" (unpublished Ph.D. dissertation), p. 202.

[88] *Ibid.*, pp. 300–301.

[89] Hart Stilwell, "Texas: Owned by Oil and Interlocking Directorates," in Robert S. Allen (ed.), *Our Sovereign State*, p. 315.

The oil and cattle industries have in fact exerted untold influence upon Texas politics and government, thereby contributing to its conservatism—a predictable situation. These industries remain to-day two of the most important components of the state's economy;[90] whether they will continue to retain their strong hold upon the political situation as the state becomes more urbanized and industrialized is problematical. One observer has summed up the situation in these terms:

> The conservative mind—in Texas a meringue of oil, rural, and Republican ideologies—governs Texas. The liberal mind—a less crusty meringue of oil-be-damned, urban, and Democratic ideologies—may possibly begin governing Texas in the 1960's. It does not seem to be more prepared to do so with wisdom than the conservatives are doing it. The liberals need a giant; the conservatives, overwhelming more than governing Texas, could win with a midget.[91]

In regard to the political ideologies that may be anticipated in the future, one feature stands out in bold relief. The South, like the United States at large, seems to be drifting more than ever toward class politics and interest-group politics.[92] The pace of this development is sure to influence the politics practiced by governors of tomorrow.

POLITICAL LEADERSHIP: PAST, PRESENT, AND FUTURE

Over the long run, the leadership role of the governor of Texas in the Democratic Party has assumed varying degrees of significance. The fluctuation has undoubtedly been affected by the mode of nomination in use at a given time, as well as by the extent to which the political philosophy espoused by the governor was attuned to the prevailing public opinion. To an even greater degree perhaps, the ability to lead has depended upon the interests and personality of the incumbent and his skill at utilizing Party machinery.

Governors nominated by conventions prior to 1906 were necessarily more cognizant of their responsibilities to the Democratic Party than have been some nominated by primaries since that time. Convention nominees found close liaison with the Party to be the only

---

90 *Texas Almanac, 1961–1962*, pp. 250, 309.
91 Fuermann, *Reluctant Empire*, p. 54.
92 O. Douglas Weeks, "The Presidential Election of 1960—Texas and the South," *Public Affairs Comment*, VII (Institute of Public Affairs, The University of Texas, January, 1961), 4.

practical route to continued political success. During that period the convention served as a forum for discussion of proposed programs and as a means of rallying support for specific causes and candidates. On the whole, the Party leadership function was of major import to the executives.

The introduction of the primary system de-emphasized for some years the role of the governor in the Party. Following the passage of the Terrell Election Law, primaries virtually displaced conventions in the eyes of the public. Attendance at and interest in Party conclaves was small and unrepresentative, and during the 1920's the Party role of the chief executive continued to decline proportionately, reaching an all-time low in the early 1940's when the governor largely divorced himself from Party affairs.

The division within the Texas Democratic Party, dating from the latter part of the New Deal of Franklin D. Roosevelt, may have been the turning point in a revival of the functioning of Party conventions and in the political role of the chief executive. All signs point to the fact that since 1944 governors have been more alert to the potentialities of Party (or factional) leadership, and firmer control of Party machinery has been exhibited by those sitting in the gubernatorial chair. Governors Jester, Shivers, and Daniel have taken an active part in organizing conventions and in the selection of the State Democratic Executive Committee, and Governor Connally has shown that he intends to take a strong hand in Party matters.

Increased attention to the governor's role as a political leader raises the broader question of the impact of the Democratic Party, of which he is the titular head, upon Texas state government. One-party politics are a tradition and a habit with citizens of this state. Most Southerners, because they are accustomed to fighting out their differences in primaries and conventions, accept the one-party situation unquestionably and do not fully comprehend the meaning of "a responsible two-party system."[93] Residents of Texas even seem to take for granted the multifactionalism that has characterized the Democratic fold in this state for many years. Today, politics in the state revolves around three major groups: "traditional" Democrats, who hold staunchly conservative views; "loyalist" Democrats, who are devoted liberals; and a large group of "independents" in the center, who shift from one side to the other and form some unusual coalitions upon particular issues. In 1957 Professor O. Douglas Weeks said this

[93] O. Douglas Weeks, "Republicanism and Conservatism in the South," *Southwestern Social Science Quarterly*, 36 (December, 1955), 249.

fluidity could classify Texas as a "one-party state," a "no-party state," or a "multi-party state"—depending upon one's choice.[94]

Obviously, the kaleidoscopic nature of Texas Democratic politics has impeded the over-all influence of the Party upon state government. In fact, it may be argued that the Party per se is unimportant and that it is the factions which count for most. Professor Key believes that the loose factional system is a "poor contrivance for recruiting and sifting out leaders of public affairs"[95] and that it "lacks the power to carry out sustained programs of action."[96] He continues:

> . . . at times state-wide campaigns are but personal rivalries. . . . The issue becomes one of who is the "best man" or the "most competent" man to carry out what everyone is agreed upon. In a broader sense, the politics of such a situation amounts to control, whatever governor is in office, by the conservative groups of the state who squabble among themselves for the perquisites of office, which are, after all, relatively minor in the total flow of income and in the total status system of a society.[97]

Certainly his analysis is appropriate for Texas, because the shifting factions have coalesced repeatedly to keep governors of conservative persuasion in office most of the time. In this, they frequently have been joined by Republicans participating in Democratic primaries.

A perennial question is whether Texas is on the brink of abandoning its factional politics in favor of a full-fledged two-party system. Recent elections in which Republicans have won or made significant showings have given some hope to the advocates of two-party politics. No doubt such a development would create a more felicitous political climate by providing greater responsibility in the state government and placing the titular heads of the parties in stronger leadership roles. To become a genuine two-party state, however, Republicans would have to develop grass-roots organizations and nominate complete slates of candidates. So far this has not been done in Texas, as many national Republican leaders tend to think of their Party in the South as a permanently minority organization, which in presidential elections and Democratic primaries will serve its purpose by making temporary alliances with conservative Democrats.[98] Although the *esprit de corps* of Texas Republicans has been high since the election

[94] Weeks, *Texas One-Party Politics in 1956*, p. 50.
[95] Key, *Southern Politics*, p. 304.
[96] *Ibid.*, p. 308.
[97] *Ibid.*
[98] Weeks, "Republicanism and Conservatism in the South," *Southwestern Social Science Quarterly*, 36 (December, 1955), 251–252.

of one of their number (John Tower) to the United States Senate in 1961, it is debatable whether the enthusiasm generated in that race will solidify the group sufficiently to create a lasting organization. Even if the Republicans pursue the goal of shaping an effective party organization, it may be some time before Texas becomes a true two-party state.

Pending the day when a governor of Texas may be the leader of a political party which faces a comparably vigorous opposition party and which exerts stronger influence upon state government than at present, the state's chief executive must continue to be the leader of a faction within the Democratic Party, or must attempt the exceedingly difficult task of uniting factions. Experience has demonstrated that governors can ill afford to brush aside the political role. It is a useful, albeit limited, medium for exercising leadership in governmental affairs.

When the political role is coupled ingeniously with the leadership opportunities afforded by his roles as executive-administrator and as legislative leader, a governor can lead the state effectively. The combination of the roles appears to have worked reasonably satisfactorily over the years, for Texas has continued to occupy an increasingly important position among the states of the Union—a fact which is some tribute to the leadership in the state.

Legally, the governor of Texas occupies a relatively weak position in comparison to that of chief executives in some of the other states, and his leadership potentialities would be strengthened materially by the removal of some of the archaic circumscriptions upon the office. However, the mere legal status of his position fails to portray the total picture, for, in actuality, the governorship in Texas can be a much stronger office than would seem to be the case from a cursory examination of constitutional and legal powers.

As the governor's activities are curbed by innumerable limitations, the incumbent of the office must be constantly alert to search out avenues of leadership available to him—ones which may be less obvious than specific legal authorizations, perhaps even devious, and which are, no doubt, tedious to find. The long and honorable development of the office of governor of Texas has accumulated many opportunities for exercising leadership, but in view of the difficulties which he must overcome to be effective in office, perhaps the title bestowed upon the leader of the state government in Texas is really a misnomer. Instead of the "Chief Executive of Texas," under existing laws he might more accurately be labelled the "Chief Persuader of Texas."

APPENDIX I

Comparison of Powers Vested in Texas Chief Executives
Under the State's Several Constitutions

Powers of Governor	Under Constitution of:						
	1827	1836	1845	1861	1866	1869	1876
I. *Legislative Duties*							
Call Special Sessions	x[a]	x	x	x	x	x	x
Recommend Legislation	x	x	x	x	x	x	x
Sign or Veto Laws	x[b]	x	x	x	x	x	x
Veto Items in Appropriations Bills	..	..	..	..	x	x	x
Call Special Election To Fill Legislative Vacancies	..	..	x	x	x	..	x
II. *Military Duties*							
Act as Commander in Chief of State Militia	x	x	x	x	x	x	x
III. *Executive Duties*							
Appointment Powers							
Appoint Ministers and Consuls	..	x	..	..	..	..	..
Appoint Judges	..	x	x[c]	..	..	..	..
Appoint Department Heads	x	x	x	..	..	x[d]	..
Make Recess Appointments in Executive and Judicial Branches	..	..	x	x	x	x	x
Removal Powers							
Remove Officers on Joint Address of the Legislature	..	..	x	x	x	x	x
Suspend and Fine Executive Employees	x	..	..	..	..	..	..
Require Information from Department Heads	..	..	x	x	x	x	x
Inspect Books and Vouchers of those Handling Public Funds	..	..	..	..	..	..	x
Administer and Collect State Rents	x	..	..	..	..	..	..
Faithfully Execute Laws	x[e]	x[f]	x[g]	x[g]	x[g]	x[g]	x[h]
See that Justice Is Administered by Courts and Decisions are Enforced	x	..	..	..	..	..	..

APPENDIX I   (Continued)

Comparison of Powers Vested in Texas Chief Executives
Under the State's Several Constitutions

Powers of Governor	Under Constitution of:						
	1827	1836	1845	1861	1866	1869	1876
Issue Regulations for Better Government of Departments	x	..	..	..	..	..	..
IV. *Pardoning Power*							
Issue Reprieves and Pardons	x	x	x	x	x	x	x[i]
V. *Miscellaneous Duties*							
Keep State Seal	..	x	x	x	x	x	..
Commission the Elected and Appointed Officers	..	x	x	x	x	x	x
Negotiate Treaties	..	x	..	..	..	..	..
Superintend Manufacture of Tobacco	x	..	..	..	..	..	..
Authorize Contracts for Construction and Maintenance of Churches	x	..	..	..	..	..	..
Conduct Relations with U.S. and Other States	..	..	..	..	..	..	x

[a] Upon advice from Executive Council.
[b] Promulgation Power.
[c] After 1850 judges were elected under terms of constitutional amendment.
[d] Appointed attorney general.
[e] He shall see that the "laws be fulfilled."
[f] He shall "see that the laws be faithfully executed."
[g] He shall "take care that the laws be faithfully executed."
[h] He shall "cause" the laws to be faithfully executed.
[i] Assisted by Board of Pardons and Paroles since 1936.

APPENDIX II

Length of Terms, Qualifications, and Salary of Chief Executives Under the Several Constitutions of Texas

Constitution	Article	Citizenship	Age	Residence	Term (Years)	Re-eligibility	Salary*
1827	Title II	Mexican**	30	Inhabitant of state 5 years, 2 immediately prior to election	4	Ineligible	$4,000
1836	III, VI	Republic of Texas	35	Inhabitant of Republic 3 years prior to election	3	Ineligible	$10,000
1845	V	U.S. or Texas	30	Resident of State of Texas 3 years; 2 years prior to election	2	No more than 4 years in any 6	$2,000
1861	V	Texas	30	Resident of State of Texas 3 years prior to election	2	No more than 4 years in any 6	$3,000
1866	V	U.S. or Texas	30	Resident of State of Texas 6 years prior to election	4	No more than 8 years in any 12	$4,000
1869	IV	U.S.	30	Resident and citizen of Texas 3 years preceding election	4	No limit	$5,000
1876	IV	U.S.	30	Resident of Texas 5 years preceding election	2	No limit	$4,000

* Salary fixed at time of adoption of the Constitution.
** Citizen "in the exercise of his rights"; born in territory of the Republic of Mexico. Ecclesiastics and military officials ineligible.

APPENDIX III

Personal Data on Governors of Texas (1876–1963)

Governor	Term	Birthplace	Date of Birth	Age when Inaugurated	Occupation of Father	Religio
Richard Coke	1874–76[a]	Williamsburg, Virginia	March 13, 1829	44	Unknown	Episcopa
Richard B. Hubbard	1876–79	Walton County, Georgia	Nov. 1, 1832	43	Soldier	Baptist
Oran M. Roberts	1879–83	Laurens Dist., S. Carolina	July 9, 1815	63	Farmer	Methodi
John Ireland	1883–87	Hart County, Kentucky	Jan. 1, 1827	56	Farmer	Methodi
Lawrence S. Ross	1887–91	Bentonsport, Iowa	Sept. 27, 1838	48	Ranger captain	Methodi
James S. Hogg	1891–95	Rusk, Texas	March 24, 1851	39	Farmer	Baptist
Charles A. Culberson	1895–99	Dadeville, Alabama	June 10, 1855	39	Lawyer	Baptist
Joseph D. Sayers	1899–1903	Grenada, Mississippi	Sept. 23, 1841	57	Doctor	Methodi
Samuel W. T. Lanham	1903–07	Spartanburg, S. Carolina	July 4, 1846	56	Farmer	Methodi
Thomas M. Campbell	1907–11	Rusk, Texas	April 22, 1856	50	Farmer	Presbyte
Oscar B. Colquitt	1911–15	Camilla, Georgia	Dec.16, 1861	49	Farmer	Methodi
James E. Ferguson	1915–17[b]	Salado, Texas	August 31, 1871	43	Minister	Methodi
William P. Hobby	1917–21	Moscow, Texas	March 26, 1878	39	Lawyer	Methodi
Pat M. Neff	1921–25	McGregor, Texas	Nov. 26, 1871	49	Farmer	Baptist
Miriam A. Ferguson	1925–27 1933–35	Bell County, Texas	June 13, 1875	{49 57}	Farmer	Episcop
Dan Moody	1927–31	Taylor, Texas	June 1, 1893	33	Merchant	Baptist
Ross S. Sterling	1931–33	Anahuac, Texas	Feb. 11, 1875	55	Farmer	Christia
James V. Allred	1935–39	Bowie, Texas	March 29, 1899	35	Mail carrier	Christia
W. Lee O'Daniel	1939–41[a]	Malta, Ohio	March 11, 1890	48	Farmer	Christia
Coke R. Stevenson	1941–47	Mason County, Texas	March 20, 1888	53	Teacher-Surveyor	Methodi
Beauford H. Jester	1947–49[c]	Corsicana, Texas	Jan. 12, 1893	54	Lawyer	Methodi

‚ducation	Profession	Military Service	Member-ship in Masonic Lodge	Number of Children	Date of Death
liam & Mary College	Lawyer-Farmer	Yes	Yes	4	May 14, 1896
:cer Univ. vard Law School	Lawyer	Yes	Yes	0	July 12, 1901
v. of Alabama	Lawyer-Teacher	Yes	Yes	7	May 19, 1898
lic school ✓ office	Lawyer	Yes	Yes	3	March 15, 1896
lor Univ. sleyan Univ. f Alabama	Soldier–Farmer	Yes	Yes	8	Jan. 4, 1898
lic school ✓ office	Lawyer–Newspaper editor	No	No	4	March 3, 1907
;inia Mil. Inst. v. of Virginia	Lawyer	No	Yes	1	March 25, 1925
trop Mil. Inst. ✓ office	Lawyer	Yes	Yes	0	May 15, 1929
lic school ✓ office	Lawyer	Yes	Yes	8	July 29, 1908
uity Univ. ✓ office	Lawyer– Railroad ex.	No	No	5	April 1, 1923
ngerfield College	Lawyer–Editor	No	No	5	March 8, 1940
do College ✓ office	Banker–Lawyer	No	Yes	2	Sept. 21, 1944
lic school ✓	Editor	No	Yes	2	
lor Univ. v. of Texas	Lawyer	No	Yes	2	Jan. 19, 1952
do College lor College (Belton)	Housewife	No	No	2	June 25, 1961
v. of Texas	Lawyer	Yes	Yes	2	
lic school	Oil Company Executive	No	Yes	5	March 25, 1949
‚ Institute berland Univ.	Lawyer	Yes	Yes	3	Sept. 24, 1959
lic school	Flour sales	No	Yes	3	
lic school ✓ office	Lawyer–Rancher	No	Yes	2	
v. of Texas vard Law School	Lawyer	Yes	Yes	3	July 11, 1949

APPENDIX III (Continued)

Personal Data on Governors of Texas (1876–1963)

Governor	Term	Birthplace	Date of Birth	Age when Inaugurated	Occupation of Father	Religion
Allan Shivers	1949–57	Lufkin, Texas	Oct. 5, 1907	41	Lawyer	Baptist
Price Daniel	1957–63	Dayton, Texas	Oct. 10, 1910	46	Editor–Real Estate	Baptist
John Connally	1963–	Floresville, Texas	Feb. 27, 1917	45	Farmer	Methodist

a Resigned before expiration of term.
b Impeached and removed from office.
c Died before expiration of term.

ducation	Profession	Military Service	Member-ship in Masonic Lodge	Number of Children	Date of Death
v. of Texas	Lawyer	Yes	Yes	4	
lor Univ.	Lawyer–Editor–Rancher	Yes	Yes	4	
v. of Texas	Lawyer–Rancher	Yes	No	3	

ource: Compiled from
James T. DeShields, *They Sat in High Place: The Presidents and Governors of Texas* (San Antonio: The Naylor Co., 1940).
Hugh N. Fitzgerald, *Governors I Have Known* (Austin: American-Statesman Publishing Co., 1927).
Paul Bolton, *Governors of Texas* (Corpus Christi: Caller-Times Publishing Co., 1947).
Who's Who in Texas (Dallas: Who's Who Publishing Co., 1931).
Texian Who's Who (Dallas: The Texian Co., 1937).
Texas Almanac, 1959 (Dallas: A. H. Belo Corp., 1959).
Biographical Files, Governors of Texas, Barker Texas History Center, The University of Texas.

APPENDIX IV

Professional Data on Governors of Texas (1876–1963)

Governor	Term	Age at Inauguration	Length of Tenure (Years)	Official Residence Section of State
Richard Coke	1874–76	44	2	Waco (Central)
Richard B. Hubbard	1876–79	43	3	Tyler (East)
Oran M. Roberts	1879–83	63	4	Tyler (East)
John Ireland	1883–87	56	4	Seguin (Central)
Lawrence S. Ross	1887–91	48	4	Waco (Central)
James S. Hogg	1891–95	39	4	Tyler (East)
Chas. A. Culberson	1895–99	39	4	Dallas (North)
Joseph D. Sayers	1899–1903	57	4	Bastrop (Central)
Samuel W. T. Lanham	1903–07	56	4	Weatherford (West)
Thomas M. Campbell	1907–11	50	4	Palestine (East)
Oscar B. Colquitt	1911–15	49	4	Terrell (North)
James E. Ferguson	1915–17	43	2½	Temple (Central)
William P. Hobby	1917–21	39	3½	Beaumont (Southeast)
Pat M. Neff	1921–25	49	4	Waco (Central)
Miriam A. Ferguson	1925–27	49	2	Temple (Central)
	1933–35	57	2	
Dan Moody	1927–31	33	4	Taylor (Central)
Ross S. Sterling	1931–33	55	2	Houston (Southeast)
James V. Allred	1935–39	35	4	Wichita Falls (North)
W. Lee O'Daniel	1939–41	48	2½	Fort Worth (North)
Coke R. Stevenson	1941–47	53	5½	Junction (West)
Beauford H. Jester	1947–49	54	2½	Corsicana (North)
Allan Shivers	1949–57	41	7½	Port Arthur (Southeast)
Price Daniel	1957–63	46	6	Liberty (Southeast)
John Connally	1963–	45		Fort Worth (North)

Years of Experience in Public Office Prior to Election

Lieu-tenant Governor	Attorney General	U.S. Congress	Texas Legisla-ture	Judicial[c]	State Ad-ministra-tion	Local Offices	Office Held When Elected Governor
--	--	--	--	4	--	--	None
2	--	--	2	--	--	--	Lieutenant Governor[a]
--	--	--	--	20	--	--	Ch. Justice, Tex. Sup. Ct.
--	--	--	--	9	--	7	None
--	--	--	2	--	--	2	None
--	4	--	--	7	--	7	Attorney General
--	4	--	--	--	--	--	Attorney General
2	--	14	2	--	--	--	U.S. House of Rep.
--	--	16	--	5	--	--	U.S. House of Rep.
--	--	--	--	--	--	--	None
--	--	--	4	--	9	--	R.R. Com. of Texas
--	--	--	--	--	--	2	None
2½	--	--	--	--	--	--	Lieutenant Governor[a]
--	--	--	4[b]	6	--	--	None
--	--	--	--	--	--	--	None
--	2	--	--	3	--	--	Attorney General
--	--	--	--	--	4	--	Ch., Texas Hwy. Com.
--	4	--	--	3	--	--	Attorney General
--	--	--	--	--	--	--	None
2½	--	--	10[b]	--	--	7	Lieutenant Governor[a]
--	--	--	--	--	4	--	R.R. Com. of Texas
2½	--	--	12	--	--	--	Lieutenant Governor[a]
--	6	4	6[b]	--	--	--	United States Senator
--	--	--	--	--	--	--	None[d]

Succeeded to office when vacancy occurred.
Served as speaker of the House of Representatives.
Includes service as county attorney and district attorney.
Resigned as United States Secretary of the Navy to run for Governor.

Source: Compiled from Biographical Files on Texas Governors, Barker Texas History Center, University of Texas; and Scrapbooks on Texas Governors, The University of Texas Archives.

APPENDIX V

Itinerary of the Governor of Texas During 1954
(Exclusive of Campaign Appearances)

Date	Place	
Jan. 13	New York*	Southern Society meeting
Jan. 21	San Antonio*	A. B. Frank Company luncheon
Jan. 22	Austin*	Dedication of State Bar Building
Jan. 24	Brownsville	Joint dedication of Fort Brown Memorial Center
Jan. 25	Washington, D.C.	Commission on Intergovernmental Relations
Jan. 26	Austin*	Facts Forum
Jan. 29	Fort Worth*	Weatherford Civic Club and Fort Worth Stock Show
Feb. 3	San Antonio*	Texas Federated Women's Clubs luncheon
Feb. 4	Corpus Christi*	Dedication of terminal grain elevator
Feb. 10	East St. Louis, Ill.*	Illinois Bankers' Association dinner
Feb. 16	Washington, D.C.	Veterans of Foreign Wars banquet and Commission on Intergovernmental Relations
Feb. 16	Stephenville	Annual Chamber of Commerce banquet
Feb. 21	Washington, D.C.	American Good Government Society
Feb. 23	Waxahachie	First Baptist Church Men's Bible Class
Feb. 26	Mineral Wells	Texas Young Democrats meeting
Mar. 2	Huntsville*	75th Anniversary, Sam Houston State College
Mar. 9	Fort Worth*	Methodist group
Mar. 14	Austin*	Opening of special session of Legislature
Mar. 22	Dallas	Reception and dinner for Ben Wooten
Mar. 26	Fort Worth	Gridiron Dinner
Mar. 27	Woodville	Dogwood Festival
Mar. 29	Austin*	Cancer Crusade broadcast
Mar. 29	San Angelo	West Texas Chamber of Commerce
Apr. 12	Wichita Falls	Frank Wood Awards Dinner
Apr. 19	Houston	Gridiron Dinner
Apr. 21	Beaumont	Rotary Club
Apr. 21	Bryan*	A. & M. College Annual Muster
Apr. 23	San Antonio*	South Texas Press Association
Apr. 24	Rockdale*	Dedication of ALCOA plant
Apr. 24	Dallas*	State Democratic Executive Committee
Apr. 26	Washington, D.C.	Conference with President Eisenhower
Apr. 30	Lampasas*	School board banquet
May 3	Old Point Comfort, Virginia	Southern Regional Conference of Council of State Governments
May 13	Brady*	Chamber of Commerce banquet
May 14	Longview*	Resistol hat plant
May 14	Glen Rose*	Optimist Club banquet
May 15	Tyler	Shrine banquet
May 20	San Francisco	Trip to Korea
May 31	St. Louis*	Southern Baptist convention
June 4	Houston*	University of Houston commencement
June 8	Odem	Kiwanis district convention dinner

APPENDIX V (Continued)

Itinerary of the Governor of Texas During 1954
(Exclusive of Campaign Appearances)

Date	Place	
June 9	San Antonio*	Preflight class graduation, Lackland AFB
June 10	Dallas*	Campaign luncheon for Wallace Savage, candidate for Congress
June 12	Austin*	Physically Handicapped Week address, Texas Employment Commission
June 14	Houston	Texas Cotton Seed Crushers' Association
June 17	Corpus Christi	Lon Hill testimonial dinner
June 18	Fort Worth & Arlington*	TPA Convention and Chamber of Commerce banquet
June 19	North Fort Hood	Governor's Day Review, 36th Division
June 20–August 28		Campaign for third term as Governor**
Sept. 13	Mineral Wells*	State Democratic Executive Committee and Convention
Sept. 19	California	Vacation for ten days
Oct. 5	New Orleans, La.*	Banquet for Governor Kennon of Louisiana
Oct. 9	Dallas	Open State Fair; Texas-Oklahoma football game
Oct. 12	Houston*	National Retail Druggist convention
Oct. 23	Houston*	Dedication of M. D. Anderson Hospital; Texas-Rice football game
Oct. 25	Houston*	Grand Chapter, Eastern Star of Texas
Oct. 28	Phoenix, Arizona*	Press Club; Arizona Livestock Show
Nov. 1	Nacogdoches*	Texas Fox and Wolf Hunters at Camp Tonkawa
Nov. 5	Waco	Baylor University Conference on American Ideals (Governor Frank Clement and Dr. Billy Graham, Speakers)
Nov. 8	Chicago	Governor's Conference, Special Highway Committee
Nov. 10	Boca Raton, Florida	Southern Governors' Conference
Nov. 17	Birmingham, Alabama*	Alabama Chamber of Commerce dinner
Nov. 30	Dallas*	Prededication tour of Republic National Bank, dinner and show
Dec. 1	Chicago	Board of Managers, Council of State Governments
Dec. 3	Chicago*	Interstate Oil Compact Commission
Dec. 12	Port Arthur	Annual duck hunt
Dec. 17	Austin*	Advisory Committee to State Hospital Board

* Speech delivered by Governor Shivers.
** Itinerary of the campaign appearances June–August, 1954, shown in Chapter 12.
Source: Appointment books of Governor Allan Shivers, 1954. (Provided by Weldon Hart, executive secretary to Governor Shivers.)

APPENDIX VI

An Illustration of the Appointing Process and the Practice of
Senatorial Courtesy

(Source: Correspondence Files of Governor Beauford H. Jester, Box
GC–79, Texas State Archives.)

October 2, 1947

Mr. A. G. Blackwelder
Post Office Service Station
Gonzales, Texas

Dear Arthur:

Beauford called me this morning, and said that he had been informed by
the District Judge in Gonzales County that the District Attorney expected
to resign sometime about the last of October, and that he had called you
and mentioned several with whom you could get together and give him
a recommendation for a replacement. He asked me to write you and find
out what the situation is up to date, and what youall have in mind. Will
you please let me know as early as possible? Beauford does not want to
let the announcement of the resignation get very wide-spread publicity,
before he has decided upon who should be appointed in lieu of the present
District Attorney. By doing this, he will be able to keep his friends from
getting into a fuss between themselves.

With best wishes for you always, and assuring you that it was a pleasure
to see you at Corsicana, I am

Sincerely yours,
Paul H. Brown

PHB: kcs

APPENDIX VI (Continued)

Gonzales, Texas
October 3, 1947

Hon. Paul H. Brown
Secretary of State
Austin, Texas

Dear Paul:

I am in receipt of your letter of October 2nd in regard to the vacancy of the District Attorney's Office that is being created in the 25th Judicial District by the resignation of Mr. Denver E. Perkins.

I talked to Mr. Perkins last Saturday, and he told me that he intended to send in his final resignation on Saturday, October 4th or Monday, October 6th.

As a result of the phone call that I had with the Governor, I checked with the various parties that he requested me to check with, and they are unanimous in the question that Willis E. Ellison, present County Judge of Gonzales County, be appointed to the office of District Attorney that is being vacated by Mr. Perkins.

Please give my best wishes to the Governor.

Yours truly,
A. G. Blackwelder

Austin, Texas
October 8, 1947

(11:35 a.m.)

SENATOR RUDOLPH A. WEINERT
SEGUIN, TEXAS

HONORABLE DENVER E. PERKINS, DISTRICT ATTORNEY OF THE 25TH. JUDICIAL DISTRICT AT GONZALES HAS HANDED ME HIS RESIGNATION. I DESIRE TO APPOINT WILLIS E. ELLISON THE PRESENT COUNTY JUDGE OF GONZALES COUNTY TO THIS POSITION PROVIDED THAT YOU HAVE NO OBJECTIONS. WILL YOU PLEASE ADVISE ME BY WIRE COLLECT AT YOUR EARLIEST CONVENIENCE? BEST REGARDS.

BEAUFORD H. JESTER, GOVERNOR

APPENDIX VI (Continued)

1947 Oct 8 PM 4 01

D.SJA1013 PD=SEGUIN TEX 8 327P
GOV BEAUFORD JESTER=
    AUSTIN TEX

IN RE YOUR WIRE DISTRICT ATTORNEYS OFFICE APPOINT-
MENT OF JUDGE WILLIS ELLISON OF GONZALES COUNTY EN-
TIRELY SATISFACTORY TO ME=

R A WEINERT

October 9, 1947

MR. WILLIS E. ELLISON
GONZALES, TEXAS
IT IS MY PLEASURE TO APPOINT YOU DISTRICT ATTORNEY OF
THE 25TH JUDICIAL DISTRICT TO FILL UNEXPIRED TERM OF
HONORABLE DENVER E. PERKINS, RESIGNED. BEST WISHES.

BEAUFORD H. JESTER

EXECUTIVE DEPARTMENT
Austin, Texas

Beauford H. Jester
    Governor

October 10, 1947

Colonel Paul H. Brown
Secretary of State
Austin, Texas

Dear Paul:

I am today appointing Willis E. Ellison of Gonzales, Gonzales County,
to be District Attorney of the 25th Judicial District to fill the unexpired
term of Honorable Denver E. Perkins, resigned.

Please issue commission to Mr. Ellison as soon as he has qualified.
With best wishes, I remain

Most sincerely yours,
Beauford H. Jester

APPENDIX VII

Schedule of Governor John Connally for Week of May 6, 1963
(Legislature in Session)

Monday, May 6
A.M.:

7:30—Breakfast with Senate members at the Mansion
9:00—Conference with administrative assistants re legislation, itinerary, and state legal matters, including clemency
10:30—Greeted Mark Connally's (Governor's youngest son) class in Reception Room. The class was making a tour of the Capitol
10:45—State Board of Barber Examiners re upcoming appointment to that Board
11:00—Recent appointee (woman) to a State University Board of Regents
11:30—Consul General of Japan, courtesy call
Noon:
12:00—Texas Automobile Dealers Association luncheon, speech

P.M.:

2:15—Man re educational program
2:45—Man re county and local politics
3:00—Man re possible legislation
3:30—State senators (3) re legislation
4:00—Architect delivering plans for proposed renovation of Governor's Offices
4:20—Staff meeting
7:30—Discussion with State senator in elevator and en route to car re legislation (This happened a great deal during the session, but it was difficult to keep track of these meetings.)

Tuesday, May 7
A.M.:

7:30—Breakfast at the Mansion with House members
9:00—Judge, announcing his intention to retire
10:00—School Land Board meeting
11:30—Men re labor
11:50—Greeted and talked with Senior Class in Reception Room. This class was on its Senior trip and the Governor talked with them about continuing their education.
Noon:
12:00—Lunch with staff

P.M.:

1:15—Have picture made for House and Senate composite photographs
2:00—Proclamations and bill signing

3:00—School Land Board meeting (to finish business on the morning's agenda)
4:45—State senator re legislation
5:10—State senator re legislation
5:25—State representative re legislation
6:30—Conference with Austrian Ambassador at Mansion

Wednesday, May 8

A.M.:

7:30—Breakfast with staff at the Mansion
9:30—Building Commission meeting
11:00—Man re Latin American citizens of Texas
11:30—Board of Directors of a state association to endorse pending legislation
Noon:
12:00—Luncheon with friends, including speaker of the House of Representatives

P.M.:

2:00—State senator and two of his constituents re legislation
2:15—Man re appointment to a state board
2:30—State representative seeking assistance on pending legislation
2:45—Man re new industry in the state
3:20—Administrative assistant re legislation (joined later by two more assistants)
5:30—State representative re proposed bill
7:00—Party for all members of the Legislature, Mansion

Thursday, May 9

A.M.:

8:00—Meeting with staff re legislation
9:15—Man re legislation and invitation to East Texas
9:30—Building Commission meeting
11:00—Man re appointment to a judgeship
11:30—Welcome visiting governors of Mexico (5) in Reception Room, exchange of gifts, tour of capitol, tour of Governor's Mansion
Noon:
12:45—Luncheon honoring governors of Mexico

P.M.:

3:00—Man re pending legislation
3:45—Man re politics within the senatorial district in which he lives
4:00—State representatives (2) re bill they intended to sponsor
4:20—Men (2) re matters relating to atomic energy
5:00—Visited personal physician for belated checkup following surgery
6:30—Dinner at Mansion with family and Mrs. Connally's parents

Friday, May 10

A.M.:

8:30–Staff conference
10:00–Press conference
10:45–Man re appointment to a state commission
11:00–Swearing-in for the State Textbook Committee, Reception Room
11:15–Bill signing (Sponsors of successful bills and Governor have picture taken while bill is being signed.)

P.M.:

2:00–Depart Austin for Fort Worth
5:00–Meet and present Honorary Texan Certificate to dignitary visiting from another state
7:00–Exchange Club Golden Deeds Award Banquet
(Governor Connally was honored as Fort Worth's Outstanding Citizen for 1963.)

Saturday, May 11

A.M.:

Morning spent attending to personal business in Fort Worth
Noon: Luncheon with friends

P.M.:

Early–Returned to Austin
3:45–Reviewed bills passed by Legislature awaiting his signature (The Governor and an administrative assistant attended to this job at least once a week and on occasion twice a week during the session.)

Schedule of Governor John Connally for Week of August 5, 1963

(Legislature Not in Session)

Monday, August 5

A.M.:

9:30–Man re Regulatory Loan Commission
10:00–Man re proposed trip for Governor Connally
10:30–Man re politics in his county
11:45–Man re policy, Department of Public Safety
12:00–Old friend of the Governor's who dropped by
Noon:
12:00–Luncheon with friends

P.M.:

2:00—State representative, State senator and one man re possible appointment to a state board
3:00—Administrative assistant re itinerary
4:30—Administrative assistant re legal matters
6:00—Man re candidate for appointment to a judgeship

Tuesday, August 6

A.M.:

9:00—Texas Southern University Board of Directors
10:00—School Land Board meeting
11:00—Filmed introduction to industrial film to be distributed over all U.S.
11:30—Man re civil rights

P.M.:

4:00—Depart Austin for flight to San Angelo
5:30—Meeting re higher education
7:30—San Angelo College Appreciation Dinner, speech

Wednesday, August 7

A.M.:

8:00—Breakfast with friends
10:00—Depart San Angelo for return flight to Austin
11:30—Meeting with administrative assistants
Noon:
12:30—Luncheon with department head re change in policy

P.M.:

2:30—Meeting with administrative assistant re speech schedule, topics
4:00—State senator re district matters and invitation to visit that district
5:15—Man re attracting industry to the state

Thursday, August 8

A.M.:

10:00—Committee of sportsmen re new Parks and Wildlife Commission
10:30—Meeting with administrative assistant re clemency matters
11:30—State department executive re state highways
Noon:
12:00—Lunch with staff (administrative assistants)

P.M.:

3:30—Committee (25 men) re screwworm program
4:45—Administrative assistant re itinerary
7:00—Dinner with friends (Governor and Mrs. Connally)

Friday, August 9

A.M.:

10:30—British Consul General paid courtesy call and discussed proposed visit of British Ambassador to Texas

11:00—Proclamations: Parent-Teacher Week, Building Trades Week
Presentation of gift to Governor from Swedish Consul General (presentation made by a friend of the Consul General's)

11:30—Filming of safety spot with director of department of Public Safety

Noon:

12:00—Texas Legal Reserve Officials Association luncheon, speech (Mrs. Connally accompanied the Governor.)

P.M.:

2:30—Man re industrial possibilities in East Texas

3:00—Men (2) re contacting Civil Aeronautics Board pertaining to retaining a city's service by an airline

3:30—Committee re job opportunities

5:30—Meeting at the Mansion with daughter of former Governor of Texas (They discussed higher education and an existing educational foundation which she helped to establish.)

7:00—Dinner with chairman and executive secretary of the State Democratic Executive Committee

Saturday, August 10

A.M.:

9:00—Man re water conservation

10:00—Parade Marshall for Austin Aqua Festival Parade

P.M.:

2:30—Administrative assistants re appointments to various state boards and commissions

Source: Governor Connally's office

BIBLIOGRAPHY

CONSTITUTIONS AND STATUTES

Acta Constitutiva de Federacion Mexicana de 1824.
Constitution of the State of Coahuila and Texas, 1827.
Constitution of the Republic of Texas, 1836.
Constitution of Texas, 1845.
Constitution of Texas, 1861.
Constitution of Texas, 1866.
Constitution of Texas, 1869.
Constitution of Texas, 1876.
General and Special Laws of the State of Texas, 1876–1961.
Index Digest of State Constitutions. 2d ed. New York: Legislative Drafting
    Fund of Columbia University, 1959.
Laws and Decrees of the State of Coahuila and Texas. Translated by J. P.
    Kimball, M.D.
Vernon's Annotated Civil Statutes, State of Texas. Kansas City & Vernon Law
    Book Co., 1961.

JOURNALS OF CONSTITUTIONAL CONVENTIONS

Debates in the Texas Constitutional Convention of 1875. Edited by S. S. McKay.
    Austin: University of Texas Press, 1930.
Debates of the Texas Constitutional Convention of 1845. William F. Weeks,
    Reporter. Houston: J. W. Cruger, 1846.
Journal of Secession Convention of Texas, 1861. Ed., E. W. Winkler. Austin:
    Austin Printing Co., 1912.
Journal of the Reconstruction Convention. Austin: Tracy, Siemering and Co.,
    Printers, 1870.
Journal of the Constitutional Convention Begun and Held in Austin, September
    6, 1875. Galveston: Galveston News Co., 1875.

ARCHIVAL MATERIALS

Allred, James V. Files containing public papers. Texas State Archives.
———. Scrapbook. The University of Texas Archives.
Biographical File (on each governor of Texas from 1876 to 1962, containing
    newspaper clippings, campaign literature, inaugural programs, miscellane-
    ous personal letters, etc.). Barker Texas History Center, The University of
    Texas.
Coke, Richard. Scrapbook. The University of Texas Archives.
Colquitt, Oscar B. Public Papers (collection appearing under title of Colquitt
    Papers). The University of Texas Archives.
———. Scrapbook. The University of Texas Archives.
Democratic Conventions in Texas Scrapbook. The University of Texas Archives.
Executive Record Books (containing copies of proclamations, pardons, and re-
    mission of fines). Texas State Archives.
Ferguson, James E. Scrapbook. The University of Texas Archives.
Ferguson, Miriam A. Files containing public papers. Texas State Archives.
———. Scrapbook. The University of Texas Archives.
"Governors' Races in Texas." Scrapbook. The University of Texas Archives.
Governors' Letters Received 1876–1931 (chronologically arranged in 50 file
    drawers). Texas State Archives.
Governors' Letters Sent 1876–1925. Texas State Archives.

Governors' Messages, Coke to Ross, 1874–1891. Texas State Archives.
Hogg, James S. Public Papers (collection appearing under title of Hogg Papers). The University of Texas Archives.
Jester, Beauford H. Files containing public papers. Texas State Archives.
Moody, Dan. Scrapbook. The University of Texas Archives.
Neff, Pat M. Scrapbook. The University of Texas Archives.
O'Daniel, W. Lee. Files containing public papers. Texas State Archives.
———. Scrapbook. The University of Texas Archives.
Stevenson, Coke R. Files containing public papers. Texas State Archives.

GOVERNMENT DOCUMENTS AND PUBLICATIONS

Reports of the Adjutant General of Texas. Issued intermittently, 1921–1960.
Attorney General of Texas. *Biennial Report 1918–1920.*
———. Opinion No. 0–308, February 9, 1939.
Annual Reports of the Comptroller of Public Accounts. State of Texas, 1884–1961.
Annual Report on Condition and Fiscal Operation of the State of Texas, 1939.
State Board of Control. *Biennial Appropriations Budgets,* 1921–1948.
Citizens Advisory Committee on Revision of the Constitution of Texas, *Interim Report to the 56th Legislature and the People of Texas,* March 1, 1959.
Commission on Intergovernmental Relations. *A Report to the President for Transmittal to the Congress.* H. R. Doc. 198, Eighty-fourth Congress, first session, 1955.
———. *Survey Report on the Impact of Federal Grants-in-Aid on the Structure and Functions of State and Local Governments.* Washington: Government Printing Office, 1955.
"Duties and Powers of the Governor of Texas." Prepared and distributed by the staff of Governor Price Daniel, n.d. (Mimeographed.)
Marburger, Harold J. (comp.). "Veto Messages by the Governors of Texas, 1931–1957."
Proclamation No. 13406, by Governor Miriam A. Ferguson, 1933. Original on file in Texas State Archives, Austin, Texas.
Proclamations of Governor James V. Allred, 1936. Bound volume in Texas State Archives, Austin, Texas.
Proclamation No. 1836 by Governor W. Lee O'Daniel, 1940. Original on file in the office of the secretary of state, Austin, Texas.
Proclamations of Governor W. Lee O'Daniel, 1941. Bound volume in office of the secretary of state, Austin, Texas.
Proclamation No. 7039, June 25, 1943. Original on file in office of the secretary of state, Austin, Texas.
Texas Election Code, 1958.
Texas Good Neighbor Commission. *Texas: Friend and Neighbor,* 1961.
Texas Insurance Code, 1957.
Texas Legislative Council. *An Inventory of Special Funds Outside the State Treasury—A Report to the 56th Legislature.* (Report 55–58, December, 1958).
Texas Legislative Council and Institute of Public Affairs, The University of Texas. *A Guide to Texas State Agencies* (1956) with 1960 *Supplement.*
Texas Legislative Council. *Manual of Texas State Government.* Staff Research Report 51–56. Compiled by H. A. Calkins, Austin, 1950, 1953.
Texas Legislature. *House Journals,* 1876–1961.
Texas Legislature. *Senate Journals,* 1876–1961.

Texas Legislature, Joint Legislative Committee on Organization and Economy. *The Government of the State of Texas*, Pts. I–XIII, 1933.
Vetoed Bills, 1920–1963. (Bound volumes containing bills vetoed by each Governor of Texas after adjournment of sessions of the Texas Legislature, on file in the office of the secretary of state, Austin.)
U. S. Department of Commerce, Bureau of the Census. *Census of 1960.* Washington: Government Printing Office, 1961.
U. S. Department of Commerce. *Statistical Abstract of the United States, 1958.* Washington: Government Printing Office, 1959.
U. S. President's Committee on Administrative Management. *Report With Special Studies.* Washington: Government Printing Office, 1937.

CASES

A. P. Norman v. W. P. Hobby. 56th District Court of Texas, August 10, 1920.
Arnold v. State. 9 S.W. 120 (1888).
Carter v. Tomlinson. 227 S.W. (2d) 795 (1950).
Constantin v. Smith. 57 Fed. (2d) 236 (1932).
Denison v. State. 61 S.W. (2d) 1017 (1933).
Ex Parte Daily. 246 S.W. 91 (1922).
Ex Parte Lefors. 303 S.W. (2d) 394 (1957).
Ferguson v. McCallum, Secretary of State; Sterling v. Ferguson, 53 S.W. (2d) 753 (1932).
Ferguson v. Maddox. 263 S.W. 888 (1924).
Ferguson v. Wilcox, et al. 28 S.W. (2d) 526 (1930).
Fulmore v. Lane. 140 S.W. 405 (1911).
Knox v. Johnson. 141 S.W. (2d) 698 (1941).
Missouri, Kansas, and Texas Ry. Co. of Texas v. Shannon. 100 S.W. 138 (1907).
Neff v. Elgin. 270 S.W. 873 (1925).
Pickle v. McCall. 24 S.W. 265 (1893).
Rose Mfg. Co. v. Western Union Telegraph Co. 251 S.W. 337 (1923).
Seay v. Latham. 182 S.W. (2d) 251 (1944).
Sterling v. Constantin. 53 S.Ct. 190 (1932).
Terrell, Comptroller of Public Accounts v. Middleton. 187 S.W. 367 (1916).
United States v. Wolters. 268 Fed. 69 (1920).
Walker v. Baker, Chairman of Board of Control, et al. 196 S.W. (2d) 324 (1946).

BOOKS, MONOGRAPHS, AND PAMPHLETS

Abernethy, Byron R. *Some Persisting Questions Concerning the Constitutional State Executive.* Governmental Research Series, No. 23. Lawrence: University of Kansas, 1960.
Adams, Frank C. (ed.). *A Centennial History of Politics and Personalities of the Democratic Party—1836–1936.* 4 vols. Austin: Democratic Historical Association, 1937.
Adrian, Charles R. *State and Local Governments: A Study in the Political Process.* New York: McGraw-Hill Book Co., 1960.
Allen, Robert S. (ed.). *Our Sovereign State.* New York: The Vanguard Press, 1949.
Allred, James V. *Legislative Messages of the Honorable James V. Allred, Governor of Texas, 1935–1939.* Austin: n.p., 1939.

American Assembly, Graduate School of Business, Columbia University. *The Forty-Eight States: Their Tasks as Policy Makers and Administrators.* New York: Arden House, 1955.

Anderson, William, Clara Penniman, and Edward W. Weidner. *Government in the Fifty States.* New York: Holt, Rinehart and Winston Inc., 1960.

Anderson, William, and Edward W. Weidner. *State and Local Government in the United States.* New York: Henry Holt & Co., 1951.

Babcock, Robert S. *State and Local Government and Politics.* New York: Random House, 1957.

Benton, Wilbourn E. *Texas: Its Government and Politics.* Englewood Cliffs, New Jersey: Prentice-Hall, Inc., 1961.

Biggers, Don H. *Our Sacred Monkeys or 20 Years of Jim: A Thousand Chuckles and a Thousand Facts Showing the Amusing Humbuggery of the Whole Business Particularly Since Jim Broke Into the Game in 1914.* No publisher indicated, 1933.

Bolton, Paul. *Governors of Texas.* Corpus Christi: Caller-Times Publishing Co., 1947.

Book of the States, The, 1960–61. Chicago: Council of State Governments, 1960.

Bryce, James. *The American Commonwealth.* 2 vols. Reprint of 1888 ed. New York: The Macmillan Co., 1931.

Buck, A. E. *The Reorganization of State Governments in the U.S.* New York: Columbia University Press, 1938.

Burkhead, Jesse. *Government Budgeting.* New York: John Wiley & Sons, Inc., 1956.

Cagle, Alvah P. *Fundamentals of the Texas Constitution.* Waco: Baylor University Press, 1957.

Clark, James A., and Weldon Hart. *The Tactful Texan: A Biography of Governor Will Hobby.* New York: Random House, 1958.

Cotner, Robert C. *James Stephen Hogg, A Biography.* Austin: The University of Texas Press, 1959.

Council of State Governments. *The Book of the States, 1960–61.* Chicago: Council of State Governments, 1960.

———. *The Governor and Public Information: Selected Methods Employed by Governors' Offices in Communicating with the Public.* Chicago: Council of State Governments, 1961.

———. *The Governors—Personal Histories.* Chicago: Council of State Governments, 1960.

———. *The Governors—Their Backgrounds.* Chicago: Council of State Governments, 1960.

Crawford, Finla G. (ed.). *Readings in American Government.* Revised edition. New York: F. S. Crofts & Co., 1933.

Current, R. N., T. Harry Williams, and Frank Friedel. *American History: A Survey.* New York: Alfred A. Knopf, 1961.

DeShields, James T. *The Fergusons, "Jim and Ma": The Stormy Petrels in Texas Politics.* Dallas: Clyde C. Cockrell Publishing Co., 1932.

———. *They Sat in High Place: The Presidents and Governors of Texas.* San Antonio: The Naylor Company, 1940.

Douglas, C. L., and Francis Miller. *The Life Story of W. Lee O'Daniel.* Dallas: Regional Press, 1938.

Ewing, Cortez A. M. *Primary Elections in the South: A Study in Uniparty Politics.* Norman: University of Oklahoma Press, 1953.

Farmer, Hallie. *The Legislative Process in Alabama.* University, Alabama: Bureau of Public Administration, University of Alabama, 1949.

Fitzgerald, Hugh N. *Governors I Have Known*. Austin: American-Statesman Publishing Co., 1927.

Fuermann, George. *Reluctant Empire*. Garden City, New York: Doubleday & Co., 1957.

Graves, W. Brooke. *American State Government*. Fourth edition. Boston: D. C. Heath Co., 1953.

———— (ed.). *Major Problems in State Constitutional Revision*. Chicago: Public Administration Service, 1960.

Goodwyn, Frank. *Lone Star Land: Twentieth-Century Texas in Perspective*. New York: Alfred A. Knopf, 1955.

Haines, Charles G. *The Movement for the Reorganization of State Administration*. Austin: "The University of Texas Bulletin," No. 1848, August 25, 1918.

Hamilton, Alexander, James Madison, and John Jay. *The Federalist*. New York: Everyman's Library, 1932.

Havard, William C. *The Government of Louisiana*. Baton Rouge: Bureau of Public Administration, Louisiana State University, 1958.

Heady, Ferrel. *State Constitutions: The Structures of Administration*. State Constitutional Studies Project, No. 4. New York: National Municipal League, 1961.

Heard, Alexander. *The Costs of Democracy*. Chapel Hill: The University of North Carolina Press, 1960.

————. *Money and Politics*. Public Affairs Pamphlet, No. 242. New York: Public Affairs Committee, Inc., 1956.

————, and Donald Strong. *Southern Primaries and Elections, 1920–1949*. University, Alabama: University of Alabama Press, 1949.

Hogg, James Stephen. *Addresses and State Papers of James Stephen Hogg*. Edited by Robert C. Cotner. Austin: University of Texas Press, 1951.

————. *Speeches and State Papers of James Stephen Hogg*. Edited by C. W. Raines. Austin: The State Printing Company, 1905.

Howard, L. Vaughan, and John H. Fenton. *State Governments in the South: Functions and Problems*. New Orleans: The Southern Assembly, Tulane University, 1956.

Institute of Public Affairs, The University of Texas. *The Fifty-sixth Legislature: A Review of Its Work*. Austin: Institute of Public Affairs, 1959.

————. *The Texas Constitutional Amendments of 1960*. Austin: Institute of Public Affairs, 1960.

Jennings, Eugene E. *An Anatomy of Leadership: Princes, Heroes, and Supermen*. New York: Harper & Bros. ,1960.

Johnson, Claudius O. *American State and Local Government*. Second edition. New York: Thomas Y. Crowell Co., 1956.

Kelley, Stanley, Jr. *Political Campaigning*. Washington: Brookings Institution, 1960.

Key, V. O., Jr. *American State Politics: An Introduction*. New York: Alfred A. Knopf, 1956.

————. *Southern Politics in State and Nation*. New York: Alfred A. Knopf, 1949.

Kingrea, Nellie Ward. *History of the First Ten Years of the Texas Good Neighbor Commission*. Fort Worth: Texas Christian University Press, 1954.

Lasswell, Harold D. *Power and Personality*. New York: W. W. Norton Co., Inc., 1948.

————. *Psychopathology and Politics*. Chicago: University of Chicago Press, 1930.

Lipson, Leslie. *The American Governor from Figurehead to Leader*. Chicago: University of Chicago Press, 1938.

MacCorkle, Stuart A., and Dick Smith. *Texas Government*. Fourth edition. New York: McGraw-Hill Book Co., 1960.

McCleskey, Clifton. *The Government and Politics of Texas*. Boston: Little-Brown and Company, 1963.

McCraw, William. *Professional Politicians*. Washington: The Imperial Press, 1940.

McKay, Seth S. *Making the Texas Constitution of 1876*. Philadelphia: University of Pennsylvania Press, 1924.

————. *Seven Decades of the Texas Constitution of 1876*. Lubbock: Texas Tech Press, 1942.

————. *Texas Politics, 1906–1944*. Lubbock: Texas Tech Press, 1952.

————. *W. Lee O'Daniel and Texas Politics, 1938–1942*. Lubbock: Texas Tech Press, 1944.

Macdonald, Austin F. *American State Government and Administration*. Sixth edition. New York: Thomas Y. Crowell Co., 1960.

Madden, James William. *Charles Allen Culberson: His Life, Character and Public Service*. Austin: Gammel's Book Store, 1929.

Marburger, Harold J. *Texas Elections, 1918–1954*. Austin: Texas State Library, Legislative Reference Division, 1956.

Matthews, Donald R. *The Social Background of Political Decision-Makers*. Garden City, New York: Doubleday & Co., Inc., 1954.

Maxey, Chester C., and Robert Y. Fluno. *The American Problem of Government*. Sixth edition. New York: Appleton-Century-Crofts, Inc., 1957.

Michie, Allan A., and Frank Rhylick. *Dixie Demagogues*. New York: The Vanguard Press, 1939.

Mills, Warner E., Jr. *Martial Law in East Texas*. University, Alabama: Inter-University Case Program, No. 53, University of Alabama Press, 1960.

Morris, Richard B. (ed.). *Encyclopedia of American History*. New York: Harper and Bros. Inc., 1961.

Myres, S. D., Jr. (ed.). *The Government of Texas: A Survey*. Dallas: Arnold Foundation, Southern Methodist University, 1934.

Nalle, Ouida Ferguson. *The Fergusons of Texas or "Two Governors for the Price of One."* San Antonio: The Naylor Company, 1946.

Neff, Pat M. *Messages of Pat M. Neff*. Austin: A. C. Baldwin and Sons, 1921.

————. *The Battles of Peace*. Fort Worth: Pioneer Publishing Co., 1925.

Patterson, C. Perry, Sam B. McAlister, and George C. Hester. *State and Local Government in Texas*. Third edition. New York: The Macmillan Co., 1961.

Phares, Ross. *Texas Tradition*. New York: Henry Holt & Co., 1954.

Porter, Kirk H. *State Administration*. New York: F. S. Crofts & Co., 1938.

Ransone, Coleman B., Jr. *The Office of Governor in the South*. University, Alabama: Bureau of Public Administration, University of Alabama, 1951.

————. *The Office of Governor in the United States*. University, Alabama: University of Alabama Press, 1956.

Reinsch, Paul S. *American Legislatures and Legislative Methods*. New York: The Century Co., 1907.

Rich, Bennett M. *State Constitutions: The Governor*. New York: State Constitutional Studies Project, No. 3, National Municipal League, 1960.

Richardson, Rupert N. *Texas, The Lone Star State*. Second edition. Englewood Cliffs, New Jersey: Prentice-Hall Co., 1958.

Roosevelt, Theodore. *An Autobiography*. New York: Scribners & Co., 1920.

Scace, Homer E. *The Organization of the Executive Office of the Governor.* New York: Institute of Public Administration, 1950.
Schlesinger, Joseph A. *How They Became Governor.* East Lansing: Governmental Research Bureau, Michigan State University, 1957.
Shartle, Carroll L. *Executive Performance and Leadership.* Englewood Cliffs, New Jersey: Prentice-Hall, Inc., 1956.
Sheppard, John Ben. *A Bureaucrat's Dilemma: Ex-Officio Boards.* Austin: No publisher indicated, 1954.
Shirley, Emma Morill. *The Administration of Pat M. Neff, Governor of Texas, 1921–1925.* Waco: "Baylor University Bulletin," Vol. XLI, No. 4, 1938.
Sindler, Allen P. *Huey Long's Louisiana: State Politics, 1920–1952.* Baltimore: Johns Hopkins University Press, 1956.
Smith, Arthur D. H. *Mr. House of Texas.* New York: Funk, Wagnalls & Co., 1940.
———. *The Real Colonel House.* New York: George H. Doran Co., 1918.
Smith, Robert H. *Address to the Citizens of Alabama on the Constitution and Laws of the Confederate States of America.* Mobile, Alabama: n.p., n.d.
Steen, Ralph W. *The Texas Story.* Austin: The Steck Co., 1948.
———. *Twentieth Century Texas: An Economic and Social History.* Austin: The Steck Co., 1942.
Still, Rae Files. *The Gilmer-Aikin Bills: A Study in the Legislative Process.* Austin: The Steck Co., 1950.
Tansill, Charles S. (ed.). *Formation of the Union of American States.* Washington: Government Printing Office, 1927.
Texian Who's Who. Dallas: Texian Co., 1937.
Texas Almanac, 1961–1962. Dallas: A. H. Belo Publishing Co., 1961.
Thompson, John T. *Public Administration of Water Resources in Texas.* Austin: Institute of Public Affairs, The University of Texas, 1960.
Truman, David B. *The Governmental Process.* New York: Alfred A. Knopf, Inc., 1951.
Tugwell, Rexford G. *The Enlargement of the Presidency.* Garden City, New York: Doubleday & Co., Inc., 1960.
Utecht, Byron C. *The Legislature and the Texas People.* San Antonio: The Naylor Co., 1937.
Webb, Walter Prescott, and H. Bailey Carroll (eds.). *The Handbook of Texas.* 2 vols. Austin: Texas State Historical Assn., 1952.
Weeks, O. Douglas. *Research in the American State Legislative Process.* Ann Arbor: J. W. Edwards, 1947.
———. *Texas in the 1960 Presidential Election.* Austin: Institute of Public Affairs, The University of Texas, 1961.
———. *Texas One-Party Politics in 1956.* Austin: Institute of Public Affairs, The University of Texas, 1957.
———. *Texas Presidential Politics in 1952.* Austin: Institute of Public Affairs, The University of Texas, 1953.
Who's Who in Texas: A Biographical Dictionary. Dallas: Who's Who Publishing Co., 1931.
Wilson, Woodrow. *The State and Federal Governments of the United States.* Boston: D. C. Heath & Co., 1889.
Winkler, E. W. *Platforms of Political Parties in Texas.* Austin: The State Publishing Co., 1916.
Wolters, Jacob F. *Martial Law and Its Administration.* Austin: Gammel's Book Store, Inc., 1930.

Wooten, Dudley Goodall (ed.). *A Comprehensive History of Texas, 1865–1897.*
    Dallas: William G. Scarff, 1898.
Zeller, Belle (ed.). *American State Legislatures.* A Report of the Committee on
    American Legislatures, American Political Science Association. New York:
    Thomas Y. Crowell Co., 1954.
Zink, Harold. *Government and Politics in the United States.* Third edition. New
    York: Macmillan Co., 1951.

ARTICLES AND PERIODICALS

Ahlberg, Clark D., and Daniel P. Moynihan. "Changing Governor—and Poli-
    cies," *Public Administration Review,* XX (Autumn, 1960), 195–204.
Anderson, H. D. "Educational and Occupational Attainment of Our Rulers,"
    Scientific Monthly, 40 (September, 1935), 512–530.
Appleby, Paul H. "The Role of the Budget Division," *Public Administration
    Review,* XVII (Summer, 1957), 156–158.
Bane, Frank. "On Governors," *Public Administration Review,* IV (Spring, 1944),
    153–155.
———. "The Job of Being a Governor," *State Government,* XXXI (Summer,
    1958), 184–189.
Bendiner, Robert. "How Much has TV Changed Campaigning?" *New York
    Times Magazine* (November 2, 1952), 71–72.
Blachly, Frederick F., and Miriam E. Oatman. "Methods by Which the Ad-
    ministration Influences the Legislature," *Southwestern Political and Social
    Science Quarterly,* V (September, 1924), 160–177.
Bosworth, Karl A. "The Politics of Management Improvement in the States,"
    American Political Science Review, XLVII (March, 1953), 84–99.
Bowles, Chester. "A Governor's Job as Seen by a Governor," *New York Times
    Magazine* (July 24, 1949), 8, 30–31.
Brooks, Raymond. "Middle of the Road," *Austin American-Statesman* (March
    2, 1958), B–2.
Brown, David S. "The Public Advisory Board as an Instrument of Government,"
    Public Administration Review, XV (Summer, 1955), 196–204.
Brownlow, Louis. "Lowden of Illinois," *National Municipal Review,* XLVI
    (October, 1957), 446–449, 468.
Burdine, J. Alton. "Constitutional Revision—the Governor, the Administrative
    System, and Local Government." *Texas Law Review,* XXI (May, 1943),
    500–513.
Burdine, J. Alton, and Tom Reavley. "Toward a More Effective Administra-
    tion," *Texas Law Review,* 35 (October, 1957), 939–953.
"Business of Being Governor," *State Government,* XXXI (Summer, 1958),
    145–149. Summary of a round table discussion headed by Governor R. B.
    Meyner of New Jersey at the National Governors' Conference, Bal Harbour,
    Florida, May 18, 1958.
Caldwell, Lynton K. "Perfecting State Administration, 1940–1946," *Public
    Administration Review,* VII (Winter, 1947), 25–36.
Calkins, Howard A. "The Need for Constitutional Revision in Texas," *Texas
    Law Review,* XXI (May, 1943), 479–489.
Carleton, William G. "The Southern Politician—1900 and 1950," *Journal of
    Politics,* 13 (May, 1951), 215–231.
Cater, Douglass. "The Trouble in Lyndon Johnson's Back Yard," *The Reporter*
    (December 1, 1955), 32–35.

Duckworth, Allen. "Democratic Dilemma in Texas," *Southwest Review*, XXXII (Winter, 1947), 34–40.

Dugger, Ronnie. "What Corrupted Texas?", *Harpers* (March, 1957), 68–74.

Dunn, Roy. " 'New Deal': Made in Texas by a Texan," *Texas Parade* (April, 1961), 7–8.

Egger, Rowland A. "Power is not Enough," *State Government*, XIII (August, 1940), 149–150, 160–161.

Ewing, Cortez A. M. "Southern Governors," *Journal of Politics*, 10 (May, 1948), 385–409.

Fairlie, John A. "The Executive Power in the State Constitution," *Annals of the American Academy of Political and Social Science*, CLXXXI (September, 1935), 59–73.

———. "The State Governor," *Michigan Law Review*, X (March, 1912), 370–383.

———. "The State Governor," *Michigan Law Review*, X (April, 1912), 458–475.

Fairman, Charles. "Martial Rule in the Light of *Sterling* v. *Constantin*," *Cornell Law Quarterly*, XIX (1933–1934), 20–34.

Friedrich, Carl J. "Political Leadership and the Problem of the Charismatic Power," *Journal of Politics*, 23 (February, 1961), 3–24.

Gallagher, Herbert R. "State Reorganization Surveys," *Public Administration Review*, IX (Autumn, 1949), 252–256.

Gambrell, Herbert. "James Stephen Hogg: Statesman or Demagogue," *Southwest Review*, XIII (April, 1928), 338–366.

Graves, W. Brooke. "Criteria for Evaluating the Effectiveness of State Government," *American Political Science Review*, XXXII (June, 1938), 508–514.

———. "Some New Approaches to State Administrative Reorganization," *Western Political Quarterly*, IX (September, 1956), 743–754.

Gravlin, Leslie M. "An Effective Chief Executive," *National Municipal Review*, XXXVI (March, 1947), 139.

Gurwell, John K. "Governors of the States," *State Government*, XIV (July, 1941), 157–158.

Hardeman, D. B. "Shivers of Texas: A Tragedy in Three Acts," *Harpers*, (November, 1956), 50–56.

Heady, Ferrel. "States Try Reorganization," *National Municipal Review*, XLI (July, 1952), 334–338.

Kallenbach, Joseph E. "Constitutional Limitations on Re-eligibility of National and State Chief Executives," *American Political Science Review*, XLVI (June, 1952), 438–454.

Koenig, Louis W. "The Man and the Institution," *Annals of the American Academy of Political and Social Science*, 307 (September, 1956), 10–14.

Kohler, Walter J., Jr. "The Governor's Office," *Wisconsin Magazine of History*, XXXV (Summer, 1952), 243–245.

Lehman, Harvey C. "The Age of Eminent Leaders: Then and Now," *American Journal of Sociology*, 52 (January, 1947), 342–356.

Lipson, Leslie. "Influence of the Governor on Legislation," *Annals of the American Academy of Political and Social Science*, 195 (January, 1938), 72–78.

———. "The Executive Branch in New State Constitutions," *Public Administration Review*, IX (Winter, 1949), 11–21.

Lomax, John A. "Governor Ferguson and the University of Texas," *Southwest Review*, XXVIII (Autumn, 1942), 13–21.

MacCorkle, Stuart A. "The Pardoning Power in Texas," *Southwestern Social Science Quarterly*, XV (December, 1934), 218–228.

McGeary, M. Nelson. "The Governor's Veto in Pennsylvania," *American Political Science Review*, XLI (October, 1947), 941–946.

McGee, Vernon A. "A Legislative Approach to State Budgeting," *State Government*, XXVI (August, 1953), 200–204.

McKay, S. S. "O'Daniel, Roosevelt, and the Texas Republican Counties," *Southwestern Social Science Quarterly*, XXVI (June, 1945), 1–21.

McLean, Joseph E. "Early Modern Governor," *National Municipal Review*, XLVI (January, 1957), 20–22.

Macdonald, Austin F. "American Governors, 1900–1910," *National Municipal Review*, XVI (November, 1927), 715–719.

Martin, Roscoe C. "The Grange as a Political Factor in Texas," *Southwestern Political and Social Science Quarterly*, VI (March, 1926), 363–383.

Mathews, John M. "The New Role of the Governor," *American Political Science Review*, VI (May, 1912), 216–228.

Mauck, Elwyn A. "Some Problems in State Budgetary Administration," *State Government*, XXVI (February, 1953), 40–42.

Middleton, Annie. "The Texas Convention of 1845," *Southwestern Historical Quarterly*, XXV (July, 1921), 26–62.

Monypenny, Phillip. "The Changing Position of the Department Head in State Government," *State Government*, XXIV (April, 1951), 112–114.

Morrison, Donald. "Public Administration and the Art of Governance," *Public Administration Review*, V (Winter, 1945), 83–87.

Negley, Glenn R. "The Executive Veto in Illinois," *American Political Science Review*, XXXIII (December, 1939), 1052–1056.

Ogg, Frederic A. "Impeachment of Governor Ferguson," *American Political Science Review*, XII (February, 1918), 111–115.

Perkins, J. A. "American Governors, 1930–1940," *National Municipal Review*, XXIV (March, 1940), 178–184.

Pfiffner, John M. "The Personnel Function in Government," *Public Personnel Review*, 17 (October, 1956), 181–185.

Pitchell, Robert J. "The Influence of Professional Campaign Management Firms in Partisan Elections in California," *Western Political Quarterly*, XI (June, 1958), 278–290.

Prescott, Frank W. "The Executive Veto in American States," *Western Political Quarterly*, III (March, 1950), 97–111.

———. "The Executive Veto in Southern States," *Journal of Politics*, X (November, 1948), 659–675.

Reston, James. "Our Campaign Techniques Re-examined," *New York Times Magazine*, (November 9, 1952), 62–64.

Richardson, Rupert N. "Edward M. House and the Governors," *Southwestern Historical Quarterly*, LXI (July, 1957), 51–65.

———. "Framing the Constitution of the Republic of Texas," *Southwestern Historical Quarterly*, XXXI (January, 1928), 191–220.

Rogan, Octavia F. "Texas Legislation, 1925," *Southwestern Political and Social Science Quarterly*, VI (September, 1925), 167–178.

Scace, Homer E. "The Governor Needs Staff," *National Municipal Review*, XL (October, 1951), 462–467, 479.

Schmidhauser, John R. "The Justices of the Supreme Court: A Collective Portrait," *Midwest Journal of Political Science*, III (February, 1959), 1–58.

Scott, Elizabeth McK. "State Executive Departments Play Growing Part in Lawmaking," *National Municipal Review*, XXXII (November, 1943), 529–534.

Scott, Elizabeth McK., and Belle Zeller. "State Agencies and Lawmaking," *Public Administration Review*, II (Summer, 1942), 205–220.
Shivers, Allan. "Dynamic and Responsible State Government," *State Government*, XXVI (September, 1953), 214, 232.
Smith, Alfred E. "How We Ruin Our Governors," *National Municipal Review*, X (May, 1921), 277–280.
Smith, Dick. "Administrative Reorganization in Texas—a Reappraisal," *State Government*, XVIII (May, 1945), 86–87.
Smith, Harold D. "The Budget as an Instrument of Legislative Control and Executive Management," *Public Administration Review*, IV (Summer, 1944), 181–190.
Solomon, Samuel R. "American Governors Since 1915," *National Municipal Review*, XX (March, 1931), 152–158.
———. "Governors: 1950–1960," *National Civic Review*, XLIX (September, 1960), 410–416.
———. "The Governor as Legislator," *National Municipal Review*, XL (November, 1951), 515–520.
———. "U. S. Governors, 1940–1950," *National Municipal Review*, XLI (April, 1952), 190–197.
Spicer, George W. "Gubernatorial Leadership in Virginia," *Public Administration Review*, I (November, 1941), 441–457.
Steen, Ralph W. "The Ferguson War on the University of Texas," *Southwestern Social Science Quarterly*, 35 (March, 1955), 356–362.
Stevenson, Adlai E. "Reorganization from the State Point of View," *Public Administration Review*, X (Winter, 1950), 1–6.
Stewart, Frank M. "Impeachment in Texas," *American Political Science Review*, XXIV (August, 1930), 652–658.
Stokes, Thomas L. "The Governors," *State Government*, XVII (June, 1944), 343–345.
Stratton, William G. "The Governors' Conference Through Fifty Years—and Tomorrow," *State Government*, XXXI (Summer, 1958), 125–126.
Thomas, A. J., Jr., and Ann Van Wynen Thomas. "The Texas Constitution of 1876," *Texas Law Review*, 35 (October, 1957), 907–918.
Wall, E. L. "Biggest Job in the Biggest State," *Houston Chronicle Magazine* (April 27, 1947), 12–13.
Walker, Harvey. "The Legislature Today," *National Civic Review*, XLIX (November, 1960), pp. 530–536.
Weeks, O. Douglas. "Initiation of Legislation by Administrative Agencies," *Brooklyn Law Review*, IX (January, 1940), 117–131.
———. "Recent Developments in the State Legislative Process," *State Government*, XVI (July, 1943), 162–166.
———. "Republicanism and Conservatism in the South," *Southwestern Social Science Quarterly*, 36, (December, 1955), 248–256.
———. "The Presidential Election of 1960—Texas and the South," *Public Affairs Comment*, VII (Institute of Public Affairs, The University of Texas, January, 1961).
———. "The Texas-Mexican and the Politics of South Texas," *American Political Science Review*, XXIV (August, 1930), 606–627.
———. "Toward a More Effective Legislature," *Texas Law Review*, 35 (October, 1957), 926–938.
White, Leonard D. "On Governors," *Public Administration Review*, IV (Winter, 1944), 68–70.

———, and Harvey M. Sherman. "The Governors March On," *State Govern-ment,* 13 (February, 1945), 69–73.
Whitman, Willson. "Can a Wife be Governor?" *Colliers,* 76 (September 5, 1925), 5–6.
Young, William H. "The Development of the Governorship," *State Government,* XXXI (Summer, 1958), 178–183.

NEWSPAPERS

Amarillo Globe-Times, September 10, 1952.
Austin American, 1920–1963.
Austin Daily Tribune, November 19, 1939.
Austin Statesman, 1875–1963.
Beaumont Enterprise, 1938–1963.
Corpus Christi Caller-Times, November 5, 1959.
Dallas Morning News, 1900–1963.
Fort Worth Star-Telegram, 1900–1963.
Galveston News, 1875–1900.
Houston Chronicle, 1940–1963.
Houston Post, 1892–1963.
Houston Telegraph, October 8, 1875.
New York Times, 1917–1963.
Port Arthur News, May 5, 1946.
San Antonio Express, 1918–1963.
San Antonio Herald, September 20, 1875.
San Antonio Light, June 3, 1945.
State Observer (Texas), 1943–1963.

UNPUBLISHED MATERIAL

Baker, Marvin P. "The Executive Veto in Texas." Unpublished M.A. thesis, The University of Texas, 1933.
Barksdale, Mary Louise Wimberly. "The Gubernatorial Administration of James Stephen Hogg." Unpublished M.A. thesis, The University of Texas, 1932.
Bellush, Jewell L. "Selected Case Studies of the Legislative Leadership of Governor Herbert H. Lehman." Unpublished Ph.D. dissertation, Columbia University, 1959.
Brandenberger, William S. "The Administrative System of Texas, 1821–1836." Unpublished M.A. thesis, The University of Texas, 1912.
Burlage, Robb K. "James V. Allred—Texas' Liberal Governor." Unpublished research paper, The University of Texas, May, 1959.
Ferguson, Miriam A. "A Partial List of Outstanding Achievements of the Fergu-son Administration," Austin, n.d. (mimeographed).
Gorvine, Albert. "The Governor and Administration, State of Nevada." Un-published Ph.D. dissertation, New York University, 1950.
Grant, Daniel Ross. "The Role of the Governor of Arkansas in Administration." Unpublished Ph.D. dissertation, Northwestern University, 1948.
Huckaby, George P. "Oscar Branch Colquitt: A Political Biography." Un-published Ph.D. dissertation, The University of Texas, 1946.
Kennedy, Mizell F. "A Study of James Stephen Hogg, Attorney General and Governor." Unpublished M.A. thesis, The University of Texas, 1919.
Lanham, Martha A. "Life of Governor S. W. T. Lanham." Unpublished M.A. thesis, Baylor University, 1930.

Llewellyn, Sarah A. "Martial Law in Texas." Unpublished M.A. thesis, The University of Texas, 1932.
McBride, Travis. "The Office of Lieutenant Governor in Texas with Emphasis on Recent Administrations." Unpublished research paper, The University of Texas, Summer, 1959.
McCamy, James L. "Governmental Reporting in Texas State Administration." Unpublished M.A. thesis, The University of Texas, 1932.
Martin, Roscoe C. "The Farmers in Texas Politics, 1875–1900." Unpublished M.A. thesis, The University of Texas, 1925.
Martindale, Robert Rene. "James V. Allred: The Centennial Governor of Texas." Unpublished M.A. thesis, The University of Texas, 1958.
Mills, Warner E., Jr. "The Public Career of a Texas Conservative: A Biography of Ross Shaw Sterling." Unpublished Ph.D. dissertation, Johns Hopkins University, 1956.
St. Clair, Grady S. "The Hogg-Clark Campaign." Unpublished M.A. thesis, The University of Texas, 1927.
Sanderford, Ghent. "The Ferguson Era, 1914–1944." Ms. submitted to Winston Publishing Co., for incorporation into book on Texas history, 1955. Copy of ms. furnished by Mr. Sanderford.
Smith, Maggie R. "The Administration of Governor John Ireland, 1883–1887." Unpublished M.A. thesis, The University of Texas, 1934.
Steen, Ralph W. "The Political Career of James E. Ferguson, 1914–1917." Unpublished M.A. thesis, The University of Texas, 1929.
Street, Katherine. "Philosophy of and Plans for Education Found in Legislative Messages of the Chief Executives of Texas." Unpublished M.A. thesis, Baylor University, 1940.
Stroud, Roy W. "The Run-Off Primary." Unpublished M.A. thesis, The University of Texas, 1941.
Wagner, Robert L. "The Gubernatorial Career of Charles Allen Culberson." Unpublished M.A. thesis, The University of Texas, 1954.
Whatley, William A. "The Formation of the Mexican Constitution of 1824." Unpublished M.A. thesis, The University of Texas, 1921.
Webb, Juanita Oliver. "The Administration of Governor L. S. Ross, 1887–1891." Unpublished M.A. thesis, The University of Texas, 1935.
Weeks, O. Douglas. "The Presidential Election of 1960." Paper read before the meeting of the Southwestern Social Science Association, Dallas, Texas, March 31, 1961.
Wood, Robert C. "The Metropolitan Governor." Unpublished Ph.D. dissertation, Harvard University, 1950.

PERSONAL INTERVIEWS

Allred, Mrs. James V.
Brooks, Raymond, Capitol correspondent, *Austin American-Statesman*; former secretary to Governor W. P. Hobby.
Calvert, Robert S., comptroller of public accounts, State of Texas.
Calvert, Robert W., chief justice, Supreme Court of Texas; former speaker, Texas House of Representatives; former chairman, State Democratic Executive Committee.
Christian, George E., former executive assistant to Governor Price Daniel; administrative assistant to Governor John Connally.
Cobb, Bill B., administrative assistant to Governor John Connally.
Connally, John, Governor of Texas.

Connerly, Doris H., director, Legislative Reference Service, Texas State Library.
Daniel, Price, former Governor of Texas.
Dewey, B. H., Jr., member, Texas House of Representatives.
Dougherty, Pat, former secretary to Governor Dan Moody and Governor Ross Sterling.
Duckworth, Allen, political editor, *Dallas Morning News*.
Duncan, Dawson, Capitol correspondent, *Dallas Morning News*.
Edgar, J. W., commissioner of education, State of Texas.
Evans, Wilbur, administrative assistant to Governor John Connally.
Ferguson, Miriam A., former Governor of Texas (Telephone interview.)
Garner, John Nance, former Vice President of the United States; former member, Texas House of Representatives.
Garrett, Glenn E., executive secretary, Texas Good Neighbor Commission.
Goldsum, John, former administrative assistant to Governor Price Daniel.
Granberry, C. Read, executive director, Texas Legislative Council; former administrative assistant to Governor Allan Shivers.
Greer, DeWitt, state engineer, Texas Highway Department. (Telephone interview.)
Hart, Weldon, former executive secretary to Governor Beauford H. Jester and Governor Allan Shivers; former member, Texas Employment Commission.
Johnson, Clyde, executive director, State Democratic Executive Committee.
Johnson, J. H., former secretary to Governor Pat M. Neff.
Lawson, William J., member, Board of Directors, A. and M. College of Texas; former executive secretary to Governor W. Lee O'Daniel.
Long, Stuart, editor, *Austin Report*; former member, State Democratic Executive Committee.
McGee, Vernon A., director, Texas Legislative Budget Board.
Manford, Durwood, member, State Board of Insurance; former chairman, Texas Board of Water Engineers; former speaker, Texas House of Representatives.
Miskell, Frank, administrative assistant to Governor John Connally; regulatory loan commissioner of Texas.
Moody, Dan, former Governor of Texas.
Patman, Wright, member, United States House of Representatives; former member, Texas House of Representatives.
Pickle, J. J., member Texas Employment Commission; former executive director, State Democratic Executive Committee.
Read, Julian, of Read and Poland, Inc., public relations firm, Ft. Worth, Texas.
Rose, Howard, executive assistant to Governor John Connally.
Rudder, Earl, president, A. and M. College of Texas; former commissioner of the General Land Office.
Sanderford, Ghent, former secretary to Governor Miriam A. Ferguson.
Shivers, Allan, former Governor of Texas.
Spears, Franklin, member, Texas Senate.
Stevenson, Coke R., former Governor of Texas.
Turman, James A., speaker, Texas House of Representatives.
Winters, John H., executive director, Texas Department of Public Welfare.

OTHER SOURCES

Austin Report. 1955–1961. A weekly newsletter edited by Stuart Long, Capitol correspondent.
Appointment books of Governor Allan Shivers, 1950–1956.
Daniel, Price. "Budget Message to the 55th Legislature." (Mimeographed.)

————. "Ten Reasons Why the Texas Escheat Law Needs Stronger Enforcement Provisions." Privately printed, 1961.

Expense Accounts of candidates for governor of Texas, filed with the secretary of state.

Files of William J. Lawson, executive secretary to Governor W. Lee O'Daniel, containing press releases from the Governor's Office, 1939–1941, and copies of miscellaneous campaign speeches and weekly broadcasts delivered by the Governor, 1939–1941; also carbon copies of all messages to the Texas Legislature by Governor O'Daniel.

Institute of Public Affairs, The University of Texas. *Organization Chart, The State Government of Texas, 1961.*

Letter of William McGill, executive secretary to Governor Allan Shivers, to Luther Gulick, Institute of Public Administration, New York, dated December 29, 1949.

Letter of R. W. Steen to Ghent Sanderford, dated April 25, 1955.

Letter of Walter Prescott Webb to Ghent Sanderford, dated April 21, 1955.

Script of television address by John Connally, June 11, 1963, concerning item vetoes in General Appropriations Bill of 1963. Furnished by Governor Connally's office.

Script of television address by John Connally, July 19, 1963, concerning civil rights legislation. Furnished by Governor Connally's office.

Shivers, Allan, "Managing the State's Business." Address to the Eleventh Conference, Texas Personnel and Management Association, in Austin, October 28, 1949.

Transcripts of interviews by Miss Pauline Yelderman, Department of Political Science, University of Houston, with Governor Allan Shivers, April 1, 1960 (filmed in KUHT-TV studios); and with Governor Price Daniel, April 5, 1960 (filmed in the Executive Office).

INDEX

A. and M. College, Texas: Ross as president of, 65; Board of Directors of, 130; and James Ferguson, 199; mentioned, 120

Acta Constitutiva de Federacion de 1824: 20

administration, state: and policy conferences with governor, 89; diffusion of power in, 108–109; as source of legislation, 192. SEE ALSO Executive Department, Texas

—system of: as restriction on governor, 14; disintegration of, 39, 109; public support of, 136–137

administrative reorganization: reforms proposed, 4, 5; as gubernatorial problem, 6; mentioned, 108, 203. SEE ALSO Administrative Reorganization Movement

Administrative Reorganization Movement: effect of, on executive departments, 5; inauguration of, 41–42; effect of, on governor's role, 135, 171; governor's budget as outcome of, 214; mentioned, 24, 73

agencies, administrative: reports of, to governor, 75; and conferences with governor, 88; requests of, for deficiency appropriations, 90; and expansion of governor's staff, 95; cooperation of, with executive secretary, 98; number of, 126–127; types of, 126–127; governor as ex-officio member of, 126–127, 165 (chart); governor's appointments to, 126–127, 243; governor's power over, 135; statements of, cleared with governor, 143; suggest legislation, 171; control of, through veto threat, 186; expansion of, 206; budget law on spending of, 215; advice to, from Legislative Budget Board, 216; source of funds for, 216–217. SEE ALSO boards and commissions

agrarian movement: 267

agriculture: and Jim Ferguson, 199, 200; marketing systems proposed for, 204

Agriculture, Department of: creation of, 37

Aguayo, Marqués de San Miguél de: governor of Texas, 16, 17

Aikin, A. M., Jr.: use of martial law by, 163; as Daniel's floor leader, 248; and Gilmer-Aikin Bills, 213, 256

Alabama: 61, 218

Alarcón, Martín de: governor of Texas, 16, 17

"Alcalde, the Old": 66

Allred, James V.: as governor, 19 (list); as federal district judge, 65; defeated for senator, 66; postgubernatorial career of, 67–68 (table); as liberal governor, 205, 324, 325–326, 327 (fig.); as campaigner, 205, 288; popularity of, 206; as attorney general, 288; role of, in conventions, 311, 312; mentioned, 19, 139, 155

—executive functions of: petitions for exercise of, 81–82; in routine duties, 90–91; in appointments, 117; in visit to Mexico City, 148; and Board of Pardons and Paroles, 153; in use of martial law, 163; in relations with press, 253

—and Legislature: social welfare program, 48, 206, 207, 241; vetoes, 180 (fig.); item veto, 184, 185; veto threat, 187; State of State messages, 205, 206; special messages, 205, 206, 207; legislative program, 205–207; special sessions, 224 n. 14, 226, 231–232 (table), 233 (fig.); endorsement of candidate for speaker, 241–242; use of floor leaders, 247

Almazán, Fernando Pérez de: governor of Texas, 17

amendments, constitutional. SEE Constitution, present Texas

American Legion: 70

American Party: 65

American Red Cross: 277

"Anti-Troop Bill": 228

Appleby, Paul H.: on budget making, 241

appointive power of governor: under Mexico, 21; under 1845 Constitution, 25, 26, 39; under 1866 Constitution, 28; under 1869 Constitution, 31, 39; in